Pascal
Programming

WILEY SERIES IN COMPUTING

Consulting Editor
Professor D. W. Barron
Computer Studies Group, University of Southampton, U.K.

BEZIER · Numerical Control—Mathematics and Applications
DAVIES and BARBER · Communication Networks for Computers
BROWN · Macro Processors and Techniques for Portable Software
PAGAN · A Practical Guide to Algol 68
BIRD · Programs and Machines
OLLE · The Codasyl Approach to Data Base Management
DAVIES, BARBER, PRICE, and SOLOMONIDES · Computer Networks
   and their Protocols
KRONSJO · Algorithms: Their Complexity and Efficiency
RUS · Data Structures and Operating Systems
BROWN · Writing Interactive Compilers and Interpreters
HUTT · The Design of a Relational Data Base Management System
O'DONOVAN · GPSS—Simulation Made Simple
LONGBOTTOM · Computer System Reliability
AUMIAUX · The Use of Microprocessors
ATKINSON · Pascal Programming
KUPKA and WILSING · Conversational Languages
SCHMIDT · GPSS-Fortran
PUZMAN/PORIZEK · Communication Control in Computer Networks
SPANIOL · Computer Arithmetic
BARRON · Pascal—The Language and its Implementation
HUNTER · The Design and Construction of Compilers

Pascal
Programming

Laurence V. Atkinson
Department of Computer Science, University of Sheffield

A Wiley–Interscience Publication

JOHN WILEY & SONS
Chichester · New York · Brisbane · Toronto

Copyright © 1980 by John Wiley & Sons Ltd.

Reprinted with corrections, July 1981
Reprinted April 1982
Reprinted May 1983

British Library Cataloguing in Publication Data:

Atkinson, Laurence V.
Pascal programming.—(Wiley series in computing).
1. PASCAL (Computer program language)
I. Title
001.6424   QA76.73.P2   80–40126
ISBN 0 471 27773 8
ISBN 0 471 27774 6 Pbk

Printed in Gt. Britain by Page Bros (Norwich) Ltd, Mile Cross Lane, Norwich, Norfolk

*Dedicated to my mother, Vera,
and to the memory of my father, Benjamin Ernest.*

Contents

Introduction   vii

Computers and Computing: Some Introductory Remarks   ix

Part A   SOME FUNDAMENTAL CONCEPTS

1. Programs and Data   3
2. Arithmetic Data Types   37
3. The Data Type *char*   51
4. Conditional Flow of Control   58
5. The Data Type *boolean*   80
6. Loops   95
7. Procedures and Functions   137
8. Program Construction   185

Part B   GENERALIZED SCALAR TYPES

9. Symbolic and Subrange Types   211

Part C   DATA STRUCTURES

10. Sets   255
11. Records   274
12. Files   288
13. Arrays   311
14. Pointers   363

Part D   EXCEPTIONAL CONTROL TRANSFER

15. The Goto-Statement   391

APPENDIXES

A. Summary of Pascal Syntax   401

B. Reserved Words   413

C. Predefined Identifiers   414

D. Operators   415

E. Some Character Sets   417

F. Exercise Notes and Hints   419

Index   425

Introduction

This book is intended both as an introductory text for those with no previous knowledge of programming and as a conversion text for those with experience of some high level programming language other than Pascal. The book's dual role has influenced its layout.

Some introductory remarks are presented for the benefit of those with no knowledge of computers.

Part A (Chapters 1–8) introduces some programming concepts fundamental to all high level sequential programming languages. These are presented here in the context of Pascal but most features will have equivalents in other languages. The lessons of good programming style are relevant whatever programming language is used. This is stressed in the discussion of loops (Chapter 6). Loops abound in most programs but are a noted source of trouble for beginners. The methodology of loop construction is given greater emphasis than in most programming texts.

Experienced programmers should be able to read these chapters quickly and acquaint themselves with the Pascal interpretation of familiar concepts. Novices should acquire a solid foundation for succeeding chapters to build upon.

Part B (Chapter 9) presents two features of Pascal which have no counterpart in any other programming language (except those developed from Pascal). These are the two most important new concepts in Pascal. They have had a far-reaching effect upon the way we think about problems, the way we express algorithms, the confidence we can place in our programs, and the speed with which programs run on the computer. Coverage of these two features, together with a discussion of their relevance to program security, constitutes a complete *Part* to emphasize their importance. The lessons to be learned from this chapter pervade the remainder of the book.

Part C (Chapters 10–14) describes the data structuring facilities available in Pascal.

Part D (Chapter 15) embodies the shortest chapter of the book. It introduces a Pascal statement you should rarely have to use.

Each chapter concludes with a set of programming exercises. Within each set these tend to be in increasing order of difficulty. If you do not have time to complete all the excercises you should attempt at least those marked with an asterisk. These form a representative sample. Because many examples appear in the book no solutions to exercises are given, but notes and hints for some exercises (marked with a dagger) are presented in Appendix F.

The book is essentially pedagogical and so should present information in the order in which it can best be assimilated by the beginner; however, it must also serve as a reference text. Inevitably, therefore, some compromises have been made. The basic ordering of the topics is sensible from a teaching (and, hence, learning) viewpoint but the depth of coverage is often greater than the novice needs during a first reading. When teaching programming, I introduce enumerated and subrange types (Chapter 9) after a shallow coverage of the first six chapters but treat recursion and backtrack programming (Chapter 7) as the last topic, while top-down design (Chapter 8) influences the whole presentation.

Programming is best learned by practice. To this end complete programs are introduced in Chapter 1 and throughout the book the emphasis is on illustration by example. The examples are taken from a variety of application areas. Few examples require more than an elementary knowledge of mathematics.

The computing world has its own jargon, familiar English words often being used but with new meanings. Each new term introduced will be enclosed within "quotation marks". Pascal text will appear in **bold** or *italicized* type.

Computers and Computing: Some Introductory Remarks

A computer is a machine. Our aim is to make the machine perform some specified actions. With some machines we might express our intentions by depressing keys, pushing buttons, rotating knobs, etc. For a computer we construct a sequence of instructions (this is a "program") and present this sequence to the machine. If we have a "terminal" (rather like an electric typewriter, possibly with a display screen in place of paper) connected to the computer we can type our program directly. An alternative method is to type the information onto a "punched card", a rectangular piece of high quality card (typically 19 cm by 8 cm). A "card punch" is a machine capable of punching patterns of holes in any of 80 columns across the card. In any column of the card is a pattern of holes and no-holes which can be sensed by a "card reader". A light shines onto one side of the card and the positions of the holes are determined by a bank of photoelectric cells on the other. Thus the information we type is recorded in a sort of Morse code. Many such cards can be collected together and fed to the computer as a "deck". There are other ways of getting information into a computer but you are unlikely to meet them in the context of an introductory programming course.

When the computer has done something, hopefully what we wanted it to, we require it to produce some "output". If we are communicating with the machine via a terminal we would expect the output to appear at the terminal. If we are communicating via any other medium, output will probably be produced by a "line printer". This machine handles continuous stationery folded into pages (typically 36 cm wide and 28 cm high) and is so called because it produces its print in units of a line (unlike a typewriter which produces its type one character at a time).

The particular system available to you will depend upon the "operational environment" of your computer installation. Pascal programs as presented in this book are independent of the operational environment but the conventions of your installation will dictate the way programs are supplied to the computer.

When specifying our intentions to the computer we must be precise. The computer has no intelligence but merely responds in a certain well-defined way to each correctly supplied instruction. Natural English is prone to ambiguity and so is not a suitable language in which to express our instructions. Accordingly languages have been developed for the specific purpose of communicating with computers. These languages are called "programming languages".

Every computer has a basic set of instructions which it can obey directly but writing programs in this "machine code" is very tedious and error prone. Accordingly "high level languages" have been developed to make life easier for us. Some are designed for use in particular problem areas but some are called "general purpose languages". Two of the earliest languages developed (in the late 1950s) were *Fortran* for numerical computing and *Cobol* for commercial applications. In 1960 the language *Algol 60* appeared and although intended for scientific use it paved the way for the general purpose languages which followed it during the 1960s. Prominent among these are *PL/I*, *Simula 67*, and *Algol 68*.

In 1971 we have the appearance of *Pascal* designed by Professor Niklaus Wirth of Eidgenossische Technische Hochschule in Zurich. Pascal was intended as a vehicle for teaching programming systematically and to provide means of efficient implementation on existing computers. In the eyes of many it is superior to any other programming language in general use today and its spread throughout the computing world has been extensive. The language, as described in this book, conforms to the BSI/ISO draft Standard for Pascal.

Part A

SOME FUNDAMENTAL CONCEPTS

1

Programs and Data

1.1 Programs

1.1.1 Algorithms, programs, and sequential flow

An "algorithm" is a description of a process expressed as a sequence of steps. For example, the following constitutes an algorithm:

Step 1. Mix eggs, flour, sugar, margarine, and butter.
Step 2. Place mixture in a cake tin.
Step 3. Bake in a moderate oven for 30 minutes.

In computing we are concerned with presenting algorithms to computers. We must therefore adopt some notation in which to express our algorithms. This notation is called the "programming language". The actions to be carried out for each step of an algorithm are described by what programming languages call "statements". A complete sequence of statements is called a "program" and when a computer "runs" a program it "obeys" each statement in turn.

1.1.2 Compilation and execution

The computer does not obey each statement as it is presented; instead it attempts to translate each statement into machine code. This translation process (called "compilation") is carried out by a program written specially for the purpose. It is possible to define an algorithm for translating from one specified computer language (the "source language") into another (the "target language"). Hence it is possible to write a program to perform the translation. Such a program is called a "compiler".

A "Pascal compiler" for a particular computer is a program which translates Pascal programs into the machine code of that computer. Pascal programs can be run on any computer with a Pascal compiler. The compiler will usually "list" (i.e. print out) the program, numbering the lines consecutively. Throughout this book programs are often presented in this way: the line numbers are not supplied by the programmer.

A program may fail to compile. This happens if the program is incomplete or contains some misuse of the source language. The rules of grammar of a language are called the "syntax" of the language and, in programming terms, a violation of these constitutes a "syntax error" or "syntactic error". Thus the English sentence

Programming (with Pascal is, fun.

contains two syntax errors:

1. A comma should not appear between *is* and *fun.*
2. Either the opening bracket should not be present or a closing bracket should follow *Pascal.*

Notice, as in the second case above, that there may be several ways to correct a syntax error. Thus a compiler may detect the *presence* of an error but be unable to inform you as to the precise *location* or *nature* of the error.

A sentence, though syntactically correct, may be meaningless. Consider an example. A simple English sentence may have the form:

Noun phrase – verb – noun phrase.

Both the following sentences are therefore syntactically correct:

1. *A girl recites a poem.*
2. *A poem recites a girl.*

The meaning of the second is somewhat obscure! The meanings of programs are described as "semantics". More will be said later about syntactic and semantic errors.

If the compiler detects the presence of syntactic or semantic errors the computer will make no attempt to run the program. No statement will be obeyed until the complete program has been successfully compiled. The program must be corrected and recompiled. When a complete program has been successfully compiled "execution" may be attempted (i.e. the program can be run). Most computer systems can be arranged to run a program automatically upon successful compilation. Your particular installation will have details of this facility.

Errors may occur during execution. For instance, one may (presumably unintentionally) ask a program to print out the letter following *Z* in the alphabet. You will see later why this would not usually be detected until run-time. If you are running your program from a terminal you may be allowed to correct some run-time errors as they occur and continue execution. If you are not using a terminal, program execution will be terminated in the event of a run-time error. The program must then be corrected, recompiled, and (when successfully compiled) run again.

1.1.3 Program output

All your programs should generate output and, as mentioned earlier, it will probably be produced by a terminal or line printer. It is possible that no lower case letters will be available on these devices, in which case all letters printed will be upper case (i.e. capitals).

In Pascal, output is generated by the

> *write*

and

> *writeln*

procedures. A "procedure" is a set of instructions which performs some specified task.

"Parameters", enclosed within parentheses and separated by commas, may be supplied to indicate any entities needed for the task. For *write* and *writeln* the parameters specify what is to be printed. The procedures are supplied by the system; the parameters must be supplied by the user.

Output is discussed in more detail at the end of this chapter; for the present an introduction to *writeln* will suffice. No parameters need be supplied. When the statement

> *writeln*

is obeyed at run-time the print head of the output device will position itself at the start of the next line. If parameters are supplied, the "value" of each in turn is printed along the line from left to right; the print head then returns to the beginning of the next line. In the simplest case the parameters might be numbers or strings of one or more characters. In Pascal, "strings" are enclosed within "quotes", (').

Examples of writeln-statements are as follows:

1. *writeln (2001)*
2. *writeln (−9)*
3. *writeln ('I think therefore I am')*
4. *writeln*
5. *writeln ('A prime number:', 17, 'two more:', 5, 7)*

If the five writeln-statements above were obeyed one after another the output would be:

2001
−9
I think therefore I am

A prime number: 17two more: 5   7

Integers (whole numbers) are output to a predefined "field width", but this varies from one compiler to another. The number of spaces preceding each integer printed will therefore be dependent upon your particular implementation. No extra spaces are output with strings but, as in examples 3 and 5, spaces may be included within a string.

Numbers with fractional parts are called "real numbers" or simply "reals" and are printed in "standard floating point form". This comprises a "coefficient" and a "scale factor" separated by the letter E. The form $\alpha E \beta$ corresponds to the value $\alpha \times 10^{\beta}$. The coefficient is a number with absolute magnitude greater than or equal to unity but less than ten, expressed to some predefined, but implementation dependent, number of decimal places. The scale factor is a signed integer. Here are some real numbers and, assuming coefficients contain six decimal places, their standard floating point equivalents:

Real number	S.f.p. form
14.2	$1.420000E + 01$
-613.94173258	$-6.139417E + 02$
3.14159265358979323846	$3.141593E + 00$
0.00000123456789	$1.234568E - 06$
97.0	$9.700000E + 01$

It is possible to output the values of "arithmetic expressions". The statement

   writeln (4, '+', 19, '=', 4 + 19)

produces the output

   4 +   19 =   23

Note that digits may be interpreted as characters as well as constituting integers:

   writeln ('4 ∗ 19 =', 4 ∗ 19)

would produce

   4 ∗ 19 =   76

When *4 ∗ 19* appears between quotes it is just a character string ("four", "asterisk", "one", "nine"); when it appears without quotes it means "4 times 19".

   Arithmetic expressions are fully explained in Chapter 2. It is also possible to output the value of a "boolean expression"; these are described in Chapter 5.

1.1.4 A complete program

Every Pascal program starts with a line something like

program α (*output*);

where a "program name" is substituted for α. The program name identifies the program but has no significance within the program.

Names in Pascal are called "identifiers" and all identifiers must start with a letter. Upper and lower case letters are equivalent within an identifier. The initial letter can be followed by any number of letters or digits or both. Pascal imposes no restriction on the length of an identifier but, since an identifier cannot contain a space or an end of line, your implementation will impose some limit. Further, it is possible that your Pascal compiler will not examine every character in a very long identifier. So long as all the characters are legal the number regarded as "significant" is unfortunately as few as eight in some implementations. This would mean that two identifiers agreeing in their first eight characters would be treated as the same identifier by the compiler. Do not let this discourage you from using long identifiers; readability of program text is very important and is heavily dependent upon the use of meaningful identifiers. So that your programs will run under any Pascal system it is worth ensuring that distinct identifiers differ in their first eight characters.

The word **program** is a "reserved word" and cannot be used in any context other than that for which it is intended. To indicate this it appears here in bold-face type. When writing programs with pencil and paper it is conventional to underline reserved words. When preparing a program for the computer reserved words are typed like any other identifier. However, if your input device provides both upper and lower case letters you are strongly recommended to use upper case letters for reserved words and lower case letters for identifiers. We shall use upper case letters within program names.

The parameter following the program name enables the program to communicate with its operational environment. If lineprinter or terminal output is required (as is the case with all the programs in this book) the name of the "standard output file", *output*, must appear.

The statements constituting the program are enclosed between the statement brackets **begin** and **end** and the **end** is followed by a period. The following is a complete Pascal program:

```
0    program OurFirstProgram (output);
1    begin
2        writeln ('Yippee – it works!')
3    end.
```

The line numbers are purely for reference and are not part of the program.

Successive statements are separated by semi-colons. Conventionally a semi-colon immediately follows the first of two statements it separates, but should still be thought of as a separator and not a terminator. Accordingly no semi-colon need follow a statement immediately preceding **end**. Pascal allows "empty statements" and so an extra semi-colon before an **end** is permitted in some contexts. This semi-colon is said to separate an empty statement (between ; and **end**) from the preceding statement. Throughout this book we shall have an empty statement only if we need one and, consequently, we shall never have a semi-colon immediately preceding **end**. Here is a program containing two statements:

```
0    program Add7and16 (output);
1    begin
2        writeln ('This is our second program');
3        writeln ('it adds 7 and 16 to give', 7 + 16,'.')
4    end.
```

When this program is executed it produces

This is our second program
it adds 7 and 16 to give   23.

If the second parameter $(7 + 16)$ of the call of *writeln* on line 3 were replaced by $7 - 16$ the program would produce the following output:

This is our second program
it adds 7 and 16 to give   −9.

We would still have a complete program which generates no compilation errors, executes successfully, and terminates normally. However, the program contains a "logical" error; it is wrong in the sense that it has not done what we presumably intended. It has done what we told it to but not what we intended to.

In this simple case it is easy to spot that the output is suspect. In more complex situations this is not so but you must always be on your guard: *the fact that a program runs to completion does not imply that the output must be correct.*

1.1.5   Layout of program text

1.1.5.1   *Comments*

It is often useful to include descriptive information within a program for the (human) reader's benefit but which will be ignored by the compiler. In Pascal anything between braces ({ and }) is ignored by the compiler; this is called a "comment". Note that a comment cannot contain the character "}". If your computer character set does not include braces you must enclose your comments between the symbols (* and *).

Comments are useful in three main areas:

1. To associate a particular symbol with some other symbol elsewhere in the program text (e.g. to associate an **end** with its corresponding **begin**).
2. To clarify the intent of a statement whose purpose is not obvious from the program text (but note that the purpose of a statement should usually be apparent).
3. To give an outline description of the purpose of a group of statements. In particular, it is usual to have a comment at the. head of the whole program to indicate the program's function.

1.1.5.2 *Significance of comments, spaces, and ends of lines*

Comments, spaces, and ends of lines are called separators. Wherever a reserved word is adjacent to an identifier, numeric constant, or other reserved word the two must be separated by at least one of these separators.

To enhance readability additional separators may be introduced between consecutive symbols anywhere in the program. Separators cannot occur within a symbol. Reserved words, identifiers, numbers, (* and *) are considered complete symbols and we shall meet other symbols containing more than one character. Note, however, that a space is a member of the printable character set of all computers and so a space is allowed within a string but is not interpreted as a separator in this context. Comments are not allowed within a string and you should avoid ends of lines occurring within a string.

1.1.5.3 *Indentation*

Throughout this book certain layout conventions will be adhered to. You may wish to form layout conventions of your own but you are advised not to stray too far from those presented here. If you are lucky you may have a compiler which indents your program listing automatically.

The layout of a program is of no concern to the compiler. The program

```
program  Our First Program                                            (
    output                                              );begin
    writeln(                               'Yippee − it works!') end.
```

is exactly the same, so far as the compiler is concerned, as the neater presentation we produced earlier. The tidier layout is for the benefit of the human reader. Some comments on the indentation policy within this book now follow.

A program will usually contain several **begin–end** pairs. Each **end** will be vertically aligned with its corresponding **begin** and nothing (except spaces) will precede **begin** or **end** on a line. The first **begin** (and hence the last **end**) will align with **program**. Nothing, except perhaps a comment, will follow **begin** on a line and all lines between **begin** and **end** will be indented, usually two or three spaces.

A number of short statements may be grouped together on one line but nothing on the same line will precede any statement which is not entirely contained on one line.

Further layout conventions will become apparent in subsequent chapters.

1.1.6 Presenting your program to the computer

If your input device provides both upper and lower case letters you should adopt the typing convention suggested. If it does not, all letters will be upper case.

The conventions for submitting a "job" to a computer vary widely, not only from one computer to another but possibly even from one installation to another when both installations have the same type of computer. You will probably have to supply at least one line before the Pascal program and possibl one or more at the end. You must determine the convention of your own installation—no further mention of this is made here.

When presented with your program the computer will list it (i.e. print out your program text with the lines numbered). If you are submitting your program from a terminal you may wish to suppress this listing; this should be possible.

If the compiler detects any errors these will be listed and the job will be abandoned at that stage. If compilation is successful you will be informed of the fact and the program can be run. Execution will probably be initiated automatically but, again, implementations differ.

1.1.7 Syntax diagrams

The syntax of a programming language can be conveniently illustrated by "syntax diagrams". Syntax diagrams for the whole of Pascal are presented in Appendix A. Throughout the text we shall use simplified forms of these to define the syntax of each new language construct we encounter.

The following diagram defines the syntax of programs we have met so far:

PROGRAM

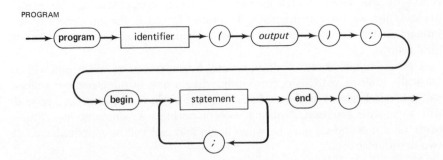

Entities within rectangular boxes require further definition and entities within rounded boxes are actual characters which must appear within the program text. Every syntax diagram has an "entry point" at the left and an "exit point" at the right. All legal constructs of the type named (PROGRAM in the above example) are defined by the possible paths in the direction of the arrows through the diagram from entry to exit.

Notice that the diagram above defines an infinite number of programs. There is no limit to the number of statements that can appear between **begin** and **end**; the only constraint is that adjacent statements must be separated by a semi-colon.

Identifiers are defined as follows:

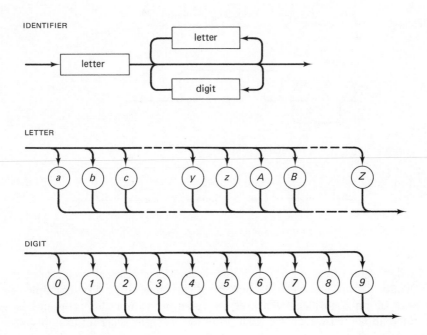

We shall not attempt a full definition of STATEMENT but, if we assume that each parameter of *writeln* is a simple value (not an expression) we get the following definitions:

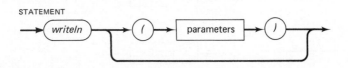

12

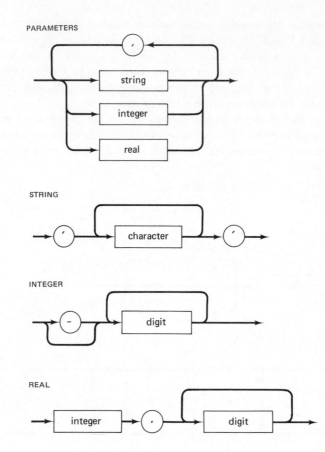

PARAMETERS

STRING

INTEGER

REAL

The definition of CHARACTER is implementation dependent so we omit it.

Syntax definitions are independent of the semantics. For example, the syntax of an identifier, whatever its function within the program, is as defined above. However, we shall often use a syntax diagram to imply some semantics. If two constructs α and β each involve an identifier, but of different kinds (say of type γ for α and type δ for β), we might use syntax diagrams of the form

α

β

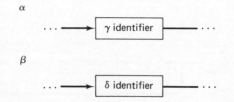

but γ *identifier* and δ *identifier*, unless defined elsewhere, are understood to be syntactically synonymous with *identifier*.

1.2 Data

1.2.1 Distinction between program and data

Returning to the cookery algorithm of Section 1.1.1 we can observe two types of information: *mix, place,* and *bake* are verbs specifying actions to be carried out upon certain entities; the entities involved are *eggs, flour, sugar, margarine, butter, cake tin, oven,* and *minutes* and can be regarded as the "data" to be processed. By specifying different quantities of ingredients different cakes will result but the same algorithm is being performed. Thus the actions to be carried out can be considered separately from the entities which the actions involve. For a complete recipe for one type of cake we must specify the quantities of each ingredient to be used. For example,

> 50 g   *margarine*
> 50 g   *butter*
> 100 g *sugar*
> 100 g *flour*
> 2   *eggs*

The recipe begins to resemble a computer program if we write it in the following form:

$$b = 50; \ s = 100; \ f = 100; \ e = 2;$$

1. $m := b;$
2.   **mix** *m grams of margarine + b grams of butter +*
          s grams of sugar   + f grams of flour +
          e eggs;
3.   **place** *in baking tin;*
4.   **bake** *in 175° oven for 30 minutes.*

$m := b$ is read "*m* becomes *b*" and implies that the value associated with *m* is to be the same as that denoted by *b*.

Written in this way the recipe can be adapted to different tastes by changing the specification of *b, s, f,* or *e*, but will still use margarine and butter in equal quantities. If we were to continue this analogy we would have to specify the size of baking tin and oven required and these would, of course, be dependent upon the size of the cake being baked. The size of cake tin required could be computed by writing, between lines 2 and 3,

$$t := 10\sqrt{b + m + s + f + 50e}$$

and replacing line 3 by

3. **place** *in a baking tin of t mm diameter.*
Large cakes would be rather flat using this formula, but do not worry if you do not follow this, we leave its pursuit to any interested reader!

1.2.2 Conceptual model of computer store

Programs and the data upon which they operate are held inside the computer "store" (often called "memory"). We can regard this store as a collection of "boxes" or "pigeon holes" each capable of holding instructions or values and some capable of having names stuck on. When we supply a sequence of statements in the form of a program the machine code equivalents of these statements are stored in boxes (during compilation) for subsequent execution. The system provides two boxes, one called *write* and one called *writeln*. These contain instructions and, as we have seen, when we quote the name of the box the computer obeys the instructions inside it. Boxes are available for holding values and we can invent our own names (identifiers) for these.

1.2.3 Distinction between constants and variables

We distinguish two types of data object within a program: "constants" which always denote the same value and "variables" which may represent different values at different times during the execution of a program.
   In the cookery algorithm of Section 1.2.1,

   50, 100, 2, 175, and *30* are predefined constants,
   b, s, f, and *e* are user-defined constants, and
   m (and *t* introduced later) is a variable.

At the start of execution the values of *m* and *t* are "undefined". At subsequent points during execution their values are changed. It would be possible to change their values again at other points during execution but this does not happen in this particular algorithm.

1.2.3.1 *Constant declarations*

The compiler recognizes unnamed constants of type character, string, integer, and real and so no "declaration" of these needs to be made. A character is a string of length 1. If we wish to introduce our own name for a constant we must declare this fact to the compiler. We precede a sequence of constant declarations by the reserved word

   const

Each declaration takes the following form:

For example,

    const *pi = 3.14159;   hisname = 'Fred'; hyphen = '–';*
       votingage = 18;   blank = ' ';

This introduces five user-defined constants: *pi* (of type real), *hisname* (of type string), *hyphen* (of type character), *votingage* (of type integer), and *blank* (of type character).

No attempt must be made to change the value of a constant within a program.

```
0   program Box (output);
1
2       { Computes the areas of the base, sides, and ends and
3             the volume of a rectangular box. The dimensions of the
4             box are supplied as user-defined constants. }
5
6   const
7       length = 26;     width = 11;     depth = 7;
8
9   begin
10      writeln ('For a box with dimensions');
11      writeln (length, ' cm *', width, ' cm *', depth, ' cm :–')
12
13      writeln ('the area of the base is', length * width, ' sq cm');
14
15      writeln ('the area of each side is', length * depth, ' sq cm');
16
17      writeln ('the area of each end is', width * depth, ' sq cm and');
18
19      writeln ('the volume of the box is', length * width * depth, ' cc.')
20  end.
```

OUTPUT:
For a box with dimensions.
    *26 cm *   11 cm *   7 cm :–*
the area of the base is   286 sq cm
the area of each side is   182 sq cm
the area of each end is   77 sq cm and
the volume of the box is   2002 cc.

Figure 1.1   Example 1.1

Example 1.1

Write a program which, given the length, width, and depth of a rectangular box, computes its volume and the areas of the base, sides, and ends. Treat the dimensions of the box as constants and consider a box 26 cm by 11 cm by 7 cm. □
  A listing of the program and the output it produces are given in Figure 1.1. ■

To apply the program to a different box we simply modify the constant declarations; the rest of the program remains the same.

1.2.3.2 *Variable declarations*

Every variable used in a program must be declared: we introduce all variable identifiers and state the type of value each can represent. We precede a sequence of variable declarations by the reserved word

var

Each declaration takes the following form:

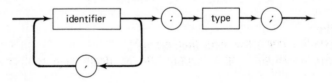

All variables declared in one list will have the type specified.
  Three standard types in Pascal are character (denoted by *char*), *integer*, and *real*. These are called "scalar types". For example,

> **var** *age, noofchildren, housenumber : integer;*
> *income : real;*
> *initial : char;*

declares five variables:

> *age, noofchildren* (number of children), and *housenumber* are integer variables so all values they take will be whole numbers;
> *income* is a real variable so it takes numeric values, but it may take a value which is not a whole number;
> *initial* is a character variable and so can take as its value any member of the character set implemented.

Note Variables of type *string* are not allowed in this simple context—we shall learn of them later.

The declarations effectively allocate boxes capable of holding values of the appropriate type and stick on the specified names. However, the boxes are empty; they contain no values. More correctly, they will probably contain whatever was left in them the last time they were used. We say that *the values of all variables are initially undefined.* Any attempt to reference an undefined value constitutes an error.

Variable declarations must appear between the **program** line and **begin** and must come after the constant declarations if any are present.

When choosing names for variables (or for anything else) pick meaningful names. Always use a name that implies the role of the object it is naming.

1.2.4 Simple assignments

The value associated with a variable can be changed by an "assignment statement":

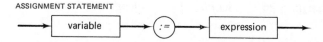

ASSIGNMENT STATEMENT

The assignment operator (:=) is read as "becomes". The expression on the right is evaluated and the resultant value assigned to the variable on the left. The previous value of the variable is destroyed (the technical term is "overwritten"). In terms of storage boxes we can think of an assignment as removing any value currently sitting in a specified box and replacing it by a new value.

Usually the variable and the value to be assigned to it must have the same type (e.g. *char, integer, real*) but it is acceptable to assign an integer value to a real variable. Note, however, that a real value must not be assigned to an integer variable.

We can now see how semantic errors can occur. The assignment statement

$x := 2.1$

is syntactically correct. It is semantically correct only if x has been declared as a real variable.

Correction of a semantic error often involves changing the program at some point well before the point at which the compiler reports the error. Inserting or changing a declaration is an example of this. Correction of a syntax error usually requires only a local alteration. You need not be concerned with the distinction between syntactic and semantic errors. The important thing is that both constitute compile-time errors.

The type of an expression is the same as that of the value it delivers. More will be said about expressions later; the following examples should suffice for the present.

18

Example 1.2

Notice that, in Figure 1.1, the expression *length* ∗ *width* appears twice (lines 13 and 19). This means that the computer must compute this, the base area of the box, twice. As *length* and *width* are both constants their values must be the same on line 19 as on line 13. The resultant value of *length* ∗ *width* must therefore be the same in both cases. We need compute the value only once; we can store this value and then recall it when it is needed.   □

```
 0    program BoxWithaVariable (output);
 1
 2          { Computes the areas of the base, sides, and ends and
 3            the volume of a rectangular box. The dimensions of the
 4            box are supplied as user-defined constants. }
 5
 6    const
 7       length = 26;      width = 11;      depth = 7;
 8
 9    var
10       basearea : integer;
11
12    begin
13       writeln ('For a box with dimensions');
14       writeln (length, ' cm *', width, ' cm *', depth, ' cm :-');
15
16       basearea := length * width;
17       writeln ('the area of the base is', basearea, ' sq cm');
18
19       writeln ('the area of each side is', length * depth, ' sq cm');
20
21       writeln ('the area of each end is', width * depth, ' sq cm and');
22
23       writeln ('the volume of the box is', basearea * depth, ' cc.')
24    end.
```

Figure 1.2   Example 1.2

This is done in the program of Figure 1.2. The integer variable *basearea* (declared on line 10) is assigned (on line 16) the value of the product of *length* and *width*. It will retain this value until any other value is subsequently assigned to it. In this program no further assignments to *basearea* occur. If *length* and *width* had been variables, instead of constants, we could have changed their values within the program. It is important to realize that any changes to *length* or *width* after the assignment on line 16 would not affect the value of the variable *basearea*.

The output from this program is, of course, the same as that produced by the earlier program. ■

We now compare these two programs and note four differences:

1. *space:* the modified program uses more store. It requires a storage location to hold the value of the variable *basearea.*
2. *time:* the modified program requires less time. It saves one multiplication (a slow operation) at the expense of an assignment (a fast operation).
3. *correctness:* the modified program is less error prone. The more times we write an expression the more likely we are to make a mistake in doing so.
4. *transparency:* the modified program is more readable (the program intent is more "transparent"). The name *basearea* is more informative than the expression *length ∗ width.*

In such a small program these differences are minor but as programs become larger the effects of such differences become much more significant. The principles are therefore important and so some further remarks are in order.

A space/time trade-off is a common feature of many programs. Many computations involve repeated use of some computed information. One has the choice of **either** computing this information each time it is required even though the same result will be obtained each time **or** computing the information once and storing the results for future reference. The former approach takes more time and the latter more store. If the computation time is large but the resultant information requires little store the second approach would be better; if the computation involved is slight but large volumes of data are involved the first approach may be better. In many cases it is difficult to decide which is preferable.

Transparency and correctness are interlinked. The easier it is to see what a program is doing, the easier it is to spot errors. Thus we are less likely to make mistakes if our programs are readable.

Example 1.3

Tom, Dick, and Harry are candidates in an election. Given the number of votes cast for each, compute their average vote and state by how much their votes differ from the average. □

The program listing is given in Figure 1.3. Each vote total is a whole number so we store these as integers. The average, and hence the differences from the average, may not be whole numbers so we use real variables to compute these. ■

We need not have stored the differences from the average; we could have omitted *tomsdiff, dicksdiff,* and *harrysdiff* from the program. In lines 27, 28, and 29 we would then have had *tomsvotes − averagevote* instead of *tomsdiff,*

```
0   program TomDickandHarry (output);
1
2       { The number of votes polled by Tom, Dick, and Harry
3         are supplied as user-defined constants. The program
4         computes their average vote and quotes the deviation
5         of each from the average. }
6
7       const
8         tomsvotes = 12;     dicksvotes = 27;     harrysvotes = 19;
9         indent = '    ';
10
11      var
12        averagevotes, tomsdiff, dicksdiff, harrysdiff : real;
13
14  begin
15      writeln ('Tom has polled', tomsvotes, ' votes');
16      writeln ('Dick has polled', dicksvotes, 'votes');
17      writeln ('Harry has polled', harrysvotes, ' votes');
18
19      averagevotes := (tomsvotes + dicksvotes + harrysvotes) / 3;
20      writeln ('Their average poll is', averagevotes, ' votes');
21
22      tomsdiff := tomsvotes - averagevotes;
23      dickdiff := dicksvotes - averagevotes;
24      harrysdiff := harrysvotes - averagevotes;
25
26      writeln ('They differ from the average as follows');
27      writeln (indent, 'Tom: ', tomsdiff);
28      writeln (indent, 'Dick: ', dicksdiff);
29      writeln (indent, 'Harry:', harrysdiff)
30  end.
```

OUTPUT:
```
Tom has polled      12 votes
Dick has polled     27 votes
Harry has polled     19 votes
Their average poll is 1.933333E+01
They differ from the average as follows
     Tom:  - 7.333333E+00
     Dick:   7.666667E+00
     Harry: -3.333333E-01
```

Figure 1.3   Example 1.3

dicksvotes – *averagevote* instead of *dicksdiff,* and *harrysvote* – *averagevote* instead of *harrysdiff.* However, in its present form the function of the program is a little clearer. Also, any future modification or extension of the program might well involve the differences and so will be accommodated more easily if they have been stored.

Modification of a program is a point which should always be borne in mind. In real life, many programs are never actually finished; they are being continually modified to meet changing requirements. For example, a payroll program must keep abreast of changing taxation laws. In fact many professional programmers never write any new programs: they just keep changing existing ones!

When a program is being written it is, of course, impossible to predict all future changes that might be required, but it is usually possible to identify some areas of potential change. A good programmer recognizes these and reflects this in the design of his program.

Example 1.4

For a given integer and each of its two successors produce the number, its double, and its triple. □

We could achieve this with the statements

```
writeln (n, n * 2, n * 3);
writeln (n + 1, (n + 1) * 2, (n + 1) * 3);
writeln (n + 2, (n + 2) * 2, (n + 2) * 3)
```

and would do so if *n* were a constant. In Figure 1.4 we adopt a different approach to illustrate that an assignment statement of the form

$$n := n + 1$$

can be sensible if *n* is a variable. It means "increment the current value of *n* by *1*". ■

Finally, to stress the dynamic nature of assignments we consider a section of program to interchange the values of two integer variables *i1* and *i2*.

Our first attempt at this might be

$$i1 := i2; \quad i2 := i1$$

but this does not work. Let us draw some boxes to prove it. When *i1* and *i2* are first declared their values are undefined; we can represent this as follows:

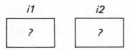

```
0   program IncDoubleTriple (output);
1
2       { For a given integer and each of its two
3           successors the program prints the number,
4           its double, and its triple. }
5
6   const
7       giveninteger = 97;
8
9   var
10      n : integer;
11
12  begin
13      n := giveninteger;
14      writeln ('    n      2 * n      3 * n');
15      writeln (n, 2 * n, 3 * n);
16      n := n + 1;    writeln (n, 2 * n, 3 * n);
17      n := n + 1;    writeln (n, 2 * n, 3 * n)
18  end.
```

OUTPUT :

n	2 * n	3 * n
97	194	291
98	196	294
99	198	297

Figure 1.4   Example 1.4

We now assume that some values (say 47 and 6) have been assigned to $i1$ and $i2$:

$i1 := 47;$ $i2: = 6$

If the first assignment ($i1 := i2$) is now obeyed, $i1$ takes the value 6 (and the value of $i2$, of course, remains unaltered):

$i1 := i2$

The second assignment $(i2 := i1)$ now has no effect because $i1$ and $i2$ have the same value:

$i2 := i1$

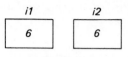

What we want is

Performing the assignments in reverse sequence does not help:

$i2 := i1; \quad i1 := i2$

What are we doing wrong? We are overwriting a value which is needed for subsequent processing. How can we avoid losing this value? Store a copy for future use.

To do this we introduce a temporary storage location, say *temp*, and interchange the values of $i1$ and $i2$ with the following sequence of three assignment statements:

$temp := i1; \quad i1 := i2; \quad i2 := temp$

Again we assume that $i1$ and $i2$ have the values 47 and 6 and consider the assignments one at a time:

temp	i1	i2
?	47	6

$temp := i1$

temp	i1	i2
47	47	6

$i1 := i2$

temp	i1	i2
47	6	6

$i2 := temp$

temp	i1	i2
47	6	47

The sequence

$$temp := i2; \qquad i2 := i1; \qquad i1 := temp$$

works equally well.

1.2.5 Program input

Each program considered so far will produce the same output each time it is run. If we wish to apply the program of Figure 1.2 to a different box we must alter the program, recompile it, and re-run it. Presumably we would wish to consider a different box each time the program is run so this is inconvenient. It would be better if we could arrange to specify the dimensions of the box at run-time rather than compile-time. We could then keep the compiled form of the program (i.e. the machine code) and run this on subsequent occasions to avoid the overhead of repeatedly recompiling the same program. If you are running your program from a terminal the benefits are immediately apparent; you can run a compiled program several times with different data each time.

We wish to utilize *length*, *width*, and *depth* as variables within the program but assign initial values to them at run-time. The process of run-time acquisition of supplied values is known as "reading".

We now regard a program and its data as being quite separate. A program is compiled and will probably include some constants but the data, apart from these constants, is not included. We arrange for the program to request data as needed and we supply the data at run-time. If you are running your program from a terminal this means that you will have to type each value when the program requests it. If not you will probably have to supply your data along with the program when it is compiled but the data will not be read until the program is run.

If a program requires "input" we must ensure that the standard "input file", *input*, has been specified in the **program** line.

Pascal provides two procedures to read data: *read* and *readln*.

1.2.5.1   *read*

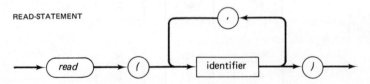

READ-STATEMENT

The procedure *read* is followed by one or more variables, separated by commas and enclosed within parentheses. When a read-statement is obeyed, values are read from the data and, in the order in which the values are encountered, are assigned to the variables in the order in which they occur in the read-statement. Each variable must have type *integer, real,* or *char.* Within the data successive numbers must be separated by at least one space if more than one are supplied on a line. Successive characters on a line cannot be separated because, in this context, a space is a valid (i.e. significant) character. More is said about arithmetic input in Chapter 2 and about character input in Chapter 3.

```
0    program BoxWithRead (input, output);
1
2        { Computes the area of the base, sides, and ends and
3            the volume of a rectangular box. The dimensions of the
4            box are supplied as run-time data. }
5
6    var
7        length, width, depth, basearea : integer;
8
9    begin
10       read (length, width, depth);
11       writeln ('For a box with dimensions');
12       writeln (length, ' cm *', width, ' cm *', depth, ' cm :-');
13
14       basearea := length * width;
15       writeln ('the area of the base is', basearea, ' sq cm');
16
17       writeln ('the area of each side is', length * depth, ' sq cm');
18
19       writeln ('the area of each end is', width * depth, 'sq cm and');
20
21       writeln ('the volume of the box is', basearea * depth, ' cc.')
22   end.
```

INPUT:
34   13   8

OUTPUT:
For a box with dimensions
    *34 cm *   13 cm *   8 cm :−*
the area of the base is   442 sq cm
the area of each side is   272 sq cm
the area of each end is   104 sq cm and
the volume of the box is   3536 cc.

Figure 1.5   Example 1.5

26

Example 1.5

We return to the box program of Figure 1.2 but modify it so that the dimensions are read at run-time. □

The program listing is given in Figure 1.5. If this program is supplied with the input data

26   11   7

it produces the same output as the programs of Figures 1.1 and 1.2. To apply the program to a different box we do not change the program, we merely supply different data. ■

```
0    program TomDickandHarryWithRead (input, output);
1
2        { The number of votes polled by Tom, Dick, and Harry
3            are supplied as input data. The program computes
4            their average vote and quotes the deviation of each
5            from the average. }
6
7        const
8          indent = '      ';
9
10       var
11         tomsvotes, dicksvotes, harrysvotes : integer;
12         averagevotes, tomsdiff, dicksdiff, harrysdiff : real;
13
14   begin
15       read (tomsvotes, dicksvotes, harrysvotes);
16       writeln ('Tom has polled', tomsvotes, ' votes');
17       writeln ('Dick has polled', dicksvotes, ' votes');
18       writeln ('Harry has polled', harrysvotes, ' votes');
19
20       averagevotes := (tomsvotes + dicksvotes + harrysvotes) / 3;
21       writeln ('Their average poll is', averagevotes, ' votes');
22
23       tomsdiff := tomsvotes − averagevotes;
24       dicksdiff := dicksvotes − averagevotes;
         harrysdiff := harrysvotes − averagevotes;
26
27       writeln ('They differ from the average as follows');
28       writeln (indent, 'Tom: ', tomsdiff);
29       writeln (indent, 'Dick: ', dicksdiff);
30       writeln (indent, 'Harry:', harrysdiff)
31   end.
```

INPUT:
13   4   36

OUTPUT:
Tom has polled   13 votes
Dick has polled   4 votes
Harry has polled   36 votes
Their average poll is 1.766667E + 01 votes
They differ from the average as follows
    Tom: −4.666667E + 00
    Dick: −1.366667E + 01
    Harry: 1.833333E + 01

Figure 1.6   Example 1.6

Example 1.6

Modify the Tom, Dick, and Harry program of Figure 1.3 to read the votes. □

The program listing is given in Figure 1.6. The three vote totals must now be supplied, in the correct order, as run-time data. ∎

Example 1.7

Write a program to compute the diameter, circumference, and area of a circle of given radius. For a circle of radius r the diameter is $2r$, the circumference is $2\pi r$, and the area is πr^2. □

A listing of the program, together with sample input is presented in Figure 1.7. The value of *pi* will be the same each time the program is run and remains constant throughout execution; *pi* is therefore supplied as a constant. ∎

1.2.5.2   readln

The procedure *readln* is similar to *read* but need not be supplied with parameters:

READLN-STATEMENT

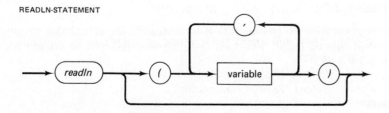

```
 0    program Circle (input, output);
 1
 2        { Computes the diameter, circumference, and area
 3            of a circle of given radius. }
 4
 5    const
 6        pi = 3.14159;
 7
 8    var
 9        radius, diameter, circumference, area : real;
10
11    begin
12        read (radius);
13
14        diameter := 2 * radius;
15        circumference := pi * diameter;
16        area := pi * radius * radius;
17
18        writeln ('For a circle of radius', radius, ' cm');
19        writeln ('the diameter is', diameter, ' cm');
20        writeln ('the circumference is', circumference, ' cm');
21        writeln ('and the area is', area, ' sq cm')
22    end.
```

INPUT :
4.7

OUTPUT :
For a circle of radius   4.700000E + 00 cm
the diameter is   9.400000E + 00 cm
the circumference is   2.953095E + 01 cm
and the area is   6.939772E + 01 sq cm

Figure 1.7   Example 1.7

The effect of

readln

when supplied with no parameters is to disregard the remainder (if any) of the current line of input. The next datum requested will be sought on the next line of data.

When supplied with parameters

readln $(\alpha, \beta, \ldots, \gamma)$

is equivalent to

$$read\ (\alpha, \beta, \ldots, \gamma);\qquad readln$$

the equivalent call of *read* (i.e. with the same parameters in the same order) followed by a call of *readln* with no parameters.

Example 1.8

A pet shop keeps a record of its current livestock. Typical data might be

8	KITTENS
4	PUPPIES
1	CANNIBAL FISH
128	RABBITS

Assuming a shop has only four types of pet and the data is provided in the format illustrated, write a program to compute the total number of pets in the shop. □

The program listing is given in Figure 1.8. Note that *readln* has been used for all four values; *read* could have been used for the fourth but the

---

```
0   program PetShop (input, output);
1
2       { Computes the total pet shop population assuming
3         four kinds of pet and data values supplied
4         one per line. }
5
6   var
7       pet1s, pet2s, pet3s, pet4s, totalpets : integer:
8
9   begin
10      readln (pet1s);   readln (pet2s);   readln (pet3s);   readln (pet4s);
11      totalpets := pet1s + pet2s + pet3s + pet4s;
12      writeln ('Total pet population is', totalpets)
13  end.
```

INPUT :
4 PUPPIES
8 KITTENS
1 CANNIBAL FISH
128 RABBITS

OUTPUT :
Total pet population is   141

Figure 1.8   Example 1.8

---

program would then have left part of the data unread and this is not very tidy. In future modifications to the program a subsequent read-statement would pick up *RABBITS* and this would probably not be what was intended. It is better therefore to use *readln* for all four values. ■

Example 1.9

A message has been encoded by reversing each word in the message and then replacing each letter by the character which follows it in the computer character set. These characters are then placed in groups of varying length at the front of consecutive lines of character data.

Write a program to decode a four-letter, single-word message supplied on three lines, given that the encoded characters are the first character of each of the first two lines and the first two characters of the third. □

The program is listed in Figure 1.9. ■

```
0    program Decode (input, output);
1
2        { This program decodes a four-letter, single-word
3            message supplied on three lines, given that the
4            encoded characters, in reverse order, are the first character
5            of each of the first two lines and the first two
6            of the third. }
7
8        var
9            ch1, ch2, ch3, ch4 : char;
10
11    begin
12        readln (ch1);   readln (ch2);   read (ch3, ch4);
13        writeln ('Message is: ',
14            pred (ch4), pred (ch3), pred (ch2), pred (ch1) )
15    end.
```

INPUT :
FINISHED
OR
PENDING?

OUTPUT :
Message is: DONE

Figure 1.9   Example 1.9

1.2.6 Presenting the data

When a program is supplied on cards it is customary to supply the data on cards immediately following the program. Your installation may provide alternatives but this will be the simplest. When the program has run you will not know what values have been read from the data unless you print out the values input. That is why the program of Figure 1.5 outputs (on line 12) the input dimensions of the room, the program of Figure 1.6 outputs (on lines 16, 17, and 18) the votes input, and the program of Figure 1.7 outputs (on line 18) the value read in as the radius. It is a good idea to output values which have been input otherwise you will have no way of knowing if the program has been supplied with incorrect data.

When a program is being run from a terminal the program will request each datum as it needs it. It will probably do this by displaying a particular character (called the "invitation-to-type" character or "prompt") at your terminal. You will then type the appropriate datum. It is now not quite so necessary (but sometimes still advisable) that your program outputs the values input. Because you have typed the values they are there before you to be seen. The problem is, however, that whilst the program is running you must be constantly aware of the order in which data items will be required. This is greatly simplified if you make your program tell you what information it is requesting. Thus, for terminal use, each read-statement should be preceded by a writeln-statement indicating the information required by the ensuing read-statement. To illustrate this, the programs of Figures 1.6 and 1.7 are modified for terminal use and listed in Figures 1.10 and 1.11.

The purpose of the extra writeln-statements on line 21 of Figure 1.10 and line 19 of Figure 1.11 is to produce two blank lines at the terminal display between the typed input and the program ouput. Although not produced by these programs, blank lines at the end of the output are helpful in distinguishing program output from other displayed information.

For the remainder of the programs in this book it is assumed that data will not be supplied from a terminal.

1.3 More about output

1.3.1 *write*

write differs from *writeln* only in that it must be supplied with at least one parameter and does not cause the print head to move to the start of the next line. The two statements

write $(\alpha, \beta, \ldots, \gamma)$;   writeln

obeyed in sequence have the same effect as the one statement

writeln $(\alpha, \beta, \ldots, \gamma)$

```
0    program TomDickandHarryFromaTerminal (input, output);
1
2         { The number of votes polled by Tom, Dick, and Harry
3            are supplied from a terminal. The program computes
4            their average vote and quotes the deviation of each
5            from the average. }
6
7    const
8         indent = '      ';
9
10   var
11        tomsvotes, dicksvotes, harrysvotes : integer;
12        averagevotes, tomsdiff, dicksdiff, harrysdiff : real;
13
14   begin
15        writeln ('How many votes have been polled by');
16        writeln ('Tom?');   read (tomsvotes);
17        writeln ('Dick?');   read (dicksvotes);
18        writeln ('Harry?');   read (harrysvotes);
19
20        averagevotes := (tomsvotes + dicksvotes + harrysvotes) / 3;
21        writeln;   writeln;
22        writeln ('Their average poll is ', averagevotes, ' votes');
23
24        tomsdiff := tomsvotes - averagevotes;
25        dicksdiff := dicksvotes - averagevotes;
26        harrysdiff := harrysvotes - averagevotes;
27
28        writeln ('They differ from the average as follows');
29        writeln (indent, 'Tom: ', tomsdiff);
30        writeln (indent, 'Dick: ', dicksdiff);
31        writeln (indent, 'Harry: ', harrysdiff)
32   end.
```

Figure 1.10

The effect of the following sequence of calls is self-evident:

```
write ('this and');
write ('this will be on the');
writeln ('same line');
write ('but this and this will');
writeln ('be on the next');
writeln ;
writeln ('and a blank line will precede this')
```

```
 0    program CircleFromaTerminal (input, output);
 1
 2        { Computes the diameter, circumference, and area of
 3            a circle whose radius is supplied from a terminal. }
 4
 5        const
 6          pi = 3.14159;
 7
 8        var
 9          radius, diameter, circumference, area : real;
10
11    begin
12        writeln ('Please type the radius of your circle, in cm');
13        read (radius);
14
15        diameter := 2 * radius;
16        circumference := pi * diameter;
17        area := pi * radius * radius;
18
19        writeln;   writeln;
20        writeln ('For a circle of radius', radius, ' cm');
21        writeln ('the diameter is', diameter, ' cm');
22        writeln ('the circumference is', circumference, ' cm');
23        writeln ('and the area is', area, ' sq cm')
24    end.
```

Figure 1.11

1.3.2 page

page is a procedure which needs no parameters. If output is being produced by a line printer, a call of

    page

will cause ensuing output to appear at the top of the next page. If output appears at a terminal the concept of a page may not be applicable; the effect of the procedure is then implementation dependent and may give a few blank lines.

1.3.3 Formatting

Control of the lines upon which output is to appear is by appropriate use of writeln and page. Control of the layout of information on a line is by format information which may follow any parameter supplied to write or writeln.

```
0    program TomDickandHarryFormatted (input, output);
1
2        { The number of votes polled by Tom, Dick, and Harry
3          are supplied as input data. The program computes
4          their average vote and quotes the deviation of each
5          from the average. }
6
7      const
8        space = ' ';
9
10     var
11       tomsvotes, dicksvotes, harrysvotes : integer;
12       averagevotes, tomsdiff, dicksdiff, harrysdiff : real;
13
14   begin
15     read (tomsvotes, dicksvotes, harrysvotes);
16     writeln ('Tom has polled ', tomsvotes :1, ' votes');
17     writeln ('Dick has polled ', dicksvotes :1, ' votes');
18     writeln ('Harry has polled ', harrysvotes :1, ' votes');
19
20     averagevotes := (tomsvotes + dicksvotes + harrysvotes) / 3;
21     writeln ('Their average poll is', averagevotes : 5 : 2, ' votes');
22
23     tomsdiff := tomsvotes − averagevotes;
24     dicksdiff := dicksvotes − averagevotes;
25     harrysdiff := harrysvotes − averagevotes;
26
27     writeln ('They differ from the average as follows');
28     writeln (space :5, 'Tom: ', tomsdiff :6:2,
29              space :5, 'Dick: ', dicksdiff :6:2,
30              space :5, 'Harry: ', harrysdiff :6:2)
31   end.
```

INPUT:
13   4   36

OUTPUT:
Tom has polled 13 votes
Dick has polled 4 votes
Harry has polled 36 votes
Their average poll is 17.67 votes
They differ from the average as follows
  Tom: −4.67   Dick: −13.67   Harry: 18.33

Figure 1.12 Example 1.6 with formatting incorporated

A desired "field width" may be specified after a parameter, the two being separated by a colon:

write (α:β)

where β is an "integer expression", outputs the value of α right justified in a field of width β. This means that if fewer than β characters are needed to print the value α an appropriate number of spaces will be added at the left-hand end. If the field width specified is too small it will be ignored and the minimum field width necessary will be assumed. Specifying a field width of unity therefore ensures that the output value will occupy no more spaces than necessary.

For reals a second format parameter (preceded by :) may be specified to indicate the number of decimal places required. The value is then rounded to the appropriate number of decimal places and printed in "fixed point form" (this is the usual mathematical notation for a real number):

write (3.14159265:10:6)

will produce

3.141593

Figure 1.12 shows the program of Figure 1.6 with formatting incorporated.

1.4 Exercises

The programs for Exercises 1 to 6 need no variables. Any values required can be supplied as user-defined constants at the head of the program.

*1. Charlie is looking forward to his retirement when he reaches 65 but cannot work out when that will be. Write a program that will tell Charlie how many years he has to wait if he supplies his age.
  2. Write a program which prints the number of electricity units used if the present and previous meter readings are supplied.
†*3. Write a program to convert a length in yards, feet, and inches to inches.
  4. Write a program to print the perimeter and area of a rectangular field of given length and breadth.
  5. Write a program to draw the following triangle.

*6. Write a program to print your name and address within a border. Use any character of your choice for the border.

The programs for Exercises 7, 8, and 9 should use variables. Until you are familiar with reading values for variables you may supply values as user-defined constants {but you should eventually incorporate read-statements}.

*7. The first two terms in the "Fibonacci sequence" are 0 and 1 and each successive term is the sum of the previous two. Thus the sequence starts 0, 1, 1, 2, 3, 5, 8, 13, ... Write a program which, given two consecutive Fibonacci numbers, produces the next three.

†8. Write a program which will print the net price of an item, the tax payable on the item, and the total cost of the item. The net price in pence is supplied and the tax percentage is quoted as an integer.

*9. A capital invested and the interest rates for each of three successive years are supplied. Interest is calculated at the end of each year and added to the current sum invested. Write a program to print the original sum, the interest awarded each year, and the total investment at the end of the three years.

No user-defined constants should appear in the programs for Exercises 10 and 11.

†*10. Write a program to read a four-letter word and print it backwards.

†11. Write a program to read three lines of data and print the first character of the first line, the second character of the second line, and the third character of the third line.

2

Arithmetic Data Types

2.1 The data type *integer*

Nearly all programs are involved with integers in one way or another. Even if not processing integers explicitly a program is probably counting something somewhere, and counting involves sequencing through the integers. A basic familiarity with processing integers is therefore fundamental to programming.

Integers should be used in any context which dictates that only whole numbers can occur. Examples might be recording someone's age in years, the number of days between two dates, the number of employees within a firm, or the number of children in someone's family.

The type *integer* has already been mentioned as one of the standard scalar types. For reasons which will be explained in Section 2.2 the type *integer* is also classified as an "ordinal" type. It embraces all the integral values (whole numbers), positive, negative, and zero, between two extremes determined by your particular computer. Pascal provides a predefined constant *maxint* with an implementation dependent value. For your compiler *maxint* will be the largest integer your computer can represent. Typically this might be about 32,000 for a small computer or perhaps up to 300,000,000,000,000 for a large one. The smallest integer (i.e. the negative integer with the largest absolute magnitude) it can represent should be assumed to be -*maxint*.

Any attempt to produce an integer outside the permitted range is said to cause "overflow" and constitutes an error. In the absence of overflow all operations on integers are exact.

Within a program or within data an integer "denotation" is a sequence of digits possibly preceded by a plus or minus sign:

INTEGER DENOTATION

UNSIGNED INTEGER

Neither spaces nor commas may appear within an integer constant.

Five arithmetic operators are provided for integers. Each yields an integer result when supplied with two integer operands:

+	*addition*
−	*subtraction*
*	*multiplication*
div	*integer division (divide and round towards 0)*
mod	*modulo reduction (a* **mod** *b is the remainder when a is divided by b)*

The subtraction operator may be used as a unary minus and supplied with one operand. The operations **div** and **mod** may be unfamiliar, so here are some examples:

$$17 \ \textbf{div} \ 6 = 2 \qquad 17 \ \textbf{mod} \ 6 = 5$$
$$6 \ \textbf{div} \ 17 = 0 \qquad 6 \ \textbf{mod} \ 17 = 6$$
$$18 \ \textbf{div} \ 6 = 3 \qquad 18 \ \textbf{mod} \ 6 = 0$$

The operations **div** and **mod** are not defined if the left-hand operand is negative or the right-hand operand is negative or zero.

If you are a mathematical genius it will be obvious to you that, for non-zero m and positive n,

$$((m \ \textbf{div} \ n) * n) + (m \ \textbf{mod} \ n) = m$$

If not, do not worry, but check that this works for $m = 17$ and $n = 6$.

```
0    program ReverseInt (output);
1         { Takes a positive user-defined three-digit integer and
2             prints its value backwards. }
3    const
4        n = 472;
5    var
6        units, tens, hundreds : integer;
7    begin
8        units := n mod 10;
9        tens := (n mod 100) div 10;
10       hundreds := n div 100;
11
12       writeln (n :3, ' reversed is ', units :1, tens :1, hundreds :1)
13   end.
```

OUTPUT:
472 reversed is 274

Figure 2.1   Example 2.1

Example 2.1

Write a program to print out backwards a three-digit integer supplied as a user-defined constant. □

A program operating upon the value *472* is given in Figure 2.1. To show that it works, at least for the value *472*, we work through it line by line:

8	*units*: = *472* **mod** *10*	{ =2}
9	*tens*: = (*472* **mod** *100*) **div** *10*	{ =72 **div** 10 =7}
10	*hundreds*: = *472* **div** *100*	{ =4}
12	*472 reversed is 274*	

Note that we could form the integer value whose digits are those of *n* in reverse order with the expression

(*hundreds* * 100) + (*tens* * 10) + *units* ∎

Pascal provides four standard functions which deliver an integer result if supplied with an integer operand. The operand need not be simply an integer constant or variable but may be any expression of type *integer:*

succ (i)	the successor of *i* ($i+1$)
pred (i)	the predecessor of *i* ($i-1$)
abs (i)	the absolute magnitude of *i* ($|i|$)
sqr (i)	*i* squared (i^2)

The expression *sqr(i)* is equivalent to $i*i$ but may be compiled more efficiently.

The successor and predecessor functions are more usually applied to other scalar types we shall meet later but can be used with any ordinal operand and, hence, an integer expression. Your compiler may produce slightly more efficient code for *succ(i)* and *pred(i)* than for $i+1$ and $i-1$, but you should use whichever form you find more natural.

The value delivered by a function is said to be undefined if the value it should deliver falls outside the permitted range. Any attempt to produce a value outside the permitted range constitutes an error. In particular,

succ (maxint)   and   *pred(-maxint)*

are undefined.

Recall that a real value must not be assigned to an integer variable. Consequently Pascal provides two functions which take a real operand and produce an integer result:

round (r)	the integer closest to *r*. If *r* is equidistant between two integers (i.e. *2r* is an integer), rounding is away from 0. *round (7.5) = 8* and *round (− 7.5) = − 8*.
trunc (r)	*r* rounded towards 0. *trunc (7.5) = 7* and *trunc (− 7.5) = − 7*.

40

User-defined integer constants were introduced in Section 1.2.3.1 and integer variables in Section 1.2.3.2. An integer variable may take as its value any integer within the range -*maxint* to *maxint.*

2.2 The data type *real*

Real numbers allow complex mathematical computations to be carried out and are principally for the numerical analyst, engineer, etc. If you are likely to be involved with complex numerical computation you may benefit by following this general introduction to programming with a text specifically aimed at numerical computation. A great many programs, including most of those in this book, involve no real values at all.

Reals are used in contexts where numerical values will not necessarily be whole numbers. Examples might be distances (e.g. 14.3 metres), temperatures (e.g. −49.1762°C) and prices in pounds or dollars (e.g. £2.17, $314.56).

The set of reals in Pascal is a subset of all the values, integral and non-integral, between two implementation dependent bounds. Because real numbers are represented inside your computer in a different way to integers a much greater range of values is possible. A price one pays for this is that not all numbers (not even all whole numbers) within that range can be represented because a computer can store only a certain number of significant digits. So, unlike operations on integers, operations on reals are likely to involve some error because the values themselves may not be stored exactly. Some values must be truncated to store them in the computer. The same thing happens in ordinary decimal notation if we try to express one-third as a finite fraction. The error involved with any one operation should be small, but if many operations are carried out (and in a typical numerical program the operations on real values may number several millions) these errors accumulate and the final results may be meaningless. There are ways of dealing with this and if you are likely to be involved with large numerical calculations you should seek further advice. For the scope of this book you need no more than a general awareness of the problem as outlined in Section 2.5.

Only operations performed on real values suffer from inherent error. Consequently, it is convenient to discriminate between type *real* and other scalar types. All scalar types other than real are classed as "ordinal" types.

There are two ways to represent real values in Pascal, corresponding to the two formats available from *write* and *writeln.* Fixed point form comprises an integral and fractional part separated by a decimal point:

FIXED POINT REAL CONSTANT

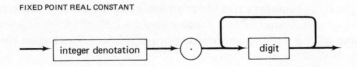

For example,

           3.1415926536
           0.1
           1.0
      123456.789
          −0.0000001
         −43.201

Floating point form comprises a coefficient and a power of ten separated by *E*:

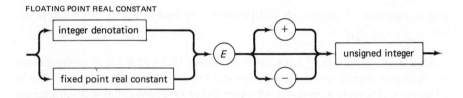

FLOATING POINT REAL CONSTANT

For example,

1E6	*{ =1000000.0}*
1.0E−6	*{ =0.000001}*
12345E5	*{ =1234500000.0}*
0.1234E−4	*{ =0.00001234}*

Real numbers expressed in either of these forms and within the range imposed by your computer are legal in both program and data. Note that spaces are not allowed within either form.

Four arithmetic operators are supplied for reals. Each yields a real result when supplied with two real operands or one real and one integer operand:

   +   *addition*
   −   *subtraction*
   *   *multiplication*
   /   *division*

The subtraction operator may be used as a unary minus and supplied with only one operand. The division operator may be supplied with two integer operands but the result will still be of type *real*.

The standard functions *abs* and *sqr* are applicable to real as well as integer operands. Each delivers a real result if supplied with a real operand. *sqr(x)* should be used in preference to *x ∗ x*. Six further standard functions deliver a real result whether supplied with an integer or a real operand:

$sin(x)$	natural sine and cosine:	$\{sin\ x\}$
$cos(x)$	x must be expressed in radians.	$\{cos\ x\}$
$arctan(x)$	inverse tangent, in radians.	$\{tan^{-1}\ x\}$
$ln(x)$	natural logarithm.	$\{log_e\ x\}$
$exp(x)$	exponential function.	$\{e^x\}$
$sqrt(x)$	positive square root.	$\{\sqrt{x}\}$

Some programming languages provide an exponentiation operator to allow a representation of expressions of the form x^y with the only restriction that y must have type *integer* if x is negative. When y is *real* the compilers then utilize the fact that

$$x^y = e^{y\ ln(x)}$$

and implement x^y as though the programmer had written

$exp\ (y * ln(x))$

This is an "expensive" expression in that it involves a lot of computation because *exp* and *ln* are each time-consuming functions. We shall see why in Chapter 6. There is a danger with these other languages that a programmer, not realizing the computation time involved with x^y, might use the exponentiation operator unwisely. Consequently the Pascal programmer must write

$exp\ (y * ln(x))$

if he requires x^y but cannot achieve it more conveniently. He will then be aware of the computation invoked and will also understand why the computer will object if x is negative (*ln* must not be supplied with a negative parameter).

Example 2.2

Write a program which prints the first five powers of a given number and the sum of the first three (i.e. x, x^2, x^3, x^4, x^5 and $x+x^2+x^3$ for some given x). □
The program is listed in Figure 2.2. ■

User-defined real constants were introduced in Section 1.2.3.1 and real variables in Section 1.2.3.2. A real variable may take as its value any representable value within the floating point range of the machine.

2.3 Arithmetic expressions

Arithmetic expressions may contain integer and real constants, variables, function "calls", arithmetic operators, and parentheses. We shall meet other possible constituents in subsequent chapters. We have met all the arithme-

```
program PowersAndSums (input, output);
      { Computes the first five powers of a given number
        and the sum of the first three powers. }
   var
      x, xsquared, xcubed : real;
begin
   read (x);
   xsquared := sqr(x);     xcubed := x * xsquared;

   writeln ('The first 5 powers of ', x, ' are');
   writeln (x, xsquared, xcubed, sqr (xsquared), xsquared * xcubed);

   writeln ('The sum of the first 3 powers is ',
      x + xsquared + xcubed)
end.
```

INPUT:
49.56

OUTPUT:
The first 5 powers of 0.495600E + 02 are
  0.495600E + 02   0.245619E + 04   0.121729E + 06   0.603289E
                                            + 07   0.298990E + 09
The sum of the first 3 powers is 0.124235E + 06

Figure 2.2   Example 2.2

---

tic operators and standard arithmetic functions available and have encountered some simple arithmetic expressions. We now look at the "precedence rules" governing the evaluation of arithmetic expressions.

The operators

   * / **div mod**

are called "multiplying operators" and

   + −

are "adding operators". The multiplying operators take precedence over the adding operators. This means that multiplying operators will be applied before adding operators in the same expression unless parentheses indicate otherwise. Any expression within parentheses is evaluated independently of any preceding or succeeding operators. At any one precedence level operators are applied in order from left to right.

Some expressions in conventional mathematical notation and in Pascal form are as follows:

Conventional	Pascal
$(a+b)(c+d)$	$(a+b) * (c+d)$
$\dfrac{a}{bc}$	$a / (b * c)$ {not $a / b * c$}
$\sqrt{b^2 - 4ac}$	$sqrt\,(sqr\,(b) - 4 * a * c)$
$x^2 \sin x^2$	$sqr\,(x) * sin\,(sqr\,(x))$

Note that the multiplication operator ($*$) must appear explicitly in Pascal. Some Pascal expressions are evaluated:

$3/2 * 4 = (3/2) * 4 = 1.5 * 4 = 6.0$ {real}
$3/(2 * 4) = 3/8 = 0.375$ {real}
3 **div** $2 * 4 = (3$ **div** $2) * 4 = 1 * 4 = 4$ {integer}
$trunc\,(- sqrt(sqr(17$ **mod** $5) * 2 * (15$ **div** $2) + sqr(1/2)))$
$= trunc\,(- sqrt(sqr(2) * 2 * 7 + sqr(0.5)))$
$= trunc\,(- sqrt(4 * 2 * 7 + 0.25))$
$= trunc\,(- sqrt(56.25))$
$= trunc\,(- 7.5) = -7$ {integer}

```
program FahrenToCenti (input, output);
     { Reads a Fahrenheit temperature and converts it
        to Centigrade. }

  var
     fahrentemp, centitemp : real;
  begin
     read (fahrentemp);

     centitemp := (fahrentemp - 32) * 5 / 9;

     writeln ('The centigrade equivalent of ',
        fahrentemp :6:2, 'F is ', centitemp :6:2, ' C')
  end.
```

INPUT:
14.9

OUTPUT:
The centigrade equivalent of 14.90 F is −9.50 C

Figure 2.3   Example 2.3

To aid readability it is often useful to include extra parentheses:

$a * b$ **div** c **mod** $d + e$

is perhaps clearer if written

$((a * b)$ **div** $c)$ **mod** $d + e$

Example 2.3

Write a program to convert a Fahrenheit temperature into Centigrade:

$$\frac{\text{Fahrenheit} - 32}{9} = \frac{\text{Centigrade}}{5} \quad \square$$

The program listing is given in Figure 2.3. ∎

```
program RealRoots (input, output);
      { Computes the roots of a quadratic equation
        assuming the equation has real roots. }
   var
      a, b, c, sqroot, twoa, x1, x2 : real;
begin
   read (a, b, c);
   writeln ('2' :26);
   writeln ('The equation ', a :10:4, 'x   + ',
      b :10:4, 'x + ', c :10:4, ' = 0');

   sqroot := sqrt (sqr (b) − 4 * a * c);
   twoa := 2 * a;

   x1 := (−b + sqroot) / twoa;
   x2 := (−b − sqroot) / twoa;

   writeln ('has roots', x1, ' and ', x2)
end.
```

INPUT:
3.1   1.891   −8.7234

OUTPUT: *2*
The equation   3.1000 x +   1.8910 x +   −8.7234 = 0
has roots 0.140000E + 01 and −0.201000E + 01

Figure 2.4   Example 2.4

Example 2.4

Write a program which computes the roots of a given quadratic equation with real roots. The roots of the equation $ax^2 + bx + c = 0$ are

$$\frac{-b \pm \sqrt{b^2 - 4ac}}{2a} \quad \square$$

The program is listed in Figure 2.4. ■

2.4 Integer overflow

Integers should be used in preference to reals in any context where only whole numbers can occur. Unfortunately the range limitation of integers can sometimes prevent this. A program dealing with population sizes of large cities may produce values greater than *maxint*. A program to compute the factorial function can easily generate overflow:

{factorial (n) $\equiv 1 \times 2 \times 3 \times \cdots \times n$ for integral n.
factorial (10) = 3,628,800.
factorial (15) = 1,307,674,368,000.}

In such cases we must use real variables and expressions.

Note that overflow can occur at any point during the evaluation of an expression. Although the final value of the expression

maxint ∗ 2 **div** 3

would be within range, overflow occurs when the computer attempts to evaluate

maxint ∗ 2

and so the final value will never be computed. Rewriting *maxint* ∗ 2 as

maxint ∗ 2.0

avoids the overflow at this point (because the expression is now of type real) but we must resist any temptation to write

round (*maxint* ∗ 2.0) **div** 3

because the call of *round* will fail (overflow again). Instead, we must write the expression in the form

trunc (*maxint* ∗ 2.0/3)

Substitute some small values for *maxint* to convince yourself that this gives the same answer as the original expression.

2.5   Precision of reals

Inside a computer a real value is represented by a fixed number of significant digits along with a record of where the point should be. These digits are binary digits and the point is a binary point, but the principles involved are exactly the same in decimal form so we can illustrate some problems with reals by considering a hypothetical decimal machine.

Let us assume our machine can store five significant digits (and, if appropriate, a minus sign). It would then represent the value

123.45

by storing the two values

12345 and 3

to indicate that the value is

0.12345×10^3

(i.e. the point is three places in from the left). The digit string 12345 is called the "mantissa" and 3, the power of ten, is called the "exponent".

The value

0.000012345

would be represented by

12345 and -4

corresponding to

0.12345×10^{-4}

Just as there is a limit to the number of digits which can be stored for the mantissa, so there is a limit on the size of the exponent. Let us assume that our decimal computer imposes a limit of one digit (and, if appropriate, a minus sign). The largest number we can then store is

0.99999×10^9 $(\equiv 999\,990\,000)$

Notice that the next largest value we can represent exactly is

0.99998×10^9 $(\equiv 999\,980\,000)$

and that these differ by $10,000$. Any value between these two will be stored as one of these values so a value in this range can be in error by up to 5,000!

Leading zeros in the mantissa are not stored (i.e. the first digit must be non-zero) so the smallest positive value that can be stored is

0.10000×10^{-9} $(\equiv 0.000\,000\,000\,1)$

and then any value less than

$$0.5 \times 10^{-10} \quad (\equiv 0.000\,000\,000\,05)$$

will be stored as *0.0*.

This can cause problems. Consider the expression

$a/(b * c)$

where $a = 0.000\,000\,4$, $b = 0.000\,01$, and $c = 0.000\,004$. Mathematically the value delivered by the expression is *10,000* but, in our computer, evaluation of $b * c$ produces

0.000 000 000 04

which is less than 0.5×10^{-10} and so is stored as *0.0*. Upon attempting to evaulate $a/0.0$ the computer naturally objects (overflow).

We now evaluate some expressions subject to the constraint that each intermediate result will be truncated to five significant digits.

(a) *10000+0.5*

The addition should produce

10000.5

but rounding to 5 significant digits gives

10001.0.

The result is in error by *0.5*.

(b) *10/3 * 3*

Mathematically the value is, of course, *10* but our computer produces a different result. Dividing *10* (integer) by *3* (integer) gives

3.3333 (real)

and multiplying this by *3* (integer) gives

9.9999 (real)

The result is in error by *0.0001*.

(c) *2 * 5000.7 − (9000 + 1000.6)*

Mathematically the value is *0.8*; our computer produces *0.0*. The product

*2 * 5000.7*

produces *10001.4* which, to five significant digits, is

10001.0

and the sum

9000 + 1000.6

produces *10000.6* which also, to five significant digits, is

10001.0

Fortunately the number of significant binary digits stored by a computer should be equivalent to more than five decimal digits; the significance is typically between seven decimal digits for a small computer to fourteen for a large one. The representational errors inherent in real numbers are therefore less than those indicated in the examples above but, as the computation proceeds, these errors accumulate. Be on your guard!

2.6 Arithmetic input

When a request is made for input to a real or integer variable the computer expects to find, in the data, a character sequence satisfying the syntax for numbers in Pascal text. Any preceding spaces or ends of lines will be skipped. Reading will cease whenever the next character to be input cannot possibly be part of the number (or sooner if overflow occurs).

The value read and the variable to which the value is to be assigned must be **assignment** compatible. Just as one cannot assign a real value to an integer variable with an assignment statement, neither can this be achieved by *read* or *readln*. If an attempt is made to read a real value for an integer variable, the variable will be assigned the value represented by the digit sequence preceding *E* or the decimal point and *E* or the decimal point will be the next character waiting to be read.

Consider the statement

read (i, ch, r)

in the context of the declaration

var *i* : *integer*;   *ch* : *char*;   *r* : *real*;

If the data supplied were

*1 * 2.3*

the value of the variables would become

i = 1   ch = ''   r = 2.3*

but the data

*1.0 * 2.3*

would give

i = 1   ch = '.'   r = 0.0

2.7 Exercises

*1. Write a program to determine the length of the hypotenuse of a right-angled triangle, given the lengths of the other two sides.

 2. Write a program to compute the area of a triangle using the fact that, for a triangle with sides of length a, b, and c, the area is given by

$$\sqrt{s\,(s-a)\,(s-b)\,(s-c)}$$

where

$$s = \frac{a+b+c}{2}$$

†*3. A secret service organization uses numeric codes for agents and cities. When spy α is to go to city β a coded message is sent to central intelligence. Instead of referring to the agent and the destination directly the message incorporates the two values $\alpha - \beta$ and $\alpha^2 - \beta^2$. Write a decoding program which, given these two coded values, deduces which agent and city are involved.

†4. Carol wishes to lay one course of carpet tiles across her bedroom. Assuming the width of her bedroom is supplied as an integral number of feet and the width of a carpet tile is given as an integral number of inches write a program to tell Carol how much she will have to cut off the last tile to be laid.

†*5. Write a program to produce change from £1 for any purchase less than £1 not involving $\frac{1}{2}$ p. The program is to indicate which coins are to be paid and should minimize the number of coins. Denominations available are 50 p, 10 p, 5 p, 2 p, and 1 p.

†*6. Using a 24-hour clock a time can be represented by an integer in the range 0 {midnight} through 1200 {noon} to 2359 {11.59 pm}. Write a program to add a given duration, expressed in hours and minutes, to a specified time.

3

The Data Type *char*

In our everyday life more information is conveyed to us through general characters (letters, punctuation, etc., as well as digits) than through numbers alone. Much of the information presented to computers must be processed on a character by character basis. A compiler is an example of a program which is supplied with a sequence of characters (your program) which it must process. In fact, even when you supply an arithmetic datum to a program the *read* procedure scans the number character by character and builds up the value in the process. We shall see how in Chapter 6.

3.1 Characters

The ordinal data type *char* embraces all the characters available on your computer. If your output is produced by a line printer it may only make sense to consider your computer's set of printable characters. If you are communicating via a terminal you may be able to utilize some non-printable characters. For example, most terminals recognize a character which cannot be printed and sound a buzzer or ring a bell. Throughout this book we shall consider only printable characters.

The set of characters for a computer is small (typically 64 or 128 members), implementation dependent (different computers may provide different characters), and ordered. The ordering associated with the character set (called the "lexicographic order") varies from one computer to another but we can assume that all computers will regard the digits 0 to 9 as contiguous, that most regard the letters *A* to *Z* as contiguous, and that they regard the letters *a* to *z*, if they are available, as contiguous.

You should determine the underlying character set of your computer and its lexicographic ordering. Be wary, though, of letting your programs place too much dependence upon this ordering. A well-written program is easily "portable" from one computer to another. A program exploiting special features of a particular lexicographic ordering will not transport easily. Throughout this book we shall keep programs as portable as possible and will clearly indicate any situations where modifications might be necessary if the program were moved to another computer.

The ISO-ASCII character set presented in Appendix E is a standard 128-character set but, since many input/output devices can handle only 64 characters, only a subset may be available. Different computers implement different subsets and impose different lexicographic orderings. Some implemented character sets, with the lexicographic orderings indicated, are included in Appendix E. All the programs presented in this book have been run on either an ICL 1900 computer or a Prime computer, and so each assumes either the ICL 1900 or Prime character set. In particular, it is assumed that all letters occurring within supplied data will be upper case.

We saw how to represent a character value in Section 1.1.3.1; the character is enclosed within quotes. To represent the quote character itself it is typed twice. Some examples of character constants are

$$'F', '3', '?', '''', ' ', '+'$$

Note that '3' (a character) is not the same as 3 (an integer) and may well be represented quite differently inside the computer. For example, *sqr(3)* is a valid expression (delivering the value 9) but *sqr('3')* is undefined and will fail to compile (incorrect type of operand).

Note also that a space is a valid character.

User-defined character constants were introduced in Section 1.2.3.1 and character variables in Section 1.2.3.2. A character variable may take as its value any character from the implemented set.

3.2 Standard functions

The standard functions *succ* and *pred* are applicable to operands of type *char*. Note that the values of *succ* and *pred* are undefined if they are applied to, respectively, the last and first member of the character set.

We can assume that

$$pred\ ('7') = '6'$$

and, if the letters *A* to *Z* are represented contiguously, that

$$succ\ ('A') = 'B',$$
$$succ\ ('B') = 'C',$$
$$pred\ ('Z') = 'Y'$$

and so on, but

$$pred\ ('A'), \quad succ\ ('Z'), \quad pred\ ('0'), \quad and \quad succ\ ('9')$$

are implementation dependent; in fact, some may not exist at all (i.e. the value delivered by the function may be undefined).

Associated with each character is an "ordinal number", its position within the ordered set. The first character in the set has the ordinal number 0. Two standard functions are defined to determine the ordinal number of any character and to deduce a character from its ordinal number:

ord (c)   ordinal number of character *c*
chr (n)   character with ordinal number *n*

The following relationships should be apparent (assuming *c* has type *char*, *i* has type *integer*, and no attempt is made to produce a character outside the set):

pred (succ (c))   = *c*
succ (pred (c))   = *c*
ord (succ (c))   = *ord (c) + 1*
succ (ord (c))   = *ord (c) + 1*
ord (pred (c))   = *ord (c) − 1*
pred (ord (c))   = *ord (c) − 1*
ord (chr (i))   = *i*
chr (ord (c))   = *c*
chr (ord (c) + 1) = succ (c)
chr (ord (c) − 1) = pred (c)

To aid portability we should not make a program's function dependent upon the absolute ordinal numbers of any characters, but we may use relative ordinal numbers of letters or digits. For example, the position in the alphabet of a letter *l* will be given by the expression

ord (l) − ord ('A') + 1

whatever the underlying character set, so long as the letters *A* to *Z* are contiguous.

```
program FirstAndLastChars (output);
      { Prints the first and last characters in the available
        character set if told the set size. }
   const
      noofcharsinset = 64;
   begin
      writeln ('First and last characters of the lexicographic ',
         'ordering are,');
      writeln ('respectively, ', chr (0), ' and ',
         chr (noofcharsinset − 1))
   end.
```

OUTPUT:
First and last characters of the lexicographic ordering are, respectively, 0 and ←

Figure 3.1   Example 3.1

```
program FiveLetters (input, output);
    { Given a letter between C and X inclusive, the
      program prints five alphabetically contiguous letters
      centred on the given letter. }
var
    letter : char;
begin
    read (letter);
    writeln ('Five letters centred on ', letter, ' are ',
        pred (pred(letter)), pred (letter), letter,
        succ (letter), succ (succ (letter)))
end.
```

INPUT:
R

OUTPUT:
Five letters centred on R are PQRST

Figure 3.2   Example 3.2

Example 3.1

Write a program which prints the first and last characters in the ordered character set if told how many characters the set contains.   □
    The program is listed in Figure 3.1.   ■

Example 3.2

Given a letter between C and X inclusive, write a program which prints five alphabetically contiguous letters with the given letter in the middle. For example, given the letter *K* the program should produce *IJKLM*.   □
    The program is listed in Figure 3.2.   ■

3.3 Character input

When an arithmetic datum is sought any preceding spaces or ends of lines are ignored, but this is not the case when a character is requested. The next character in the input stream is read, whatever it may be. A space is a significant character in this context and the end of a line is interpreted as a space. Each line should therefore be regarded as having an extra space at the end. It is possible to distinguish this artificial space from real spaces, but discussion of this is deferred to Chapter 5.

Example 3.3

The British convention for expressing a date is

   day/month/year

The American convention is

   year/month/day

Write a program which reads a date typed in the British convention and outputs it in the American form. Allow for separators other than "/" to occur but assume that each separator will immediately follow the preceding digit.   □

   The program is presented in Figure 3.3.   ■

   We sometimes wish to "skip" the next character in the input stream. This is achieved by the statement

   get (input)

To read two characters separated by some arbitrary character we could write

   read (ch1);   get (input);   read (ch2)

using the two character variables *ch1* and *ch2*.

   It is often useful for a program to be able to "look at" the next character in the data without having to read it in. Reading implies extracting a value

```
program UKtoUSdate (input, output);
     { Reads a date in British form and outputs it in US form. }
   var
     day, month, year : integer;
     sep1, sep2 : char;
begin
   read (day, sep1, month, sep2, year);
   writeln ('Date in US form is ',
     year :2, sep1, month :2, sep2, day :2)
end.

INPUT:
25/9/81

OUTPUT:
Date in US form is 81/9/25
```

Figure 3.3   Example 3.3

56

```
program TwoCharsThreeTimes (input, output);
    { Prints the first character from each of two lines
      of data three times but reads none from
      the second line. }
  var
    ch : char;
begin
  read (ch);
  writeln ('First line: ', ch, ch, ch);
  readln;
  writeln ('Second line: ', input↑, input↑, input↑)
end.
```

INPUT:
ABRACADABRA
*? * % & !*

OUTPUT:
First line: AAA
Second line: ???

Figure 3.4   Example 3.3(b)

from the data so that it is no longer accessible for subsequent input. A program processing an address might want to know whether the address starts with a house name or a number; if the first character is a digit it can read a number, but if not it must read characters. It must determine which course of action to adopt before reading the first character. We shall see in Chapter 4 how a program can vary its course of action as a result of tests it can make.

The next character in the input stream can be determined by inspecting

input↑

the "input window"; *input↑* can be thought of as a window one character wide which slides along a line of data in front of the read head. Thus *input↑* exists only if *input* appears in the program parameter list and is then effectively a character variable which cannot be assigned to. It is automatically assigned to each time *read* or *readln* is called. For a character variable *ch*,

read (ch)

is equivalent to

ch := input↑;   get (input)

When execution commences, the value of *input*↑ is the very first character of the data. When the last character of a line is read *input*↑ = ' '. When this artificial space is read the value of *input*↑ becomes the first character of the next line of data. If there is no next line of data the value of *input*↑ is undefined. Any attempt to read data when *input*↑ is undefined constitutes an error.

Example 3.4

Write a program which is to be supplied with two lines of data and is to output the first character of each line three times but is not to read any data from the second line. □

The program is listed in Figure 3.4. Note the following points:

1. *readln* is used to move *input*↑ to the start of the second line after the first character of the first line has been read.
2. Reference to *input*↑ does not change its value; each of the three references produces the same value.
3. If a further *read(ch)* followed the *write* the value *ch* would acquire would be the first character of the second line; no datum has been read (i.e. extracted) from the second line. ■

3.4 Exercises

Assume the letters *A* to *Z* are contiguous.

*1. A simple way to encode a message which does not contain the letter *Z* is to replace each letter by its alphabetic successor. Write a program which reads a coded three-letter word and decodes it.
†2. Write a program which states the position in the alphabet of a given letter.
†*3. Write a program to print a letter, given its position in the alphabet.
*4. Write a program which states how far apart in the alphabet two given letters are.

4

Conditional Flow of Control

It was stated in Section 1.1.1 that "control" passes sequentially from one statement to the next when a program is being obeyed. This is strictly true only in the simplest of programs. In this chapter we see how the flow of control can be dependent upon the outcome of tests made at run-time.

4.1 The if-statement

There are two variants of the if-statement.

4.1.1 if ... then ...

This is the simpler of the two forms:

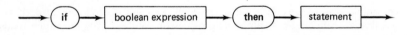

We consider "boolean expressions" in detail in Chapter 5 but for the moment regard them as simple tests involving one or more variables in the program. Simple tests may be made using the following relational operators:

<	*less than*
>	*greater than*
=	*equal to*
<=	*less than or equal to*
>=	*greater than or equal to*
<>	*not equal to*

These operators can be used to compare two operands of any scalar type. Both operands must have the same type unless one is real and the other integer. The result of the comparison (i.e. the value of the boolean expression) is said to be either *true* or *false*. Accordingly, *true* and *false* are called "boolean values".

We use this form of the if-statement when we wish to perform some action only under certain conditions. At run-time the boolean expression is evaluated (i.e. the test is made) and if it delivers the result *true* (i.e. the condition tested holds) the statement after **then** is obeyed. If the boolean expression delivers the result *false* (i.e. the condition tested does not hold) the statement after **then** is ignored. In either case control then passes to the statement following the if-statement.

For example,

$n = 3$

is a boolean expression and so

if $n = 3$ **then** *write* *('n is 3')*

is a legal if-statement if *n* has type *integer*. The expression $n = 3$ is evaluated. We can regard this expression as a statement of fact—it is either *true* or *false* (unless the value of *n* is undefined in which case the value of the boolean expression is undefined). The write-statement after **then** is obeyed only if the current value of *n* is *3*.

Notice that no semi-colons appear within the if-statement.

```
program BankBalance (input, output);
   var
      balance, withdrawal : real;
begin
   read (balance, withdrawal);
   writeln ('Current balance : £', balance :7:2);

   writeln ('After withdrawing £', withdrawal :6:2);
   balance := balance - withdrawal;
   writeln ('   the resultant balance is £', balance :7:2);

   if balance < 0 then
      writeln ('Your account is overdrawn—',
               'Please see the manager!')
end.
```

INPUT:
246.43
317.82

OUTPUT:
Current balance : £ 246.43
After withdrawing £ 317.82
*   the resultant balance is £ −71.39*
Your account is overdrawn—Please see the manager!

Figure 4.1   Example 4.1

60

Example 4.1

Write a program which reads a current bank balance and a withdrawal amount and computes the resultant balance. An appropriate message should be output if the account becomes overdrawn. □
 The program is given in Figure 4.1. ∎

Example 4.2

Write a program to read an integer and to print its modulus without using the function *abs*. The modulus of a number is its absolute magnitude. □
 The program listing is given in Figure 4.2. When run with the datum −856 it produces 856 as the modulus and when run with the datum 27 it produces 27. ∎

Example 4.3

Write a program which reads a letter and, unless this letter is Z, prints the letter following it in the alphabet. If the letter supplied is Z the Z is to be reproduced. □
 The program listing is given in Figure 4.3. ∎

```
program Modulus (input, output);
     { Reads an integer and computes its modulus. }
  var
     n : integer;
begin
  read (n);
  writeln ('The supplied integer is ', n);

  if n < 0 then
     n := −n;
  writeln ('Its modulus is ', n)
end.
```

INPUT:
−856

OUTPUT:
The supplied integer is   −856
Its modulus is   856

Figure 4.2   Example 4.2

```
program NextLetter (input, output);
     { Reads a letter and, unless this letter is Z,
       prints its successor. Z is merely reproduced. }
   var
     letter : char;
begin
   read (letter);
   writeln ('Supplied letter is ', letter);

   if letter < > 'Z' then
     letter := succ (letter);
   writeln ('Unless this letter is Z its successor is ', letter)
end.
```

Figure 4.3   Example 4.3

Relational operators have lower precedence than all the other operators so an expression such as

$a + b < c * d$

can be written without parentheses because it is equivalent to

$(a + b) < (c * d)$

4.1.2 if ... then ... else ...

This is the full if-statement:

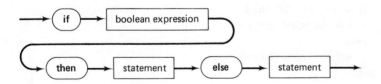

At run-time the boolean expression is evaluated and, assuming no error results from this evaluation, control passes to either the statement after **then** or the statement after **else**. If the boolean expression delivers *true* the statement after **then** is obeyed. If the boolean expression delivers *false* the statement after **else** is obeyed. Control then passes to the statement after the if-statement.

We use this form of the if-statement when we wish to perform one, but only one, of two distinct actions and the computer is to determine which.

62

Example 4.4

Write a program which reads a letter and outputs the next letter of the alphabet if the supplied letter is in the first half of the alphabet and outputs the preceding letter if the supplied letter is in the second half of the alphabet. □

The program is given in Figure 4.4. Notice that the if-statement could equally well have been written with the test "inverted" and the statements interchanged:

```
if letter > 'M' then
    writeln (pred (letter))
else
    writeln (succ (letter))
```

We need not have used an else-clause at all. We could have used two if–then-statements instead:

```
program PredSuccLetter (input, output);
        { Reads a letter and outputs its predecessor or successor
          depending upon the half of the alphabet in
          which the supplied letter falls. }
    var
        letter : char;
    begin
        read (letter);
        writeln ('Supplied letter is ', letter);

        write ('Desired adjacent letter is ');

        if letter <= 'M' then
            writeln (succ (letter))
        else
            writeln (pred (letter))
    end.
```

INPUT:
S

OUTPUT:
Supplied letter is S
Desired adjacent letter is R

Figure 4.4   Example 4.4

---

if *letter* <= *'M'* **then** *writeln (succ (letter))*;
if *letter* > *'M'* **then** *writeln (pred (letter))*

Use of one if-statement with an else-part is better for the following three reasons:

1. The if–then–else form is more transparent. It tells us immediately that one, and only one, of the writeln-statements will be obeyed. This is not apparent in the two-if version until we realize that the two tests are "complementary" (i.e. if one is *false* the other is *true*).
2. If we have to write two tests, one of which is the inverse of the other, we may get one wrong. We are less likely to make a mistake if we make only one test and do not need to work out its inverse.
3. Why make the computer do more work than is necessary? The outcome of the first test tells us what the outcome of the second will be. Making the second test is therefore both illogical and inefficient. ■

Example 4.5

Write a program which reads two integers and outputs the modulus of their difference but does not use the function *abs*. □
   The program is given in Figure 4.5. ■

Example 4.6

Write a statement to determine whether or not two characters *ch1* and *ch2* are the same. □
   Here are two such statements:

1. **if** *ch1 = ch2* **then**
      write ('same')
   else
      write ('different')
2. **if** *ch1* <> *ch2* **then**
      write ('different')
   else
      write ('same') ■

This example is presented to illustrate the undesirability of negation in program logic. Our mental faculties can cope reasonably with a single level of negation when they must, but we have trouble with double or triple negatives.
   The else-part of an if-statement embodies an implicit negation. To discern the conditions under which control will reach the else-part we must mentally

64

```
program ModDiff (input, output);
    { Outputs the modulus of the difference between
        two supplied integers. }
    var
        int1, int2 : integer;
begin
    read (int1, int2);
    write ('The modulus of the difference between ',
        int1 :1, ' and ', int2 :1, ' is ');

    if int1 > int2 then
        writeln (int1 - int2)
    else
        writeln (int2 - int1)
end.
```

INPUT:
−47   263

OUTPUT:
The modulus of the difference between −47 and 263 is 310

Figure 4.5   Example 4.5

invert (i.e. negate) the test following the appropriate preceding **if**. Thus, in version 1 above, control reaches the else-part if it is not the case that *ch1* = *ch2*. We easily recognize this as meaning when *ch1* and *ch2* differ.

If the test following **if** involves a negation we then have to unravel a double negative to decide how control reaches the else-part. This happens in version 2. Control reaches the else-part if it is not the case that *ch1* does not equal *ch2*. A conscious mental effort is now required before we realize that this means *ch1* and *ch2* agree.

The moral is: when an **if** has an associated **else** try to avoid involving negation in the test. *Think positively*!

4.2   The case-statement

The if-statement provides a two-way choice based upon a boolean expression. The case-statement provides a multi-way choice based upon expressions of other types as well as *boolean*. We return later to the generality of the case-statement but consider here the case-statement with boolean, character, and integer "selectors".

4.2.1 Two-way selection with boolean selector

In the particular case of a boolean selector the case-statement has one of the two forms:

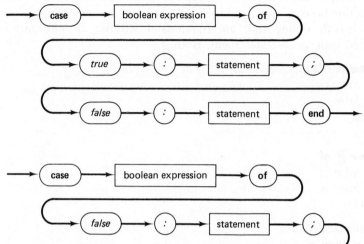

and

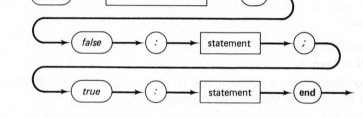

These two forms are equivalent and have the same effect as the full if–then–else-statement. The boolean expression is evaluated and, depending upon the result obtained, the appropriate statement is obeyed. It is customary to follow an **end** associated with **case** by the comment { case }.

The if-statement of Figure 4.4 could be written as

```
case letter <= 'M' of
    true :  writeln (succ (letter));
    false : writeln (pred (letter))
end { case }
```

and the if-statement of Figure 4.5 as

```
case int1 > int2 of
    true :  writeln (int1 - int2);
    false : writeln (int2 - int1)
end { case }
```

Which style you prefer is very much a matter of personal taste. You will find that most Pascal texts will use if-statements, probably to the exclusion of the case-statement with a boolean selector. Do not be misled into thinking that the if-statement must therefore be superior. This form of if-statement has been with us since the inauguration of Algol 60, but the Pascal case-statement is a more recent innovation. Most Pascal programmers are still more familiar with **if**. Experience shows, however, that many people meeting Pascal for the first time are happier with **case**. We shall see later (as in Figures 7.13 and 7.14) that the **case** form can be attractive when used in conjunction with user-defined boolean constants. Both forms will be used in this book.

It is worth noting that an if-statement without an else-part can be simulated using a case-statement. Both

> **case** β **of**
> > *true* : α;
> > *false* :
> **end**

and

> **case** β **of**
> > *false* : ;
> > *true* : α
> **end**

are equivalent to

> **if** β **then** α

Case-statements of this form will rarely be used in this book—the effect of the if-statement is usually more obvious.

4.2.2 Multi-way selection

A case-statement controlled by a boolean selector can only provide a two-way choice mechanism because a boolean expression can only deliver one of two values, *true* or *false*. Case-statements may be supplied with selectors of any ordinal type.

For a boolean selector we list the values the selector could produce and follow each by an appropriate statement. We do the same thing for selectors of other types and, in general, there will be more than two possible values. The value of the selector is determined and the appropriate statement within the case-statement is obeyed. Control then passes to the statement following the case-statement.

Example 4.7

Write a program which outputs one of the names Amanda, Bernard, Christine, or Frank when given the initial letter. □

The program is given in Figure 4.6. We note the following points:

1. The selector is not an expression involving an operator (but in general it can be). A variable is a simple case of an expression and the value delivered by the expression is just the current value of the variable.
2. The selector values quoted are called "case labels". The case labels need not appear in any particular order. The program would be nicer if they

```
0   program Names (input, output);
1       { Outputs a name given the initial. }
2   var
3       initial : char;
4   begin
5     read (initial);
6
7     case initial of
8       'F' : writeln ('Frank');
9       'C' : writeln ('Christine');
10      'A' : writeln ('Amanda');
11      'B' : writeln ('Bernard')
12    end { case }
13  end.
```

INPUT:
C

OUTPUT:
Christine

Figure 4.6   Example 4.7

did appear in the order 'A', 'B', 'C', 'F', but they have been jumbled to show that this is not necessary.
3. Not all the values that can be taken by the selector need be quoted within the case-statement. ■

A statement may be preceded by more than one case label. A number of case labels, separated by commas, may be supplied. If Amanda is known to her friends as Mandy, an appropriate modification to the program of Figure 4.6 might be the replacement of line 10 by

10   'M', 'A' : writeln ('Amanda');

The program will now produce her name when prompted with either M or A.

We can now formalize the syntax of a case-statement:

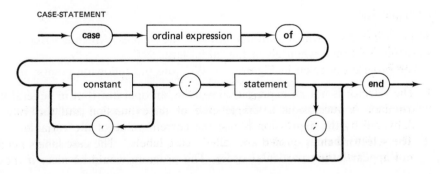

If the value of the selector is not present as one of the case labels the effect of the case-statement is undefined. A program such as the one just considered should therefore check that the value of the selector is appropriate before obeying the case-statement. We shall do this in various ways in later examples.

We now consider an example involving an integer selector.

Example 4.8

Write a program that states in which quadrant a given angle, expressed in degrees, lies. An angle α is said to be in the

first quadrant if in the range $0 \leq \alpha < 90$
second quadrant if in the range $90 \leq \alpha < 180$
third quadrant if in the range $180 \leq \alpha < 270$

and

fourth quadrant if in the range $270 \leq \alpha < 360$ □

We can determine the quadrant by dividing the angle by 90 and considering the integer part of the result. This will give us an integer in the range 0 to 3 corresponding to quadrants 1 to 4 respectively. The program is listed in Figure 4.7. We should check that the value of *angle* does lie within the range $0 \leq angle < 360$ before entering the case-statement. We return to this later. ■

The amount of storage space needed for the run-time case limb selection mechanism depends upon the range of the case labels. A case-statement may be unacceptably expensive in this respect if the range of the case labels is large but the number of limbs is small. For example, the machine code produced by your compiler for the statement

```
case i of
    1000 : . . . ;
    2000 : . . .
end
```

will probably contain about 1,000 instructions more than that produced for

```
if i = 1000 then . . . . . else
    if i = 2000 then . .
```

```
program Quadrant (input, output);
     { Determines which quadrant contains a given angle,
       assumed to be in the range 0 < = angle < 360. }
  var
    angle : real;
begin
  read (angle);      { angle must be expressed in degrees }
  write ('The supplied angle is ', angle :6:2,
    'degrees and lies in the ');

  case trunc (angle / 90) of
    0 : write ('first');
    1 : write ('second');
    2 : write ('third');
    3 : write ('fourth')
  end { case } ;

  writeln (' quadrant')
end.
```

INPUT:
247.29

OUTPUT:
The supplied angle is 247.29 degrees and lies in the third quadrant

Figure 4.7   Example 4.8

4.3   Compound-statements

If, in an arithmetic expression, we wish to refer to the product of a with the sum of b and c we write $a*(b+c)$. We bracket $b+c$ to indicate that $b+c$, and not just b, is the right-hand operand of $*$. Similarly, we have occasion to bracket statements to indicate that a group of statements is to be considered where only one would otherwise be. Such a situation arises if we wish to obey more than one statement after **then**, **else**, or a case label.

begin and **end** are statement brackets. A group of (zero or more) statements, separated by semi-colons and enclosed between **begin** and **end**, is called a "compound-statement". The main body of a program is a compound-statement.

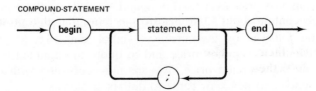

70

```
program DoublePrice (input, output);
    { Doubles a price supplied in sterling or US currency. }
    var
        lowprice : integer;
        highprice : real;
        units : char;
begin
  case input↑ of
    '£', '$' :
      begin
        read (units, highprice);
        writeln ('Supplied price is ', units, highprice :6:2);
        writeln ('Doubled price is ', units, highprice * 2 :7:2)
      end;
    '1', '2', '3', '4', '5', '6', '7', '8', '9' :
      begin
        read (lowprice, units);
        writeln ('Supplied price is ', lowprice :2, units);
        writeln ('Doubled price is ', lowprice * 2 :3, units)
      end
  end { case }
end.
```

INPUT:
$17.59

OUTPUT:
Supplied price is $ 17.59
Doubled price is $ 35.18

Figure 4.8   Example 4.9

A compound-statement may be used at any point where any other statement may be used. At the moment its usefulness to us, except as a program body, is restricted to the three situations mentioned above.

Example 4.9

A price is quoted in either sterling (pounds or pence) or US currency (dollars or cents). A price expressed in pounds or dollars will be *preceded* by the currency symbol (e.g. £17.32, $4.18) but a price expressed in pence or cents will be *followed* by the currency symbol (e.g. 48 c, 86 p). Write a program to double a supplied price and to quote the doubled price in the same units as the supplied price. We are not concerned with converting pence to pounds and pence or cents to dollars and cents.

We assume the first character of the price is the first character of the data. □

This could be done (with difficulty) without a compound-statement but the natural way to express the algorithm is to look at the first character of the data (but not read it) to determine whether the price is high (i.e. pounds or dollars) or low (pence or cents) and then both read the currency symbol and the figure in the appropriate order and write the doubled price, again with the currency symbol and figure in the appropriate order. The program is given in Figure 4.8. ■

4.4 Nested conditionals

The statement following **then** or **else** or a case label may be conditional. We then say the conditionals are "nested". We isolate two particular cases of interest.

```
program JackandJill (input, output);
    { States the age difference of Jack and Jill. }
  var
    jacksage, jillsage : integer;
begin
  read (jacksage, jillsage);
  writeln ('Jack is ', jacksage :2, ' and Jill is ', jillsage :2);

  if jacksage > jillsage then
    writeln ('Jack is ', jacksage – jillsage :2,
      ' years older than Jill')
  else
    if jacksage < jillsage then
      writeln ('Jill is ', jillsage – jacksage :2,
        ' years older than Jack')
    else
      writeln ('Jack and Jill are the same age')
end.
```

INPUT:
19   19

OUTPUT:
Jack is 19 and Jill is 19
Jack and Jill are the same age

Figure 4.9   Example 4.10

72

4.4.1   if *following* else

if β_1 **then** α_1 **else**
  if β_2 **then** α_2 **else** α_3

If β_1 is *true* then α_1 is obeyed. If β_1 is *false* control passes to the second if-statement, whereupon if β_2 is *true* α_2 is obeyed and if β_2 is *false* α_3 is obeyed.

We have arranged for two tests to be made in sequence, the second being made only if the first one fails (i.e. delivers *false*).

Example 4.10

Write a program which, given the ages in years of Jack and Jill, states who is the elder and by how much. If Jack and Jill are the same age the program should mention this.   □
We have three possible states:

1. Jack is older than Jill.
2. Jack is younger than Jill.
3. Jack and Jill are both the same age.

We can determine the state by making, at most, two tests. The program is given in Figure 4.9.   ∎

Example 4.11

Modify the program of Figure 4.7 to check that the supplied angle is in the range $0 \le angle < 360$.   □
The program is given in Figure 4.10. Note the use of the compound-statement within the second if-statement.   ∎

The principle can be extended:

if β_1 **then** α_1 **else**
  if β_2 **then** α_2 **else**
    if β_3 **then** α_3 **else**
      . . .
        if β_n **then** α_n **else** α_{n+1}

A series of tests is made until one delivers *true* and the appropriate statement is then obeyed. If no test delivers *true* the action specified after the final **else** is carried out. If the final if-statement has no else-part and all the tests deliver *false* no action is carried out.

This effect is similar to that of a case-statement. The case-statement of

```
program QuadrantWithCheck (input, output);
      { Determines which quadrant contains a given angle and checks
        that the angle is in the range 0 <= angle < 360. }
var
   angle : real;
begin
   read (angle);      { angle must be expressed in degrees }
   writeln ('The supplied angle is ', angle :6:2, ' degrees');

   if angle < 0 then
     writeln ('Negative angles are not catered for')
   else
     if angle >= 360 then
        writeln ('This angle is too large') else
     begin      { angle is in required range }
        write ('The angle lies in the ');

        case trunc (angle / 90) of
           0: write ('first');
           1: write ('second');
           2: write ('third');
           3: write ('fourth')
        end { case };

        writeln (' quadrant')
     end
end.
```

INPUT :
372.9

OUTPUT :
The supplied angle is   372.90 degrees
This angle is too large

Figure 4.10   Example 4.11

Figure 4.10 has the same effect as the following sequence of nested **if**s:

if *trunc (angle/90) = 0* **then** *write ('first')* **else**
   if *trunc (angle/90) = 1* **then** *write ('second')* **else**
      if *trunc (angle/90) = 2* **then** *write ('third')* **else**
         write ('fourth')

To save repeated evaluation of the expression *trunc (angle/90)* we could store its value in a variable:

```
quad := trunc (angle/90);
if quad = 0 then write ('first') else
  if quad = 1 then write ('second') else
    if quad = 2 then write ('third') else
      write ('fourth')
```

The case-statement is still preferable for two reasons:

1. The case-statement is more transparent. It shows immediately that the choice of statement to be obeyed is dependent only upon the value of one expression and clearly states what the possible values are.
2. The case-statement is more efficient. The choice of statement to be obeyed is made directly upon evaluation of the selector. The nested **if**s involve a possible series of tests being made.

The case-statement is appropriate for the program of Figure 4.10 because the choice of inner statement is dependent solely upon the value of one expression and the possible values are few and known. We now consider an example where this is not so. Several courses of action are possible and the tests for each either involve different expressions or involve an expression with many possible values.

We consider the problem of finding the roots of the general quadratic equation

$$ax^2 + bx + c = 0$$

If $b^2 - 4ac$ (called the "discriminant") is positive two distinct real roots exist and we can compute these as in Figure 2.4. If the discriminant is zero two equal real roots exist. If the discriminant is negative we have two complex roots. For example, the equation

$$x^2 + 2x + 5 = 0$$

has complex roots

$$-1 + 2i \qquad \text{and} \qquad -1 - 2i$$

The computer knows nothing of complex numbers but we can easily arrange for it to produce character strings such as the two roots above.

We must be careful when testing the value of the discriminant. We should never test two real values for equality or inequality. The dangers of doing so are apparent from the discussion of Section 2.5. Instead, if we wish to test two reals for equality we must test to see if their absolute difference does not exceed some very small number which, considering the limited precision of reals, we are prepared to regard as zero. This is illustrated in the following example.

```pascal
program Quadratic (input, output);

    {                              2
        Solves the quadratic equation ax + bx + c = 0 }
    const
        assumedzero = 1E - 6;
    var
        a, b, c, discriminant, x1, x2, realpart, imagpart : real;
begin
    read (a, b, c);
    writeln ('2' : 24);
    writeln ('The equation ', a :8:4, ' x  +',
        b :8:4, ' x +', c :8:4, '= 0');

    if abs (a) <= assumedzero then
        writeln ('is not quadratic') else
    begin { true quadratic }
        discriminant := sqr (b) - 4 * a * c;

        if abs (discriminant) <= assumedzero then
            writeln ('has two equal roots :', -b/(2 * a) :8:4)
        else

            if discriminant > assumedzero then
            begin { distinct real roots }
                x1 := (-b + sqrt (discriminant)) / (2 * a);
                x2 := (-b - sqrt (discriminant)) / (2 * a);
                writeln ('has distinct real roots :',
                    x1 :8:4, ' and ', x2 :8:4)
            end { distinct real roots } else

                begin { complex roots }
                    realpart := -b / (2 * a);
                    imagpart := sqrt (-discriminant) / (2 * a);
                    writeln ('has complex roots :');
                    writeln (realpart :8:4, ' +', imagpart :8:4, ' i');
                    writeln (realpart :8:4, ' -', imagpart :8:4, ' i')
                end { complex roots }
    end { true quadratic }
end.
```

INPUT :
1 -4   5

76

OUTPUT :   2
The equation   1.0000 x +   −4.0000 x+   5.0000 = 0
has complex roots   :
   2.0000 +   1.0000 i
   2.0000 −   1.0000 i

Figure 4.11   Example 4.12

Example 4.12

Write a program to compute the roots of the quadratic equation $ax^2 + bx + c = 0$. □

The program is listed in Figure 4.11. ■

4.4.2 **if** *following* **then**

First, note that the following two statements have different effects:

(a) **if** β_1 **then**
     begin
        if β_2 **then** α **else** γ
     end
(b) **if** β_1 **then**
     begin
        if β_2 **then** α
     end
   else γ
The statement

   if β_1 **then**
      if β_2 **then** α
   else γ

could be interpreted either way. For this reason some languages forbid this form and insist that the statement be written as in (a) or (b). Pascal permits this form and decrees that it is equivalent to (a). The **else** is associated with the closest preceding outstanding **then**. If we want the effect of (b) we must write it as in (b). If we want the effect of (a) it is a good idea, in order to reduce the possibility of (human) misinterpretation, to write it as in (a). Another way to make the program intent clear is to replace the second **if** by **case**:

(a)* **if** β_1 **then**
        case β_2 **of**
           true : α ;
           false : γ
        end { case }

```
program NamesWithCheck (input, output);
    { Outputs a name, given an appropriate initial. }
    var
        initial : char;
begin
    read (initial);

    if initial >= 'A' then
        if initial <= 'F' then
            if initial <> 'D' then
                if initial <> 'E' then
                    case initial of
                        'A' : writeln ('Amanda');
                        'B' : writeln ('Bernard');
                        'C' : writeln ('Christine');
                        'F' : writeln ('Frank')
                    end { case }
end.
```

Figure 4.12   Example 4.13

So, the effect of

if β_1 **then**
    if β_2 **then** α **else** γ

is that if β_1 is *false* no action is taken and if β_1 is *true* then depending upon β_2 either α or γ is obeyed.

Extending the idea to

if β_1 **then**
  if β_2 **then**
    if β_3 **then**
      . . .
        if β_n **then** α **else** γ

we see that α is obeyed only if $\beta_1, \beta_2, \ldots, \beta_n$ are all *true* and γ is obeyed only if $\beta_1, \beta_2, \ldots, \beta_{n-1}$ are all *true* and β_n is *false*.

If β_1 to β_{n-1} are not all *true* no action is taken.

Example 4.13

Modify the program of Figure 4.6 to ensure that the case-statement is not obeyed if the supplied initial is not appropriate.   □

The program is given in Figure 4.12. This solution is purely to illustrate the effect of nested **if**s following **then**. This is *not* the way this example should be programmed. We shall soon discover better ways. The nested **if** approach is appropriate when we need to arrange for tests to be made in sequence (see Section 5.3). ■

4.5 Exercises

  1. Write a program to print two supplied integers in ascending order.

†*2. Write a program to determine which of three given letters occurs first in the alphabet.

  3. Write a program to state whether three supplied letters are in alphabetical order.

 *4. Write a program to determine whether a five-letter word is palindromic. A palindrome reads the same backwards and forwards.

†5. (a) Write a program to determine whether a given triangle is right-angled. Assume the length of each side is specified as an integral number of units.

    (b) Include data validation: your program is to check that the supplied lengths do specify a triangle.

†6. Write a program to determine whether two three-letter words are supplied in alphabetical order.

†*7. Write a program to tell a person's age in years (not years, months, and days). The person's birthdate and the current date are given, each in the form of three integers—day, month, year.

†8. We wish to print the sum of two supplied integers unless this falls outside the range *[-maxint, maxint]*, in which case we wish to know which end of the range is exceeded and by how much. Assume that each of the two supplied integers is within the range *[-maxint, maxint]* and write two different programs to achieve this. In the first, convert integers to real form within the program as appropriate; in the second, make no use of type *real.*

Test your program with several pairs of integers including various combinations of *maxint, -maxint, (maxint* **div** *3)∗2, -(maxint* **div** *3)∗2,* and *0.*

 *9. A program is to be supplied with the first letter of one of the five messages "Get well soon", "Congratulations", "Happy Birthday", "Bon Voyage", and "Merry Christmas" and is to output the corresponding message. When a birthday greeting is required, an age will follow the letter *H* and this age is to be included within the message. Write the program.

10. Write a program to print the Morse code of any supplied letter.

†11. Write a program to accept a date typed in the form

    day/month/year

with the year specified by two digits, and to expand it by naming the month, quoting the full four digits of the year and following the day by *st, nd, rd,* or *th* as appropriate.

    For example,

    23/5/81

should appear as

    23rd May 1981

†12. The motor insurance brokers U. Crash and I. Pay have eight categories of insurance based upon an applicant's age and occupation. Only people aged over sixteen but not over seventy are eligible and occupations are classified into

three risk groups. The table below illustrates the applicable insurance categories:

	Low risk	Medium risk	High risk
17–20	6	7	8
21–24	4	5	6
25–34	2	3	5
35–64	1	2	4
65–70	2	3	5

Write a program to state the appropriate category for a given age and risk group (specified by one of the letters *L*, *M*, *H*). The program must ensure that the applicant is of eligible age.

5

The Data Type *boolean*

5.1 Boolean constants

There are two boolean values: *true* and *false*. It is quite legal (but pointless) to write

>**if** *true* **then** α **else** γ

or

>**if** *false* **then** α **else** γ

for some statements α and γ. In the first case α will be obeyed and in the second case γ will be obeyed.

There is more point in having a user-defined boolean constant in such a context. We can then steer control through chosen branches of if- and case-statements.

Example 5.1

Modify the pet shop program of Figure 1.8 so that it could easily be adapted to accepting data with no associated text and with several values on each line. □

This flexibility is displayed by the program of Figure 5.1. As written the program accepts data presented one value per line with associated text but if we redefine *onevalueperline* as *false* it will assume no text is present in the data and several values may be on one line. We indicate the effect we want merely by changing the value of a user-defined constant. This is easier, and safer, than altering statements within the body of the program. ∎

A common use of this technique is to control the points at which a program will generate output. When we are developing a program we often wish to see how computation is progressing at certain points in the program so that we may check that all is well.

Example 5.2

Provide the quadratic equation example of Figure 4.11 with the option of producing the value of the discriminant and, for real roots, the values c/a,

```
program PetShop (input, output);
    { Computes the total pet population assuming four kinds of pet
      and can be made to take each datum from a new line. }
const
    onevalueperline = true;
var
    pet1s, pet2s, pet3s, pet4s, totalpets : integer;
begin
    if onevalueperline then
    begin
        readln (pet1s);   readln (pet2s);   readln (pet3s);   readln (pet4s)
    end else
        read (pet1s, pet2s, pet3s, pet4s);

    totalpets := pet1s + pet2s + pet3s + pet4s;
    writeln ('Total pet population is ', totalpets : 1)
end.
```

Figure 5.1   Example 5.1

```
program Quadratic (input, output);
    {                                    2
        Solves the quadratic equation ax  + bx + c = 0. }
const
    assumedzero = 1E - 6;
    extraoutput = true;
var
    a, b, c, discriminant, x1, x2, realpart, imagpart : real;
begin
    read (a, b, c);
    writeln ('2' : 24);
    writeln ('The equation ', a :8:4, ' x  + ',
        b :8:4, ' x +', c :8:4, ' = 0');

    if abs (a) <= assumedzero then
        writeln ('is not quadratic') else
    begin { true quadratic }
        discriminant := sqr (b) - 4 * a * c;

        if extraoutput then
            writeln ('has discriminant ', discriminant, ' and');

        if abs (discriminant) <= assumedzero then
            writeln ('has two equal roots :', -b / (2 * a) :8:4)
        else
```

```
        if discriminant > assumedzero then
        begin {distinct real roots}
            x1 := (−b + sqrt (discriminant)) / (2 * a);
            x2 := (−b − sqrt (discriminant)) / (2 * a);
            writeln ('has distinct real roots :',
                x1 :8:4, ' and ', x2 :8:4);
            if extraoutput then
            begin
                writeln;
                writeln ('Sum of roots : ', x1 + x2);
                writeln ('−b/a : ', −b/a);
                writeln;
                writeln ('Product of roots : ', x1 * x2);
                writeln ('c/a :', c/a)
            end
        end {distinct real roots} else

        begin {complex roots}
            realpart := −b / (2 * a);
            imagpart := sqrt (−discriminant) / (2 * a);
            writeln ('has complex roots :');
            writeln (realpart :8:4, ' +', imagpart :8:4, ' i');
            writeln (realpart :8:4, ' −', imagpart :8:4, ' i')
        end {complex roots}
    end {true quadratic}
end.
```

Figure 5.2   Example 5.2

$−b/a$, the product of the roots, and the sum of the roots. Mathematically, for two real roots α and β of the equation $ax^2 + bx + c = 0$, $\alpha\beta = c/a$ and $\alpha + \beta = −b/a$. □

The program of Figure 5.2 produces this extra output. If *extraoutput* is defined to be *false* the program has the same effect as the original. ∎

Program transparency can sometimes be improved when user-defined constants are used in place of the predefined boolean values.

```
    const
        positive = true;   negativeorzero = false;
        ...
    case (a + b) * c > 0 of
        positive: ... ;
        negativeorzero: ...
    end { case }
```

is perhaps more informative than

if $(a+b)+c>0$ **then**
   ...
else
   ...

5.2   Standard functions

The function *ord* may be applied to a boolean expression:

ord (false) = 0   and   *ord (true) = 1*

and hence

false $<$ *true*

Pascal provides three standard functions which deliver a boolean result.

5.2.1   *odd*

The function *odd* (α) is defined for any valid integer expression α and delivers *true* if α is odd and *false* if α is even. We could test the parity of a given integer *n* (i.e. whether *n* is odd or even) with the test

n **div** $2*2 = n$ {delivers *true* if *n* is even}

but *odd(n)* will implement the test more efficiently. For example,

if *odd (n)* **then**
  write (n, ' is odd')
else
  write (n, ' is even')

5.2.2   *eoln*

When the end of a line of data has been reached (i.e. the last character of the line has been read and *input*↑ indicates the artificial space), the function *eoln* delivers *true*. At all other times it delivers *false*. It is thus possible to distinguish the artificial space inserted at the end of each data line from spaces actually present in the data.

Unless a non-standard input file is being used (see Chapter 12) *eoln* need not be supplied with a parameter.

Example 5.3

Write a section of program to inspect the next character in the data and to classify it as non-space, genuine space, or end of line, as appropriate.   □

84

There are several ways to achieve this. Here are two:

1. **if** *input↑ < >*' ' **then**
      write (*'non-space'*)
   else
     if *eoln* **then**
       write (*'end of line'*)
     else
       write (*'space'*)
2. **if** *input↑* =' ' **then**
     case *eoln* **of**
       true : write (*'end of line'*);
       false : write (*'space'*)
     end { case }
   else
     write (*'non-space'*)

Version 2 is easier to "verify" than version 1; convincing yourself that the presented solution works will probably take longer for version 1 than for version 2. This is because an if-statement in version 1 has an else-part and embodies a negation within its test. Remember, think positively! ■

5.2.3 *eof*

When the last character and the artificial space at the end of the last line of data have been read the program is said to have reached the end of the input file. When this is the case the boolean function *eof* delivers the value *true*. It will also deliver *true* if *input* has been specified in the program parameter list but no data has been supplied. At all other times, assuming *input* has been specified, *eof* delivers *false*.

When data is supplied directly from a terminal, implementations differ in the way they allow the end of the input file to be indicated. Some implementations do not recognise the end of the input file at all in this situation.

Unless a non-standard input file is being used (see Chapter 12) *eof* need not be supplied with a parameter.

Example 5.4

Write a program which states whether it is supplied with no data, one line of data, or more than one line of data. □
The program listing is given in Figure 5.3. ■

A program will fail if an attempt is made to read data when *eof* is *true*.

5.3 Boolean operators

5.3.1 and

In previous examples we have seen the need to make compound tests

```
program HowMuchData (input, output);
    { States whether the program is supplied with no data,
        one line of data, or more than one line of data. }
begin
    write ('This program has been supplied with ');

    if eof then
        writeln ('no data') else
    begin
        readln;

        if eof then
            writeln ('one line of data')
        else
            writeln ('more than one line of data')
    end
end.
```

INPUT :

'TWAS BRILLIG, AND THE SLITHY TOVES

OUTPUT :

This program is supplied with one line of data

Figure 5.3   Example 5.4

composed of several simple tests. For example, the program of Figure 4.12
makes several tests (*initial* $> =$ 'A', *initial* $< =$ 'F', *initial* $< >$ 'D', *initial*
$< >$ 'E'), all of which must yield *true* before the ensuing statement will be
obeyed.

If the order in which the tests are made is not important a statement of
the form

(1) **if** β_1 **then**
       if β_2 **then**
          if β_3 **then**
             . . .
                if β_n **then** α

can be written

(2) **if** (β_1) **and** (β_2) **and** (β_3) . . . **and** (β_n) **then** α

The whole test is regarded as *true* only if β_1 and β_2 and β_3 . . . and β_n are

all *true*. Thus

> **if** *initial* $>=$ $'A'$ **then**
>   **if** *initial* $<=$ $'F'$ **then**
>   **if** *initial* $<>$ $'D'$ **then**
>   **if** *initial* $<>$ $'E'$ **then**
>   **case** . . .

can be replaced by

> **if** *(initial* $>=$ $'A')$ **and** *(initial* $<=$ $'F')$**and**
>   *(initial* $<>$ $'D')$ **and** *(initial* $<>$ $'E')$ **then**
>   **case** . . .

The operator **and** is a boolean operator which must be supplied with two boolean operands and delivers the value *true* only if **both** its operands deliver *true*. In the above example each **and** is applied to two operands because

> **if** β_1 **and** β_2 **and** β_3 **and** β_4 **then** . . .

is equivalent to

> **if** $((\beta_1$ **and** $\beta_2)$ **and** $\beta_3)$ **and** β_4 **then** . . .

Notice that an expression of the form

> $(x > 1)$ **and** (<10)

is illegal because **and** has not been supplied with two boolean operands, and that

> $(x > 1)$ **and** $(x < 10)$

is legal. The operator **and** is classed as a multiplying operator and so takes precedence over relational operators. So the parentheses in an expression such as

> $(x > 1)$ **and** $(x < 10)$

are necessary. The expression

> $x > 1$ **and** $x < 10$

is equivalent to

> $x > (1$ **and** $x) < 10$

which is nonsense!

Example 5.5
To vote in a general election in the United Kingdom a person must be at least eighteen years of age but not yet sixty-five. Write a program which

reads a person's age (as a whole number of years) and states whether the person is of voting age.   □

The program is illustrated in Figure 5.4. ■

Note that the two forms (1) and (2) are not equivalent if the ordering of the tests is important. When a compound test is expressed as a set of nested if-statements no further tests will be made when one constituent test delivers *false*. When a compound test is expressed as a set of tests joined by **and** the computer may evaluate all the constituent tests before deciding whether the compound test is *true* or *false*.

Thus a statement of the form

(a) **if** $x > 0$ **then**
     if *sqrt (x)* > 10 **then** . . .

is not the same as

(b) **if** $(x > 0)$ **and** *(sqrt (x)* $> 10)$ **then** . . .

If the value of x is positive or zero both (a) and (b) have the same effect. If the value of x is negative (a) does nothing and passes control to the next statement in sequence, but (b) might attempt to evaluate *sqrt (x)* which will produce an execution error (*sqrt* must not be supplied with a negative operand).

The definition of Pascal does not stipulate whether the second constituent test will be made or not. Some systems will decide that the compound test must be *false* as soon as $x > 0$ is discovered to be *false*, but some will go ahead with the evaluation of *sqrt(x)* > 10 regardless.

Further mention of this point will be made in section 6.1.5.

```
program Voter (input, output);
      { Given a person's age the program states whether
        that person is eligible to vote. }
   var
      age : integer;
begin
   read (age);
   if (age >= 18) and (age < 65) then
      write ('Yes—eligible to vote')
   else
      write ('No—not eligible');

   writeln (' at ', age :2)
end.
```

Figure 5.4   Example 5.5

5.3.2 or

Another frequent occurrence is the need to perform some action if **at least one** of a number of tests holds. Suppose a particular process is applicable to all integers over 100 but only to odd integers less than 100. An integer n is suitable if n is odd or n exceeds 100 (or both). This can be expressed in Pascal as

>**if** *odd (n)* **or** *(n > 100)* **then** ...

The operator **or** is a boolean operator which must be supplied with two boolean operands and delivers the result *true* if both its operands are valid and **at least one** delivers *true*.

Thus further alternatives for the nested if-statements of Figure 4.12 are

>**if** *(initial = 'A')* **or** *(initial = 'B')* **or**
>*(initial = 'C')* **or** *(initial = 'F')* **then** ...

and

>**if** *((initial >= 'A')* **and** *(initial <= 'C'))* **or** *(initial = 'F')* **then** ...

The operator **or** is classed as an adding operator and so has lower precedence than **and**. We could therefore omit one pair of parentheses from this last example. Thus

>**if** *(initial >= 'A')* **and** *(initial <= 'C')* **or** *(initial = 'F')* **then** ...

has the desired effect.

5.3.3 not

The operator **not** is a boolean operator which must be supplied with one boolean operand and delivers the result *true* if its operand is *false* and *false* if its operand is *true*; it **inverts** a test.

Suppose we wish to carry out some process only if a given integer m is even. We require a statement of the form

>**if** *m is even* **then** ...

A standard function is supplied to test for m being odd; but how can we test for m being even? We use **not** because we wish to invert the result produced by *odd*:

>**if not** *odd (m)* **then** ...

Reconsider the situation that an integer n is suitable for some process if it is odd or greater than 100. Suppose we wish to print a message if n is unsuitable; we require a statement of the form

>**if** *n is unsuitable* **then** *write (n, ' is unsuitable')*

The test we must make is the inverse of the test we made the last time we considered this example. With some thought you should be able to convince yourself that

if *(***not** *odd (n))* **and** *(n <= 100)* **then**

has the desired effect. However, less thought is required to see that

if not *(odd (n)* **or** *(n > 100))* **then** ...

is applying the inverse test.

So, to invert a test simply stick **not** in front and apply parentheses if necessary. The operator **not** has a higher priority than any other operator so parentheses are usually necessary after **not**.

Example 5.6

A program is supplied with three, four, or five integers typed one per line. Compute their average. □
   The program of Figure 5.5 does this. ■

```
program Average345 (input, output);
      { Averages three, four, or five integers supplied one per line. }
   var
      n, n1, n2, n3, noofints, sum : integer;
begin
   readln (n1, n2, n3);
   sum := n1 + n2 + n3;   noofints :=  3;

   if not eof then
   begin
      readln (n);   sum := sum + n;   noofints := 4;

      if not eof then
      begin
         readln (n);   sum := sum + n;   noofints :=  5
      end
   end;

   writeln ('The average of the ', noofints : 1,
      ' supplied integers is ', sum/noofints : 7:2)
end.
```

Figure 5.5   Example 5.6

90

5.3.4 in

The operator **in** is really a relational operator, not a boolean operator, but it is convenient to introduce it in the present context.

5.3.4.1 *Set constructors*

Pascal allows the use of "sets". Sets are described fully in Chapter 10. In the present chapter we consider only the simple use of "set constructors".

A set is a collection of values all of the same type {called the "base type" of the set}. The base type of a set may be any ordinal type. To construct a set the values are listed in any order, separated by commas and enclosed within square brackets. The following are examples of sets:

    [1980, 1981, 1982, 1983, 1984, 1985]   {set of *integer*}
    ['M', 'F', 'D', 'B', 'Z', 'C', 'A']   {set of *char*}
    [false]   {set of *boolean*}

All values within a specified interval can be implied by quoting the lower and upper bounds of the interval separated by **..**. The first two sets above could be expressed as follows:

    [1980 .. 1985]
    ['A' .. 'D', 'F', 'M', 'Z']

Each value supplied need not be a constant but can be any expression delivering a value of the appropriate type. Thus, in the scope of

    var *ch* : *char*;   *i, j* : *integer*;

the two sets

    ['2' .. '6', *ch*, *pred (input↑) .. succ (input↑)]*

and

    [*i* − 5 .. *j* + 2, *i* ∗ *j* .. 100, 17]

are legal assuming all the expressions deliver defined values.

5.3.4.2 *Testing set membership*

The operator **in** takes two operands. The right-hand operand is a set and the left-hand operand is an expression whose type must be the same as the base type of the set:

    α **in** β

is *true* if the value produced by α is currently a member of the set β.

Thus, the nested **if**s of Figure 4.12 could (and, indeed, should) be written

    if *initial* **in** ['A' .. 'C', 'F'] **then** . . .

As a further example we can determine if the next character in the input stream is "alphanumeric" (i.e. letter or digit) by writing

if *input*↑ **in** *['0'..'9','A'..'Z']* **then** ...

This is neater, and also more efficient, than

if *(input*↑ >= *'0')* **and** *(input*↑< = *'9')* **or**
    (input↑ >= *'A')* **and** *(input* ↑< = *'Z')* **then** ...

which is semantically equivalent.

5.3.4.3 *Implementation dependence of sets*

The set facility of Pascal provides a natural means of expressing certain frequent computing operations and it is intended that the implementation of sets should be efficient. To achieve this efficiency most implementations impose a restriction on the number of members a set may contain. Typically this could be 64. Thus a set such as

[1812..1914]

will probably be rejected by your compiler.

Furthermore, most implementations restrict the permitted range of ordinal numbers of set members (typically 0 to 63). Thus the set

[1980..1985]

will probably be rejected by your compiler even though it contains only six members and, depending upon the lexicographic ordering of your computer's character set, even

['A'..'Z']

might be unacceptable. You have my sympathy if your compiler excludes any character from set membership!

Throughout this book we shall assume that negative integers will be unacceptable as set members and that the maximum ordinal value permitted for any set member is not less than 63.

5.4 Boolean variables

Boolean variables are very useful in other programming languages. Because Pascal permits user-defined scalar types (discussed in Chapter 9), boolean variables appear less frequently in a well-written Pascal program than they might if the program were written in some other language.

A boolean variable may take as its value one of the two values *true* or *false*. We can imagine a boolean variable to be a box with a name stuck on and containing a piece of paper on which is written either "yes" or "no". The purpose of a boolean variable is to record the result of a test. Then, if

92

the program, at some later point, wishes to know what the outcome of the test was, it need merely look inside the box to see if the test held—i.e. to see if the value of the variable is *true* ("yes") or *false* ("no").

Example 5.7

A person's age (as a whole number of years) and height (to the nearest centimetre) are supplied. A program is to classify the person's age as

either under 12 *or* 12 or over

and height as

either over 180 cm *or* 180 cm or under

The program is to produce an appropriate message if it encounters anyone under the age of twelve who is taller than 180 cm. □
This could be done as shown in Figure 5.6.

```
0    program AgeAndHeight (input, output);
1      var
2        age, height : integer;
3    begin
4      read (age, height);
5      writeln ('Person"s age is ', age : 1,
6        ' years and height is ', height :1, ' cm');
7
8      write ('Age classification is ');
9      case age < 12 of
10       true : writeln ('under 12');
11       false : writeln ('12 or over')
12     end { case };
13
14     write ('Height classification is ');
15     case height > 180 of
16       true : writeln ('over 180 cm');
17       false : writeln ('180 cm or below')
18     end { case };
19
20     if (age < 12) and (height > 180) then
21       writeln ('Tall for your age aren"t you!')
22   end.
```

Figure 5.6   Example 5.7

Alternatively, the if-statement on lines 20 and 21 could be removed and instead line 16 could be modified to

```
true :   begin
             writeln ('over 180 cm');
             if age < 12 then
                 writeln ('Tall for your age aren"t you!')
         end;
```

but the effect of the program listed is perhaps more obvious.

In either case at least one test may be repeated. A better approach is illustrated in Figure 5.7. Each test is made only once and the results are stored for subsequent reference. In the if-statement the tests are not repeated; instead, the values previously obtained are consulted. ∎

```
program AgeAndHeightWithBooleans (input, output);
   var
       age, height : integer;
       young, tall : boolean;
begin
   read (age, height);
   writeln ('Person"s age is ', age :1,
       ' years and height is ', height :1, ' cm');

   young := age < 12;
   write ('Age classification is ');

   case young of
       true : writeln ('under 12');
       false : writeln ('12 or over')
   end { case };

   tall := height > 180;
   write ('Height classification is ');

   case tall of
       true : writeln ('over 180 cm');
       false : writeln ('180 cm or below')
   end { case };

   if young and tall then
       writeln ('Tall for your age, aren"t you!')
end.
```

Figure 5.7   Example 5.7

In other languages boolean variables are particularly useful in loops (discussed in Chapter 6) but because Pascal provides a better alternative (presented in Chapter 9) their use within this book is occasional.

5.5 Exercises

1. The insurance brokers of Exercise 4.5.11 have restricted their cover to certain occupations. These fall into the three risk groups as follows:

   Low: magicians, burglars, undertakers, and teachers
   Medium: dentists and zookeepers
   High: actors, footballers, guitarists, executives, and students

   Extend the program of the Exercise 4.5.10 to include classification of the applicant's occupation, assuming the initial letter of the occupation replaces the *L*, *M*, or *H* originally suggested.

†*2. Write a program which states whether a given positive integer less than 64 is odd or even and, if it is odd and greater than 1, whether it is a prime number.

†*3. Write a program to state whether a given word contains 1, 2, 3, or more than 3 letters. The word contains only letters and is immediately followed by an end-of-line marker.

4. Write a program to accept an integer and the bounds of two integer ranges and to classify the integer as

   in the first range only,
   in the second range only, or
   in both ranges.

6

Loops

Many computations can be expressed in the form of repeating an action a number of times. The value 2^{10} could be computed by obeying the statement

> *powerof2*: = *2*

once and then repeating the statement

> *powerof2*: = *powerof2 * 2*

nine times.

The sum of a sequence of numbers can be found by repeatedly reading numbers and adding them into a running total. The two statements

> *read (number);   sum* : = *sum + number*

obeyed 100 times and preceded by

> *sum* : = *0*

will sum 100 numbers.

Loops are essentially of two types. If we know how many times we wish to execute a loop the situation is said to be "deterministic"; if we do not, it is said to be "non-deterministic". The two examples above illustrate deterministic loops.

Consider slight modifications to these examples. Suppose we wish to compute the smallest power of 2 which exceeds some specified bound or to accumulate the sum of supplied numbers only until the sum exceeds some specified value. We could still use the same "loop bodies" as previously but now we cannot predict, in advance, how many repetitions will be required. These situations are non-deterministic.

6.1   Non-deterministic loops

A non-deterministic loop is implemented by a while-statement or a repeat-statement.

6.1.1 While-statement

WHILE-STATEMENT

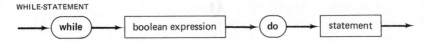

Prior to each execution of the loop body (the statement after **do**) the boolean expression is evaluated. Looping continues only so long as this evaluation delivers *true*. When the boolean expression delivers *false* the loop body is not obeyed; instead, control leaves the loop and passes to the statement next in sequence after the while-statement. If the boolean expression delivers *false* upon entry to the while-statement the loop body is not executed at all; control passes directly to the statement following the while-statement:

> *The body of a while-loop will not necessarily be executed.*

We use a while-statement in a *non-deterministic* situation when we may wish to perform *0 iterations* and so require the loop test to be made *prior* to the first execution of the loop body.

Example 6.1

Consider evaluation of the smallest power of 2 greater than some specified bound. □

This is achieved by the program of Figure 6.1.

To illustrate the effect of the loop we follow the action of this program when supplied with the datum 11:

1. The read-statement on line 6 gives *bound* the value 11.
2. The assignment on line 7 gives *powerof2* the value 2.
3. Control now reaches the while-statement on line 8; the boolean expression (*powerof2* <= *bound*) is evaluated and delivers *true* (2 <= 11) and so the loop body (line 9) is executed.
4. The assignment on line 9 gives *powerof2* the value 4(= 2 * 2).
5. The boolean expression following **while** is now evaluated again and once more yields *true* (4 <= 11). Accordingly the loop body is executed again.
6. The assignment on line 9 gives *powerof2* the value 8(= 4 * 2).
7. The boolean expression following **while** is evaluated again and once more yields *true* (8 <= 11). Accordingly the loop body is executed again.
8. The assignment on line 9 gives *powerof2* the value 16(= 8 * 2).
9. The boolean expression following **while** is evaluated again but this time delivers *false* (16 <= 11), so control leaves the while-statement and passes to the next statement in sequence.
10. The writeln-statement on line 11 produces

> *The smallest power of 2 greater than 11 is 16*

```
0   program MinPowerOf2 (input, output);
1       { Computes the smallest power of 2
2           greater than some specified bound. }
3     var
4       bound, powerof2 : integer;
5   begin
6     read (bound);
7     powerof2 := 2;
8     while powerof2 <= bound do
9       powerof2 := powerof2 * 2;
10
11    writeln ('The smallest power of 2 greater than ',
12        bound :1, ' is ', powerof2 :1)
13  end.
```

INPUT :
11

OUTPUT :
The smallest power of 2 greater than 11 is 16

Figure 6.1   Example 6.1

Notice that we do not wish the loop body to be entered if the supplied bound is less than 2. The loop test must therefore be made *before* execution of the loop body and so we use a while-statement. ∎

The loop body must be expressed as a single statement. If we wish to repeat a group of statements we must bracket the statements with **begin** and **end** to form a compound statement.

Example 6.2

Modify the program of Figure 6.1 to state the power to which 2 has been raised as well as the final value. ☐

Inside the loop we now wish to increment a variable recording the power as well as doubling the power of 2. We must therefore bracket two statements together. The program is presented in Figure 6.2. ∎

Example 6.3

The Fibonacci sequence is

0, 1, 1, 2, 3, 5, 8, 13, . . .

98

---

program *MinPowerOf2 (input, output);*
    { Computes the smallest power of 2 greater than
        some specified bound and states the power. }
  var
    bound, powerof2, power : integer;
begin
  read (bound);
  powerof2 := 2; power := 1;
  while *powerof2 <= bound* **do**
  begin
    *powerof2 := powerof2 * 2; power := power + 1*
  end;

  writeln ('The smallest power of 2 greater than ',
    bound :1, ' is ', powerof2 :1);
  writeln ('This is 2 raised to the power ', power :1)
end.

INPUT :
1000

OUTPUT :
The smallest power of 2 greater than 1000 is 1024
This is 2 raised to the power 10

Figure 6.2   Example 6.2

With the exception of the first two values each term in this sequence is the sum of its two preceding terms. Write a program to compute the smallest Fibonacci number not less than some specified value. □

The program listing is given in Figure 6.3.

This program is worthy of careful study. It illustrates a very frequent situation; during each "iteration" (i.e. each time round the loop) we compute some new value but must keep a record of the previous value. In fact, here we must keep a record of the previous two values. If we tried to use only two variables and computed a new term with the statement

    thirsterm: = thisterm + prevterm

we would be unable to compute the next term. Try it!

Within the loop we utilize three variables:

  termbeforethat   *prevterm*   *thisterm*
    α β γ

```
0   program MinFibonacci (input, output);
1       { Computes the smallest Fibonacci number
2           not less than a specified bound. }
3   var
4     minvalueaccepted,
5     thisterm, prevterm, termbeforethat : integer;
6   begin
7     read (minvalueaccepted);
8     thisterm := 1;  prevterm := 0;
9     while thisterm < minivalueaccepted do
10    begin
11      termbeforethat := prevterm;
12      prevterm := thisterm;
13      thisterm := prevterm + termbeforethat
14    end;
15
16    writeln ('The smallest Fibonacci number not less than ',
17        minvalueaccepted :1, ' is ', thisterm :1)
18  end.
```

INPUT :
20

OUTPUT :
The smallest Fibonacci number not less than 20 is 21

Figure 6.3   Example 6.3

Immediately upon entry to the loop we "shuffle down" (lines 11 and 12) the values of *thisterm* and *prevterm* into *prevterm* and *termbeforethat*:

termbeforethat	*prevterm*	*thisterm*
β	γ	γ

Notice that the ordering of these two assignment statements is important; the program will not produce the desired effect if they are interchanged.

We then compute the next term in the sequence (line 13):

termbeforethat	*prevterm*	*thisterm*
β	γ	$\beta + \gamma$

Another notable feature of this program is the fact that *thisterm*, the variable involved in the while-test, receives its new value as the *last* action of the loop body. This means that loop exit is considered *immediately* the new value is computed. This is a good thing and will be mentioned again in Section 6.1.3. ∎

A problem such as that of Example 6.3 would be regarded as trivial by an experienced programmer. It might surprise you therefore to learn that some programmers might produce a program inferior to that presented here. For instance, the program of Figure 6.4 produces the same output as that of Figure 6.3 but is a poor program.

Let us list its faults:

1. When the new value of *thisterm* is obtained (line 14) further processing is performed (lines 15 and 16) before this value is tested. The processing is unnecessary if we have just obtained the term we seek. It is illogical to

```
0   program PoorMinFibonacci (input, output);
1       { How not to compute the smallest Fibonacci number
2           greater than or equal to a specified bound. }
3     var
4       minvalueaccepted,
5       thisterm, prevterm, termbeforethat : integer;
6   begin
7     read (minvalueaccepted);
8     if minvalueaccepted <= 0 then
9       prevterm := 0 else
10    begin
11      termbeforethat := 0;   prevterm := 1;
12      while prevterm < minvalueaccepted do
13      begin
14        thisterm := prevterm + termbeforethat;
15        termbeforethat := prevterm;
16        prevterm := thisterm
17      end
18    end;
19
20    writeln ('The smallest Fibonacci number not less than ',
21      minvalueaccepted :1, ' is ', prevterm :1)
22  end.
```

INPUT :
20

OUTPUT :
The smallest Fibonacci number not less than 20 is 21

Figure 6.4   Example 6.3

perform unnecessary computation. The extra processing has destroyed some information; the value of the previous term but one has been lost. We may not need this value again but it is pointless to destroy information when we gain nothing by it. A good moral is: *never make a program do something until it has to.* There are exceptions, but this is a good general rule. In this example we do not need to update the values of *prevterm* and *termbeforethat* until we are about to compute a new term: so don't!

2. The loop test (*prevterm* < *minvalueaccepted*) is illogical. It implies that we are seeking that term which *follows* the first term whose value is not less than the bound. As soon as we find a term *t* which fails the test *t* < *minvalueaccepted* it is this term we want, and so it is *thisterm* we should be testing. As the program is written we cannot use *thisterm* in the while-test because its value is undefined upon entry to the while-statement. To counteract this we would have to include *thisterm*: = 1 within line 11, but this would introduce even more unnecessary processing.

3. Use of *prevterm* in the writeln-statement is illogical for reasons similar to those presented for fault 2. Again, the way the program is written prevents our using *thisterm*. If *minvalueaccepted* < = 1 the loop body will not be executed, and so the value of *thisterm* will remain undefined.

4. The interpretation of *thisterm* and *prevterm* is illogical and inconsistent. If the loop body is executed they both indicate the same value at the end of each iteration. If the loop body is not entered *prevterm* indicates the value we seek and the value of *thisterm* is undefined.

Compare the programs of Figures 6.3 and 6.4 in the light of these criticisms. We are not concerned in this book merely with programs which "work"; we are concerned with *good* programs. As a matter of natural consequence a good program will "work".

Note that the comments made above are independent of the fact that the programs are written in Pascal. The effect of the programs is clearer than it would be in most other languages, but programs equivalent to these could be written in almost any programming language. The same comments would apply. Mastery of the concepts presented in this book should equip you for good programming whatever programming languages you subsequently encounter.

6.1.2 Repeat-statement

REPEAT-STATEMENT

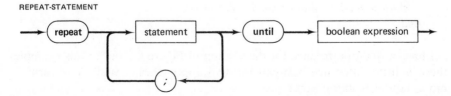

After each execution of the loop body the boolean expression is evaluated. This process continues only until the boolean expression delivers *true*. Control then leaves the loop and passes to the statement next in sequence after the repeat-statement:

The body of a repeat-loop will be obeyed at least once.

We use a repeat-statement in a *non-deterministic* situation when we require *at least one iteration* of the loop to be performed.

Notice that a group of statements may appear between **repeat** and **until** and need not be enclosed between **begin** and **end**.

Example 6.4

A company is offering shares for sale and issues them on a first-come-first-served basis until some predetermined number has been exceeded. As soon as a sale is made which takes the total sold above this bound the company's shares will be removed from the market. A program is to be supplied with the specified bound and a sequence of integers indicating the number of shares requested by buyers in the order in which the purchase requests are received. The program may assume that more shares will be requested than are offered and is to state how many shares are to be sold and how many lots these constitute. □

This involves the repeated addition of supplied numbers into a running total until the specified bound is exceeded. If the bound is sensible (>0) we must process at least one purchase request, and this suggests that a repeat-statement is appropriate. The program is presented in Figure 6.5.

Notice that *sharesissued* is initialized to 0 prior to the repeat-statement, and so we must perform one iteration of the loop before *sharesissued* can acquire a "sensible" value: we use **repeat**. Instead we could have initialized *sharesissued* to the number of shares requested by the first buyer (and *nooflots* to 1). Then we would have to use a while-loop because the bound may already have been exceeded. Thus lines 12 to 16 could be replaced by

```
read (sharesissued);  nooflots: = 1;
while sharesissued < = cutofftotal do
begin
    read (sharesrequested);  nooflots: = nooflots + 1;
    sharesissued: = sharesissued + sharesrequested
end
```

I have a slight preference for the version of Figure 6.5 but in this example there is little difference between the two approaches. Usually one form is more natural than the other.

```
0   program Shares (input, output);
1       { Totals the number of shares issued until
2           a specified cut-off total is reached. }
3   var
4       cutofftotal, nooflots,
5       sharesissued, sharesrequested : integer;
6   begin
7     read (cutofftotal);
8
9     case cutofftotal > 0 of
10    true:
11      begin
12        sharesissued := 0;   nooflots := 0;
13        repeat
14          read (sharesrequested);   nooflots := nooflots + 1;
15          sharesissued := sharesissued + sharesrequested
16        until sharesissued > cutofftotal;
17
18        writeln ('The number of shares issued exceeds ',
19            cutofftotal :1);
20        writeln (' as soon as ', nooflots :1,
21            ' lots have been issued');
22        writeln ('The total number of shares issued is then ',
23            sharesissued :1)
24      end;
25    false :
26        writeln ('The specified cut-off total ', cutofftotal :1,
27            ' is invalid')
28    end { case }
29  end.
```

Figure 6.5   Example 6.4

What you should *not* do is initialize *sharesissued* to 0 and then use a while-loop:

```
sharesissued: = 0;   nooflots: = 0;
while sharesissued < = cutofftotal do
begin
  read (sharesrequested);   nooflots: = nooflots + 1;
  sharesissued: = sharesissued + sharesrequested
end
```

This gives a "forced" while-loop. Processing prior to the while-statement forces the test to be *true* the first time and so at least one iteration of the loop body is guaranteed. It is illogical to make the computer perform a test whose outcome we can guarantee. Pascal provides a statement to force the first iteration of a loop: use it! This program produces the same output as the two previous versions but either of the two earlier programs is to be preferred. ■

It was mentioned in Chapter 2 that evaluation of *exp* or *ln* is expensive. This is because the functions *exp* and *ln* (and *sin*, *cos*, etc.) are defined as series and summing a series can be a time-consuming process. Your computer will not actually sum a series to evaluate these functions. It will use what are known as "rational functions", but these still involve a significant amount of processing. We now consider summation of a series.

Example 6.5

Write a program which computes π by substituting an appropriate value (in radians) into the series

$$tan^{-1}x = x - \frac{x^3}{3} + \frac{x^5}{5} - \frac{x^7}{7} + \cdots$$

and summing the series until a term with absolute magnitude less than some specified significance is encountered. □
    Knowing that

$$tan\frac{\pi}{4} = 1$$

we conclude that

$$\pi = 4 \, tan^{-1} \, 1$$

We could compute π by substituting $x = 1$ into the above series and summing terms until we encounter a term sufficiently small, say less than 10^{-6} in absolute magnitude. This would not be a very good approach. When $x = 1$ the numerator of each term is 1 and so "convergence" of the series will be very slow; each term is not much smaller than its predecessor. The first term with magnitude less than 10^{-6} is $1/(10^6 + 1)$ so our program would have to generate 500,001 terms of the series! It would be better if we could find a value less than 1 to substitute into the series. Convergence would then be faster.
    The relation

$$tan\frac{\pi}{6} = \frac{1}{\sqrt{3}}$$

gives

$$\pi = 6 \, tan^{-1} \frac{1}{\sqrt{3}}$$

The program of Figure 6.6 substitutes $x = 1/\sqrt{3}$ and sums the series. We must evaluate several terms of the series so **repeat** is appropriate. For comparison the predefined Pascal function *arctan* is used to produce a value of π. If you want to compute π to the accuracy provided by your machine, the simplest way to do it is with the expression *4 * arctan (1)*. Because your computer will use rational functions it will not suffer from the problems which would have befallen our program with $x = 1$. ■

It was mentioned in Chapter 3 that the Pascal read-statement performs character processing to transform a digit string into a numerical value. We can now simulate its actions.

Example 6.6

Write a program to convert a positive octal integer into the corresponding decimal value. The program may assume that the value will not exceed *maxint.* □
When we write the decimal integer

74203

this is a shorthand notation for

$$7 \times 10^4 + 4 \times 10^3 + 2 \times 10^2 + 0 \times 10 + 3$$

The decimal system uses "base" 10 with digits 0, 1, 2, 3, 4, 5, 6, 7, 8, and 9, but numbers can be expressed to any base. In particular, numbers inside a computer are effectively stored in binary (base 2) with digits 0 and 1. The octal system uses base 8 and digits 0, 1, 2, 3, 4, 5, 6, and 7. Thus

74203

in the octal system is equivalent to the decimal value defined by

$$7 \times 8^4 + 4 \times 8^3 + 2 \times 8^2 + 0 \times 8 + 3$$

which is *30851.*
The program of Figure 6.7 reads a sequence of octal digits and computes the decimal equivalent of the octal integer. The original problem has been generalised in that the program can convert from any base into base 10 if suitable values are specified for the user-defined constants *base* and *max-digit.* Note that we need not know the position of the digits within the computer character set; we need merely determine how far a digit is from the character 0. ■

Recall that the computer stores its values in binary. This program is converting into decimal because the *write* and *writeln* procedures convert values into base 10 for output. We can make our program convert from any base into any other base if we supply an appropriate replacement for *writeln.*

```
program PiCalculator (output);
   { Using the series
              -1        3      5     7
         tan    x = x - x /3 + x /5 - x /7 + · · ·
      the program computes pi by substituting x = 1/sqrt(3)
      to give pi/6. }
const
   significance = 1E-10;
   pifactor = 6;
var
   x, xsquared, numerator, sum, term : real;
   denominator, noofterms : integer;
begin
   x := 1 / sqrt (3);   xsquared := sqr (x);
   numerator := x;   denominator := 1;   sum := x;

   repeat
      numerator := -numerator * xsquared;
      denominator := denominator + 2;
      term := numerator / denominator;
      sum := sum + term
   until abs (term) < significance;

   noofterms := (denominator + 1) div 2;

   writeln ('For x = ', x :6:4, ' the sum of the first ',
      noofterms :1, ' terms');
   writeln (' of the series for arctan x is ', sum :12:10);
   writeln ('This includes the first term with absolute magnitude');
   writeln (' less than ', significance : 7);
   writeln ('This implies that pi = ', sum * pifactor :12:10);
   writeln;

   writeln ('For comparison, the value produced by the');
   writeln (' library routine "arctan" is ', arctan (x) :12:10);
   writeln (' which gives pi = ', arctan (x) * pifactor :12:10)
end.
```

OUTPUT :
For x = 0.5774 the sum of the first 19 terms
 of the series for arctan x is   0.5235987756
This includes the first term with absolute magnitude
 less than   0.1E-09
This implies that pi =   3.1415926537

For comparison, the value produced by the

library routine 'arctan' is   0.5235987756
which gives pi = 3.1415926536

Figure 6.6   Example 6.5

---

program *OctalRead (input, output);*
   { Reads a positive octal integer and prints
      the decimal equivalent. }
   const
      space = *' ';   zero* = *'0';*
      base = *8;   maxdigit* = *'7';*
   var
      int : integer;
begin
   { Skip any spaces or ends of lines which may be present. }
   while *input↑* = *space* **do** *get (input);*

   if *input↑* **in** *[zero .. maxdigit]* **then**
   begin
      write ('Supplied integer (base ', base :1,') : ');

      int := 0;
      repeat
         write (input↑);
         int := int ∗ base + ord (input↑) − ord (zero);
         get (input)
      until not *(input↑* **in** *[zero .. maxdigit]);*

      writeln;
      writeln ('Decimal equivalent : ', int :1)
   end else
   begin
      writeln ('Invalid numeric input—in base ', base :1);
      writeln ('   a positive integer must start with a digit in the range ',
         zero, ' to ', maxdigit)
   end
end.

INPUT :
74203

OUTPUT :
Supplied integer (base 8) : 74203
Decimal equivalent : 30851

Figure 6.7   Example 6.6

108

Example 6.7

Write a program which reads a decimal integer and outputs the corresponding octal value. □

With our present knowledge we must tackle this problem as shown in Figure 6.8. This program is rather cumbersome and we shall consider two alternative solutions later {Examples 7.6 and 13.4}. ■

We conclude this section with an example of text processing.

Example 6.8

Write a program to determine the length of the longest word in a supplied sentence. Words will contain only letters and will be separated by at least one space or end of line. The sentence may be preceded by several spaces or ends of lines and will be terminated by a period immediately following the last word of the sentence, but will contain no other punctuation. □

We shall construct the program in stages; first, a brief outline:

taking each word in the sentence **do**
    if it is longer than the longest word so far encountered
        then record its length as the largest so far encountered

So far so good—but it is not Pascal. We must now transform this outline into a program. Consider first how to arrange for processing to be applied to each word in the sentence. We do not know how many words the sentence will contain but we do know that it must contain at least one. This suggests the use of **repeat**:

repeat
    skip to next word;
    determine length of this word;
    if this length > max length so far **then**
        max length so far := this length
until at end of sentence

We are now aware that we need two integer variables *thislength* and *maxlengthsofar* and that *maxlengthsofar* must be initialized (0 would seem appropriate) prior to execution of the repeat-loop. Upon exit from the loop, *maxlengthsofar* is the value we seek. Our program fragment now stands as follows:

program *FindLengthOfLongestWord (input, output);*
    var *thislength, maxlengthsofar : integer;*
begin
    maxlengthsofar := 0;

```
program OctalWrite (input, output);
    { Converts from decimal to octal. }
  const
    base = 8;
  var
    n, ndivbase, powerofbase : integer;
begin
  read (n);
  write ('The decimal value ', n :1,
    ' expressed to base ', base :1, ' is ');

  if n = 0 then
    writeln (0 :1) else
  begin
  if n < 0 then
  begin
    write ('-');   n := -n
  end;

  ndivbase := n div base;

    { Compute max power of base <= n. }
  powerofbase := 1;
  repeat
    powerofbase := powerofbase * base
  until powerofbase > ndivbase;

    { Compute successive digits starting with the
      most significant. }
  repeat
    write (n div powerofbase :1);
    n := n mod powerofbase;
    powerofbase := powerofbase div base
  until powerofbase = 0;
  writeln
  end
end.
```

INPUT :
−30851

OUTPUT :
The decimal value −30851 expressed to base 8 is −74203

Figure 6.8   Example 6.7

```
    repeat
        skip to next word;
        determine length of this word;
        if thislength > maxlengthsofar then
            maxlengthsofar: = thislength
    until at end of sentence;
    writeln (maxlengthsofar)
end.
```

This is not complete but we are getting closer. Let us turn our attention to *skip to next word*. All words but the first will be preceded by at least one space. The first word may or may not be. Skipping to a word must therefor be implemented as a while-loop:

while *input*↑ = ' ' **do** *get (input)*

This will skip over any spaces or ends of lines and upon exit the value of *input*↑ will be the first character of the next word.

Now turn to *determine length of this word*. This involves counting the number of letters in the word and recording this value in *thislength*. We do not know how many letters there will be, but there must be at least one—so we use **repeat**:

```
repeat
    thislength: = thislength + 1;   get (input)
until not (input↑ in ['A'·-'Z'])
```

and note that

thislength: = 0;

must precede the loop. Upon exit from this loop *input*↑ indicates the character immediately following the word. We can now see how to implement our test *at end of sentence* for the outer loop. If the word just scanned is the last word of the sentence the value of *input*↑ will now be '.'. So our implementation of *at end of sentence* is

input↑ = '.'

The complete program is presented in Figure 6.9. ■

6.1.3 Data sentinels and end of file

A program often has to process a set of data of unknown length. This involves repeating some activity until the end of the data set is encountered. If no further data follows this data set the end of the data can be detected using *eof* (but recall the caveat of Section 5.2.3). If a further data set follows then some other means must be employed. The usual technique is to terminate the data set with a "data sentinel", a datum which could not possibly be part of the data set. For instance, a sequence of positive integers

```
 0    program LongestWord (input, output);
 1          { States the length of the longest word in a supplied sentence.
 2              Words are assumed to contain only letters and to be separated
 3              by least one space or end of line. A sentence is assumed
 4              to be terminated by a full stop immediately following the
 5              last word of the sentence but contains no other punctuation. }
 6    const
 7          fullstop = '.';   space = ' ';
 8    var
 9          thislength, maxlengthsofar : integer;
10    begin
11       maxlengthsofar := 0;
12       repeat
13           { Skip to next word. }
14           while input↑ = space do
15             get (input);
16
17           { Determine length of this word. }
18           thislength := 0;
19           repeat
20             thislength := thislength + 1;   get (input)
21           until not (input↑ in ['A'.. 'Z']);
22
23           { Is this the max length so far? }
24           if thislength > maxlengthsofar then
25                maxlengthsofar := thislength
26       until input↑ = fullstop;
27
28       writeln ('The longest word in the supplied sentence contains ',
29           maxlengthsofar :2, ' letters')
30    end.
```

Figure 6.9   Example 6.8

could be terminated by −1 and a sequence of names could be terminated by ZZZ. We examine the consequences of each approach: data sentinel and *eof*. Despite the earlier coveat we shall assume that *eof* will detect the end of the standard file *input*.

6.1.3.1   *Data sentinel*

Example 6.9

The Lunar Habitation Party and the Martian Nationalist Party are contesting an election. For each party the votes gained by its candidates are supplied as a sequence of integers. The LHP votes are terminated by -1 and the MNP votes by -2. Write a program to compute the total number of votes polled by each party and to state which party gains a majority. The LHP votes will precede the MNP votes in the data. □

The overall structure of the program must be

accumulate votes for LH party
accumulate votes for MN party
LHvotes > MNvotes ⇒ victory for LHP
LHvotes = MNvotes ⇒ dead heat
LHvotes < MNvotes ⇒ victory for MNP

Each party must be fielding at least one candidate otherwise there could not be an election. The data set for each party must contain at least one vote count, so this suggests the use of **repeat**. First consider the accumulation of LHP votes. We might be tempted to write the following program fragment (assuming appropriate declarations):

```
0    lunarvotes: = 0;
1    repeat
2        read (votecount);
3        lunarvotes: = lunarvotes + votecount
4    until votecount = − 1
```

This is close to what we want but is not quite right. Until the -1 is encountered all goes well; successive vote counts are read and accumulated. When the value -1 is read for *votecount* (line 2) it, too, is added into the total (by the asignment statement on line 3). The final answer we get will be 1 too low. We could rectify this by adding 1 to the accumulated total when we exit from the loop, but this not a "clean solution". It is called a "patch"—it covers a hole without considering why the hole appeared. We have failed to recognize that we are doing something illogical within the loop: we are adding in to a running vote total a value which does not represent a vote count at all but is supplied merely to act as a data sentinel. A consequence is that any change of data sentinel (perhaps a future modification to the problem specification might require -1 to indicate a candidate's withdrawal) would imply a change not only in the loop termination test (which we would expect) but also the first statement following the loop (which we would not expect).

Another approach would be to modify line 3 to

```
3    if votecount < > − 1 then lunarvotes: = lunarvotes + votecount
```

but this is clumsy because we are now making what is effectively the same test (one test and its inverse) twice for each iteration of the loop. As with the other patch, subsequent modification of the data sentinel implies two changes when only one would be expected.

Prevention is better than cure! This example stresses the significance of a remark made in Section 6.1.1—computation of a new value which directly affects the loop termination test should usually be the *last* action within the lop. We have contravened this principle. The correct approach is to make

> *read (votecount)*

the last statement of the loop. The loop body then becomes

> *lunarvotes:* = *lunarvotes* + *votecount;*
> *read (votecount)*

Accordingly, *votecount* must be given a value prior to loop entry. The most sensible value to give it is the value of the first datum, and so the solution is

```
0     lunarvotes: = 0;   read (votecount);
1     repeat
2         lunarvotes: = lunarvotes + votecount;
3         read (votecount)
4     until votecount = − 1
```

This produces the correct total. The full program is given in figure 6.10. ■

Example 6.10

Write a program to accumulate separately the cash sales, account sales and refunds for one day's transactions in a shop. Each transaction is represented by a real number followed by one of the characters +, @ or − indicating a cash sale, account sale or refund respectively. The sequence of transactions is terminated by a negative number (say −1). □

The overall structure might first be conceived as

```
zeroize three totals;
repeat
    read (price, code);
    case code of
        '+':⎫
        '@':⎬ update appropriate total
        '−':⎭
    end { case }
until price < 0
```

A little thought shows that this is inappropriate. When the dummy price (−1) is read *code* will not receive a sensible value; it will pick up the character (probably a space) that happens to follow the −1. The program will then fail when it attempts to execute the case-statement. The cause is the usual one: reading a value for *price*, the variable which controls the loop,

```
0   program MoonMarsElection (input, output);
1       { Totals two sequences of vote counts to
2           determine the outcome of an election. }
3     const
4       lunarterminator = -1;   martianterminator = -2;
5     var
6       votecount, lunarvotes, martianvotes : integer;
7   begin
8       { Total votes for Lunar Habitationists }
9       lunarvotes := 0;   read (votecount);
10    repeat
11      lunarvotes := lunarvotes + votecount;   read (votecount)
12    until votecount = lunarterminator;
13
14      writeln ('Votes polled by the Lunar Habitation Party : ',
15        lunarvotes);
16
17        { Total votes for Martian Nationalists }
18      martianvotes := 0;   read (votecount);
19    repeat
20        martianvotes := martianvotes + votecount;   read (votecount)
21    until votecount = martianterminator;
22
23      writeln ('Votes polled by the Martian Nationalist Party : ',
24        martianvotes);
25
26    if lunarvotes = martianvotes then
27        writeln ('There is a tie—how about a recount?') else
28    begin
29        write ('A majority vote has been gained by the ');
30        case lunarvotes > martianvotes of
31          true : write ('Lunar Habitation');
32          false : write ('Martian Nationalist')
33        end { case };
34        writeln (' Party')
35    end
36  end.
```

INPUT :
47   962   5471   479   684   2001   −1
837   3471   2462   1792   2482   −2

OUTPUT :
Votes polled by the Lunar Habitation Party :   9644
Votes polled by the Martian Nationalist Party :   11044
A majority vote has been gained by the Martian Nationalist Party

Figure 6.10   Example 6.9

is not the last action within the loop. The loop should be

```
repeat
    read (code);
    case code of
      . . .
    end {case};
    read (price)
until price < 0
```

and obviously the loop initialization must now include

```
read (price)
```

The full program is given in Figure 6.11. A repeat-statement is used

---

```
program CashAccountRefund (input, output);
    { Accummulates a sequence of cash sales,
      account sales, and refunds. }
const
    cashcode = '+';   accountcode = '@';   refundcode = '-';
var
    price, cashsales, accountsales, refunds : real;
    code : char;
begin
    cashsales := 0;   accountsales := 0;   refunds := 0;
    read (price);
    repeat
      read (code);
      case code of
        cashcode :
          cashsales := cashsales + price;
        accountcode :
          accountsales := accountsales + price;
        refundcode :
          refunds := refunds + price
      end { case };
      read (price)
    until price < 0;

    writeln ('The totals are :— ');
    writeln ('      Cash sales : ', cashsales :7:2);
    writeln (' Account sales : ', accountsales :7:2);
    writeln ('        Refunds : ', refunds :7:2)
end.
```

Figure 6.11   Example 6.10

---

because it is assumed that at least one transaction will be supplied. If it is considered possible that the data may contain only −1 and no transactions then one might use a while-loop instead of a repeat-loop, but a better alternative would be to use a combination of **if** and **repeat** as follows:

```
read (price);
if price > = 0 then
begin
   zeroize totals;
   repeat
     . . .
   until price < 0;
   output totals
end else
   writeln ('Where are the transactions?')  ■
```

6.1.3.2 End of file

The standard file *input* is called a "textfile". Textfiles comprise lines and the end of each line is indicated by some special marker which *eoln* recognizes but which appears as a space to *input↑*. If the processing within a loop regards the ends of lines as significant the loop body will contain calls of *readln* and possibly *eoln*. Any test for *eof* should then follow *readln*.

Example 6.11

Modify the program of Figure 1.8 to accommodate an unknown number of species. □
   We can achieve this by replacing lines 10 and 11 by

```
totalpets: = 0;
repeat
   readln (pets);   totalpets: = totalpets + pets
until eof;
```

and suitably modifying the declarations. In this case the loop termination test does not immediately follow *readln* because we must first process the data read. If we were to distinguish between the two activities of *readln*, namely reading a value and skipping to the next line, it would then be natural for *readln* to be the last action within the loop:

```
repeat
   read (pets);   totalpets: = totalpets + pets;
   readln
until eof;  ■
```

Example 6.12

Write a program to determine the average number of spaces per line in the supplied data. It is assumed that at least one line of data will be provided. □

The structure of the program is

> *nooflines*: = 0;   *noofspaces*: = 0;
> **repeat**
>   increment *noofspaces* by the number of spaces in this line;
>   *nooflines*: = *nooflines* + 1;
>   *readln*
> **until** *eof*;
> *spacesperline*: = *noofspaces* / *nooflines*

Incrementing *noofspaces* is achieved by

> **while not** *eoln* **do**
> **begin**
>   **if** *input*↑ = *space* **then**
>   *noofspaces*: = *noofspaces* + 1;
>   *get (input)*
> **end**   ■

If the ends of lines within the data are not significant we must treat character input and numeric input differently. When reading from a textfile *eof* can never be *true* immediately after reading a numeric datum (see Chapter 12 for other files) but it can be *true* after reading a character (because this character may be the artificial space at the end of the last line). *input*↑ is undefined when *eof* is *true* so when we are reading characters but not checking *eoln* we must test *eof* before referring to *input*↑ (and hence before calling *read* or *get*).

Example 6.13

Write a program to count the number of semi-colons in the data. □

The essence of the program is

> *noofsemicolons*: = 0;
> **while not** *eof* **do**
> **begin**
>   **if** *input*↑ = *semicolon* **then**
>   *noofsemicolons*: = *noofsemicolons* + 1;
>   *get (input)*
> **end**   ■

For numeric input we must skip any spaces and line markers and test *eof* before attempting to read a value. This is because an error will occur if *read* is called and *eof* then becomes *true* while a number is being sought. Discussion of the skipping process itself is deferred until Example 6.16, but the following example illustrates its use.

Example 6.14

Modify the program of Figure 6.5 to accumulate all the purchase requests, assuming that no data sentinel is supplied. □
   The main section of the program is

> *totalrequested*: = *0*;
> **repeat**
>   *read (thisrequest);*
>   *totalrequested*: = *totalrequested* + *thisrequest;*
>   *skip until significant character or end of file found*
> **until** *eof* ■

6.1.4   General considerations

Pascal provides two non-deterministic loop statements (while-loops and repeat-loops) and we have seen examples of when each is appropriate. Both have three main constituents:

1. Loop initialization
2. Loop body
3. Loop termination (we shall use this term to cover both while and repeat loops even though a while-loop must be given a loop *continuation* condition).

   We make some general observations about these in the order in which we construct them.

6.1.4.1   *Loop body*

When writing a loop body we assume it will be performed several times and write it in such a way that it will function correctly once it "gets going". We must convince ourselves that each iteration of the loop will perform the appropriate computation. Although at this stage we need not know the precise nature of the loop termination test, we must have some notion as to when we wish to exit from the loop so as to avoid superfluous (and possibly harmful) computation. When constructing the programs of Figures 6.10 and 6.11 our first outline of each loop body was modified when we considered the loop termination.
   So, when we have written a loop body we should know why we want control to leave the loop but perhaps we do not yet know how to detect the situation.

6.1.4.2 *Loop termination*

Once we know what is happening each time round a loop we can decide how to stop it. The termination condition must make use of some information which changes (or possibly changes) with each iteration, for otherwise the loop would become infinite! If the information you wish to incorporate within your test is not being changed by the loop body, then either you are thinking of the wrong test or your loop body is incomplete (or just plain wrong!). If you are sure your test is the right one then you must modify your loop body.

When you have ensured that the termination test involves information which can change within the loop you must convince yourself that it changes in such a way that the termination test will eventually be satisfied. Consider the loop

```
repeat
    if n < m then n := n + 2 else n := n - 2
until n = m
```

for two integer variables n and m. It might appear sensible at first sight; each iteration performs an assignment to n and each new value of n is apparently closer to the value of m. A little thought shows that the loop is finite only if n and m have the same parity. If one is odd and the other even the loop goes on for ever! In practice it would not be allowed to go on for ever. Your computer system will impose some time limit upon your job. A programmer can usually control this time limit but a system designed for novices will probably enforce a limit of a few seconds. A modern computer can perform thousands of Pascal statements in a second so it is unlikely that a beginner's program will genuinely need more than a few seconds of computer time.

Often an infinite loop will generate an error before the time limit is reached and this will cause the job to be terminated. If we had omitted

get (input)

from line 20 of the program of Figure 6.9 the repeat-loop of line 19 would be theoretically infinite. The program will probably generate integer overflow before the time limit is reached because the value of *thislength* is being incremented during each iteration.

When you have sorted out your loop body and the termination test you should definitely know whether you want **while** or **repeat**. If you want the termination test to be made *before* the first iteration use **while**; if not, use **repeat**.

6.1.4.3 *Loop initialization*

We have written our loop body and termination test so that all will be well so long as the loop starts off properly. Now we must ensure that the "computa-

120

tional state" is appropriate when the loop is first entered. There are two aspects to this.

6.1.4.3.1 *Implicit initialization*

We must be aware of the current computational state when control leaves the previous section of program so that we can be sure it is appropriate. For example, when control reaches the inner repeat-loop (line 19) of the program in Figure 6.9 *input*↑ indicates the first character of a word (assuming the data to be correct). It was for this reason that we used a repeat-loop here. If the supplied sentence were permitted to contain internal punctuation this would no longer be the case; *input*↑ would indicate a punctuation character (e.g. comma or semi-colon) if one followed the word just processed. This does not constitute a valid "initial state" for entry to the loop. We must either modify the previous section of program (skip to next word) or precede the repeat loop of line 19 by some instructions explicitly to initialize the loop. In this case we should modify the termination condition of the previous loop.

6.1.4.3.2 *Explicit initialization*

Explicit initialization usually refers to entities which are essentially local to the loop. Variables used inside the loop often need initializing before the loop is entered. This is particularly true for summing and counting variables. Thus in Figure 6.5 *sharesissued* and *nooflots* are initialized to 0 (line 12), in Figure 6.9 *thislength* is initialized to 0 (line 18), in Figure 6.10 *lunarvotes* (line 9) and *martianvotes* (line 18) are initialized to 0, and in Figure 6.11 *price* is initialized by a read-statement. Notice that each of these initializations is delayed as long as possible. Each initialization statement is as close to its loop as is practicable. In Figure 6.10 the statement *martianvotes* := 0 could have occurred much earlier (anywhere between lines 7 and 19) but it is bad practice to put it anywhere but where it is. This variable has nothing to do with any previous processing so it should not be mixed up with it. Try to keep together statements which are "logically connected".

6.1.5 Multiple-exit loops

All loops so far considered have been single-exit loops; there was only one reason for terminating the loop. Often we wish control to leave a loop for any of several reasons.

Example 6.15

A positive integer with no factors other than 1 and itself is said to be prime. If any other factors exist the integer is said to be composite. Write a program to determine whether a supplied positive integer is prime or composite. $\square$

If we were to divide an integer n by all integers in the range 2 to $n-1$ we would know n to be prime if no division produced a zero remainder. This is the basic approach we shall adopt but we first improve our algorithm. If n is composite it must have at least one factor which does not exceed $\sqrt{n}$. So we need consider only divisors in the range 2 to $\lfloor \sqrt{n} \rfloor$ where $\lfloor \sqrt{n} \rfloor$ (called the "floor" of $\sqrt{n}$) is the largest integer which does not exceed $\sqrt{n}$. If n is odd it will not be divisible by any even number so we need then try only odd divisors. Our algorithm is now as follows:

```
read (n);
if n < 1 then error else
    if n <= 3 then n is prime else
        if n mod 2 = 0 then n is composite else
        begin
            try successive odd integers starting with 3 until a factor of n
                is found or all these potential factors <= √n have been
                tried;
            if a factor was found then n is composite
                else n is prime
        end
```

The main part of the algorithm is a double-exit loop; we wish to exit from the loop if either of two termination conditions is satisfied. The program of Figure 6.12 implements this algorithm. The loop used is a while-loop because we need a non-deterministic loop (we do not know how many times we wish to execute the loop) and we may wish to execute the loop body zero times (n may be smaller than 16 or may be a multiple of 3). Control will exit from the loop if either

$(n \bmod potfactor = 0)$

or

$(potfactor >= sqrootofn)$

Upon exit from the loop we must test to determine the reason for exit. It is imperative that our test involve (n and $potfactor$) and not ($potfactor$ and $sqrootofn$). We must not have

```
if potfactor >= sqrootofn then
    writeln ('is prime')
else
    writeln ('is composite')
```

because we may have $potfactor = sqrootofn$ whether n is prime or composite.

```
program Prime (input, output);
    { Determines whether a supplied positive integer
      is prime or composite. }
  var
    n, potfactor, sqrootofn : integer;
begin
  read (n);   write (n, '   ');

  if n < 1 then
    writeln ('should not be less than 1')
  else
    if n <= 3 then
      writeln ('is prime')
    else
      if odd (n) then
      begin
        sqrootofn := trunc (sqrt (n));

        potfactor := 3;
        while (n mod potfactor <> 0) and (potfactor < sqrootofn) do
          potfactor := potfactor + 2;

        if n mod potfactor = 0 then
          writeln ('is composite')
        else
          writeln ('is prime')
      end else
        writeln ('is composite')
end.
```

Figure 6.12   Example 6.15

Consequently, testing

```
if potfactor <= sqrootofn then
  writeln ('is composite')
else
  writeln ('is prime')
```

is no better. Try $n = 9$ and $n = 11$—neither of these last two tests works for both.

The continuation condition of the while-loop involves two tests

$(potfactor < sqrootofn)$

and

$(n \textbf{ mod } potfactor <> 0)$

The second is the "dominant condition"; this determines whether or not the current potential factor is indeed a factor. The first is an "auxiliary condition" to reduce the number of possible divisors that might otherwise be tried; the program is still correct if we replace this auxiliary test by $(potfactor < n)$ or even $(potfactor < maxint - 2)$. Upon exit from a multi-exit loop it is imperative that we test *dominant* conditions. In this case there is only one—either $n \textbf{ mod } potfactor = 0$ or its inverse.

The program of Figure 6.12 is correct but not very transparent; even someone familiar with the algorithm would have to give it careful study to convince himself that it is correct. Don't be disheartened if you found this too! We have used meaningful identifiers for the square root of n and for each potential factor. We could perhaps improve upon n as a name for the supplied number but this would have little effect upon the overall transparency. The program's obscurity stems from its complicated boolean expressions; the significance of each expression is not apparent. One way to overcome this is to use boolean variables to record the values of the tests.

This approach is illustrated in Figure 6.13. The program is now more readable. The reasons for loop exit and the significance of the ensuing test are now immediately apparent by virtue of the names of the boolean variables used. A repeat-loop is now used in place of the while-loop because we must execute the loop at least once to give values to the two boolean variables involved in the loop termination test. This does have the slightly undesirable consequence of forcing us to initialize *potfactor* to 1. Perhaps better is

```
potfactor := 3;
factorfound := false;   allpotfactorstried := false;
repeat
   if n mod potfactor = 0 then factorfound := true else
      if potfactor >= sqrootofn then allpotfactorstried := true else
      potfactor := potfactor + 2
until factorfound or allpotfactorstried;
if factorfound then ...
```

Notice that the first test made inside the loop body concerns the dominant condition; the program would not be correct if the auxiliary condition were tested first.

Various compromises exist. For instance, we might choose to use only one boolean variable, in which case it should represent the dominant condition. Notice that we use *factorfound* and not *factornotfound* or some equivalent. When choosing names for boolean variables it is particularly important to remember the maxim: think positively!

```
program PrimeWithBooleans (input, output);
    { Determines whether a supplied integer is
      prime or composite. }
  var
    n, potfactor, sqrootofn : integer;
    factorfound, allpotfactorstried : boolean;
begin
  read (n);   write (n, '  ');

  if n < 1 then
    writeln ('should not be less than 1')
  else
    if n <= 3 then
      writeln ('is prime')
    else
      if odd (n) then
      begin
        sqrootofn := trunc (sqrt (n));

        potfactor := 1;
        repeat
          potfactor := potfactor + 2;
          factorfound := n mod potfactor = 0;
          allpotfactorstried := potfactor >= sqrootofn
        until factorfound or allpotfactorstried;

        if factorfound then
          writeln ('is composite')
        else
          writeln ('is prime')
      end else
        writeln ('is composite')
end.
```

Figure 6.13   Example 6.15

```
potfactor := 3;   factorfound := false;
repeat
  if n mod potfactor = 0 then
    factorfound := true
  else
    potfactor := potfactor + 2
until factorfound or (potfactor >= sqrootofn);
if factorfound then ...
```

An approach equivalent to one of these discussed is probably the best one can do in other languages and each provides a nice solution in Pascal. However, Pascal provides an even better approach to general multi-exit loops (using symbolic types) and we shall revisit this example when we reach Chapter 9. ■

In the example just discussed we have a free choice as to whether we use booleans or not. This is because the two loop continuation tests

(potfactor < sqrootofn)

and

(n **mod** *potfactor = 0)*

are independent: the value of one does not affect the validity of the other. When tests are not independent we may be forced into using booleans (or something similar).

Example 6.16

The skipping process outlined in Example 6.14 involves a loop with two exit conditions: either a non-space character has been located or the end of the file has been reached. But these two tests are not independent. We must not write

    while *(input↑ < >' ')* **and not** *eof* **do**
     get (input)

because *input↑* will be undefined if *eof* becomes *true*. Under some compilers the second operand of **and** is evaluated only if the first delivers *true* {because the result must otherwise be *false*}. In this case the possibility of illegal reference to *input↑* is avoided by writing

    while not *eof* **and** *(input↑ < > ' ')* **do**
     get (input)

because the second operand *(input↑ < >' ')* will not be evaluated if *eof* is *true*. Such implementation dependence should be avoided. In the interest of program portability we should rewrite the loop. We can always safely refer to *eof* but we should store the value of the other test. □

    var
     spacenext : boolean;
    . . .
    spacenext : = true;
    while *spacenext* **and not** *eof* **do**
    begin
     get (input);
     if not *eof* **then**
      spacenext : = input↑ = ' '
    end

This is clumsy because testing *spacenext* upon entry to the while-statement is redundant and, worse, because *eof* is checked twice during each iteration of the loop. The approach of Chapter 9 removes both these objections. ∎

6.2 Deterministic loops

A deterministic loop should usually be implemented with a for-statement. Pascal distinguishes two forms: "incremental" and "decremental".

6.2.1 Incremental loop

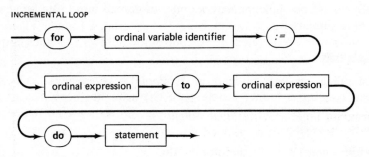

INCREMENTAL LOOP

The expressions and the variable must all have the same type and this may be any ordinal type. If the for-loop occurs within a procedure or function (described in Chapter 7) the declaration of the variable must be local to that procedure or function.

The effect of

for $\alpha := \beta$ **to** γ **do** δ

is to execute δ, the loop body,

$$ord\ (\gamma) - ord\ (\beta) + 1$$

times with α, the "control variable", taking values

$$\beta,\ succ\ (\beta),\ succ\ (succ\ (\beta)),\ \ldots,\ \gamma$$

in turn unless $\beta > \gamma$, in which case the loop body is not executed at all. Within the loop body no attempt must be made to change the value of the control variable and upon exit from the loop the value of the control variable becomes undefined.

Example 6.17

Write a program to raise 2 to some specified non-negative power. □
We know how many iterations of the loop are required so we use a for-statement. The program is presented in Figure 6.14. A more efficient version is presented in Figure 6.15. ■

If we wish the loop body to comprise a group of statements we must bracket them with **begin** and **end**.

Example 6.18

Write a program to print a specified number of terms of the Fibonacci sequence. The Fibonacci sequence was defined in Example 6.3. □
Again we know how many loop iterations we want the program to perform and so we use a for-statement. The program is listed in Figure 6.16. Notice the use of an if-statement to control the number of values output on each line. ■

```
program nthPowerOf2 (input, output);
    { Raises 2 to a specified power. }
    var
        n, powerof2, power : integer;
begin
    read (n);
    if n > = 0 then
    begin
        powerof2 := 1;
        for power := 1 to n do
            powerof2 := powerof2 * 2;

        writeln ('2 raised to the power ', n :1, ' is ',
            powerof2 :1)
    end else
        writeln ('Power is ', n :1, ' but should be positive')
end.
```

INPUT :
5

OUTPUT :
2 raised to the power 5 is 32

Figure 6.14   Example 6.17

```
program nthPowerOf2by4 (input, output);
    { Raises 2 to a specified power by raising 4 to
       half the power. }
  var
    n, powerof2, sqpower : integer;
begin
  read (n);
  if n >= 0 then
  begin
    if odd (n) then
      powerof2 := 2
    else
      powerof2 := 1;

    for sqpower := 1 to n div 2 do
      powerof2 := powerof2 * 4;

    writeln ('2 raised to the power ', n :1, ' is ',
      powerof2 :1)
  end else
    writeln ('Power is ', n :1, ' but should be positive')
end.
```

Figure 6.15   Example 6.17

6.2.2 Decremental loop

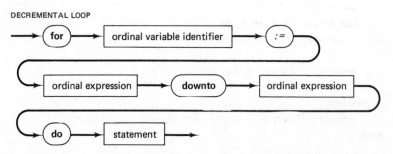

This is similar to the first form but successive values of the control variable descend. Accordingly, with the statement

for $\alpha := \beta$ **downto** γ **do** δ

the loop body is not executed if $\beta < \gamma$, but otherwise is executed

$$ord\ (\beta) - ord\ (\gamma) + 1$$

```
program nFib (input, output);
    { Prints a specified number of terms of
      the Fibonacci sequence. }
  const
    noperline = 5;
  var
    n, i, f, prevf, fbefore : integer;
begin
  read (n);
  writeln ('Fibonacci numbers up to F', n :1);

  if n < 0 then
    writeln (n :1, ' is negative')
  else
    if n = 0 then
      writeln (0) else
    begin
      write (0, 1);
      f := 1;  prevf := 0;

      for i := 2 to n do
      begin
        fbefore := prevf;  prevf := f;  f := prevf + fbefore;
        if i mod noperline = 0 then
            writeln;
        write (f)
      end
    end;
  writeln
end.
```

INPUT :
22

OUTPUT :
Fibonacci numbers up to F22
```
      0       1       1       2       3
      5       8      13      21      34
     55      89     144     233     377
    610     987    1597    2584    4181
   6765   10946   17711
```
Figure 6.16   Example 6.18

times with α taking values

β, *pred* (β), *pred* (*pred* (β)), . . . , γ

In the program of Figure 6.14 the incremental loop could be replaced by a decremental loop because the control variable is not referred to within the loop:

for $p := n$ **downto** *1* **do** *powerof2* := *powerof2* * 2

works (if p is suitably declared) but now interpretation of the control variable is less obvious. In the original version the value of the control variable (*power*) at the end of each execution of the loop body indicates the power to which 2 has been raised.

A decremental loop should be used only if it is naturally implied by the problem.

Example 6.19

Write a program to print the alphabet forwards and backwards. □
The program is in Figure 6.17. ∎

```
program Alphabets (input, output);
    { Prints the alphabet forwards and backwards. }
    var
        letter : char;
begin
    for letter := 'A' to 'Z' do
        write (letter);
    writeln;

    for letter := 'Z' downto 'A' do
        write (letter);
    writeln
end.
```

OUTPUT :
ABCDEFGHIJKLMNOPQRSTUVWXYZ
ZYXWVUTSRQPONMLKJIHGFEDCBA

Figure 6.17   Example 6.19

6.2.3   Loops with non-unit increment

Occasionally we encounter a situation where we apparently require a deterministic loop with a control variable increment (or decrement) other than unity. Many programming languages allow the increment of a deterministic loop to be specified by the user. Pascal does not. We shall not go into the reasons for this restriction but mention that languages allowing a non-unit increment insist that the type of the control variable be arithmetic (and most insist that it is integer). Pascal permits a control variable to be of types for which addition is not defined (e.g. *char*) and so the concept of an increment is less appropriate.

However, if the control variable is of type *integer* how can we simulate a non-unit increment? Suppose we wish successive values of the control variable to be

$$\alpha, \alpha + \delta, \alpha + 2\delta, \ldots, \beta$$

for $\delta > 1$. We have several lines open to us. Here are four:

1. **for** $\theta := \alpha$ **to** β **do**
   if $(\theta - \alpha)$ **mod** $\delta = 0$ **then** ...

2. **for** $\rho := 0$ **to** $(\beta - \alpha)$ **div** δ **do**
   begin
   $\quad \theta := \rho * \delta + \alpha;$
   ...
   end

3. $\theta := \alpha;$
   for $\rho := \alpha$ **to** $(\beta - \alpha)$ **div** $\delta + \alpha$ **do**
   begin
   $\quad \ldots;$
   $\quad \theta := \theta + \delta$
   end

4. $\theta := \alpha;$
   while $\theta <= \beta$ **do**
   begin
   $\quad \ldots;$
   $\quad \theta := \theta + \delta$
   end

These approaches are not all equivalent.

1. This is the most transparent. The for-statement tells us that the loop is deterministic and shows the limits of the range of values θ may assume. The if-statement shows that the loop is effective only for $\theta = \alpha$, $\alpha + \delta$, $\alpha + 2\delta$, and so on. Unfortunately this is probably the least efficient of the four in general.

2. Again the for-statement tells us that the loop is deterministic and the first statement of the loop body shows that θ goes up in steps of δ. Apart from that, little is obvious. Notice that this form is not semantically equivalent to method 1 because the division is undefined if $\beta < \alpha$ and upon exit from the loop θ remains defined.

3. As with method 2, the value of θ is defined upon exit and we know that the loop is deterministic with θ going up in steps of δ. The starting value of θ is perhaps more apparent than in method 2 but the final value taken by θ is not the same as in method 2. Upon exit the value of θ is δ greater than the last value of θ for which the loop body was performed. This is an undesirable aspect and one which will receive further attention when subrange types are discussed (Chapter 9).

4. This is beautifully simple and is probably the version most programmers would choose. Unfortunately it has two weaknesses. Use of **while** implies that it is a non-deterministic loop but the situation is undoubtedly deterministic and, as in method 3, θ assumes a value outside the range of values in which we are interested.

So, in such a circumstance, which approach should you adopt? There is no one method which is always best. You should use the approach which seems most natural for the application in hand. If you wished to consider all odd integers from 3 to 99,

> **for** i : = *3* **to** *99* **do**
>   **if** *odd (i)* **then** . . .

would be transparent and reasonably efficient. If you wished to consider all multiplies of 1,000 between 3,000 and 30,000,

> **for** i : = *3000* **to** *30000* **do**
>   **if** i **mod** *1000 = 0* **then** . . .

may be transparent but is very wasteful (i will be incremented and i **mod** $1000 = 0$ tested 27,001 times whereas each of the other forms would increment i only 28 times).

If the value of ρ in methods 2 or 3 is useful to the computation within the loop this would give weight to methods 2 and 3. Usually the simplicity of method 4 wins.

Note that method 1 is often appropriate when the increment δ can vary and there is no simple way to determine each δ. To apply a process for every non-prime less than 30,

> **for** i : = 4 **to** 28 **do**
>   **if not** *(i* **in** *[5, 7, 11, 13, 17, 19, 23])* **then** . . .

is the best approach.

6.3 Tabulated output

We often wish a program to output a table comprising several columns of information. This is achieved by using a fixed format and having each iteration of a loop output one line of the table.

Example 6.20

Write a program to output, in columns across the page, all the integers from 1 to some specified value, their squares, square roots, and reciprocals. □
The program is given in Figure 6.18. Notice that the format specified for each value to be printed is large enough to accommodate the value so all fields have the size specified. The output therefore takes the form of columns. ■

```
program Tabulation (input, output);
     { Tabulates integers, squares, square roots,
       and reciprocals. }
   var
     i, n : integer;
begin
   read (n);
   writeln ('   i       sqr(i)          1/i            sqrt(i)');
   for i := 1 to n do
      writeln (i :4, sqr(i) :8, 1/i :10:5, sqrt(i) :10:5)
end.
```

INPUT :
5

OUTPUT :

i	sqr(i)	1/i	sqrt(i)
1	1	1.00000	1.00000
2	4	0.50000	1.41421
3	9	0.33333	1.73205
4	16	0.25000	2.00000
5	25	0.20000	2.23607

Figure 6.18   Example 6.20

6.4 Post script

Discussion of loops has been detailed and several examples have been presented. This is because loops form a fundamental part of almost every program but often cause difficulty for beginners. Appreciation of the right and wrong ways to go about implementing a loop will greatly improve your programming ability. The foundations laid down here will be built upon in subsequent chapters. Nearly every example in the rest of this book will contain at least one loop.

134

6.5 Exercises

The programs for Exercises 1 to 10 should utilize non-deterministic loops; those for Exercises 11 to 22 should use deterministic loops.

*1. The equation

$$x^3 - 11x^2 - 10x - 24 = 0$$

has a solution that is a small positive integer. Write a program which finds a solution by trying in turn

$$x = 1, 2, 3, \ldots$$

2. Write a program which reads a real value s $(s \geq 1.5)$ and finds the smallest integer n such that

$$1 + \frac{1}{2} + \frac{1}{3} + \frac{1}{4} + \cdots + \frac{1}{n} > s$$

*3. Write a program to count the number of letters contained in a supplied word. The word will neither contain spaces nor be preceded by spaces but will be immediately followed by a space.

†*4. Write a program to compute the length of (i.e. the number of digits contained in) a given positive integer. The integer is to be introduced to the program as a user-defined constant.

5. If a variable x initially has the value λ and the value of x is repeatedly replaced by the value of

$$\frac{x}{2} + \frac{\lambda}{2x}$$

the values produced approach $\sqrt{\lambda}$.

Write a program which accepts as data two positive values λ and ε and uses the above technique to compute μ such that $|\mu^2 - \lambda| \leq \varepsilon$. Your program should say how many iterations are required to achieve the desired accuracy.

†*6. Write a program to produce the largest factor (other than n itself) of a given integer n.

7. Write a program to produce the largest Fibonacci number less than some specified positive value.

*8. Given two distinct positive integers n and m such that $n > m$, the hcf (highest common factor) of m and n **mod** m is the same as the hcf of n and m. Thus, if we start with two positive values α and β, repeatedly replace the larger of the two by the appropriate modulo reduction, and stop when the modulo reduction gives 0, we have computed the hcf of α and β.

Write a program to compute the hcf of two supplied integers.

9. (a) Write a program to count the number of words in a sentence. Words will contain only letters, spaces may precede the first word, and consecutive words will be separated by at least one space or end of line. The last word of the sentence will be immediately followed by a full stop.

(b) Modify the program to state the number of four-letter words present.

*10. A sequence of integers indicates the ages of owners of successive houses on the west side of a street as we go northwards. Only one owner is aged twenty-three. Write a program to read successive ages and tell us the age of the next-door neighbour, if any, on the south side of the twenty-three year old owner.

*11. Write a program to print all the members of the character set available on your computer, together with their ordinal numbers.

†12. Write a program to compute $n!$ $\{1 \times 2 \times 3 \times \cdots \times n\}$ for a given positive n.

*13. Write a program to print all the letters of the alphabet between two supplied letters (inclusive). The letters are to be printed in the order in which the specified letters are supplied. For example,

$$DH \Rightarrow DEFGH$$
$$TM \Rightarrow TSRQPONM$$

†14. An integer n is followed by n expressions, each of the form $\alpha + \beta$, $\alpha - \beta$, or $\alpha * \beta$ where α and β are integers. No spaces occur within an expression but expressions are separated by at least one space or end of line and spaces may precede the first expression. Write a program to print the value represented by each expression.

15. Write a program to tabulate $\sin\theta$, $\cos\theta$, $\tan\theta$, $\sec\theta$, and $\csc\theta$ for $\theta = 5°$, $10°$, $15°, \ldots, 85°$.

16. For a function tabulated at a set of equispaced points $x_0, x_1, x_2, \ldots, x_n$ the area beneath the curve over some range $[x_i, x_j]$ can be approximated by repeated application of the Trapezium Rule. For the range $[x_0, x_n]$ this gives

$$\int_{x_0}^{x_n} f(x)\, dx \simeq \frac{h}{2}(f_0 + f_n) + h \sum_{i=1}^{n-1} f_i$$

where h is the interval between successive x_i and $f_k \equiv f(x_k)$.

Write a program which reads a value for h and then an integer n followed by $n+1$ function values $f_0, f_1, f_2, \ldots, f_n$ and outputs an approximation to

$$\int_{x_0}^{x_n} f(x)\, dx$$

†*17. A set of measurements $x_1, x_2, \ldots, x_n$ is supplied, preceded by the value n. Write a program to compute the "mean" μ and "standard deviation" σ of this sample:

$$\mu = \frac{1}{n} \sum_{i=1}^{n} x_i$$

$$\sigma^2 = \frac{1}{n} \sum_{i=1}^{n} x_i^2 - \mu^2$$

†18. Write a program to produce all the factors of a given positive integer n.

†*19. A clothing manufacturer uses integer codes for colours. He produces T-shirts in a range of colours t_0 to t_1 and can print motifs in colours m_0 to m_1. These ranges may overlap. He wishes to produce all colour combinations of T-shirts and motifs so long as the motif on a T-shirt is not the same colour as the T-shirt.

Write a program to accept t_0, t_1, m_0, and m_1 as data and to produce all the desired combinations.

†20. An electronics firm produces resistors with impedances $r_0, r_0 + h, r_0 + 2h, \ldots, r_0 + nh$. Write a program to tabulate the values of the combined impedance of two resistors connected (a) in series and (b) in parallel for all possible pairs of impedances.

For two resistors with impedances Ω_1 and Ω_2 the combined impedance for serial connection is $\Omega_1 + \Omega_2$ and for parallel connection is $\Omega_1\Omega_2/(\Omega_1 + \Omega_2)$.

The output should appear in four columns (Ω_1, Ω_2, series, parallel) and should avoid duplication (e.g. $\Omega_1 = \alpha$ and $\Omega_2 = \beta$ is equivalent to $\Omega_1 = \beta$ and $\Omega_2 = \alpha$). r_0, h, and n are supplied as data.

*21. Write a program which takes a positive value λ and produces an inverted pyramid comprising λ lines such that the value $\lambda - i + 1$ appears $\lambda - i + 1$ times in line i of the pyramid.

For $\lambda = 5$ the pyramid should have the following form:

```
55555
4444
333
22
1
```

22. Write a program which draws a diamond of the form illustrated below. The letter which is to appear at the widest point of the figure (E in the example) is specified as input data.

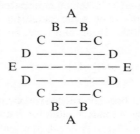

7

Procedures and Functions

We are familiar with some predefined procedures (*read, readln, write, writeln, get*) and functions (*succ, pred, ord, sin, cos, sqrt*, etc.). Pascal allows us to extend the set of procedures and functions available by defining our own.

Procedure and function declarations provide a means of associating names with sections of a program. These sections are then called "routines", and a routine is obeyed when its name is quoted. This offers two instant benefits. First, logically distinct activities can be referred to by different names thus making the program more readable; a well-chosen name will convey more immediate information than will a sequence of several statements. Second, if one activity is to be carried out at more than one point in a program we can declare the activity as a routine and merely call the routine at each point; we thus avoid writing the same sequence of statements several times. At run-time the computer obeys a routine body when it encounters its name in the program body. Upon completion of a routine the body control returns to the "point of call".

Procedure and function declarations must appear between the variable declarations (if there are any) and the **begin** of the program body.

The statements (there may be zero or more) that are to constitute the body of the routine must be bracketed between **begin** and **end** to form a compound statement and it is conventional to identify the end of the routine with a comment.

7.1 Parameterless procedures

In the simplest case a procedure declaration merely associates a name with some statements.

PARAMETERLESS PROCEDURE DECLARATION

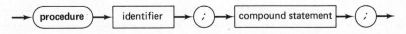

138

Example 7.1

In Figure 7.1 the program of Figure 6.9 has been rewritten to use procedures. □

Apart from two new procedure calls (and exits) performed by the program of Figure 7.1 the sequence of statements obeyed at run-time is exactly the

```
0    program LongestWordWithProcs (input, output);
1      const
2        fullstop = '.';   space = ' ';
3      var
4        thislength, maxlengthsofar : integer;
5
6      procedure DetermineLengthOfThisWord;
7          { Assumes input↑ < > space upon entry. }
8      begin
9        thislength := 0;
10       repeat
11         thislength := thislength + 1;   get (input)
12       until not (input↑ in ['A' .. 'Z'])
13     end { Determine Length of This Word };
14
15     procedure SkipToNextWord;
16     begin
17       while input↑ = space do
18         get (input)
19       { now input↑ < >space }
20     end { Skip To Next Word }
21
22   begin { program body }
23     maxlengthsofar := 0;
24     repeat
25       SkipToNextWord;   DetermineLengthOfThisWord;
26       if thislength > maxlengthsofar then
27         maxlengthsofar := thislength
28     until input↑ = fullstop;
29
30     writeln ('The longest word in the supplied sentence contains ',
31         maxlengthsofar :1, ' letters')
32   end.
```

Figure 7.1   Example 7.1

same as in the program of Figure 6.9. The advantage of the program of Figure 7.1 lies in its improved readability. To read a program containing procedures we first ignore the procedures and read the program body. Notice how the structure of the program is now more transparent. The main structure is described in a few lines (lines 24 to 28). These give the overall picture and show how each procedure fits into the total scheme. If we desire further detail of one section of the program we can examine the appropriate procedure. ■

A procedure should be declared before it is used but, subject to this constraint, the order of declaration of procedures is immaterial. It is convenient to declare procedures in alphabetic order; this considerably eases the task of finding a procedure within a large program.

Procedure names are often lengthy (if they have been created by a good programmer!) so, as with program names, we shall adopt the convention of using upper case for the first letter of each constituent word.

Example 7.2

Rewrite the program of Figure 6.10 to use procedures.   □

We could do this by defining three procedures: one to accumulate lunar votes, one to accumulate martian votes, and one to announce the result. If we did so, two of these procedures would be very similar—the process of totalling one set of votes is essentially the same as totalling the other set; only some of the names involved are different. This suggests that one procedure, rather than two, might be appropriate. The best procedure is described in Section 7.4.2 (see Figure 7.6) but first we try implementing one procedure with our present knowledge. We define a procedure to total a sequence of vote counts until a specified terminator is reached:

```
procedure TotalVotes;
begin
   totvotes:= 0;   read (votecount);
   repeat
      totvotes:= totvotes + votecount;
      read (votecount)
   until votecount = voteterminator
end { Total Votes }
```

This procedure can be accommodated if we extend the program variable declarations to include

```
totvotes, voteterminator : integer;
```

Accumulation of the LHP votes is then achieved by

```
voteterminator:= lunarterminator;
TotalVotes;
lunarvotes:= totvotes
```

```
0   program MoonMarsElectionWithaProc (input, output);
1     const
2       lunarterminator := - 1;   martianterminator := -2;
3     var
4       lunarvotes, martianvotes, voteterminator,
5       votecount, totvotes : integer;
6
7     procedure TotalVotes;
8     begin
9       totvotes := 0;   read (votecount);
10      repeat
11        totvotes := totvotes + votecount;   read (votecount)
12      until votecount = voteterminator
13    end { Total Votes };
14
15  begin
16      { Total votes for Lunar Habitationists }
17    voteterminator := lunarterminator;
18    TotalVotes;
19    lunarvotes := totvotes;
20
21    writeln ('Votes polled by the Lunar Habitation Party :',
22      lunarvotes);
23
24      { Total votes for Martian Nationalists }
25    voteterminator := martianterminator;
26    TotalVotes;
27    martianvotes := totvotes;
28
29    writeln ('Votes polled by the Martian Nationalist Party :',
30      martianvotes);
31    if lunarvotes = martianvotes then
32      writeln ('There is a tie—how about a recount?') else
33    begin
34      write ('A majority vote has been gained by the ');
35      case lunarvotes > martianvotes of
36        true : write ('Lunnar Habitation');
37        false : write ('Martian Nationalist')
38      end { case };
39      writeln (' Party')
40    end
41  end.
```

Figure 7.2   Example 7.2

A complete program using this approach is given in Figure 7.2. It must be stressed that this is not a very good program; its purpose is to pave the way for the next three sections. ■

One user-defined procedure may call another. In Example 7.2 we may decide that the overall structure splits most naturally into

> *accumulate both vote totals;*
> *announce result*

and declare one procedure to accumulate both totals. This procedure then calls *TotalVotes* twice:

```
procedure FormBothTotals;
begin
   voteterminator:= lunarterminator;
   totalvotes;
   lunarvotes:= totvotes;
   voteterminator:= martianterminator;
   totalvotes;
   martianvotes:= totvotes
end { Form Both Totals }
```

The procedure *FormBothTotals* refers to *TotalVotes* and so the declaration of *TotalVotes* must precede that of *FormBothTotals*:

```
program ...
   ...
procedure AnnounceResult;
   ...
end { Announce Result };

procedure TotalVotes;
   ...
end { Total Votes };

procedure FormBothTotals;
   ...
end { Form Both Totals };

begin { program body }
   ...
end.
```

It would seem that we are unable to maintain alphabetic ordering of the procedure declarations. We shall see how to overcome this in Section 7.6.

142

7.2 Localized information

You may have noticed a similarity between a procedure and a program. Each contains a sequence of statements (presented as a compound statement) which may refer to entities declared "outside". The procedures in Figures 7.1 and 7.2 refer to variables and constants declared in the main program just as statements within a program body can refer to *read, write, maxint, sin, cos,* etc.

This similarity extends. A program can contain declarations specifying entities which may be used by procedures which are declared within the program and by the statements of the program body. The same applies to procedures. A procedure declaration may contain its own declarations. Any entity declared within a procedure may be used by any procedure declared within the procedure and by the statements of the procedure body.

An entity does not exist outside the procedure in which it is declared. An entity declared within a procedure is said to be "local" to that procedure. An entity declared in the main program is said to be "global". The main program and each procedure or function constitutes a "block." Space for local variables is allocated when a block is entered and released when the block is exited.

It is good practice to declare variables as locally as possible. This reduces the possibility of their corruption in other parts of the program. Suppose a variable which should only be used within a ten-line procedure in a thousand-line program is acquiring a wrong value. If the variable is global you have to look through 1,000 lines of program to see if it has been used inappropriately. If the variable is local to the procedure you have only ten lines to worry about; if the variable had been referred to outside the procedure the program would not have compiled.

Localizing variables can increase program efficiency. Local references are usually more efficient than non-local references. We shall ignore the fact that in some Pascal implementations the most efficient access is to global variables.

We can now smarten up the program of Figure 7.2 a little. The variable *votecount* is used only inside the procedure *TotalVotes* so that is where it should be declared. It should be removed from the main program declarations (line 5) and the line

    var *votecount* : *integer;*

inserted between lines 7 and 8.

We cannot move any variable declarations into *FormBothTotals* because the three variables used within *FormBothTotals* (*voteterminator, lunarvotes,* and *martianvotes*) are also used elsewhere. We could, however, declare the two constants *lunarterminator* and *martianterminator* within *FormBothTotals.*

Because constants cannot be corrupted the positioning of constant declarations is not so critical. If one constant is used by several procedures it should be declared globally. If a constant is obviously relevant for only one procedure then it may well be sensible to declare it locally; put it where you will most easily find it in case a future modification to the program specification requires a different constant.

A similar reasoning applies to procedure declarations. If one procedure is used within several other procedures it will probably have to be declared globally. If it is used within only one other procedure it is nice to declare it within the procedure which uses it. The modified program for Example 7.2, using the procedure *FormBothTotals*, could utilize this facility. The resulting program is given in Figure 7.3. Notice that the declaration of *voteterminator* and *totvotes* can now be moved inside *FormBothTotals*.

```
program MoonMarsElectionWithNestedProcs (input, output);
   const
      lunarterminator = -1;   martianterminator = -2,
   var
      lunarvotes, martianvotes : integer;

   procedure AnnounceResult;
   begin
      writeln ('Votes polled by the Lunar Habitation Party :',
         lunarvotes);
      writeln ('Votes polled by the Martian Nationalist Party :',
         martianvotes);

      if lunarvotes = martianvotes then
         writeln ('There is a tie—how about a recount?') else
      begin
         write ('A majority vote has been gained by the ');
         case lunarvotes > martianvotes of
            true  : write ('Lunar Habitation');
            false : write ('Martian Nationalist')
         end { case };
         writeln (' Party')
      end
   end { Announce Result };

   procedure FormBothTotals;
      var
         totvotes, voteterminator : integer;
```

144

```
  procedure TotalVotes;
    var
      votecount : integer;
  begin
    totvotes := 0;   read (votecount);
    repeat
        totvotes := totvotes + votecount;   read (votecount)
    until votecount = voteterminator
  end { Total Votes };


begin { Form Both Totals }
  voteterminator := lunarterminator;
  TotalVotes;
  lunaravotes := totvotes;

  voteterminator := martianterminator;
  TotalVotes;
  martianvotes := totvotes
end { Form Both Totals };


begin { program body }
  FormBothTotals;
  AnnounceResult
end.
```

Figure 7.3   Example 7.2

Unfortunately procedures can be difficult to locate if deeply nested within a large program. As with constants, a procedure cannot be corrupted and so program security is not severely affected by the positioning of procedure declarations. A good strategy is to declare procedures globally in alphabetic order except, perhaps, for some obviously intended for use within only one other procedure.

7.3   Scope of identifiers

The "scope" of an identifier is that section of program in which it can be referenced. If an identifier is declared only once within a program (as has been the case with all identifiers in examples so far) its scope extends from its point of definition to the end of the current block.

In a large program several procedures may be written by different people and it would not be reasonable to insist that each programmer name his local entities differently to all other programmers on the same project. Consequently Pascal allows one identifier to be used for different purposes at different points in a program. At any one point the most local definition is the one which is in force. Figure 7.4 shows a program schema and indicates the scopes of the declared entities. Declaration of the parameters b (line 5) and q (line 8) will be explained in Section 7.4.

```
program ScopeDemo (output);

1    const a = 1;                                              a₁
2    var b, c : integer;                                       b₂
                                                          c₂
3    procedure p ;                                   p₃
4        var c : char;                            c₄
5        procedure q (b : boolean);            q₅
         begin                        b₅
         . . .
         end { q } ;                                      b₂
6        procedure r;                      r₆
7            var c : real;
             begin                c₇
             end { r } ;                   c₄
8        procedure b (var q : char);    b₈
9            var r : real;            q₈
             begin                r₉
             . . .
             end { b };          r₆  q₅
         begin { p }
         . . .
         end { p };                        c₂  b₂
     begin { program body }
     . . .
     end.
```

Figure 7.4   Illustration of scopes

146

7.4 Parameters

When we use a predefined procedure or function such as *read, write, get, sqrt, sin,* and *cos* we supply one or more parameters. This enables one process to be applied to different values or variables. We often require the same facility for user-defined procedures and functions.

We achieve this by declaring a procedure or function in terms of "formal parameters" and then supply "actual parameters" when the routine is called. The actual parameters are then substituted for the formal parameters. The order in which the parameters appear is important. An actual parameter corresponds to the formal parameter which is in the same position in the parameter list.

The scope of a formal parameter is the whole of the procedure within which it is declared.

7.4.1 Value parameters

Examine the program of Figure 7.2. The vote totalling process is applied twice: once to accumulate votes until the value −1 is read and once until the value −2 is read. We can convey this information to the procedure *TotalVotes* by introducing a "value parameter".

We remove the variable *voteterminator* from the main program and declare it as a formal value parameter of the procedure *TotalVotes*. Value parameter declarations within a procedure resemble ordinary declarations but the word **var** is missing.

>   **procedure** *TotalVotes (voteterminator : integer);*
>   **begin**
>   . . .
>   **end** { Total Votes }

We now replace

>   *voteterminator:= lunarterminator;*
>   *TotalVotes*

by

>   *TotalVotes (lunarterminator)*

and

>   *voteterminator:= martianterminator;*
>   *TotalVotes*

by

>   *TotalVotes (martianterminator)*

Notice how this approach localizes information; *voteterminator* is now local to *TotalVotes*. Within the procedure *AnnounceResult* we could localize references to *lunarvotes* and *martianvotes* by making them value parameters. This aspect would be more important if the procedure contained more non-local references, but it is worth providing the procedure with these two parameters for another reason.

The action of the procedure is governed by two values, the two vote totals. Supplying these two values as parameters highlights their significance. The procedure heading might then be

procedure *AnnounceResult (lunarvotes, martianvotes : integer);*

and the call would become

AnnounceResult (lunarvotes, martianvotes)

The same names have been chosen for the formals and actuals to show that this is legal. The formal *lunarvotes* and actual *lunarvotes* are different variables; they are two boxes in different parts of the computer but with the same name. Within the procedure *AnnounceResult* references to *lunarvotes* imply the formal parameter; elsewhere such references access the global variable.

An actual parameter corresponding to a formal value parameter may be any expression which gives a value of the appropriate type. The type of the actual and formal should usually be the same, but an integer expression may be supplied when a real parameter has been specified. This is consistent with the type compatibility demanded by assignments. The full definition of assignment compatibility is given in Section 9.3.

A formal value parameter is essentially an initialized local variable; when the procedure is called, the formal parameter is given the value of the actual parameter. Space for the formal parameter is allocated each time the procedure is called and released when the procedure is exited. We are allowed to change the value of a formal value parameter inside a procedure but this does not affect the actual parameter. The program of Figure 7.5 illustrates this. The same value is output by both writeln-statements (lines 18 and 21). When the procedure is called, the current value of *m* is assigned to *n* but subsequent changes to *n* (line 11) do not affect the value of *m*. Each procedure call generates a new *n* which starts life as a "copy" of *m*.

Value parameters transfer information into a procedure and so are sometimes called "input parameters".

7.4.2 Variable parameters

Return again to Figure 7.2. Each time the vote totalling process is activated it must not only seek a different terminating value but it must assign the total to a different variable. It is convenient therefore to supply the procedure *TotalVotes* with a variable as well as a value. We do this by giving *TotalVotes* a "variable parameter".

```
0   program AssignToValueParameter (input, output);
1     var
2       m : integer;
3
4     procedure DoubleUp (n : integer);
5       var
6         i : integer;
7     begin
8       write (n);
9       for i := 1 to 3 do
10      begin
11        n := n * 2;   write (n)
12      end;
13        writeln
14      end { Double Up };
15
16  begin { program body }
17    read (m);
18    writeln ('m has the value ', m :1);
19
20    DoubleUp (m);
21    writeln ('m now has the value ', m :1)
22  end.
```

INPUT :
27

OUTPUT :
m has the value 27
    27   54   108   216
m now has the value 27

Figure 7.5

When an actual parameter is substituted for a formal variable parameter the substitution occurs throughout the procedure. For each procedure call a formal parameter really **is** the corresponding actual parameter and not just a copy. Consequently, any attempt to change the value of the formal parameter will affect the actual parameter. The actual parameter must be a variable and so cannot be a general expression as was the case for value parameters. Variable parameters may be of any type, but the types of an actual parameter and its corresponding formal parameter must be identical. The declaration of formal variable parameters includes the word **var**.

Figure 7.6 contains the resulting program. Notice that the word **var** is

```
0    program MoonMarsElectionWithProcsandPars (input, output);
1    const
2        lunarterminator = -1;   martianterminator = -2;
3      var
4        lunarvotes, martianvotes : integer;
5
6      procedure AnnounceResult (lunarvotes, martianvotes : integer);
7      begin
8        writeln ('Votes polled by the Lunar Habitation Party :',
9           lunarvotes);
10       writeln ('Votes polled by the Martian Nationalist Party :',
11          martianvotes);
12
13       if lunarvotes = martianvotes then
14          writeln ('There is a tie—how about a recount?') else
15       begin
16          write ('A majority vote has been gained by the ');
17          case lunarvotes > martianvotes of
18             true : write ('Lunar Habitation');
19             false : write ('Martian Nationalist')
20          end { case };
21          writeln (' Party')
22       end
23     end { Announce Result };
24
25     procedure TotalVotes (var total : integer;   voteterminator : integer);
26     var
27         votecount, totvotes : integer;
28     begin
29       totvotes := 0;   read (votecount);
30       repeat
31          totvotes := totvotes + votecount;   read (votecount)
32       until votecount = voteterminator;
33       total := totvotes
34     end { Total Votes };
35
36   begin { program body }
37     TotalVotes (lunarvotes, lunarterminator);
38     TotalVotes (martianvotes, martianterminator);
39     AnnounceResult (lunarvotes, martianvotes)
40   end.
```

Figure 7.6

150

effective only up to the semi-colon. The variable *voteterminator* is still a value parameter. Notice too that semi-colons are used to separate formal parameters of different types, but no semi-colon immediately precedes the closing parenthesis.

We can declare several formal parameters of the same type by separating their names with commas. If such a list of names is preceded by the word **var** each name will constitute a variable parameter; if not, each will be a value parameter.

PROCEDURE HEADING

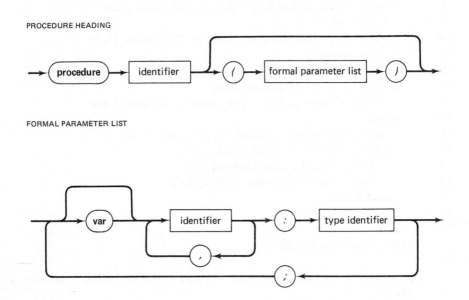

FORMAL PARAMETER LIST

In the program of Figure 7.6 we could interchange the order of the actual parameters supplied to *TotalVotes* (lines 37 and 38) if we interchange the order of the formals. The procedure heading would then be

procedure *TotalVotes (voteterminator: integer;* **var** *total: integer);*

The variable *totvotes* is not strictly needed. We could dispense with *totvotes* and use *total* wherever *totvotes* appears within the procedure body, but the version presented is better. The accumulation of votes is a process local to the procedure and so the running total should be stored in a local variable. The actual parameter supplied for *total* is interested only in the final total so, within the procedure, only the final total is assigned to the formal parameter (line 33).

It was mentioned in the previous section that supplying an expression (which may be a single variable) as an actual parameter to a procedure highlights its significance. This is particularly true for variable parameters. If a procedure may change the value of a non-local variable it is good practice to supply the variable as a parameter to stress the fact.

The two "parameter transfer mechanisms" can be described simply in terms of boxes. A formal value parameter is the name of a locally accessible box (created each time the procedure is called) and when the procedure is called, a value (the value of the actual parameter) is placed in this box. The value of the actual parameter must be defined. A formal variable parameter is a name with no associated box. When the procedure is called, a box (the box whose name is quoted as the actual parameter) is supplied. For the duration of the procedure body the formal name is stuck on to this box. It does not matter if the box contains no value when it is supplied (i.e. the value of the actual parameter may be undefined); this is the case with both calls of *TotalVotes* in Figure 7.6.

Variable parameters are used to transfer information out of a procedure and so are sometimes called "output parameters".

7.5 Functions

The predefined routine *sqrt* could have been defined as a procedure with two parameters (one value and one variable):

procedure *getsqrt (x: real;* **var** *sqrtx: real);*
   { Evaluates the square root of x and assigns
      the result to sqrtx. }
begin
   . . .
end *{ get sqrt }*

The statement

   $y := sqrt\ (y) + sqrt\ (sqrt\ (y + 1))$

would then have to be written something like

   getsqrt (y, rootofy);
   getsqrt (y + 1, rootofyplus1);
   getsqrt (rootofyplus1, fourthrootofyplus1);
   $y := rootofy + fourthrootofyplus1$

Instead it was defined as a real function with one parameter. The example above shows how much more convenient this is.

Similarly, there are times when a user-defined routine is best expressed as a function. This is when we are interested in only one value resulting from the computation invoked by the routine and when the routine produces no "side-effects". A routine is said to have a side-effect if it can cause any non-local change (i.e. change the value of a non-local variable or initiate input or output). A function with a side-effect is undesirable because functions are used in expressions and a program can be hard to follow if evaluation of an expression changes the global environment. Obscure errors can occur if a program is later modified, possibly by someone other than the original programmer, and the function is called again: the non-local changes which will occur will not be expected. Also, a function without side-effects alludes more closely to the mathematical definition—it merely delivers a value. In Pascal, a function may deliver a result of any scalar (or pointer; see Chapter 14) type. To prohibit the corruption of an actual parameter function formals should be value parameters (but Chapter 11 suggests that this constraint can sometimes be relaxed).

A function declaration differs from a procedure declaration in three respects:

1. **function** replaces **procedure**.
2. The type of the result delivered by the function is quoted (preceded by a colon) before the closing semi-colon of the function heading.
3. Within the function body there must be at least one assignment statement with the function identifier on the left-hand side.

FUNCTION HEADING

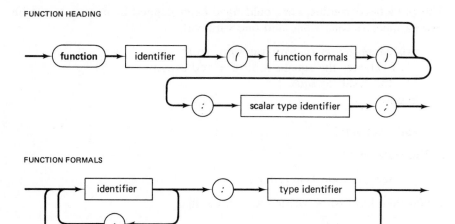

FUNCTION FORMALS

In the program of Figure 7.6 we are interested in a single integer value being returned by *TotalVotes* and so this suggests that a function might be appropriate:

```
function totalvotes (voteterminator: integer): integer;
begin
    ...
    totalvotes:= totvotes
end { total votes }
```

The two procedure calls

$\quad$ *TotalVotes (lunarvotes, lunarterminator)*$\qquad$(line 37)

and

TotalVotes (martianvotes, martianterminator)   (line 38)

would then be replaced by

lunarvotes:= totalvotes (lunarterminator)

and

martianvotes:= totalvotes (martianterminator)

respectively. We could certainly do this but we would have a function with a side-effect; each call of *totalvotes* changes the state of the input stream. The form presented in Figure 7.6 is to be preferred.

We use a function name on the left-hand side of an assignment statement when we wish to give a value to the function but a function reference in almost any other context constitutes a function call. The only exception to this is when a function name is passed as an actual parameter (corresponding to a formal function), as described in Section 7.8. In the above example we must maintain a local variable (*totvotes*) to accumulate the votes. The following function definition is illegal:

```
function totalvotes (voteterminator : integer) : integer;
  var votes : integer;
begin
  read (votes);   totalvotes:= 0;
  repeat
    totalvotes:= totalvotes + votes;
    read (votes)
  until votes = voteterminator
end { total votes }
```

The function reference on the right-hand side of the assignment statement

totalvotes:= totalvotes + votes

constitutes a recursive function call (see Section 7.7.1) with an incorrect number (zero) of parameters.

Example 7.3

Write a program to read two real numbers x and y and two positive integers m and n and to compute the values x^m, y^n, $(x^n)^m$, and $(y^m)^n$.   □

The program is given in Figure 7.7. Use of a function *power* to raise a given number to a specified power makes the program body easy to write and easy to read. Each time we raise a number to a power we are interested only in the final result and computation of this value does not affect anything outside the routine. The routine is therefore best expressed as a function. The function takes two value parameters. ∎

```
program Powers (input, output);
  var
    x, y : real;
    m, n : integer;

  function power (x : real;   n : integer) : real;
    var
      i : integer;
      p, xsquared : real;
  begin
    if n = 1 then
      power := x else
    begin
      xsquared := sqr (x);
      if odd (n) then
        p := x * xsquared
      else
        p := xsquared;

      for i := 2 to n div 2 do
        p := p * xsquared;
      power := p
    end
  end   { power };

begin { program body }
  read (x, y, m, n);
  writeln (x, ' raised to the power ', m : 2, ' =', power (x, m) );
  writeln (y, ' raised to the power ', n : 2, ' =', power (y, n) );
  writeln (x, ' raised to the power ', n :2,
    ' all raised to the power ', m :2,
    ' =', power (power (x, n), m) );
  writeln (y, ' raised to the power ', m :2,
    ' all raised to the power ', n : 2,
    ' =', power (power (y, m), n) )
end.
```

Figure 7.7   Example 7.3

Example 7.4

Write a program to decode an encoded message. The decoding process involves interchanging

the digits $0, 1, 2, \ldots, 9$ and $9, 8, 7, \ldots, 0$,
the vowels A, E, I, O, U and their successors B, F, J, P, V,

the letters C, G, K, Q, W and their successors D, H, L, R, X, and the letters M, S, Y and their successors N, T, Z,

reducing consecutive spaces to a single space and replacing any other character by a question mark. □

An improved solution will be presented in Chapter 13 but the program of Figure 7.8 serves to illustrate the use of functions. ■

```
program DecodeMessage (input, output);
    { Decoding process for one character :—
         [0, 1, . . . , 9] <−> [9, 8, . . . , 0]
         [A, E, I, O, U] <−> [B, F, J, P, V]
         [C, G, K, Q, W] <−> [D, H, L, R, X]
              [M, S, Y] <−> [N, T, Z]
       Everything else   −>  ? }
  const
    space = ' ';   query = '?';

  procedure Decode (ch : char);
    var
      decodedch : char;

    function chisadigit : boolean;
    begin
      chisadigit := ch in ['0'..'9']
    end { ch is a digit };

    function digitwithrank (n : integer) : char;
    begin
      digitwithrank := chr (ord ('0') + n)
    end { digit with rank };

    function rankofch : integer;
    begin
      rankofch := ord (ch) − ord ('0')
    end { rank of ch };

    function vowel (ch : char) : boolean;
    begin
      vowel := ch in ['A', 'E', 'I', 'O', 'U']
    end { vowel };

  begin { Decode }
    if ch = space then decodedch := space else
    if chisadigit then decodedch := digitwithrank (9 − rankofch) else
```

```pascal
        if vowel (ch) then decodedch := succ (ch) else
          if vowel (pred (ch)) then decodedch := pred (ch) else
            if vowel (pred(pred(ch))) then decodedch := succ (ch) else
              if vowel (pred(pred(pred(ch)))) then decodedch := pred (ch) else
                if ch in ['M', 'S', 'Y'] then decodedch := succ (ch) else
                  if ch in ['N', 'T', 'Z'] then decodedch := pred (ch) else
                    decodedch := query;
        write (decodedch)
      end { Decode };


      procedure DecodeWord;
      begin
        repeat
          Decode (input↑);   get (input)
        until input↑ = space
      end { Decode word };


      procedure SquashSpaces;
      begin
        if (input↑ = space) and not eoln then
        begin
          write (space);
          repeat
            get (input)
          until eoln or (input↑ <> space)
        end
      end { Squash Spaces };


    begin { program body }
      if eof then
        writeln ('No message has been supplied') else
      begin
        SquashSpaces;
        repeat
          while not eoln do
          begin
            DecodeWord;   SquashSpaces
          end;
          readln;   writeln
        until eof
      end
    end.
```

INPUT :
*OBTDBK   OQPHQBNNJMH   8019 $ − *!*

OUTPUT :
PASCAL PROGRAMMING 1980 ????

Figure 7.8   Example 7.4

7.6   Forward references

It is not always convenient to declare a procedure or function at a point within the program text at which it precedes all its references. It is possible to declare a procedure or function body and its heading at different points within the same block. The declaration of the heading must precede the declaration of the body and must precede any references to the routine. The heading is followed by the word *forward* and this constitutes a "forward reference" to the body. The body, together with any local declarations, is then preceded by a simplified heading.

FORWARD ROUTINE HEADING

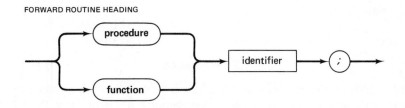

The simplified heading makes no mention of any parameters nor, in the case of a function, the type of the function.

Thus, the program of Figure 7.6 could have the form

program . . .
   . . .
procedure *TotalVotes* (**var** *total* : *integer;   voteterminator* : *integer);*
   forward;

procedure *AnnounceResult (lunarvotes, martianvotes* : *integer);*
   . . .
end { Announce Result };

procedure *FormBothTotals;*
   . . .
end { Form Both Totals };

```
    procedure TotalVotes { (var total:integer; voteterminator:integer) };
    begin
      . . .
    end { Total Votes };

  begin
    . . .
  end.
```

The parameters of the forward reference procedure have been indicated by a comment when the procedure body is declared. This improves program readability.

A program incorporating the function of Figure 7.7 as a forward reference would have the following form:

```
  program . . .
    . . .
    function power (x:real;   n:integer)   :   real;
      forward;
    . . .
    function power { (x:real;   n:integer)   :   real };
    begin
      . . .
    end { power };
    . . .
  end.
```

7.7   Recursion

In the hands of the master recursion is a powerful tool which can provide elegant solutions to some complex programming problems. For the beginner, on the other hand, it can be a difficult concept to grasp. A brief discussion of recursion is included here for completeness. You may wish to skip this section on a first reading.

It is sometimes convenient to describe a process "in terms of itself". In computing terminology this constitutes a "recursive definition" and corresponds to a procedure or function being invoked before a previous invocation has been completed.

7.7.1   Direct recursion

If a routine body includes a call of the routine this is called "direct recursion".

Example 7.5

Define a function to raise a number x to a positive integral power n in such a way that the number of arithmetic operations performed is minimized for large n.   □

This can be done if we observe that

for $n = 1$, $x^n = x$ and
for $n > 1$,
n even $\Rightarrow x^n = sqr\,(x^{n\,\mathbf{div}2})$
n odd $\Rightarrow x^n = x \;*\; sqr\,(x^{n\,\mathbf{div}2})$

For example, x^{50} can be computed as

$sqr\,(x^{25})$

with x^{25} computed as

$x * sqr\,(x^{12})$

with x^{12} computed as

$sqr\,(x^6)$

with x^6 computed as

$sqr\,(x^3)$

with x^3 computed as

$x * sqr\,(x)$

The arithmetic operations performed are

div: five times
* : twice
sqr: five times

Repeated multiplication as in Figure 6.14 would require fifty multiplications. The improved approach of Figure 7.7 would use

div: once
* : twenty-four times
sqr: once

The algorithm suggested by the above observation involves recursion: we have described the result of raising a number (x) to a power (n) in terms of raising a number (x) to a power $(n \text{ div } 2)$. The process is described in terms of itself or, to be more precise, in terms of a "subcase" of itself. This is important. If the process were literally described in terms of itself we would have infinite recursion. In the above example n is replaced by $n \text{ div } 2$ in each recursive reference and so in this case the recursion is said to be "on n". Also important is the fact that there must be at least one "explicit" definition of the process; for at least one particular case ($n = 1$ in the above example) there must be a definition which does not involve recursion. If the subcases do not eventually lead to one of these explicit cases the recursion will be infinite. In the above example we must eventually reach 1 if we start

160

with a positive integer and repeatedly halve it (taking the integer part) and so the recursion is finite.

This recursive algorithm can be implemented directly as a recursive function:

function *power (x : real;   n : integer) : real;*
　　{ Raises a number x to a positive power n with the
　　　minimum number of arithmetic operations for large n. }
begin
　if *n = 1* **then** *power := x* **else**
　　if *odd (n)* **then** *power := x * sqr (power (x, n* **div** *2))* **else**
　　　power := sqr (power (x, n **div** *2))*
end *{ power }*

Remember that new space is allocated for a value parameter each time the function is called. When the function calls are nested recursively we get a new *x* and *n* each time. To see how this function works we follow a function call:

　write (power (2.1, 6))

The call of *write* invokes the call *power (2.1, 6):*

　power is called (level 1) with *x = 2.1* and *n = 6*
　so at level 1 *power := sqr (power (2.1, 3))*
　　hence *power* is called (level 2) with *x = 2.1* and *n = 3*
　　so at level 2 *power := 2.1 * sqr (power (2.1, 1))*
　　　hence *power* is called (level 3) with *x = 2.1* and *n = 1*
　　　so at level 3 *power := 2.1*
　　　and this value is returned to level 2
　　so at level 2 *power := 2.1 * sqr (2.1)*
　　which gives *power := 9.261*
　　and this value is returned to level 1
　so at level 1 *power := sqr (9.261)*
　which gives *power := 85.766121*
　and this value is returned to the point of call

Thus the value delivered to the write-statement is

　85.766121

In this example the function takes two parameters *x* and *n* but recursion is on *n* only; *x* remains the same for each recursive call. We could therefore avoid passing *x* as a parameter through the recursion. Notice that this would necessitate the declaration of one routine within another because the recursive function (*xtothe* in the example which follows) must refer to *x*, a formal parameter of *power:*

function *power (x : real; n : integer) : real;*
　function *xtothe (n : integer) : real;*

```
    begin
      if n = 1 then xtothe := x else
        if odd (n) then
          xtothe := x * sqr (xtothe (n div 2))
        else
          xtothe := sqr (xtothe (n div 2))
    end { x to the };
  begin { power }
    power := xtothe (n)
  end { power }
```

Passing a parameter takes a certain amount of time so the function call will now be more efficient. Unfortunately references to *x* are now non-local whereas they were previously local. On balance we have possibly made a slight gain (because there will be few run-time references to *x*) but this is very much implementation dependent.

It is worth noting that this version uses less space because each time the function is called, less parameter space need be allocated. This could be important in an environment where the depth of recursion may be large. ■

Example 7.6

The program of Figure 6.8 prints an integer in octal form. A much shorter solution is available if we use recursion. A positive integer *n* will be printed in octal if we print the number *n* **div** 8 in octal and follow it by the digit *n* **mod** 8.   □

```
    procedure PrintOctal (n : integer);
    begin
      if n > 0 then
      begin
        PrintOctal (n div 8);   write (n mod 8 : 1)
      end
    end { Print Octal }  ■
```

7.7.2 Mutual recursion

If one routine calls another routine which calls another routine... which calls the first routine, these routines are said to be "mutually recursive" and the recursion is said to be "indirect".

Example 7.7

Write a program to print the value of an arithmetic expression supplied on one line as a fully bracketed triplet. Assume that permissible operators are +, −, *, and /, that no spaces will be present, and that the data is correct.

162

A "fully bracketed triplet" has the form $(\alpha\,\theta\,\beta)$ where each operand α and β may be either a single value or a fully bracketed triplet and θ is an operator. For example,

$$(((2.3 + 4.72) * (-3.9 - 6.8))/ 7.1)$$

is a fully bracketed triplet. □

The program of Figure 7.9 achieves this using two mutually recursive procedures. Notice that a forward reference is inevitable with mutually recursive procedures. In Figure 7.9 each procedure calls the other but they can not each be declared before the other. ■

```
program EvaluateFullyBracketedTriplet (input, output);
  var
    result : real;

  procedure GetNextValue (var nextvalue : real);
    forward;

  procedure GetBracExpValue (var value : real);
    var
      lhoperand, rhoperand : real;
      operator : char;
  begin
    get (input);      { to skip opening bracket }
    GetNextValue (lhoperand);
    read (operator);
    GetNextValue (rhoperand);
    get (input);      { to skip closing bracket }
    case operator of
      '+' : value := lhoperand + rhoperand;
      '-' : value := lhoperand - rhoperand;
      '*' : value := lhoperand * rhoperand;
      '/' : value := lhoperand / rhoperand
    end { case }
  end { Get Brac Exp Value };

  procedure GetNextValue { (var nextvalue : real) };
  begin
    if input↑ = '(' then
      GetBracExpValue (nextvalue)
    else
      read (nextvalue)
  end { Get Next Value };

begin { program body }
  GetBracExpValue (result);
```

---

writeln ('The supplied expression evaluates to ', result)
end.

INPUT :

$(((2.3 + 4.72) * (-3.9 - 6.8))/7.1)$

OUTPUT :

The supplied expression evaluates to $-0.105794366E + 02$

Figure 7.9   Example 7.7

7.7.3   Backtrack programming

In all the problems tackled so far we have known the initial state (the data), we have had to work out the steps required to get the answer (these constitute the algorithm), and the computer has then given us the result. With some problems the situation is rather different. We know the initial state (the data) and we also know the final state (the answer), but we want the computer to produce the steps needed to get from one to the other (the algorithm). Examples include playing solitaire, playing chess, finding a route through a maze, solving a mathematical theorem, and making a robot perform a specified task. Programs which do these things are sometimes said to display "artificial intelligence" because they are apparently being "clever". Of course, like a conjuring trick, it is not half so clever when you know how it is done!

Many such problems demand specific, highly complex programs but some can be tackled satisfactorily by a standard technique known as "backtracking". The computer tries a sequence of possible steps and if it finds this cannot lead to a solution it backtracks, undoing the effects of the steps it has just examined, and tries a different sequence. This process continues until all possible sequences have been explored (and so no solution exists) or a solution is found (or, as can easily happen, the program runs out of time!).

Example 7.8

Write a program to determine a sequence of steps which will tranform one given integer into another. The operations permitted at each step are adding 3, subtracting 4, or multiplying by 2.   □

If we consider the operations in the order mentioned and seek a solution starting from some integer i, the program must first "look ahead" in an attempt to find a solution starting from $i + 3$. If it succeeds then the solution from i is the sequence of steps it has just determined, preceded by the step "add 3". If it fails to find a solution from $i + 3$ it must, instead, try $i - 4$. Again, if it finds a solution from $i - 4$ we know the solution from i. If not it must try $i \times 2$. If no solution is found this time then no solution starting from i exists.

164

If the permitted operations were $+6, -4$, and $*2$ it would be impossible to transform any even number into an odd number. However, for the problem specified it should always be possible, in theory, to transform any integer into any other. The sequence $(+3, -4)$ is equivalent to -1 and the sequence $(+3, -4, +3, -4, +3)$ is equivalent to $+1$, and by repeatedly adding 1 or subtracting 1 we can generate all the integers. The trouble is that the program may not produce a solution in the time allowed. Consider what happens if it tries to transform 5 into 2. It explores the sequence 8, 11, 14, 17, ... because the look-ahead always tries addition first. When this sequence reaches *maxint* the program will either generate overflow or, if the programmer has guarded against this, will start backtracking and will apply other operations. In either case this is unsatisfactory; in the first case the program fails and in the second it wastes a great amount of time. To avoid this it is customary to "bound" the depth of look-ahead. Figure 7.10 illustrates the effect of transforming 5 into 2 by the previous algorithm with a depth bound of 3. The sequence discovered is $(-4, \times 2)$.

The process is usually described in terms of searching a "tree". The tree "traversed" by the process of Figure 7.10 is shown in Figure 7.11. In

```
                                                                   level
Enter problem-solving process with initial value
→5 +3                                                          0
    →8  +3                                                         1
        →11  +3                                                     2
              → 14 at bound so return to level 2                  3
             −4                                                     2
              →  7 at bound so return to level 2                  3
             ×2                                                     2
              → 22 at bound so return to level 2                  3
             no more operators so return to level 1               2
        −4                                                         1
          →  4  +3                                                 2
              →  7 at bound so return to level 2                  3
             −4                                                     2
              →  0 at bound so return to level 2                  3
             ×2                                                     2
              →  8 at bound so return to level 2                  3
             no more operators so return to level 1               2
        ×2                                                         1
          →16  +3                                                   2
              → 19 at bound so return to level 2                  3
             −4                                                     2
              → 12 at bound so return to level 2                  3
             ×2                                                     2
              → 32 at bound so return to level 2                  3
```

```
                              no more operators so return to level 1        2
                  no more operators so return to level 0              1
     −4                                                          0
       →1  +3                                                        1
           →  4  +3                                              2
                   →  7 at bound so return to level 2                3
                   −4                                            2
                   →  0 at bound so return to level 2                3
                   ×2                                            2
                   →  8 at bound so return to level 2                3
                  no more operators so return to level 1            2
           −4                                                    1
       →   − 3 +3                                                2
                   →  0 at bound so return to level 2                3
                   −4                                            2
                   →−7 at bound so return to level 2                 3
                   ×2                                            2
                   →−6 at bound so return to level 2                 3
                  no more operators so return to level 1            2
       ×2                                                        1
           →  2  solution found so return to level 1                2
       record '×2' as level 1 step and return to level 0         1
record '−4' as level 0 step and exit from process.          0
```

Figure 7.10 Transformation of 5 into 2 in Example 7.8

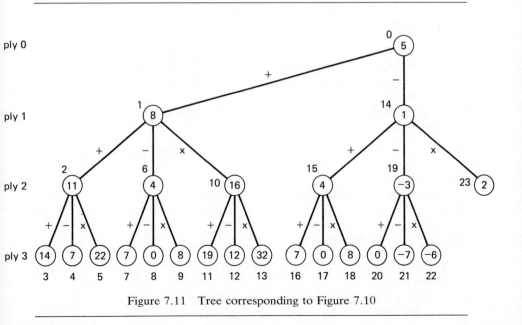

Figure 7.11   Tree corresponding to Figure 7.10

166

computing, trees grow upside down with the "root" at the top. The lines are called "branches" and represent operations and the circles are called "nodes" and represent the values examined. The nodes have been numbered in the order in which they are generated within the process described above. The term "ply" is often used to indicate depth. The root node (numbered 0 in the diagram) has ply 0.

---

if $s = S$ **then**
    return to previous level with "success"

else
    if depth bound has been reached **then**
        return to previous level with "failure" **else**

begin
    for each operator available or until a successful
        outcome is observed (whichever is the sooner) **do**

    begin
        apply the operator to s to produce a new state s';
        apply this whole process at the next level
            with s' replacing s;
        if control returns from the next level with "success" **then**
            note the last operator applied
    end;

    if a successful outcome was achieved **then**
        return to the previous level with "success"
    else
        return to the previous level with "failure"
end.

Figure 7.12 Bounded algorithm to transform s into S

The general algorithm to transform a state s into a desired state S is shown in Figure 7.12. In the context of Example 7.8 each "state" is an integer and so the algorithm can be implemented as a procedure with the following overall structure:

procedure *Try (int, intwanted, depthleft : integer;*   **var** *success : boolean);*
begin
    if *int = intwanted* **then** *success := true* **else**
      if *depthleft = 0* **then** *success := false* **else**

```
    begin
      for each operator +3, -4, ×2 applied in turn
        \ or until success do
          Try (int with operator applied, intwanted,
            depthleft - 1, success);
          if success then writeln ('Apply operator...')
      end
    end { Try };
```

A complete program utilizing such a procedure is shown in Figure 7.13. Notice that the steps required are listed in reverse order. The root node of Figure 7.11 represents the top level call of the procedure *Try*. Because *int* and *depthleft* are value parameters, new local variables will be created to accommodate them each time the procedure is called. Thus when control exits from one recursive level back to the previous level the values which were in force at the previous level will still be there. This is how the steps are "undone" during backtracking. The parameter *intwanted* always has the same value (the value of *finalint*) so it need not be passed as a parameter through the recursion; *finalint* could be accessed globally. ∎

```
    program TransformInt (input, output);
        { Program attempts to transform one supplied integer
          into another by a sequence of additions, subtractions,
          and multiplications. }
    const
        addint = 3;  subint = 4;  multint = 2;
        space = ' ';
        yes = true;  no = false;
    var
        initialint, finalint, maxopsallowed : integer;
        solved : boolean;

    procedure Try (intwanted, depthleft : integer;
                      var solutionfound : boolean);
        var
          success : boolean;
    begin
        if int = intwanted then solutionfound := true else
        if depthleft = 0 then solutionfound := false else
        begin
            Try (int + addint, intwanted, depthleft - 1, success);
            if success then
                writeln ('Add ', addint :1) else
```

```
      begin
         Try (int – subint, intwanted, depthleft – 1, success);
         if success then
            writeln ('Subtract ', subint :1) else
         begin
            Try (int * multint, intwanted, depthleft – 1, success);
            if success then
               writeln ('Multiply by ', multint :1)
         end
         end;
         solutionfound := success
      end
   end { Try };

begin { program body }
   read (initialint, finalint, maxopsallowed);
   writeln ('We wish to transform ', initialint :1,
      ' into ', finalint :1);

   writeln ('The permitted operations are');
   writeln (space :5, 'adding ', addint);
   writeln (space :5, 'subtracting ', subint);
   writeln (space :5, 'multiplying by ', multint);
   writeln;

   writeln ('The solution steps will be printed in reverse order');
   writeln;

   Try (initialint, finalint, maxopsallowed, solved);

   writeln;
   case solved of
      yes : write ('A');
      no : write ('No')
   end { case };
   writeln (' solution has been found')
end.
```

INPUT :
5   2   3

OUTPUT :
We wish to transform 5 into 2
The permitted operations are
    adding   3

subtracting   4
multiplying by   2
The search will be bounded at depth   3

The solution steps will be printed in reverse order

Multiply by 2
Subtract 4

A solution has been found

Figure 7.13   Example 7.8

Example 7.9

A man wishes to cross a river with a goat, a wolf, and a cabbage. He has a boat which he can use but he can not transport more than one thing at once. He has no string with which to tether the goat or the wolf and does not know how he is going to get everything safely to the opposite bank. His problem is that he must not leave the wolf with the goat (because the wolf would eat the goat) nor the goat with the cabbage (because the goat would eat the cabbage).

Write a program to tell the man what to do. □

This problem is essentially the same as the previous one. We wish to transform an initial state (all on the left bank) into a final state (all on the right bank) by a legal sequence of operations (crossing the river, in either direction, alone or with one thing, subject to peaceful relations existing on the bank left behind). The basic structure of the programs will therefore be similar but this program is more complicated. These operations are more difficult to describe in a programming language and representation of a state is more complex.

Each operation transforms one state into another so we must choose a representation for states before we can define the operations. At the same time, we should choose a representation which will simplify definition of the operations. The state representation must indicate the whereabouts of the man and each of his companions. We need not concern ourselves with the man when he is in the boat; we need worry only about the collection he has left on one bank when he has just reached the other bank. Thus there are only two possible locations of interest for each participant: left bank or right bank. With our present knowledge this suggests the use of booleans (see Example 10.9 for a better representation). We shall use *true* to represent the right bank and *false* the left. Again, we implement the algorithm as a recursive procedure and this time the procedure heading is

procedure *Try (here, cabbage, goat, wolf : boolean;*
                   depthleft : integer;   **var** *outcome : boolean);*

The current state in the search is represented by the four boolean value parameters. When the procedure is called each of the four corresponding actual parameters will be either *true* (implying that particular thing is on the right bank) or *false* (it is on the left bank). We use the name *here* rather than *man* to represent the man's position because of the way we shall be using it within the procedure body. Before the man can take a particular object we must ensure that it and the man occupy the same bank of the river. We must check that the parameter indicating the man's position and the parameter indicating the object's position have the same value. A statement of the form

if *object* = *here* **then** . . .

reads better than

if *object* = *man* **then** . . . .

When choosing names for entities always choose a name which is sensible in the context in which it is *used*. This point will be stressed when arrays are discussed (Chapter 13).

Initially all four participants are on the left bank so the top level call has the form

Try (onlbank, onlbank, onlbank, onlbank, maxdepth, outcome)

and will be followed by

```
case outcome of
  success: . . . ;
  failure: . . .
end { case }
```

We shall have to declare appropriate constants:

```
const
  onrbank = true;   onlbank = false;
  success = true;   failure = false;
  maxdepth = 9;
```

and a boolean variable to supply as the output parameter

```
var
  outcome : boolean;
```

The state we seek is that in which all four are on the right bank. This is the case in the program when all four variables *here*, *cabbage*, *goat*, and *wolf* take the value *true*. So, we have reached our goal state when the expression

here **and** *cabbage* **and** *goat* **and** *wolf*

is *true*.

Crossing the river is represented by inverting a boolean value. If the man

crosses the river alone we simulate this by a call of *Try* with the value of
here inverted and, of course, with *depthleft* decremented:

> *Try* (**not** *here, cabbage, goat, wolf, depthleft* − *1, solved*)

This assumes that *Try* contains a local boolean variable *solved*. If the man
takes something with him we must also invert the value which indicates that
thing's position. A crossing with, say, the wolf is simulated by

> *Try* (**not** *here, cabbage, goat,* **not** *wolf, depthleft* − *1, solved*)

When the man has attempted a crossing from one side to the other, he
must look back at the bank he has just left to see if anything is being eaten.
In real life he would have to think ahead and only make his crossing when
he has decided it is safe to do so. In backtrack programming it is often easier
to attempt something and then, if it is apparent that it should not have been
attempted, backtrack. Remember, all changes represented by value parameters in a recursive procedure call revert when we backtrack. If the goat has
been devoured, it will be reincarnated when we backtrack! Trouble is afoot
on the opposite bank (the bank which the man does not currently occupy) if
the cabbage is left with the goat or the goat is left with the wolf. This is the
situation when

> *(cabbage* < > *here)* **and** *(goat* < > *here)* **or**
> *(goat* < > *here)* **and** *(wolf* < > *here)*

The full program is shown in Figure 7.14. Two boolean constants, *hostile*
and *peaceful*, have been introduced to improve program transparency when
the situation on the opposite bank is being determined. Also, for conceptual
convenience (and, hence, transparency), crossing the river is handled by a
procedure *Cross*. This procedure must be capable of changing the value of
solved so we use a variable parameter to emphasize the fact. ▪

```
program ManCabbageGoatWolf (output);
   const
      onrbank = true;  onlbank = false;
      success = true;  failure = false;
      maxdepth = 9;
   var
      outcome : boolean;

   procedure Try (here, cabbage, goat, wolf : boolean;
                     depthleft : integer; var outcome : boolean);
      const
         peaceful = true;  hostile = false;

      function allonrbank : boolean;
```

172

```
begin
   allonrbank := here and cabbage and goat and wolf
end { all on r bank };

function situation (there : boolean) : boolean;
begin
   if (cabbage = there) and (goat = there) or
      (goat = there) and (wolf = there) then
      situation := hostile
   else
      situation := peaceful
end { situation } ;

procedure Cross (var solnfound : boolean);
   var
      solved : boolean;
begin
   solved := false;
   if cabbage = here then
      Try (not here, not cabbage, goat, wolf, depthleft-1, solved);
   if solved then
      writeln ('Man takes cabbage') else
   begin
      if goat = here then
         Try (not here, cabbage, not goat, wolf, depthleft-1, solved);
      if solved then
         writeln ('Man takes goat') else
      begin
         if wolf = here then
            Try (not here, cabbage, goat, not wolf, depthleft-1,
                 solved);
         if solved then
            writeln ('Man takes wolf') else
         begin
            Try (not here, cabbage, goat, wolf, depthleft-1, solved);
            if solved then
               writeln ('Man crosses alone')
         end
      end
   end;
   solnfound := solved
end { Cross } ;

begin { Try }
   if allonrbank then outcome := success else
```

```
        if depthleft = 0 then outcome := failure else
          case situation (not here) of
            peaceful : Cross (outcome);
            hostile  : outcome := failure
          end { case }
    end { Try } ;

begin { program body }
    writeln ('Man, cabbage, goat, and wolf are initially on ',
      'the left bank of the river');
    writeln;
    writeln ('The actions the man is to perform will be listed ',
        'in reverse order');
    writeln;

    Try (onlbank, onlbank, onlbank, onlbank, maxdepth, outcome);
    writeln;

    case outcome of
      success :
        writeln ('All are now safely on the right bank');
      failure :
        writeln ('No solution has been found')
    end { case }
end.
```

OUTPUT :
Man, cabbage, goat, and wolf are initially on the left bank of the river

The actions the man is to perform will be listed in reverse order

Man takes goat
Man crosses alone
Man takes wolf
Man takes goat
Man takes cabbage
Man crosses alone
Man takes goat
Man takes goat
Man takes goat

All are now safely on the right bank

Figure 7.14   Example 7.9

174

7.7.3.1 Accelerating the search

It is often possible to speed up the searching process we have been
describing by reducing the number of nodes the program examines. We can
often guide the search so that states which are "good" in some sense are
explored before those that are not so good. Guidance is the key to successful
artificial intelligence programs. The better their choice of "moves" from one
state to another the cleverer they appear to be. Such programs usually
deviate from the standard backtrack algorithm of Figure 7.12 and employ
what is known as "heuristic search". We shall consider an example of
heuristic search in Section 14.5.1. For the moment we restrict our attention
to the standard backtracking algorithm and return to our friend in the boat.

He will probably find a solution sooner if he distinguishes between the
two crossing directions. When crossing from left to right, he should consider
accompanied crossings before exploring the possibility of crossing alone, but
when crossing from right to left, the reverse applies. In the program of
Figure 7.14 the value of *here* indicates the man's whereabouts. It is a simple
matter to modify the procedure *Cross* so that solo crossings are considered
first when *here = onrbank* and last when *here = onlbank*. The program of
Figure 7.14, using a depth bound of 9, examines 111 nodes before it finds a
solution. The guided version with the same depth bound reduces this
number to 54. Inclusion of this modification is left as an exercise for the
reader.

Another technique to shorten the search is to prune the search tree. We
may know that a particular state cannot lead to a solution and so can
abandon this line of search when the state is encountered. As an example
consider a robot planning a route from room A to room B and seeking a
solution by entering room C. If room C has only one doorway, this branch of
the search can be cut off immediately; there is no point in entering room C.
This effectively prunes the search tree (fewer nodes will be generated) but
does not guarantee a faster search. Checking for special states imposes a
time overhead and this may be greater than the time possibly saved by the
pruning.

One particular pruning mechanism which is obviously beneficial is the
avoidance of consecutive applications of inverse operations. Many state
transformations have an inverse. For example, having just crossed with the
goat, our friend could turn his boat round and bring the goat back. This is
exactly what happens in the solution produced in Figure 7.14. Even when
the program of Figure 7.14 is modified to encourage accompanied crossings
from left to right and solo trips in the other direction, the man soon finds
himself ferrying his cabbage to and fro. The search process, as far as ply 6, is
shown in Figure 7.15. The program's performance will improve if we impose
the constraint that the boat's occupants must differ on successive trips. The
man is always one occupant. There are four possibilities as to his companion: nothing, cabbage, goat, or wolf. We can represent each by an integer in

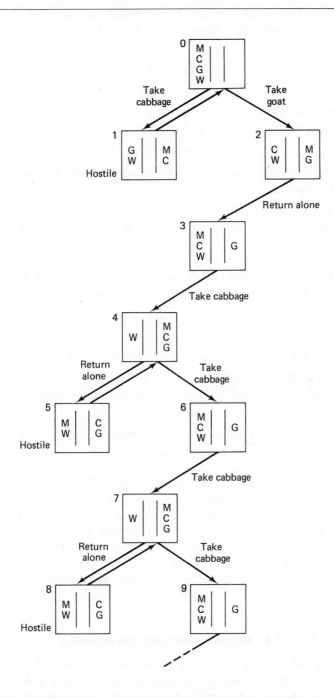

Figure 7.15   Man ferrying cabbage   Example 7.9

the range 0 to 3 {a better representation should be apparent when you have read Chapter 9; see also Example 10.9} and so we introduce four constants:

takesomething = 0;   leavecabbage = 1;
leavegoat = 2;   leavewolf = 3;

The heading of procedure *Try* is modified to

procedure *Try (here, cabbage, goat, wolf : boolean;*
            constraint, depthleft : integer;   **var** *outcome : boolean);*

and within the body of *Cross* we test the constraint prior to each attempted crossing. For example,

if *cabbage = here* **then**
    *Try (**not** here, **not** cabbage, goat, wolf, depthleft − 1, solved)*

becomes

if *(cabbage = here)* **and** *(constraint < > leavecabbage)* **then**
    *Try (**not** here, **not** cabbage, goat, wolf, leavecabbage, depthleft − 1,*
        solved)

and trying an unaccompanied crossing becomes

if *constraint < > takesomething* **then**
    *Try (**not** here, cabbage, goat, wolf, takesomething, depthleft-1, solved)*

The top level call of *Try* becomes
    Try (onlbank, onlbank, onlbank, onlbank, takesomething, maxdepth,
        outcome)

If the two directions of travel are distinguished, a search bounded at any depth greater than six finds a solution when only ten nodes have been examined.

Coverage of this example may seem excessive. The problem of the man with his goat, wolf, and cabbage can be solved in a few seconds without the aid of a computer. The example was chosen because it illustrates some general, but powerful, techniques. The problem itself is not important. Several exercises at the end of this and subsequent chapters involve backtracking. Many more example may occur to you. Try them! The programming techniques involved may be quite sophisticated. Programming a computer to play games and solve puzzles is not only fun but is educational too.

7.8 Formal procedures and functions

It is possible to make one routine a parameter of another. A procedure to tabulate a function could be an example of this. We may wish to tabulate different functions at different times, so it is convenient to supply the function as a parameter to the procedure. The procedure heading will therefore include a formal function. The declaration of a formal procedure or function takes the same form as a normal procedure or function heading. We must modify our previous definition of a formal parameter list.

FORMAL PARAMETER LIST

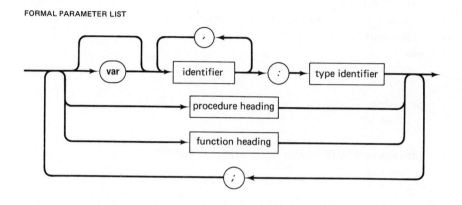

A procedure to tabulate a supplied function might have a heading of the form

procedure *Tabulate (***function** *f (x : real) : real;*
  firstpt, lastpt : real;   noofpts : integer);

Choice of the identifier *x* as the name of the formal parameter of the formal function *f* is entirely arbitrary: this variable cannot be referred to anywhere. The procedure body could contain statements such as

  writeln (f (firstpt))

and, if your compiler allows it, a suitable call of the procedure might be

  Tabulate (sqrt, 0, 2.5, 51)

Some implementations forbid the use of a standard function or procedure as an actual parameter. Of course, a user-defined function may be supplied. Figure 7.16 presents a program where this is done. The program plots a supplied function $\{y = \sin x/(x + 1)\}$ with the y axis printed horizontally and the x axis vertically. Figure 7.17 shows the output produced by the program. Construction of the program is described in the next chapter.

---

  program *PeriodicFunctionPlot (output);*
    const
      noofperiods = 3;   noofintsperperiod = 15;
      pagesize = 65;
      nameoffn = 'sin x / (x + 1)';

```
procedure PlotPeriodicFn
      (function f (r : real) : real;
         noofperiods, intsperperiod, pagewidth : integer);
   const
      pi = 3.14159;
      plotch = '*';   xaxisch = 'I';   yaxisch = '-';
      borderch = '#';   space = ' ';
   var
      period, pagecentre : integer;

   procedure DrawLine (ch : char;   length : integer);
      forward;

   procedure PlotTheValue (y : real);
      forward;

   procedure DrawHorizontalBorder;
   begin
      DrawLine (borderch, pagewidth + 2);   writeln
   end { Draw Horizontal Border };

   procedure DrawLine { (ch : char;  length : integer) };
      var
         chcount : integer;
   begin
      for chcount := 1 to length do
         write (ch)
   end { Draw Line };

   procedure DrawYaxis;
      var
         plotposn : integer;
   begin
      plotposn := round ((pagecentre - 1) * (f(0) + 1) + 1);
      write (borderch);
      DrawLine (yaxisch, plotposn - 1);   write (plotch);
      DrawLine (yaxisch, pagewidth - plotposn);   writeln (borderch)
   end { Draw Y axis };

   procedure MoveAlong (distance : integer);
   begin
      DrawLine (space, distance)
   end { Move Along };
```

```pascal
procedure MoveDown (drop : integer);
  var
    line : integer;
begin
  for line := 1 to drop do
  begin
    write (borderch);   MoveAlong (pagewidth);   writeln (borderch)
  end
end { Move Down };


procedure PlotOnePeriod (x : real;   intsperperiod : integer);
  var
    interval : real;
    point : integer;
begin
  interval := 2 * pi / intsperperiod;
  for point := 1 to intsperperiod do
  begin
    x := x + interval;   PlotTheValue ( f(x) )
  end
end { Plot One Period };


procedure PlotTheValue { (y : real) };
  var
    plotposn, halfthepage : integer;
begin
  halfthepage := pagecentre - 1;
  plotposn := round (halfthepage * (y + 1) + 1);
  write (borderch);
  if plotposn < pagecentre then
  begin
    MoveAlong (plotposn - 1);   write (plotch);
    MoveAlong (halfthepage - plotposn);   write (xaxisch);
    MoveAlong (halfthepage)
  end else
    if plotposn > pagecentre then
    begin
      MoveAlong (halfthepage);   write (xaxisch);
      MoveAlong (plotposn - pagecentre - 1);   write (plotch);
      MoveAlong (pagewidth - plotposn)
    end else
    begin
      MoveAlong (halfthepage);   write (plotch);
```

```
              MoveAlong (halfthepage)
          end;
        writeln (borderch)
      end { Plot The Value };

  begin { Plot Periodic Fn }
    if odd (pagewidth) then
      pagewidth := pagewidth − 2
    else
      pagewidth := pagewidth −3;
    pagecentre := pagewidth div 2 + 1;

    DrawHorizontalBorder;   MoveDown (2);
    DrawYaxis;
    for period := 1 to noofperiods do
      PlotOnePeriod ((period-1) * 2*pi, intsperperiod);
    MoveDown (2);   DrawHorizontalBorder
  end { Plot Periodic Fn };

  function sinxoverxplus1 (x : real) : real;
  begin
    sinxoverxplus1 := sin (x) / (x + 1)
  end { sin x over x plus 1 };

begin { program body }
  writeln (noofperiods, ' periods of ', nameoffn, ' against x');
  writeln;   writeln;
  PlotPeriodicFn (sinxoverxplus1, noofperiods, noofintsperperiod,
                  pagesize)
end.
```

Figure 7.16

Notice that the main procedure, *PlotPeriodicFn*, is "self-contained"; its only non-local references are to standard predefined procedures. It can be lifted out of this program and transferred to any other program. A self-contained routine can be incorporated within a program without knowledge of its internal workings. All one needs to know is the order and types of the parameters and their interpretation. This is the basis of "subroutine libraries". Routines have been written for many common computational tasks and are stored in what are called libraries. Your computer probably has access to several such libraries. If you become a serious programmer you will need to know more about these.

Note. If your compiler does not conform to the BSI/ISO standard for Pascal it will probably not accept formal routines in the way described. Instead, it will probably insist that parameters are not specified for formal routines and that actual routines have only value parameters.

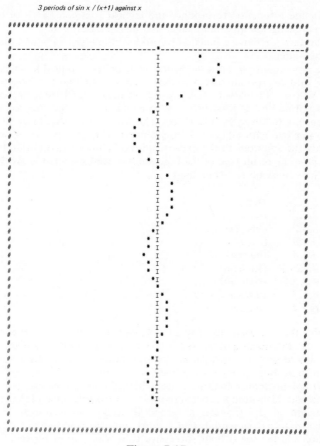

Figure 7.17

7.9 Exercises

*1. (a) Define a boolean function which determines whether two real values agree within some specified tolerance.

(b) Define three boolean functions to check whether a triangle, specified by three lengths, is equilateral (all three sides of equal length), isosceles (two sides equal), or scalene (no two sides equal). Two values are to be regarded as equal if they differ by less than some accepted tolerance.

(c) Define three boolean functions to check whether a triangle is acute (all angles $<90°$), right-angled (one angle $=90°$), or obtuse (one angle $>90°$).

(d) Define a boolean function to check that three supplied lengths do constitute a triangle.

(e) Write a program incorporating these functions to classify a sequence of supposed triangles.

*2. Define a function to compute the cube root of a supplied real value. The cube root of a value λ can be computed by an algorithm similar to that described in Exercise 6.5.5 but with x repeatedly replaced by

$$\frac{2x}{3} + \frac{\lambda}{3x^2}$$

†*3. (a) Define a function to produce the highest common factor of two positive integers using the algorithm suggested in Exercise 6.5.8.

(b) Produce a recursive function to produce the highest common factor of two positive integers.

4. Write a procedure to print the Morse code of any supplied letter {see Exercise 4.5.9} and incorporate this procedure within a program to translate a sentence into Morse code. Assume each word contains only letters, successive words are separated by at least one space or end of line, and the last word of the sentence is followed by a full stop. The Morse code should be produced one word per line with adjacent letters separated by at least one space.

5. Modify the solutions to the exercises listed below to incorporate functions. In each case the result type of the function has been specified in brackets. All the functions must be self-contained:

2.7.1	*(real)*
2.7.2	*(real)*
3.4.2	*(integer)*
3.4.3	*(char)*
3.4.4	*(integer)*
4.5.5(a)	*(boolean)*
4.5.5(b)	*(boolean)*
4.5.7	*(integer)*
6.5.4	*(integer)*

6. Modify the solution to Exercise 6.5.17 to utilize a procedure which computes the mean and standard deviation of a supplied sample. The procedure should accept n as a parameter and, rather than output μ and σ, should return these two values via parameters.

*7. (a) Write a procedure to print a given character a specified number of times.

(b) Include this within a procedure to draw a triangle. One parameter specifies the height of the triangle, a second indicates the character of which the triangle is to be composed, and a third stipulates the number of spaces that will precede the apex. Four successive calls with parameter sets

$(3, '*', 10)$ $(5, '+', 10)$ $(7, '-', 10)$ $(2, '@', 10)$

should produce the output shown below:

8. A complex number may be represented by two values: the real part and the imaginary part. Write three procedures to process a complex number:

> one to read it,
> one to print it, and
> one to form its conjugate,

and three procedures to process a pair of complex numbers:

> one to form the sum,
> one to form the difference, and
> one to form the product.

Incorporate these within a program to read four complex numbers a, b, c, d and print the values of $ab + cd$ and $ab - cd$ together with their conjugates.

9. Write a (recursive) procedure to read a word and print it backwards. Assume that the supplied word is followed by either a space or end of line.

†*10. "Towers of Hanoi" is a game involving n holed discs, each of a different size, and a board with three pegs. Initially the discs are stacked on the leftmost peg to form a pyramid:

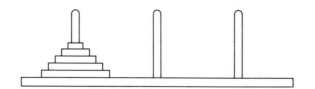

The object of the game is to move the pyramid to the rightmost peg subject to the contraints that discs must be moved one at a time from one peg to another and at no time must any disc be above a smaller one. Thus, if $n = 3$, the discs must be moved in the following sequence:

> left   → right
> left   → centre
> right → centre
> left   → right
> centre → left
> centre → right
> left   → right

Write a (recursive) program to print the moves requires for any given n.

11. Write a (backtracking) program to solve the "missionaries and cannibals" problem. m missionaries and c cannibals $(m \geq c)$ must cross a river using a boat which can hold at most p $(p > 1)$ passengers. The missionaries are wary of the cannibals' intentions and insist that the boat must always carry at least one missionary and that missionaries must never be outnumbered by cannibals whenever the boat reaches a bank. The program must identify the boat's occupants for each successive crossing. For example, for $m = c = p = 2$ a solution is

> 1 missionary and 1 cannibal cross
> 1 missionary returns
> 2 missionaries cross
> 1 missionary returns
> 1 missionary and 1 cannibal cross

12. Write a (backtracking) program to solve the "three beakers" problem. Three beakers have capacities $c1$, $c2$, and $c3$ and initially contain volumes $v1$, $v2$, and $v3$ of water. Water must be poured from beaker to beaker until a desired quantity q is isolated in one beaker. No water must be spilled and each pouring operation must either completely fill or completely empty a beaker.

8

Program Construction

Little has been said so far about the process of constructing a program. Most programs have been presented as a *fait accompli*. When we read a program we do not start at the beginning and work our way steadily to the end. We start with the program body and then examine the procedures in some order, referring to the declarations when appropriate. We write a program the same way. We start with the program body and then work our way through the procedures inserting declarations as appropriate. This is called "top-down design" and the particular approach we shall take is known as "stepwise refinement". We start with the top level of the "program logic" and then develop the lower levels in simple steps. Each step constitutes a refinement of the program.

Unless a program is short (and this is a relative term; a program considered short by the expert may seem very long to the novice), we do not write the whole program before running it. Instead we execute the program at various stages of its development in the hope that any mistakes we make might be spotted as we proceed. Thus our top-down design process incorporates "top-down testing".

8.1 Case Study 1

We consider construction of the program of Figure 7.16. You are advised to construct the program yourself by following the steps outlined below.

Our aim is to write a program which draws three periods of the function *sin x / (x + 1)*, plotting each period over fifteen intervals. We wish to do this in such a way that the plotting process is self-contained.

We first give thought to the program body. We want to output some title and then call a procedure to do the plotting for us:

> **begin**
>   *output title;*
>   *plot periodic function*
> **end**

What information must we supply to *plot periodic function* if it is to be self-contained? It will obviously need to know the function it is supposed to plot and it will also need to know how many periods are to be plotted and over how many intervals. It seems natural to supply the number of intervals per period rather than the total number of intervals. This suggests a procedure call of the form

PlotPeriodicFn (sinxoverxplus1, noofperiods, noofintsperperiod)

We can now decide how we are going to specify the number of periods and number of intervals. We could read them as run-time data or we could supply them as compile-time constants. Let us supply them as constants. Our program now has the following form:

```
program PeriodicFunctionPlot (output);
   const
      noofperiods = 3;   noofintsperperiod = 15;
      nameoffn = '(sin x) / (x + 1)' ;
   function sinxoverxplus1 (x : real) : real;
   begin
   end { sin x over x plus 1 };
   procedure PlotPeriodicFn
      (function f (r : real) : real;   noofperiods, intsperperiod : integer);
   begin
   end { Plot Periodic Fn };
begin { program body }
   writeln (noofperiods,' periods of ', nameoffn, ' against x');
   writeln;   writeln;
   PlotPeriodicFn (sinxoverxplus1, noofperiods, noofintsperperiod)
end.
```

We now turn our attention to the body of *PlotPeriodicFn*. We ignore the axes and concentrate on plotting the function values at the desired points. The process of plotting one period will be the same for each period except that the period will start at a different place each time. The first period starts at $x = 0$, the second at $x = 2\pi$, the third at 4π, and so on. This suggests the structure

```
for period := 1 to noofperiods do
   PlotOnePeriod ((period - 1) * 2 * pi)
```

We now insert declarations of *period* (integer variable) and *pi* (real constant).

The number of intervals over which each period is to be plotted will obviously be of importance to *PlotOnePeriod* so it is reasonable to supply this value as a parameter. It could be argued that the function is also relevant and so should be passed as a parameter but it is to be expected that the function will be relevant to almost everything so we shall confine our attention to scalar parameters. We now have

```
for period := 1 to noofperiods do
   PlotOnePeriod ( (period - 1) * pi,   intsperperiod )
```

We now examine this level of program logic for two purposes:

1. We convince ourselves that this level is correct (i.e. it will do what we intend it to do) if all lower levels are correct. In this case there is only one lower level: *PlotOnePeriod.*
2. We ascertain a specification for the lower level (i.e. what it must do) so that this present level of the program logic will be correct.

These two activities are interdependent and so proceed in parallel. When we examine the for-statement we find something amiss. If *PlotOnePeriod* plots both end points of the period all end points except the first and last points of the whole range will be plotted twice (because the last point of one period is the first point of the next). On the other hand, if it only plots one end point then either the first or the last point of the range will not be plotted. The simplest way to solve this is to

either   plot f at $x = 0$ before we enter the for-loop

    and   arrange for *PlotOnePeriod* to plot all but the first point of a period

or   arrange for *PlotOnePeriod* to plot all but the last point of a period

    and   plot f at $noofperiods * 2\pi$ upon exit from the for-loop

If we were using an output device which permitted "overprinting" (printing one character on top of another), plotting one point twice would be illogical but not critical. Devices intended for graphical output permit printing at any point of a designated area, but we are assuming the use of a line printer or character terminal. Our output device "moves on" when one character has been printed so we must adopt one of the two proposed solutions. There are three reasons for choosing the first alternative:

1. Treating $x = 0$ as a special case seems natural.
2. Plotting $x = 0$ first can be interpreted as loop initialization—a natural activity.
3. In this particular example we shall eventually need to consider drawing a y axis and this will include the plotted value $f(0)$ and so $x = 0$ must then be treated as a special case anyway.

The body of *PlotPeriodicFn* has now been amended to

```
PlotTheValue (f (0));
for period := 1 to noofperiods do
    PlotOnePeriod ( (period − 1) * 2 * pi, intsperperiod )
```

and we can be reasonably confident that the function will be plotted over the full range so long as

1. *PlotTheValue* plots the specified value and
2. *PlotOnePeriod* plots all but the first point of the specified period.

We now have a specification of the lower levels {*PlotTheValue* and *PlotOnePeriod*} so far as their "interface" with this level is concerned.

188

Plotting a period will involve plotting values so it is wise to consider *PlotOnePeriod* first:

```
procedure PlotOnePeriod (x : real;  intsperperiod : integer);
   var
      interval : real;
      point : integer;
begin
   interval : =  2 * pi / instperperiod;
   for point : =  1  to  intsperperiod  do
   begin
      x := x + interval;   PlotTheValue (f(x))
   end
end { Plot One Period }
```

Again we examine this level of logic before proceeding to lower levels. This procedure should plot all but the first point of the period x to $x + 2\pi$ and our specification for *PlotTheValue* remains unaltered.

When we have defined *PlotTheValue* (and any routines this may need) and supplied the body of *sinxoverxplus1* we will have a complete program but, before doing this, we can test what we have already written. If we have made a mistake it will be easier to find now than when the program is longer. So, for the moment, we simplify our specification of *PlotTheValue*. We will be able to check the output if we simply print the values. *PlotTheValue* becomes

```
procedure PlotTheValue (y : real);
begin
   writeln (y)
end {Plot The Value }
```

Before we plot values of the function we ultimately want it is a good idea to check that any supplied function will be plotted at the right points. We can do this by giving *sinxoverxplus1* the body

$$sinxoverxplus1 := x$$

When testing a program, supplied data should be simplified. For this example we should test the program with some small number of periods and intervals, even if we intend to apply the final program to many periods each with many intervals. We could reduce the number of intervals to, say, five. If we now run the program {run number 1} we should get a tabulation of sixteen equally spaced values from 0 to 6π. If not, something is wrong and we must correct the program.

When our points are correctly tabulated we can substitute the actual function we require and run the program again {run number 2}. Figure 8.1 shows the program we now have. We check a few values in the output in case we have made a mistake in our definition of the function.

```pascal
program PeriodicFunctionPlotRun2 (output);
  const
    noofperiods = 3;   noofintsperperiod = 5;
    nameoffn = 'sin x / (x + 1)';


  procedure PlotPeriodicFn
      (function f (r : real) : real;
       noofperiods, intsperperiod : integer);
    const
      pi = 3.14159;
    var
      period : integer;


    procedure PlotTheValue (y : real);
      forward;

    procedure PlotOnePeriod (x : real;   intsperperiod : integer);
      var
        interval : real;
        point : integer;
    begin
      interval := 2 * pi / intsperperiod;
      for point := 1 to intsperperiod do
      begin
        x := x + interval;   PlotTheValue ( f(x) )
      end
    end { Plot One Period };


    procedure PlotTheValue { (y : real) };
    begin
      writeln (y)
    end { Plot The Value };

  begin { Plot Periodic Fn }
    PlotTheValue ( f(0) );
    for period := 1 to noofperiods do
      PlotOnePeriod ((period-1) * 2 * pi, intsperperiod)
  end { Plot Periodic Fn };

  function sinxoverxplus1 (x : real) : real;
  begin
    sinxoverxplus1 := sin (x) / (x + 1)
  end { sin x over x plus 1 };
```

```
begin { program body }
    writeln (noofperiods, ' periods of ', nameoffn, ' against x');
    writeln;   writeln;
    PlotPeriodicFn (sinxoverxplus1, noofperiods, noofintsperperiod)
end.
```

Figure 8.1 Tabulation of function.

Programs have a habit of going wrong in "special cases" so, in addition to a general case such as that of Figure 8.1, we should test as many special cases as possible. In this example having only one period or one interval per period could be regarded as special cases, so we should check that the program works with $noofperiods = 1$ and $noofintsperperiod = 1$ {run number 3}.

When we are happy with the program in its present form we continue our process of stepwise refinement and run the program after appropriate refinements. Our attention must focus on *PlotTheValue*. The output device operates in terms of lines and so plotting a value involves printing a character at the correct position on a line and then moving on to the next line. Producing axes will only complicate matters so we continue to ignore them.

If we assume that the supplied function will produce a result in the range -1 to 1 we can use the left-hand edge of the page to represent $y = -1$ and the right-hand edge for $y = 1$ with the origin $(y = 0)$ in the middle of the page. This implies that *PlotPeriodicFn* must be told the page width that is to be utilized. Our task will be simplified if we ensure that the number of character positions available on each line is odd so that there is a central character position.

To plot a value y in the range $[-1, 1]$ we must transform it into an integer in the range $[1, pagewidth]$. This determines the position on the line at which a character must be printed. To transform the range $[-1, 1]$ into the range $[1, pagewidth]$ we

> add 1 to give $[0, 2]$,
> multiply by *pagewidth* **div** 2 (remember *pagewidth* is odd) to give $[0, pagewidth - 1]$ and then
> add 1 to give $[1, pagewidth]$.

We round the resulting value to transform it to an integer. So the plot position on the line is

*round (pagewidth **div** 2 * (y + 1) + 1)*

To print a character at character position p on a line we print $p - 1$ spaces and then print the character.

Figure 8.2 shows the program with these refinements and, again, we run the program {run number 4}. Its output is shown in Figure 8.3.

```
program PeriodicFunctionPlotRun4 (output);
  const
    noofperiods = 3;  noofintsperperiod = 5;
    pagesize = 25;
    nameoffn = 'sin x / (x + 1)';

  procedure PlotPeriodicFn
      (function f (r : real) : real;
       noofperiods, intsperperiod, pagewidth : integer);
    const
      pi = 3.14159;
      plotch = '*';  space = ' ';
    var
      period, pagecentre : integer;

    procedure PlotTheValue (y : real);
      forward;

    procedure PlotOnePeriod (x : real;  intsperperiod : integer);
      var
        interval : real;
        point : integer;
    begin
      interval := 2 * pi / intsperperiod;
      for point := 1 to intsperperiod do
      begin
        x := x + interval;  PlotTheValue (f(x))
      end
    end { Plot One Period };

    procedure PlotTheValue { (y : real) };
      var
        plotposn : integer;
    begin
      plotposn := round ((pagecentre - 1) * (y + 1) + 1);
      if plotposn > 1 then
        write (space : plotposn - 1);
      writeln (plotch)
    end { Plot The Value };
  begin { Plot Periodic Fn }
    { ensure pagewidth is odd }
    if not odd (pagewidth) then
      pagewidth := pagewidth - 1;

    pagecentre := pagewidth div 2 + 1;
    PlotTheValue (f(0));
```

```
    for period := 1 to noofperiods do
        PlotOnePeriod ((period-1) * 2*pi, intsperperiod)
    end { Plot Periodic Fn };


    function sinxoverxplus1 (x : real) : real;
    begin
      sinxoverxplus1 := sin (x) / (x + 1)
    end { sin x over x plus 1 };

  begin { program body }
    writeln (noofperiods, ' periods of ', nameoffn, ' against x');
    writeln; writeln;
    PlotPeriodicFn    (sinxoverxplus1,  noofperiods,  noofinstsperperiod,
                       pagesize)
  end.
```

Figure 8.2

Now we can consider production of the axes. The y axis is to be drawn across the page and will contain the plotted value $f(0)$. We cannot draw the x axis before we plot the function values because the output device is incapable of moving back up the page. We must print part of the x axis each time we plot a value (unless the plotted value falls on the axis). This turns out to be the most complicated part of the program!

3 periods of sin x / (x + 1) against x
```
     *
         *
       *
     *
   *
     *
      *
      *
    *
    *
     *
      *
     *
    *
   *
   *
```

Figure 8.3 Output from Figure 8.2

Let us consider the y axis first. Drawing the y axis replaces the call *PlotTheValue (f(0))* and the algorithm is

> print consecutive hyphens up to the plot position;
> print the plotting character;
> print consecutive hyphens up to the edge of the page.

The program of Figure 8.4 implements this and defines *noofintsperperiod* to be 15. When run {run number 5}, it produces the output shown in Figure 7.17, but for the x axis and the border.

```
program PeriodicFunctionPlotRun5 (output);
  const
    noofperiods = 3;   noofintsperperiod = 15;
    pagesize = 65;
    nameoffn = 'sin x / (x + 1)';

  procedure PlotPeriodicFn
      (function f(r : real) : real;
      noofperiods, intsperperiod, pagewidth : integer);
    const
      pi = 3.14159;
      plotch = '*';   yaxisch = '-';
      space = ' ';
    var
      period, pagecentre : integer;

    procedure PlotTheValue (y : real);
      forward;

    procedure DrawLine (ch : char;   length : integer);
      var
        chcount : integer;
    begin
      for chcount := 1 to length do
        write (ch)
    end { Draw Line };

    procedure DrawYaxis;
      var
        plotposn : integer;
    begin
      plotposn := round ((pagecentre - 1) * (f(0) + 1) + 1);
      DrawLine (yaxisch, plotposn - 1);   write (plotch);
      DrawLine (yaxisch, pagewidth - plotposn);   writeln
    end { Draw Y axis };
```

```
procedure PlotOnePeriod (x : real; intsperperiod : integer);
  var
    interval : real;
    point : integer;
begin
  interval := 2 * pi / intsperperiod;
  for point := 1 to intsperperiod do
  begin
    x := x + interval;   PlotTheValue (f(x))
  end
end { Plot One Period };


procedure PlotTheValue { (y : real) };
  var
    plotposn : integer;
begin
  plotposn := round ((pagecentre − 1) * (y + 1) + 1);
  DrawLine (space, plotposn − 1);   writeln (plotch)
end { Plot The Value };

begin { Plot Periodic Fn }
  if not odd (pagewidth) then
    pagewidth := pagewidth − 1;
  pagecentre := pagewidth div 2 + 1;
  DrawYaxis;
  for period := 1 to noofperiods do
    PlotOnePeriod ((period − 1) * 2*pi, intsperperiod)
end { Plot Periodic Fn } ;


function sinxoverxplus1 (x : real) : real;
begin
  sinxoverxplus1 := sin (x) / (x + 1)
end { sin x over x plus 1 };


begin { program body }
  writeln (noofperiods, ' periods of ', nameoffn, ' against x');
  writeln;   writeln;
  PlotPeriodicFn (sinxoverxplus1, noofperiods, noofintsperperiod,
                  pagesize)
end.
```

Figure 8.4

```
procedure PlotTheValue (y : real);
  var
    plotposn, halfthepage : integer;
begin
  halfthepage := pagecentre −1;
  plotposn := round (halfthepage * (y + 1) + 1);
  if plotposn < pagecentre then
  begin
    MoveAlong (plotposn − 1);   write (plotch);
    MoveAlong (halfthepage − plotposn);   writeln (xaxisch)
  end else
    if plotposn > pagecentre then
    begin
      MoveAlong (halfthepage);   write (xaxisch);
      MoveAlong (plotposn − pagecentre − 1);   writeln (plotch)
    end else
      begin
        MoveAlong (halfthepage);   writeln (plotch)
      end
end { Plot The Value }
```

Figure 8.5   Production of x axis

The x axis will be produced by *PlotTheValue* and the algorithm is as follows:

```
if plot position < page centre then
begin
   print plotting character at plot position;
   print x-axis character at page centre
end else
   if plot position > page centre then
   begin
      print x-axis character at page centre;
      print plotting character at plot position
   end else
      print plotting character at page centre;
writeln
```

The modified procedure is shown in Figure 8.5. The following procedure

```
procedure MoveAlong (distance : integer);
  var
    d : integer;
```

```
begin
    for d := 1 to distance do    { or, simply,                    }
        write (space)            { DrawLine (space, distance) }
    end { Move Along }
```

is incorporated, the appropriate constants defined and the program run {run number 6}. The output is as in Figure 7.17 but without the border. All that remains now is to add any finishing touches. The program of Figure 7.16 incorporates the refinements needed to produce the border {run number 7}.

8.2 Dummy routines

During the construction of a program we often introduce a routine to indicate its role in the overall structure but wish to run the program before considering the routine body. A program to read an integer and perform different processing according as the integer is positive, negative, or zero might have the following structure:

```
read (n);
if n > 0 then ProcessPositive (n) else
    if n < 0 then ProcessNegative (n) else
        ProcessZero
```

We may wish to implement *ProcessZero* and test the program before we define *ProcessPositive* and *ProcessNegative*. We must supply declarations of these two other procedures or the program will not compile. We therefore supply them as "dummy procedures". If we ensure that n acquires the value 0 these two dummy procedures will not be called so their bodies are of no significance. Consequently we can give them "empty bodies". A compound statement may contain zero statements (i.e. one empty statement) so we can define our two dummy procedures as follows:

```
procedure ProcessPositive (n : integer);
begin
end { Process Positive };

procedure ProcessNegative (n : integer);
begin
end { Process Negative };
```

When the program compiles it can be run.

Your compiler should object if you supply an empty body for a function because the body must contain an assignment to the function identifier. We can produce a dummy function by assigning any value of the appropriate type. For example,

```
function fun ( ... ) : integer;
begin
    fun := 0
end { fun }
```

If an empty procedure is called it has no apparent effect; when control reaches the empty body it immediately returns to the point of call. However, it would be nice to know that the routine had been called. In the above example we may wish to define all the procedures as dummy routines and run the program three times, supplying a different value of *n* each time, to test the decision logic of the program body. On the other hand, if we expected to test *ProcessZero* but *ProcessZero* was not called it would be beneficial to know which, if either, of the other two routines had been activated. It is conventional, therefore, for a dummy routine to write its name:

```
procedure ProcessPositive (n: integer);
begin
    writeln ('Process Positive')
end { Process Positive };
```

```
procedure ProcessNegative (n : integer);
begin
    writeln ('Process Negative')
end { Process Negative };
```

8.3 Top-down design and top-down testing

The case study of Section 8.1 illustrates the ideal situation. We define the top level of program logic and work our way steadily through the lower levels, never taking a false step. This is our hope for every program we write. Sometimes we achieve it. Sometimes we do not. We may need to modify a design decision in the light of subsequent refinements. In the case study, we could have chosen to treat as a special case the last point of each period rather than the first. It would not be apparent that this is illogical until we consider production of the *x* axis some time later. We would then have to backtrack and change an earlier refinement. This often involves modifying other refinements which were dependent upon the one we are now changing. The term "backtrack" is used because the process we go through is essentially that implemented by the programs of Section 7.7.3. There are two ways to reduce the need for backtracking during the design stages of a program:

1. Defer design decisions as long as possible.
2. Think ahead.

We define one level of program logic by giving names to the activities involved. To refine this we replace the named activities by groups of statements to perform the tasks or make them procedure or function calls and decide what parameters, if any, are needed. Those named activities which do not contribute to the next run of the program can be incorporated as dummy routines. Those which are significant must be further refined until we can make our next test run.

If an error comes to light it is probably caused by the changes we have made since the previous run. This knowledge considerably speeds up the process of locating and correcting errors. It is easier (and quicker in the long run) to run ten programs, each an extension of the previous one but each containing a (different) error, than to try sorting out all ten errors from one program (especially when more errors have crept in because of our ignorance of the errors we made early in the design process). This is particularly true of large programs containing thousands of lines.

Hopefully, if you implemented the program described in the case study, you ran seven correct programs. If you had to correct errors (and it is to be expected that a beginner will make mistakes) you should now appreciate the merits of developing and testing the program in the stages described.

It is an oft-quoted fact that running a program can only detect the presence of errors and not prove their absence. This is because a program can usually be supplied with an infinite number of different data sets, but running the program can show only that the program performs satisfactorily for those sets actually tried. In the case study we showed little more than the fact that the program worked for one particular function and certain numbers of periods and intervals. Nevertheless, our confidence in the program is increased by the additional runs. There is every reason to expect the program to work for more periods and more intervals and it should work for other well-behaved functions whose results lie in the range $[-1, 1]$ (but notice $sin\,x\,/\,x$ would upset it).

It is possible to verify the correctness of a program by constructing a rigorous mathematical proof, but that is beyond the scope of this book. In general the proof is longer than the program so one has a greater chance of making a mistake whilst formulating the proof than when writing the program! Automatic program verification is a topic of current research in computer science. Programming languages are being developed which enable the programmer to make "assertions" about his program and the compiler attempts to prove (or disprove) these assertions. If an assertion is disproved (proved to be false) the program fails to compile. You will be happy to learn that these languages are based on Pascal.

Top-down design aims at getting the "control structure" of the program right. Locating and correcting simple errors such as forgetting to initialize a variable prior to entry to a loop or writing $n := n + 1$ instead of $n := n - 1$ is relatively straightforward. Errors in the control structure are far more troublesome. The control structure would be wrong if, for example, the test after an **if** or **while** is incorrect or, worse, an if-statement appears where a while-statement should be. Top-down testing aims at checking the control structure at regular intervals.

Always design a program with its full specification in mind, but test the overall structure on a simplified problem as soon as possible. Thereafter apply no more refinements between successive runs than you feel you can implement without error. As you improve, the number of error-free refinements you can introduce will increase. Good luck!

8.4   Case Study 2

We are going to write a program to "say" the name of any integer whose absolute magnitude is less than a million. For example, when provided with the value −617489, the program should produce the output

MINUS SIX HUNDRED AND SEVENTEEN THOUSAND FOUR HUNDRED AND EIGHTY NINE.

As with the previous case study you are advised to implement the program yourself as our discussion proceeds. If *maxint* is less than a million on your computer you will have to consider a slightly modified problem: perhaps, to output the name of an integer with absolute magnitude less than *maxint.*

There are four aspects to this problem. We must produce names corresponding to digits or digit pairs (*SIX, SEVENTEEN, FOUR, EIGHTY, NINE*), names of powers of ten indicating the weight of each constitutent digit group (*HUNDRED, THOUSAND*), a possible sign (*MINUS*), and, when appropriate, the word *AND.* We consider each aspect individually and, in accordance with the philosophy outlined in the preceding section, develop our program in stages.

8.4.1   Digit groups

We assume, for the moment, that the number is positive and contains six non-zero digits. We concentrate on the names associated with the digits. To produce these we must determine the appropriate grouping of the digits. In the example above, but ignoring the sign, 617489 splits, first, into two groups: 617 (the number of thousands) and 489 (the number that is left if all the thousands are ignored). So, to name a number less than a million we must be able to name two numbers, each less than a thousand. Expressed in programming terms this means that the process

NameLtMillion (617489)

must be broken down into

NameLtThousand (617);   NameLtThousand (489)

and so, in general,

NameLtMillion (n)

becomes

*NameLtThousand (n **div** 1000);   NameLtThousand (n **mod** 1000)*

200

To form the appropriate grouping for a three-digit integer we isolate the first digit (the number of hundreds) and treat the last two as a pair:

NameLtThousand (617)

must be broken down into

NameUnit (6);   NameLtHundred (17)

and, in general,

NameLtThousand (n)

becomes

*NameUnit (n **div** 100);   NameLtHundred (n **mod** 100)*

Before we worry about producing names for the digits, let us make sure that our strategy is correct so far. Figure 8.6 shows a program which breaks down a six-digit integer into its digit groups. Try it for yourself {run number 1}.

```
0    program NameIntegerRun1 (input, output);
1      var
2        n : integer;
3
4      procedure NameUnit (n : integer);
5        { 0 <= n <= 9 }
6      begin
7        write (n : 5)
8      end { Name Unit };
9
10     procedure NameLtHundred (n : integer);
11       { 0 <= n <= 99 }
12     begin
13       write (n : 5)
14     end { Name    < 100 };
15
16     procedure NameLtThousand (n : integer);
17       { 0 <= n <=  999 }
18     begin
19       NameUnit (n div 100);   NameLtHundred (n mod 100)
20     end { Name    < 1000 };
21
22     procedure NameLtMillion (n : integer);
23       { 0 <= n <= 999999 }
24     begin
25       NameLtThousand (n div 1000);   NameLtThousand (n mod 1000)
```

```
26    end { Name   < 1 000 000 };
27
28  begin { program body }
29    repeat
30      readln (n);   write (n, ':');
31      if (n >= 0) and (n < 1000000) then
32        NameLtMillion (n)
33      else
34        write (' out of range');
35      writeln
36    until eof
37  end.
```

INPUT :
617489
30600
100001
203040
12

OUTPUT :

617489 :	6	17	4	89
30600 :	0	30	6	0
100001 :	1	0	0	1
203040 :	2 ,	3	0	40
12 :	0	0	0	12

Figure 8.6

Apart from a few superfluous zeros when the number contains zeros or has fewer than six digits, we see that the grouping is correct. The only time we use the name *ZERO* is when the supplied number is itself 0. We can treat this as a special case by replacing (line 32)

   NameLtMillion (n)

by

```
if n = 0 then
  write ('ZERO')
else
  NameLtMillion (n)
```

and can suppress the superfluous zeros by changing the bodies of *NameUnit* and *NameLtHundred* {lines 7 and 13} to

```
if n > 0 then write (n : 5)
```

Incorporate these refinements within your program and test them {run number 2}.

As an aside, notice that the identifier *n* has several different meanings within the program of Figure 8.6. At any point, of course, only one interpretation applies. Within the program body {lines 28 to 37} any reference to *n* implies the variable declared in the outer block {line 2}, but within a procedure body a reference to *n* implies the value that was supplied as the actual parameter when that particular procedure was called.

8.4.2 Digit group names

If we continue to ignore the weighting of the digit groups we only name numbers less than 100. We use three sets of names:

    1 to   9 : the name of the digit
    10 to 19 : the name of the digit pair
    20 to 99 : the name of the multiple of 10 followed by
                the name of the unit (unless the unit is 0)

In programming terms we can define

   NameLtHundred (n)

as

```
if n < 10 then
  NameUnit (n)
else
  if n < 20 then
    NameTeen (n) else
  begin
    NameTy (n div 10);   NameUnit (n mod 10)
  end
```

The definition of *NameUnit, NameTeen,* and *NameTy* is straightforward. Each uses a case-statement to output the appropriate name. Try it {run number 3}.

8.4.3 The weights

The points at which a weight must be introduced are apparent from the initial discussion of this case study. For a six-digit number the word *THOUSAND* must appear between the two three-digit groups and, for a three-digit number, the word *HUNDRED* must appear between the first digit and the remaining digit pair. This is easily achieved by including appropriate write-statements within the bodies of *NameLtMillion* and *NameLtThousand.* All is now well, provided that the number really does contain six digits and that the first and fourth are non-zero. In other circumstances we get inappropriate appearances of the weights. If you don't believe me, try it! {run number 4}.

We must modify the program so that the word *THOUSAND* does not appear if the number being processed is less than a thousand and the word *HUNDRED* does not appear if the number is less than a hundred. We could modify the body of *NameLtMillion* to

```
if n >= 1000 then
begin
   NameLtThousand (n div 1000);   write ('THOUSAND')
end;
NameLtThousand (n mod 1000)
```

and make a similar change to *NameLtThousand*. This will work but it is a little illogical. What is the point of evaluating *n* **mod** *1000* when we have just made a test which can tell us that *n* is less than 1000? Better is

```
1   if n < 1000 then
2      NameLtThousand (n) else
3   begin
4      NameLtThousand (n div 1000);
5      write ('THOUSAND ');
6      NameLtThousand (n mod 1000)
7   end
```

with a similar approach for *NameLtThousand*:

```
1   if n < 100 then
2      NameLtHundred (n) else
3   begin
4      NameUnit (n div 100);
5      write ('HUNDRED ');
6      NameLtHundred (n mod 100)
7   end
```

Refine your program accordingly and confirm that no superfluous output appears {run number 5}.

8.4.4 The sign

This is easily accommodated. We process a negative *n* with

```
begin
   write ('MINUS ');   NameLtMillion (−n)
end
```

and treat non-negative values as previously. Do this {run number 6}.

8.4.5 The word *AND*

This is tricky! Before we can expect our program to print *AND* in the right places we must be clear in our own minds where *AND* should appear. If you try a few examples it should become apparent that *AND* appears only before a number less than 100 and does so if some hundreds or thousands have preceded it. *AND* never appears before a unit if the unit is immediately preceded by a non-zero digit or if (in the context of our program) the unit is a number of hundreds.

Right! How do we get this into our program? As usual, we start at the top and work down. The top level of the naming process is the body of *NameLtMillion*. When each of the two procedure calls on lines 2 and 4 produces the name of its parameter we know that no *AND* will be needed if the parameter is less than 100. When the procedure call on line 6 produces the name of its parameter, on the other hand, the word *AND is* needed if its parameter is less than 100. To convey this information to the called procedure we need to supply a second parameter. The body of *NameLtMillion* must take the form

```
if n < 1000 then
    NameLtThousand (n, no) else
begin
    NameLtThousand (n div 1000, no);
    write ('THOUSAND');
    NameLtThousand (n mod 1000, yes)
end
```

There are only two possible situations, *yes* and *no*, so a boolean value is appropriate. We can write the body of *NameLtMillion* exactly as above if we define

```
const
    yes = true;   no = false;
```

and the procedure *NameLtThousand* takes two value parameters

procedure *NameLtThousand (n : integer;   andneeded : boolean);*

We must modify the body of *NameLtThousand* accordingly. When the value of *andneeded* is *no* its inclusion within the procedure body could be similar to that in *NameLtMillion:*

```
1    if n < 100 then
2        NameLtHundred (n, no) else
3    begin
4        NameUnit (n div 100, no);
5        write ('HUNDRED ');
6        NameLtHundred (n mod 100, yes)
7    end
```

but, if the value of *andneeded* is *yes*, we must change the first appearance of *no* {line 2} to *yes*. In other words, the value of the second parameter supplied to *NameLtHundred* on line 2 must be the same as the value of *andneeded*. Consequently, we supply *andneeded* as the second parameter in this call.

We now move down one level to *NameLtHundred*. We observed earlier that it is only numbers less than 100, but greater than zero, that ever need be preceded by *AND*. Consequently, the first statement of this procedure body becomes

if *(n > 0)* **and** *andneeded* **then** *write ('AND ')*

and if we were to supply a second parameter to the calls of *NameTy*, *NameTeen*, and *NameUnit* it would be *no* in each case because none need output the word *AND*. When we considered the body of *NameLtThousand* it was apparent that, if *NameUnit* took a second parameter, it would be *no*. Since the second parameter supplied to *NameTy*, *NameTeen*, and *NameUnit* would always be *no*, there is no point in having the second parameter. These three procedures need give no consideration to *AND*. The final program therefore has the form shown in Figure 8.7 {run number 7}.

```
program NameIntegerRun7 (input, output);
  const
    amillion = 1000000;
    yes = true;   no = false;
    indent = '    ';
  var
    n : integer;

  procedure NameUnit (n : integer);
      { 0 <= n <= 9 }
  begin
    case n of
      0 : ;
      1 : write ('ONE ');
      2 : write ('TWO ');
      3 : write ('THREE ');
      4 : write ('FOUR ');
      5 : write ('FIVE ');
      6 : write ('SIX ');
      7 : write ('SEVEN ');
      8 : write ('EIGHT ');
      9 : write ('NINE ')
    end { case }
  end { Name Unit };
```

```
procedure NameTeen (n : integer);
   { 10 <= n <= 19 }
begin
  case n of
    10 : write ('TEN ');
    11 : write ('ELEVEN ');
    12 : write ('TWELVE ');
    13 : write ('THIRTEEN ');
    14 : write ('FOURTEEN ');
    15 : write ('FIFTEEN ');
    16 : write ('SIXTEEN ');
    17 : write ('SEVENTEEN ');
    18 : write ('EIGHTEEN ');
    19 : write ('NINETEEN ')
  end { case }
end { Name Teen };

procedure NameTy (n : integer);
   { 2 <= n <= 9 }
begin
  case n of
    2 : write ('TWENTY ');
    3 : write ('THIRTY ');
    4 : write ('FORTY ');
    5 : write ('FIFTY ');
    6 : write ('SIXTY ');
    7 : write ('SEVENTY ');
    8 : write ('EIGHTY ');
    9 : write ('NINETY ')
  end { case }
end { Name Ty };

procedure NameLtHundred (n : integer;   andneeded : boolean);
   { 0 <= n <= 99 }
begin
  if (n > 0) and andneeded then
    write ('AND ');

  if n < 10 then
    NameUnit (n)
  else
    if n < 20 then
      NameTeen (n) else
    begin
      NameTy (n div 10);   NameUnit (n mod 10)
```

```
        end
    end { Name   < 100 };

  procedure NameLtThousand (n : integer;   andneeded : boolean);
      { 0 <= n <= 999 }
  begin
    if n < 100 then
      NameLtHundred (n, andneeded) else
    begin
      NameUnit (n div 100);   write ('HUNDRED ');
      NameLtHundred (n mod 100, yes)
    end
  end { Name   < 1000 };

  procedure NameLtMillion (n : integer);
      { 0 <= n <= 999999 }
  begin
    if n < 1000 then
      NameLtThousand (n, no) else
    begin
      NameLtThousand (n div 1000, no);   write ('THOUSAND ');
      NameLtThousand (n mod 1000, yes)
    end
  end { Name   < 1 000 000 };
begin { program body }
  repeat
    readln (n);
    writeln ('The value ', n : 1, ' is');
    write (indent);

    if abs (n) < amillion then
      if n = 0 then
        write ('ZERO')
      else
        if n > 0 then
          NameLtMillion (n) else
        begin
          write ('MINUS ');   NameLtMillion (- n)
        end
    else
      write (' out of range');
    writeln
  until eof
end.
```

Figure 8.7

As a final observation, notice that our logical approach when avoiding the appearance of superfluous weights paid off. The handling of *AND* would have been less straightforward if we had chosen the approach first suggested when our program would call

NameLtThousand (n **mod** *1000)*

even when *n* is less than 1,000 and

NameLtHundred (n **mod** *100)*

even when *n* is less than 100. The need for *AND* depends upon whether any previous hundreds or thousands have been processed. With the illogical constructs this information is not apparent when these two procedure calls occur. With our logical approach this information is evident when we need it. The moral is clear. Always avoid anything illogical. A logical approach makes a program easier to understand, easier to modify later, and, as an added bonus, improves overall efficiency.

8.5 Exercises

*1. Write a program to print a calendar with each month displayed as a block in seven columns labelled *Sun, Mon, ...* , *Sat.* The year should appear at the top and each month should be named.

Input to the program comprises the year and the date (expressed as an integer in the range 1 to 7) of the first Sunday of the year.

2. Write a program to scan a paragraph of text seeking application of the rule "*i* before *e* except after *c*". The program is to detect the presence of any word of three or more letters which contains either *ei* or *ie* other than as the first two letters. The paragraph is to be reproduced with all such words immediately followed by either an asterisk, indicating adherence to the rule, or a question mark, indicating contravention. The rule is observed if a word contains either *cei* or *αie* where *α* is not *c* (e.g., *receive, deceit, siege, pie*). The rule is violated if a word contains either *cie* or *αei* (e.g. *concierge, efficient, seize, veil*).

When the entire paragraph has been processed the program is to state how many words have been encountered in each of the four categories (*cei, αie, cie, αei*) and, consequently, how many words contravened the rule.

Part B

GENERALIZED SCALAR TYPES

9

Symbolic and Subrange Types

The topics covered in this chapter make a great contribution to Pascal's superiority over most other programming languages. Symbolic and subrange types aid our ability to express program intent naturally and encourage us to give more information to the compiler. Three benefits are transparency, security, and efficiency.

Transparency concerns the ease with which we can see what a program is doing. The more transparent a program is, the more confident we can be that it is doing what we intend and the easier it is to spot (and to correct) errors.

Security concerns the number of errors which can be detected by the computer. If you have been running programs you will, no doubt, have experience of both compile-time errors (such as misspelling the name of a variable or omitting a comma) and run-time errors (such as supplying insufficient data or accessing a variable whose value is undefined). You will know therefore that it is usually much easier to correct errors trapped at compile-time than it is to correct errors which are not detected until the program is run. Also, several errors can be spotted during one compilation; execution is terminated as soon as one run-time error occurs. Pascal enables more errors to be detected than does any of its predecessors and most can be trapped at compile-time.

Efficiency concerns both the amount of storage space a program needs and the time a program takes to run. As has been mentioned, there is often a trade-off between the two. There is also a trade-off between efficiency and security. In most programming languages increased security can be achieved only by including run-time checks; this increases execution time. Use of symbolic and subrange types can increase the security of a program without affecting its efficiency. In fact, efficiency can sometimes be improved at the same time! Efficiency is very much implementation dependent; it varies from one compiler to another. Consequently we disregard efficiency for the moment and expand our notions of transparency and security.

212

9.1 Transparency and security

Suppose we are asked to write a program which reads the number of daily visitors to a park during one particular week to compare its popularity mid-week with that at the weekend.

Assuming the data to comprise seven integers, the attendances for Monday, Tuesday, . . . , Sunday, we might produce the program of Figure 9.1. If we realize that the process of summing the mid-week attendances is the same as that of summing the weekend attendances we can introduce a procedure to perform the summing. Such a procedure might be supplied with two parameters: one, a value, to indicate the number of days and the other, a variable, to record the total. See Figure 9.2. The two totals would

```
program Park1 (input, output);
  var
     i, attendance, midweektotal, weekendtotal : integer;
begin
     {Sum attendances from Monday to Friday }
     midweektotal := 0;
     for i := 1 to 5 do
     begin
       read (attendance);
       midweektotal := midweektotal + attendance
     end;

     { Sum attendances of Saturday and Sunday }
     read (weekendtotal, attendance);
     weekendtotal := weekendtotal + attendance;

     writeln ('Park attendance is as follows');
     writeln (' mid-week : ', midweektotal);
     writeln (' week-end : ', weekendtotal)
end.
```

INPUT :
2   4   6   8   10
1   3

OUTPUT :
Park attendance is as follows
  mid-week :   30
  week-end :   4

Figure 9.1

```
procedure SumAttendances (noofdays : integer;   var total : integer);
   var
      day, attendance, sum : integer;
begin
   sum := 0;
   for day := 1 to noofdays do
   begin
      read (attendance);   sum := sum + attendance
   end;
   total := sum
end { Sum Attendances }
```

Figure 9.2

---

then be computed by two procedure calls:

SumAttendances (5, midweektotal);
SumAttendances (2, weekendtotal)

We could make our program slightly more informative by giving the procedure not the number of days, but the range of days. See Figure 9.3. The corresponding procedure calls could then be

SumAttendances (1, 5, midweektotal);
SumAttendances (6, 7, weekendtotal)

or, better,

SumAttendances (monday, friday, midweektotal);
SumAttendances (saturday, sunday, weekendtotal)

assuming we have defined the integer constants

monday = 1;   friday = 5;   saturday = 6;   sunday = 7;

We have improved the transparency of the program. The statement

SumAttendances (monday, friday, midweektotal)

makes its intent clear even if the reader is not familiar with the program. You might claim that the comments of Figure 9.1 are even more informative, but this is not the same thing. Comments merely state what we *say* the program will do; the program statements dictate what is *actually done*. The more obvious we can make the intent of each statement the better.

If our program contained the statement

SumAttendances (monday, saturday, weekendtotal)

it should be immediately apparent that something is illogical. Unfortunately, if we did not notice this the program would compile and, depending upon

214

```
procedure SumAttendances (firstday, lastday : integer;
                              var total : integer);
   var
      day, attendance, sum : integer;
   begin
     sum := 0;
     for day := firstday to lastday do
     begin
       read (attendance);   sum := sum + attendance
     end;
     total := sum
   end { Sum Attendances }
```

Figure 9.3

the data supplied and upon the computation performed by the rest of the
program, might even run to completion. We might never discover that the
output is suspect. Worse, the statement

*SumAttendances (monday * saturday, friday * sunday −25,
midweektotal)*

might not stop it running and, if the program also processed some monthly
figures and included the user-defined constant

december = 12;

it might run with the statement

SumAttendances (sunday, december, midweektotal)

We would not intentionally write these statements but we can all make
mistakes! It would be nice if a program containing such illogical statements
did not run to completion. It would be particularly nice if it did not run at all
and these statements were rejected by the compiler. Many such errors are
trapped at compile-time when we use symbolics.

As well as protecting ourselves against inadvertently performing illogical
operations such as multiplying two days of the week together or looping
from Sunday to December we can guard against variables and expressions
acquiring illogical values. For example, if the procedure of Figure 9.3
contained the statement

sum := 1 instead of *sum := 0* or
sum := sum − attendance instead of *sum := sum + attendance*

sum would acquire an illogical value. Subrange types give us some control
over this.

9.2   User-defined types

The predefined Pascal data types allow us to process numbers (integers and reals), truth values (*true* and *false*), and characters. We often wish to represent other things. The program of the previous section involves days of the week. Other examples might be directions of travel (north, south, east, west) or pieces in a chess game (pawn, knight, bishop, rook, queen, king). We often wish to group data items together: we might have a collection of details of an employee or a set of candidates in an election. We sometimes wish to define relationships within a collection of data: a family tree would be one example.

Accordingly, Pascal allows us to define our own data types. In this chapter we shall learn to define new types to represent scalars (single items) and in subsequent chapters we shall see how data can be grouped together in different ways. In this section we consider some general aspects of user-defined types.

Some contexts permit the use of "named" types only: we must associate a name with each new type and then refer to a type by its name. In other contexts we can use "anonymous" types: we indicate the values that are to constitute the new type and no name is associated with the type. Named types are usually to be preferred so we shall concentrate on these first.

9.2.1   Type declarations

The declaration of a new type has the form

and a group of such declarations must be preceded by the reserved word

type

Type declarations must appear between constant declarations (if there are any) and variable declarations (if there are any). Thus the order of declarations within any one block is

constants
types
variables
procedures and functions

You might find this ordering easier to remember if you memorize a phrase such as

*c*hilles *t*aste *v*ery *p*ungent

or

*c*ats *t*ails *v*ary *p*rofusely

216

or, perhaps if you are a vegetarian,

cook **t**extured **v**egetable **p**rotein

It does not matter what nonsense you come up with if it helps you to get your declarations in the right order!

One possible *specification of type* is simply the name of a previously named type. If we have a program which is going to compute pressures at points on a beam we could define

type
    pressures = real;
    points = integer;

We have simply introduced an alternative name for *real* and an alternative name for *integer*. The declarations

var
    p : *pressures*;
    point : *points*;

are equivalent to

var
    p : *real*;
    point : *integer*;

So what have we gained? The answer is 'two things'.

First, we have improved the transparency of our program; we can distinguish those real variables we intend to use for pressures from other real variables in the program by giving them the type *pressures* rather than *real* and we can, similarly, identify those integer variables which are to represent points. If our program contains the declarations

type
    temperatures = real;

and

var
    t : *temperatures*;

we should spot that the assignment statement

    $p := p + t$

is probably wrong: we should not be adding pressures and temperatures. Of course, the compiler will not object to this statement because the types *pressures, temperatures,* and *real* are equivalent.

Second, we ease future refinement of the program. If we ever need to change the representation of points (we may wish to associate a beam number with each point) or pressures (we may need to represent a pressure by two pieces of information, a force and a direction) we simply change the definition of *points* or *pressures* and this will automatically change the type of all the appropriate variables in the program. This is a technique commonly used to simplify initial program outlines during top-down testing. See the type *cards* of Figure 9.11 and types *items* and *transactions* of Section 12.4.2 for examples of this.

9.2.2 Scope of type identifiers

The identifiers we use as names for new types are subject to scoping rules in exactly the same way as all other identifiers in a program. The scope extends from the point of definition to the end of the current block and so, within the program text, the definition of a type must precede its use (but see Chapter 14). No identifier can be declared more than once at any one block level and if an identifier currently in scope is redefined within an inner block the outer definition is inaccessible within the inner block.

Consequently, it is possible to redefine the predefined types *integer, real, boolean,* and *char*. This would usually be a foolish thing to do and your compiler may forbid it.

A user-defined type may be used anonymously in a variable declaration but must be named for parameters and function results. To use a type anonymously the *specification of type*, preceded by a colon, follows the list of variables. The scope of any identifier introduced within *specification of type* extends, as usual, from its point of occurrence to the end of the block.

9.3 Symbolic types

The ability to define our own symbolic types enables us to refer to entities by their everyday names without the need to map them onto the data types of a particular programming language. This enhances program transparency and, as we shall see, greatly improves compile-time security.

A symbolic type constitutes an ordered set of named values. The data type *boolean* is the symbolic type

> *(false, true)*

but with the property that its values have a particular significance when used with **if**, **while**, or **until**. To declare a new symbolic type we invent a name for the type and invent names for all the values we wish the type to comprise:

SYMBOLIC TYPE DECLARATION

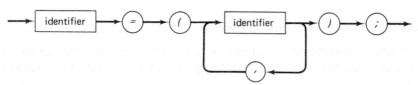

218

The name to the left of the equals sign is the name of the type and all the names inside the brackets represent constants of this new type. Remember, *all* these identifiers are subject to the usual scoping rules. Because symbolic types are defined by enumerating a list of symbolic values they are often referred to as "enumeration types" or "enumerated types".

Notice that one list of symbolic values used in declarations at two different points in a program defines two distinct types. In the following situation:

```
procedure P;
  type t = (a, b);
  var v1 : t;
  procedure Q;
    type t = (a, b);
    var v2 : t;
```

the statement $v2 := v1$, within the body of Q, would be illegal because the types of $v1$ and $v2$ are not compatible. This is a particular example of the general situation that two types t_1 and t_n are compatible only if one of the following is true:

1. They have been defined name-equivalent by a sequence of type declarations of the form $t_1 = t_2$, $t_2 = t_3, \ldots, t_{n-1} = t_n$ (in which case they are deemed identical).
2. One is a subrange of the other (see Section 9.4).
3. Both are subranges of the same host type (see Section 9.4).
4. They are both set types with compatible base types (see Chapter 10).
5. They are string types with the same number of components (see Section 13.1).

Two types are said to be assignment-compatible if neither is, nor involves, a file type (see Chapter 12) and either of the following is true:

1. One is real and the other is integer.
2. They are compatible and have possible values in common. This excludes, for example, non-overlapping subranges.

The types represented on both sides of an assignment operator must be assignment-compatible and so must the types of an actual value parameter and its corresponding formal.

You will be less likely to confuse names of types with names of constants and variables if you have a naming convention. We shall usually adopt the practice of using plurals for types.

9.3.1 Notional entities and attributes

A common application of symbolics is to give names to the entities we consider a program to be processing (e.g. chess pieces, days of the week) or to some attributes of these entities (e.g. nationalities, colours). The following constitute legal declarations (assuming none of the identifiers is declared elsewhere at the same block level):

types
    pets = (dog, cat, rabbit, hamster, mouse, snake, goldfish);
    chesspieces = (pawn, knight, bishop, rook, queen, king);
    sports = (hockey, basketball, football, athletics,
            skating, tennis, gymnastics);
    colours = (red, yellow, blue, green, brown);
    sizes = (small, medium, large);
    nationalities = (british, italian, french, belgian,
               swiss, dutch, russian, chinese,
               japanese, australian, canadian, american);
    sexes = (female, male);

The ordering associated with the values of a symbolic type is implied by the order in which the values appear in the enumerated list. If we define a type whose values are names of days we can utilize the ordering (within a for-loop) to produce a more natural version of the program of Figure 9.1. This is given in Figure 9.4. The only differences between this version and that incorporating the procedure of Figure 9.3 stem from the fact that the type of the constants *monday, tuesday,*... is now *days* rather than *integer*. This has a slight effect on transparency and a great effect upon security. An illogical statement such as

    SumAttendances (monday, saturday, weekendtotal)

would still be accepted by the compiler but expressions such as

    *monday * saturday*   and   *friday * sunday − 25*

would be rejected because we cannot supply symbolics as operands for arithmetic operators. Also, if our program contained a symbolic type *months* with *december* as one of its values, the statement

    SumAttendances (sunday, december, midweektotal)

would fail to compile: the second actual parameter *(december)* has the wrong type. We have improved the compiler's ability to spot our mistakes.

9.3.2 Standard functions and operators

The only operators which can be applied to symbolic values are the relational operators ($<, <=, =, <>, >=, >$) and the set membership operator **in**. The relational operators act upon the ordering associated with

```
program Park2 (input, output);
  type
    days = (monday, tuesday wednesday,
              thursday, friday, saturday, sunday);
  var
    midweektotal, weekendtotal : integer;

  procedure SumAttendances
      (firstday, lastday : days;  var total : integer);
    var
      attendance, tot : integer;
      day : days;
  begin { Sum Attendances }
    tot := 0;
    for day := firstday to lastday do
    begin
      read (attendance);   tot := tot + attendance
    end;
    total := tot
  end     { Sum Attendances };

begin { program body }
  SumAttendances (monday, friday, midweektotal);
  SumAttendances (saturday, sunday, weekendtotal);

  writeln ('Park attendance is as follows');
  writeln (' mid-week : ', midweektotal);
  writeln (' week-end : ', weekendtotal)
end.
```

INPUT :
49   63   51   86   172
112   207

OUTPUT :
Park attendance is as follows
   mid-week :   421
   week-end :   319

Figure 9.4

enumerated values. Thus, for the types declared in the previous section,

$$cat > dog$$
$$hamster < goldfish$$
$$king > pawn$$

and

> green > blue

Enumerated types are ordinal types so the standard functions *ord, succ,* and *pred* are applicable. The ordinal number of a symbolic value is the position of the value within the list when its type is declared. The first value has ordinal number 0, the second ordinal number 1, and so on. Thus, for the types declared in the previous section,

> ord (rabbit) = 2
> ord (king) = 5
> ord (red) = 0

and

> ord (male) = 1

The successor of a symbolic value (if it exists) is that value which immediately follows it in the declaration and the predecessor of a symbolic value (if it exists) is that value which immediately precedes it in the declaration. Any attempt to reference the predecessor of the first value in a list or the successor of the last constitutes an error. Thus, for the types declared in the previous section,

> succ (mouse) = snake
> pred (knight) = pawn
> succ (succ (football)) = skating
> pred (pred (pred (brown))) = yellow

and both

> pred (british) and succ (large) are undefined.

The following relationships, for an ordinal value α, should be apparent {assuming *pred* (α) and *succ* (α) exist}:

> pred (succ (α)) = succ (pred (α)) = α
> ord (succ (α)) = succ (ord (α)) = ord (α) + 1
> ord (pred (α)) = pred (ord (α)) = ord (α) − 1

Example 9.1

Assuming the existence of the type *days* of Figure 9.4, define a function to deliver the day after a specified day.   □

If the specified day is Sunday the following day will be Monday; otherwise the following day will be the one which appears next in the type declaration:

```
function thedayafter (today : days) : days;
    begin
        if today = sunday then
            thedayafter : = monday
```

else
    thedayafter : = *succ (today)*
end {the day after}   ■

Symbolics can be neither written nor read directly but procedures can easily be produced to achieve this.

Example 9.2

Assuming the existence of the type *chesspieces* defined in the previous section, write a procedure to output the name of a specified piece. □
  The procedure is given in Figure 9.5. ■

Example 9.3

Assuming the existence of the type *days* defined in Figure 9.4 write a procedure to read the name of a day. Assume the name may be preceded by spaces and will be followed by at least one space or end of line and that the name will be correct if its first letter is sensible. The procedure should indicate whether or not it found a name. □
  The procedure is given in Figure 9.6. The boolean variable parameter records whether a name was found and the other parameter records the day if it found one. ■

For the predefined type *char* the function *chr* is the inverse of the function *ord*. If *c* is a valid character and *n* is a valid character ordinal number then

   chr (ord (c)) = *c*   and   *ord (chr (n))* = *n*

We can easily define such an inverse function for any enumerated type.

```
procedure NamePiece (piece : chesspieces);
begin
  case piece of
    pawn   : write ('pawn');
    knight : write ('knight');
    bishop : write ('bishop');
    rook   : write ('rook');
    queen  : write ('queen');
    king   : write ('king')
  end { case }
end { Name Piece }
```

Figure 9.5   Example 9.2

```
procedure ReadaDay (var day : days;   var foundone : boolean);
  const
    space = ' ';
begin
  while input↑ = space do get (input);
  if input↑ in ['m', 't', 'w', 'f', 's'] then
  begin
    foundone := true;
    case input↑ of
      'm' :
        day := monday;
      't' :
        begin
          get (input);
          case input↑ of
            'u' : day := tuesday;
            'h' : day := thursday
          end { case }
        end;
      'w' :
        day := wednesday;
      'f' :
        day := friday;
      's' :
        begin
          get (input);
          case input↑ of
            'a' : day := saturday;
            'u' : day := sunday
          end { case }
        end
    end { case }
  end else
    foundone := false;
  repeat get (input) until input↑ = space
end { Read a Day }
```

Figure 9.6   Example 9.3

Example 9.4

Assuming the existence of the data type *sports* as in the previous section, define a function to transform an integer *n* in the range 0 to 6 into that sport whose ordinal number is *n*.   □

```
function sportwithordnum (n : integer) : sports;
  const
    firstsport = hockey;
  var
    sport : sports;
    sportnum : integer;
begin
    sport := firstsport;
  for sportnum := 1 to n do
    sport := succ (sport);
  sportwithordnum := sport
end { sport with ord num (n) }
```

Figure 9.7   Example 9.4

The function is given in Figure 9.7. Notice the use of the constant *firstsport*. This is just in case the declaration of *sports* is ever altered; it will be easy to alter the function if necessary. ■

9.3.3 State indicators

As well as giving names to notional entities and attributes as in Section 9.3.1, it is often useful to name distinct computational states of interest within a dynamic process or the possible outcomes upon completion of a dynamic process. For example, two distinct outcomes can result from a call of the procedure of Figure 9.6: either we find the name of a day or we do not. Program transparency is improved if we name these two outcomes explicitly. We achieve this by introducing a two-valued symbolic type:

> *readoutcomes = (nonamethere, anamehasbeenfound);*

The procedure heading then becomes

> **procedure** *ReadaDay* (**var** *day* : *days*;   **var** *outcome* : *readoutcomes*);

and the statements

> *foundone* : = *true*

and

> *foundone* : = *false*

become, respectively.

> *outcome* : = *anamehasbeenfound*

and

> *outcome* : = *nonamethere*

One of the most important applications of this technique is to identify states of interest within, and upon completion of, a multiple-exit loop.

Example 9.5

Reconsider Example 6.15 to determine whether a supplied positive integer is prime or composite. □

Look at the loop in the solution of Figure 6.13. At any time during this loop we (if we imagine, for the moment, that "we" are the computer) are in one of three states:

1. more potential factors to try but no factor found yet, or
2. all sensible potential factors tried but no factor found, or
3. factor found.

When we enter the loop we are in state 1 and when we exit we are in either state 2 or state 3. Upon exit from the loop we used an if-statement to determine which state applies.

In the program of Figure 6.13 the states are identified as follows:

1. *allpotfactorstried = false* (or undefined)
   and *factorfound = false* (or undefined)
2. *allpotfactorstried = true*
   and *factorfound = false*
3. *factorfound = true*
   and the value of *allpotfactorstried* is irrelevant

We can produce a nicer program if we give a name to each of these three states and use a variable to indicate the current state. A program adopting this approach is presented in Figure 9.8. This program is more transparent than that of Figure 6.13 and three particular reasons for its superiority are as follows:

1. The states of interest are identified explicitly.
2. The possible states upon exit from the loop are stated explicitly within the case-statement.
3. The initialization *potfactor := 3* is more sensible than *potfactor := 1* (this was mentioned in Section 6.1.5). ■

This state indicator approach is applicable to all multi-exit loops. Situations vary but the example we have just considered is typical and so the steps in constructing the loop are usually as follows:

1. Identify all the distinct states of interest (not forgetting the initial state) and invent a meaningful name for each.
2. Declare a symbolic type which defines all these names and introduce a variable of this type.
3. Initialize this state variable to the initial state.
4. Set up the until-test for the repeat-loop. If only one state implies continuation of the loop this test has the form

   state < > continuationstate

```
program PrimeWithStateIndicator (input, output);
     { Determines whether a supplied positive integer is prime
       or composite. }

   const
      space = ' ';

   type
      states = (tryingpotfactors, allpotfactorstried, factorfound);

   var
      n, potfactor, sqrootofn : integer;
      state : states;

begin
   read (n);   write (n, space);

   if n < 1 then
   writeln ('should not be less than 1')
   else
      if n <= 3 then
         writeln ('is prime') else

      begin
         sqrootofn := trunc (sqrt (n));
         potfactor := 3;   state := tryingpotfactors;
         repeat
            if n mod potfactor = 0 then
               state := factorfound
            else
               if potfactor >= sqrootofn then
                  state := allpotfactorstried
               else
                  potfactor := potfactor +2
         until state <> tryingpotfactors;

         case state of
            factorfound :
               writeln ('is composite');
            allpotfactorstried:
               writeln ('is prime')
         end { case }
      end
end.
```

INPUT :
143

OUTPUT :
   143 is composite

Figure 9.8   Example 9.5

as in Figure 9.8. In a more complex environment there might be several continuation states and the until-test will then be

state **in** *[termination states]*

In this case it is convenient to make the names of the termination states adjacent in the type declaration. The test will then be

state **in** *[firstterminationstate . . lastterminationstate]*

5. Supply the body of the repeat-loop, making tests for termination states when appropriate. Once a termination state has been detected no further processing should be performed. This is why each if-statement in the repeat-loop of Figure 9.8 has an else-part. Dominant conditions must be tested before auxiliary conditions.
6. Follow the loop with a case-statement which lists all the possible loop exit states (possibly with several case-labels on one limb) and carries out the processing appropriate for each state. You may be tempted to include some (or all) of this processing within the loop itself, to be obeyed when a termination state has been detected. Resist the temptation! Keep the loop as simple as possible: its function should be to perform only the processing necessary for each iteration and to detect and identify termination states. Burying, within the loop, computation which is not to be performed until the looping process is over will detract from the transparency of the program. It should be placed within the appropriate limb of the case-statement. Anyone reading the program, and this includes the person writing it, can then quickly see the conditions under which the loop will terminate and the computation consequent upon each without needing to look inside the body of the loop at all (assuming the termination states have been accurately identified and meaningfully named).

Example 9.6

Reconsider Example 6.4. Modify the program of Figure 6.5 so that it no longer assumes that the number of shares requested will exceed the cut-off total. A zero request is to signal the end of the data.   □

```pascal
program Shares (input, output);
    { Totals the number of shares issued until a specified cut-off total
      is exceeded or until a zero request is encountered. }
type
    states = (totallingrequests, toofewrequests, cutoffreached);
var
    cutofftotal, sharesrequested, sharesissued, nooflots : integer;
    outcome : states;
begin
  read (cutofftotal);
  case cutofftotal > 0 of
  true :
    begin
      sharesissued := 0;   nooflots := 0;
      outcome := totallingrequests;
      repeat
        read (sharesrequested);
        if sharesrequested = 0 then
          outcome := toofewrequests else
        begin
          nooflots := nooflots + 1;
          sharesissued := sharesissued + sharesrequested;
          if sharesissued > cutofftotal then
            outcome := cutoffreached
        end
      until outcome <> totallingrequests;

      case outcome of
        cutoffreached :
          writeln ('The number of shares issued exceeds ',
                  cutofftotal : 1);
        toofewrequests :
          writeln ('The requests are exhausted')
      end { case };
      writeln (' when ', nooflots :1, ' lots have been issued');
      writeln ('The total number of shares issued is then ',
              sharesissued :1)
    end;
  false :
    writeln ('The specified cut-off total ', cutofftotal :1,
            ' is invalid')
  end { case }
end.
```

Figure 9.9   Example 9.6

In the program of Figure 6.5 there is only one reason for control to leave the loop: *sharesissued > cutofftotal*. Now we have two reasons:

either *sharesissued > cutofftotal*
or insufficient requests have been supplied
{in which case we will encounter the zero data sentinel}

Again we have a three-state process. The program is given in Figure 9.9. Notice that the first test made inside the loop checks for the data sentinel. As in Figures 6.10 and 6.11 further processing within the loop occurs only if the value read is not the sentinel. ∎

Notice that in Figures 9.8 and 9.9, unlike the other figures in this section, the name of a user-defined type appears only in a variable declaration. Consequently, we could use the type anonymously. In Figure 9.8 we could remove

type
   states = (tryingpotfactors, allpotfactorstried, factorfound);

and replace

   state : states;

by

   state : (tryingpotfactors, allpotfactorstried, factorfound);

and in Figure 9.9 we could remove

type
   states = (totallingrequests, toofewrequests, cutoffreached);

and replace

   outcome : states;

by

   outcome : (totallingrequests, toofewrequests, cutoffreached);

We would then have less to write but if any future modification of the program needs to use one of these types for a formal parameter, function result, or local variable the type must be named. To simplify such modifications there is a lot to be said for avoiding anonymous types altogether.

9.3.4 Taxonomy

Taxonomy is a general term for the classification or categorization of information. We use it here to highlight one particular application of symbolics. In the previous sections we have seen how symbolics can be used to identify distinct entities, attributes, or computational states. A program is often not concerned with individual items or states but requires a slightly more general classification. For example, a program which declares the type

> *months = (jan, feb, march, april, may, june,*
> *july, aug, sept, oct, nov, dec)*

and a variable

> *month : months*

might include several case-statements of the form

> **case** *month* **of**
>   *march, april, may* : ... ;
>   *june, july, aug*   : ... ;
>   *sept, oct, nov*   : ... ;
>   *dec, jan, feb*   : ...
> **end** { case }

The processing within these case-statements is probably not concerned with any particular month and so is merely dependent upon the season. We can improve the program by introducing the type

> *seasons = (spring, summer, autumn, winter)*

and a variable

> *season : seasons*

and rewriting the case-statements in the form

> **case** *season* **of**
>   *spring* : ... ;
>   *summer* : ... ;
>   *autumn* : ... ;
>   *winter* : ...
> **end** { case }

If no part of the program needs to know the particular month then *months* and *month* can be removed. If the month is relevant in places, we can retain both types and both variables and update *season* appropriately whenever the value of *month* changes. We could define a function (as in Figure 9.10) to perform the taxonomy and then update *season* with the statement

> *season* : = *timeofyear (month)*

Rather than list all categories in one enumerated type it is sometimes more convenient to use what is called the "cartesian product" of two (or more) classifications. In simple terms this means that we subdivide a classification scheme. For example, a program interested in seasons might have to adjust its processing for certain months, say April, June, and

```
function timeofyear (m : months) : seasons;
begin
  case m of
    march, april, may  : timeofyear := spring;
    june, july, aug    : timeofyear := summer;
    sept, oct, nov     : timeofyear := autumn;
    dec, jan, feb      : timeofyear := winter
  end { case }
end { time of year }
```

Figure 9.10

August. The type *seasons* might then be replaced by

months = (*marchormay, april, juneoraug, july,
            autumnmonth, wintermonth*)

and the case-statements would have the form

```
case month of
  marchormay    : . . . ;
  april         : . . . ;
  juneoraug     : . . . ;
  july          : . . . ;
  autumnmonth   : . . . ;
  wintermonth   : . . .
end { case }
```

If the processing necessary for a special month differs significantly from that needed for the other months of the same season this is a reasonable approach. If, on the other hand, the processing is similar the case-statement will involve much duplicated processing. It may be better to incorporate two categories: one for the season and one to indicate whether the month is special. We would then use two types

seasons = (*spring, summer, autumn, winter*);
significances = (*ordinary, special*);

and two variables

season : *seasons*;
monthtype : *significances*;

and the case-statement acquires two levels, one to determine the season and one to distinguish the special processing:

```
case season of
    spring :  begin
                ...;
                case monthtype of
                    special : ... ;
                    ordinary : ...
                end { case };
                ...
            end;
    summer : begin
                ...;
                case monthtype of
                    special : ... ;
                    ordinary : ...
                end { case };
                ...
            end;
    autumn : ... ;
    winter : ...
end { case }
```

9.4 Subrange types

A subrange type identifies a range of contiguous values of an ordinal type. The ordinal type is then said to be the "host type". Two types with the same host type are said to be "compatible". With the exception of variable routine parameters, a subrange type is semantically equivalent to its host type but for the restriction that a variable or parameter (or function) of the subrange type cannot take (or deliver) a value outside the specified range; any attempt to do so constitutes an error. Whereas the types of a formal value parameter and its corresponding actual parameter need be only compatible, the types of corresponding variable parameters must be identical.

A sophisticated compiler will detect many subrange violations at compile-time but some subrange violations cannot be detected until run-time. To illustrate this, suppose we declare a variable x whose type is the integer subrange 1 to 50 and a variable y whose type is the integer subrange 100 to 200. The assignments

$$x := 75 \quad \text{and} \quad y := 80$$

are both illegal and your compiler should report this. The assignment

$$y := x * 2 - 1$$

would produce a value out of range because the value of *2x − 1* must lie in the range 1 to 99 and y cannot take any value in this range. Unfortunately, many compilers will not detect this but should generate a run-time check to ensure that the value assigned to y is legal. The violation would then be trapped at run-time, but only if this statement were obeyed, so the program loses both efficiency and security.

The assignment

x : = y − 100

may be legal or it may not. If the current value of y is in the range 101 to 151 it will be legal; if not, it will be illegal. Most compilers will produce a run-time check for this. A good compiler may be able to deduce from the earlier processing that the value of y is definitely within the range 101 to 151 {for instance, the previous statement might be *y : = x + 100*}, in which case it will not generate a run-time check, or that the value definitely lies outside the range 101 to 151 {for instance, the previous statement might be *y : = y + 60*} and so will report an error. A good compiler will generate the run-time check only if it is impossible to tell until the program runs whether a value is legal. For example, there is no way of knowing if *read(x, y)* will be legal until data is supplied and the program is run.

As you can see, both the security provided and the efficiency achieved by compilers varies. As more effort is put into the construction of Pascal compilers both security and efficiency will improve. You should ignore these detailed points of efficiency and concentrate on security. The intrinsic efficiency of an algorithm should always be borne in mind but a logical program usually provides a reasonably efficient implementation of the algorithm. Overall efficiency is important but security is more important. A program which produces the right answer after ten minutes is better than one which produces the wrong answer after five!

To define a subrange type we state the upper and lower bounds of the range:

SUBRANGE TYPE DECLARATION

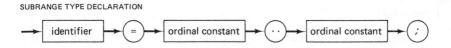

Notice that the two bounds can be neither variables nor expressions: they must be constants. Both constants must be of the same type. Each may be any valid integer, character, or boolean value, any user-defined ordinal constant currently in scope, or any symbolic value currently in scope but the ordinal number of the first must not exceed that of the second.

The following are legal subrange declarations:

posints = 1 . . maxint;
yearsthiscentury = 1900 . . 1999;

> *minus10toplus10* = -10 . . 10;
> *letters* = $'A'$ . . $'Z'$;

In the scope of the enumerated types introduced in Sections 9.3.1 and 9.3.3 so are the following:

> *furrypets* = *cat* . . *mouse*;
> *capturablepieces* = *pawn* . . *queen*;
> *europeans* = *british* . . *swiss*;
> *weekends* = *saturday* . . *sunday*;
> *primeoutcomes* = *allpotfactorstried* . . *factorfound*;

To improve security we shall give particular thought to all ordinal declarations from now on. As well as considering the basic type of a variable or parameter we must decide the smallest range of values it can sensibly assume and declare its "minimal subrange".

We have no need to introduce new examples; security can be tightened on many of the examples we have already met.

9.4.1 Previous examples revisited

We reconsider a selection of earlier examples and improve their security. In so doing, we identify eight slightly different situations. For maximum security, minimal subranging will be the aim.

9.4.1.1

Sometimes the minimal subrange of a variable is immediately apparent.

Figure 2.1

None of the variables *units, tens, hundreds* should ever take a value outside the range 0 to 9 so *integer* on line 6 should be replaced by 0 . . 9.

Figure 3.2

The supplied letter is assumed to lie between C and X (inclusive). We can enforce this by replacing *char* by $'C'$ . . $'X'$.

Figures 4.3, 4.4, and 6.17

We should replace *char* by $'A'$ . . $'Z'$.

Figure 3.3

No month contains more than thirty-one days, a year contains twelve months, and, if the year is specified by two digits, it must be in the range 0 to 99. Consequently, the declaration

> *day, month, year : integer;*

should be

> *day   : 1 .. 31;*
> *month : 1 .. 12;*
> *year   : 0 .. 99;*

Figure 4.6

We assume the supplied initial is *A, B, C,* or *F* so *char* should be *'A' .. 'F'.*

Figure 4.8

A price expressed in pence or cents will be less than 100 so *integer* should be *1 .. 99.*

Figure 8.7

Each comment states the range within which a supplied actual parameter is assumed to lie. If any value falls outside its expected range we have made a mistake. This mistake will be trapped as soon as it occurs if we specify an appropriate subrange for each formal parameter. We need the following subranges:

> **type**
> *units   = 0 .. 9;*
> *twotonine   = 2 .. 9;*
> *tentonineteen = 10 .. 19;*
> *lt100   = 0 .. 99;*
> *lt1000   = 0 .. 999;*
> *ltmillion   = 0 .. 999999;*

and the procedure headings become

> **procedure** *NameLtMillion (n : ltmillion);*
> **procedure** *NameLtThousand (n : lt1000;   andneeded : boolean);*
> **procedure** *NameLtHundred (n : lt100;   andneeded : boolean);*
> **procedure** *NameTy (n : twotonine);*
> **procedure** *NameTeen (n : tentonineteen);*
> **procedure** *NameUnit (n : units);*

9.4.1.2

In some examples we included our own checks to ensure that a value was in a desired range.

236

Figure 4.12

If we replace *char* by 'A'..'F' we can remove the first two tests. Notice that the effect of the program will change. If the program of Figure 4.12 is supplied with a character outside the range 'A'..'F' it terminates normally but produces no output. If we replace *char* by the subrange type 'A'..'F' a supplied character outside this range will cause premature termination and an error message will be printed.

Figure 6.5

If we declare *cutofftotal* to have type *1..maxint* we can remove the *false* branch of the case-statement (and, hence, lines 9, 10, 11, 24, 25, 26, 27, and 28). Again, the effect of the program will change. If we want an inappropriate value to generate the explicit error message of lines 26 and 27 we must keep the program as it is. If we are prepared to accept a system run-time error message we can use the subrange type.

9.4.1.3

As the discussion of Figure 6.5 has suggested, we sometimes wish to supply our own run-time checks. We can then produce meaningful error-messages and, if appropriate, can allow program execution to continue. This is often the case during data validation.

Figure 6.5

A request for shares should always exceed 0 so we can increase program security by giving *sharesrequested* the type *1..maxint*. If a zero or negative value is supplied a run-time error will be flagged and execution will be terminated. However, we might decide it would be better if the program were to print an appropriate message, ignore the invalid request, and carry on processing the remaining data. We would then know if any other supplied values are in error. To achieve this we leave the type of *sharesrequested* as *integer* and modify lines 14 and 15 to

```
read (sharesrequested);
if sharesrequested > 0 then
begin
  nooflots := nooflots + 1;
  sharesissued := sharesissued + sharesrequested
end else
  writeln ('Invalid request:', sharesrequested)
```

9.4.1.4

In some examples we know the range of values that one variable can take in terms of some other variables. The bounds of a Pascal subrange must be constants so it is often worth attempting to replace some variables by constants.

Figure 6.3

Assuming *minvalueaccepted* > 0, the values of *prevterm* and *termbeforethat* should always be in the range *0* to *minvalueaccepted* − *1* but, with the program in its current form, the smallest subrange we can use for *prevterm* and *termbeforethat* is *0 . . maxint*. If *minvalueaccepted* were a constant, and not a variable, program security would be improved by the use of the subrange *0 . . minvalueaccepted*. We precede the variable declarations by

const
    minvalueaccepted = *20*;   {or some other desired value}

replace the variable declarations by

    thisterm : *1 . . maxint*;
    prevterm, termbeforethat : *0 . . minvalueaccepted*;

and remove the read-statement of line 7. The program now needs no data so we remove *input* from the **program** line.

Figure 6.8

Because *n* is a variable the smallest subranges we can ascribe to *ndivbase* and *powerofbase* are *0 . . maxint* and *1 . . maxint* respectively. By making *n* a constant we can restrict these to *0 . . n* and *1 . . n*.

9.4.1.5

Often we do not wish to implement a run-time parameter as a constant (as we did in Section 9.4.1.4) and there is no unique range within which we can guarantee that sensible values will fall. In such circumstances it is often sensible to define arbitrary, but sensible, bounds.

Figures 4.9 *and* 5.4

These two programs involve ages. The subrange *0 . . maxint* is better than *integer* but is still unrealistic. We can introduce a sensible bound and enforce a much smaller subrange:

const
    maxage = *120*;
var
    age : *0 . . maxage*;

Use of a user-defined constant stresses that a maximum age has been specified.

238

Figures 5.6 *and* 5.7

These programs involve age and height. We can restrict the age range as with Figures 4.9 and 5.4. To constrain the height we should introduce both a lower and an upper bound:

```
const
    maxage = 120;
    minheight = 50;   maxheight = 250;
var
    age : 0 .. maxage;
    height : minheight .. maxheight;
```

9.4.1.6

We sometimes need to reduce or extend a "natural" subrange, usually by one value.

Figure 6.3

In Section 9.4.1.4 we noted that the values of *prevterm* and *termbeforethat* must lie within the range *0* to *minvalueaccepted* − *1*. If, in addition to *minvalueaccepted*, we introduce a constant *minvalminus1* with value 1 less, we can give *prevterm* and *termbeforethat* their minimal subrange *0 .. minvalminus1*.

Figure 6.5

The minimum number of shares sensibly requested as one lot is 1. If data validation is performed as in Section 9.4.1.3 the maximum value that *nooflots* can acquire should be *cutofftotal* + *1*. If *cutofftotal* were a constant we could introduce a second constant *cutoffplus1* and specify the minimal subrange for *nooflots*.

9.4.1.7

A subrange of characters can be implementation dependent.

Figure 6.11

The sale code can be one of only three characters so, unless we wish to perform data validation, we should use the smallest subrange which embraces all three. Such a subrange will be dependent upon the lexicographic ordering of the available character set. In the interests of portability, it might be advisable to use a full range in this case and perform data validation:

> **if** *code* **in** *[cashcode, accountcode, refundcode]* **then** ...

If a subrange is used the implementation dependence should be stressed:

> **const**
>   *cashcode* = '+';   *accountcode* = '@';   *refundcode* = '−';
>   *mincode* = *cashcode*;   *maxcode* = *accountcode*;
>   *{*** implementation dependent ***}*
> **var**
>   *code* : *mincode*..*maxcode*;

9.4.1.8

If a formal parameter or function result is to be of subrange type we must use a named type.

Figure 7.6

The total votes for a party cannot be less than 0 and the vote terminator must be either *lunarterminator* or *martianterminator*. The program declarations should include the constants

> *minterminator* = *martianterminator*;   *maxterminator* = *lunarterminator*;
>   *{*** dependent upon the defined terminators ***}*

and the types

> *nonnegints* = *0*..*maxint*;
> *terminators* = *minterminator*..*maxterminator*;

integer (lines 4 and 6) should be replaced by *nonnegints* and the procedure heading on line 25 should be

> **procedure** *TotalVotes* (**var** *total* : *nonnegints*;
>   *voteterminator* : *terminators)*;

Within the procedure *TotalVotes, tovotes* should be given the type *nonnegints* but we may wish to leave the type of *votecount* as *integer* and perform data validation.

Figure 9.7

The function is sensible only if the actual parameter lies within the range 0 to 6. A negative value causes the function to deliver *firstsport* and a value greater than 6 will result in an illegal call of *succ*. If an illogical actual parameter is supplied we should ensure that this is trapped when *sportwithordnum* is called. The (non-local) declaration of the data type *sports* should be accompanied by the declarations

> **const**
>   *maxsportordnum = 6;*
> **type**
>   *sportordnums = 0 . . maxsportordnum;*

and, within *sportwithordnum*, the type of the formal parameter *n* and the local variable *sportnum* should be *sportordnums*.

9.4.2 Overview

By reducing the range of values that a variable or expression is permitted to take we increase the probability that our mistakes will be detected. The higher this probability, the more secure our program is said to be. As we should aim for maximum security, we should, unless we have good reason for doing otherwise, use the smallest subranges possible for all ordinal types. We may have to sacrifice some flexibility to achieve this and supply, as a compile-time constant, some value we had hoped to read at run-time. The program source then has to be altered if we wish to use a different value and this inconvenience must be weighed against the gain in security. A compromise often affords the best approach: we read a value at run-time but define (constant) bounds for the value and use these bounds in the subrange declaration. It is then necessary to change the program only if we wish to supply a value outside the specified range.

Data validation is one of the few circumstances under which the use of full ranges is justified. We may prefer to check for illogical values explicitly so that we can produce appropriate error messages and avoid premature termination of execution. Notice, though, that the data validation of Section 9.4.1.3 is far from complete. Execution will be aborted if the input stream contains any non-numeric character other than + or − immediately preceding the first digit of a number.

The process described in the previous section, namely introducing subranges to existing programs, is misleading. It implies that subranges are determined by examining the program. We assumed each program to be correct and tailored the subranges so that execution of the programs is not affected if legal data is supplied. It is true that, after writing a program, we sometimes realize that closer limits can be applied, but this usually indicates a flaw in our earlier logic and is not the way to go about it. The main point of subrange types is that they help us to *develop* a *correct* program in the first place. We must decide from the *problem* context, not from the *program*, what constitutes a sensible range of values for each ordinal variable, parameter, and function result and write the program accordingly. If our range is indeed sensible, any subsequent subrange violation brings to light an error in the program. Diligent use of subrange types is a great help in developing correct programs. Throughout the remainder of this book minimal subranging will be an aim.

9.5 Case study 3

We are going to develop a program to play a single-person card game. Once again you are encouraged to implement this program yourself following the steps outlined.

9.5.1 The game

A standard pack of fifty-two playing cards is shuffled and dealt face upwards on to five piles. These piles are arranged in a circle and numbered clockwise, from 1 to 5. The first card is placed on pile 1 and dealing is initially in a clockwise direction, the second card being placed on pile 2, the third on pile 3, and so on.

When a red court card (jack, queen, king, or ace of hearts or diamonds) is played, the number of its pile is added to a running score (initially zero), and whenever a black court card is played, the direction of dealing reverses. This process continues until the entire pack has been dealt, whereupon the final score is noted.

9.5.2 Program specification

The cards will be supplied as data, each card being represented by its denomination followed by its suit. The denomination will be J for jack, Q for queen, K for king, A for ace, and a number in the range 2 to 10 for the others. The suit will be represented by its initial letter. Spaces may occur between cards but none will occur within a card.

The program should check that each datum does represent a playing card and should check that fifty-two (and only fifty-two) are supplied but need not check that all the supplied cards are different. We return to this last point in Chapters 10 and 13.

9.5.3 Initial outline

The basic process is obviously a loop: we repeatedly deal a card. We stop dealing if we have dealt fifty-two cards, if we run out of cards sooner, or if we are given an invalid card representation. The loop has multiple exits so we identify distinct states of interest. From our discussion so far we are aware of four states:

dealing,
full pack dealt,
too few cards supplied, and
invalid card representation.

This suggests an initial outline of the following form:

```
type
    states = (dealing, fullpackdealt, toofewcards, invaliddatum);
    cards = ... ;
var
    situation : states;
    thecard : cards;
    noofcards : 0 .. 52;
procedure Deal (card : cards);
    ...
procedure GetNextCard (var card : cards;   var outcome : states);
    ...

noofcards := 0;   situation := dealing;
repeat
    GetNextCard (thecard, situation);
    if situation = dealing then
    begin
        Deal (thecard);   noofcards := noofcards + 1;
        if noofcards = 52 then
            situation := fullpackdealt
    end
until situation < > dealing;

case situation of
    fullpackdealt : ... ;
    toofewcards   : ... ;
    invaliddatum : ...
end { case }
```

Notice that the loop in this outline effectively repeats a test. The test *situation = dealing* is made inside the loop and its inverse, *situation < > dealing*, at the end of the loop. This is untidy but can be avoided by our usual practice (as in Chapter 6): we move the call of *GetNextCard* to the end of the loop. We must then get the first card before we enter the loop and, in case the first card is not correctly supplied, the loop must become a while-loop.

The main purpose of *GetNextCard* is to determine the next card so we give it a variable parameter to record this. We shall also arrange for *GetNextCard* to set *situation* to *invaliddatum* or *toofewcards* if appropriate and so have transferred *situation* as a variable parameter to emphasize this fact. We should call *GetNextCard* only when *situation = dealing* but, upon return from the call, the value of *situation* might have been changed to *invaliddatum* or *toofewcards*. We can express this explicitly in the declaration of *GetNextCard*. Rather than use one (variable) parameter to record both the current value of *situation* upon entry and the resulting value upon exit we separate the two functions and use a different parameter for each. One, the input parameter, is a value parameter which can take only one value, *dealing*, and the other, an output parameter, a variable parameter capable of taking one of the three values *dealing*, *invaliddatum*, and *toofewcards*. We modify the order of enumeration of the values of the type *states* so that we can declare a subrange incorporating only these three values. Because the type of an actual variable parameter must be identically that of the formal it replaces, we cannot supply *situation* as the variable parameter; we must introduce a new variable for the purpose. We restrict the input parameter to a single value by using the subrange *dealing . . dealing* which contains only one value. This mechanism for checking that a value lies within a specified range when a procedure is called is a useful feature of Pascal. It provides a step towards the assertions mentioned in Chapter 8.

In the interest of both generality and transparency we should replace 52 by a user-defined constant *packsize*. The number of cards dealt is initially zero and we have presumably made a mistake if we ever try to deal more cards than the pack is supposed to contain; thus the minimal subrange for *noofcards* should be $0 . . packsize$. It is possible to write the program so that *noofcards* should never take a value less than 1 and, if this becomes the case, we shall tighten up the subrange.

We need to define the data type *cards* and supply bodies for the two procedures *Deal* and *GetNextCard*. Somewhere in this process we shall have to introduce a score, the piles, and some notion of the two directions of dealing. Before doing any of these things we can test our outline structure. We assume for the moment that each card is represented by an integer in the range 1 to 52. We define *cards = integer*, make *GetNextCard* read an integer which it then tests to be in the range 1 to 52, and we make *Deal* simply print the integer. We now have a program we can run. To simplify the task of supplying data for test runs we reduce the size of the pack to, say, 10, and make four test runs. For our first run we supply the correct number of cards. This is illustrated in Figure 9.11. We then try too few cards and then too many and, finally, include an invalid card representation. The output produced by the program should be different in each case.

When the program performs to our satisfaction we move on to our next refinements.

9.5.4 Subsequent refinements

We can introduce piles quite easily:

```
const
    noofpiles = 5;
```

```
program CardGameRun1 (input, output);
  const
    packsize = 10;
  type
    states = (dealing, invaliddatum, toofewcards, fullpackdealt);
    readoutcomes = dealing .. toofewcards;
    dealstates = dealing .. dealing;
    cardsdealt = 0 .. packsize;
    cards = integer;
  var
    noofcards : cardsdealt;
    situation : states;
    newsituation : readoutcomes;
    thecard : cards;

  procedure Deal (card : cards);
      { Temporary version—assumes cards = integer }
  begin
    write (card :3)
  end { Deal };

  procedure GetNextCard (var card : cards;
          state : dealstates;  var outcome : readoutcomes);
      { Temporary version—assumes cards = integer }
    var
      weare : (skipping, atendoffile, atadatum);
  begin
    weare := skipping;
    repeat
      if eof then weare := attendoffile else
        if input↑ = ' ' then get (input) else
          weare := atadatum
    until weare <> skipping;

    case weare of
      atadatum :
        begin
          read (card);
          if card in [1 .. 52] then
            outcome := state
          else
            outcome := invaliddatum
        end;
```

```
          atendoffile :
            outcome := toofewcards
        end { case }
      end { Get Next Card };


begin { program body }
    noofcards := 0;   situation := dealing;
    GetNextCard (thecard, situation, newsituation);
    situation := newsituation;

    while situation = dealing do
    begin
        Deal (thecard);   noofcards := noofcards + 1;
        if noofcards = packsize then
            situation := fullpackdealt else
        begin
            GetNextCard (thecard, situation, newsituation);
            situation := newsituation
        end
    end;
    writeln;

    case situation of
        fullpackdealt :
            writeln ('Full pack dealt');
        invaliddatum :
            writeln ('Illegal card representation supplied');
        toofewcards :
            writeln ('Too few cards supplied')
    end { case };

    writeln ('Number of cards dealt :', noofcards)
end.
```

INPUT :
27   16   11   43   19   8   51   2   13   24

OUTPUT :
27   16   11   43   19   8   51   2   13   24
Full pack dealt
Number of cards dealt : 10

Figure 9.11

type
 piles = 1 . . noofpiles;
var
 nextpile : piles;

We initialize *nextpile* to 1 and, within *Deal*, update *pile* to simulate movement in the appropriate dealing direction.

There are two directions of dealing so it seems natural to introduce a two-valued symbolic type to represent them:

type
 dealdirections = (clockwise, anticlockwise);

var
 direction : dealdirections;

Alternatively, we could replace *dealing* by two states *clockdeal* and *anticlockdeal* and then define *dealdirections* to be the subrange *clockdeal . . anticlockdeal*. This might be a good approach if the processing of a card were heavily dependent upon the current direction and were quite different for each. In this instance, though, the direction of deal affects only the updating of *pile*; everything else remains the same.

The score can be introduced as an integer subrange variable. The lowest bound of the subrange is obviously zero, but the upper bound requires more thought. A standard pack contains eight red court cards and the maximum score occurs when all eight are played on to the pile with maximum number. The upper bound is, therefore, $8 * noofpiles$.

We have still not decided upon an internal representation for cards. We are not interested in the precise identity of any card we deal. We are interested only in classifying the card as a red court card, a black court card, or neither. Consequently, the best representation is by a three-valued scalar:

type
 cards = (redcourt, blackcourt, plaincard);

Before we modify *GetNextCard* to perform this card classification we can test our inclusion of directions, piles, and scores. We can modify *GetNextCard* so that it accepts only the integers 0, 1, and 2 and maps each onto the *cards* constant with corresponding ordinal number (as in Figure 9.7) and make a further test run. Have a go!

If you want to cheat, look at Figure 9.12. This shows the final program complete with a full version of *GetNextCard* and a check for more than a full pack of cards. As usual, functions have no side-effects and, within procedures, all assignments to non-local variables are via variable parameters.

```pascal
program CardGame (input, output);
  const
    packsize = 52;  noofpiles = 5;
    maxscore = 40;  { = 8 * noofpiles }


  type
    states = (dealing, invaliddatum, toofewcards, fullpackdealt);
    readoutcomes = dealing .. toofewcards;
    dealstates = dealing .. dealing;
    dealdirections = (clockwise, anticlockwise);
    skipstates = (skipping, atendoffile, atadatum);
    piles = 1 .. noofpiles;
    skipoutcomes = atendoffile .. atadatum;
    scores = 0 .. maxscore;
    cardsdealt = 0 .. packsize;
    cards = (redcourt, blackcourt, plaincard);


  var
    noofcards : cardsdealt;
    situation : states;
    newsituation : readoutcomes;
    thecard : cards;
    direction : dealdirections;
    nextpile : piles;
    score : scores;

  procedure Skip (var outcome : skipoutcomes);
    forward;

  procedure CheckNoMore;
    var
      outcome : skipoutcomes;


  begin
    Skip (outcome);
    case outcome of
      atendoffile :
        writeln ('The correct number of cards has been supplied');
      atadatum :
        writeln ('More data follows the last card of the pack')
    end { case }
  end { Check No More };
```

```
procedure Deal (card : cards;   var score : scores;
    var pile : piles;   var dirn : dealdirections);

  function other (dir : dealdirections) : dealdirections;
  begin
    case dir of
      clockwise      : other := anticlockwise;
      anticlockwise : other := clockwise
    end { case }
  end { other };

begin { Deal }
  case card of
    redcourt    : score := score + pile;
    blackcourt : dirn := other (dirn);
    plaincard  :
  end { case };

  case dirn of
  clockwise :
    if pile = noofpiles then pile := 1 else
      pile := succ (pile);
  anticlockwise :
    if pile = 1 then pile := noofpiles else
      pile := pred (pile)
  end { case }
end { Deal };

precedure GetNextCard (var card : cards;   state : dealstates;
    var outcome : readoutcomes);
  var
    result : skipoutcomes;

  procedure ReadaCard (var card : cards;
                        var outcome : readoutcomes);
    var
      cardtype : (plain, court, illegal);
  begin
    if input↑ in ['J', 'Q', 'K', 'A'] then cardtype := court else
      if input↑ in ['2' .. '9'] then cardtype := plain else
        if input↑ = '1' then
        begin
          get (input);
          case input↑ = '0' of
```

```
              true  : cardtype := plain;
              false : cardtype := illegal
        end { case }
     end else
        cardtype := illegal;
  get (input);
  if input↑ in ['H', 'C', 'D', 'S'] then
  begin
    case cardtype of
    plain :
      card := plaincard;
    court :
      case input↑ of
        'H', 'D' : card := redcourt;
        'C', 'S'  : card := blackcourt
      end { case input↑ }
    end { case cardtype };
      get (input)
    end else
      outcome := invaliddatum
  end { Read a Card };


begin { Get Next Card }
  Skip (result);
  case result of
  atadatum :
    begin
      outcome := state;   ReadaCard (card, outcome)
    end;
  atendoffile :
    outcome := toofewcards
  end { case }
end { Get Next Card };


procedure Skip { (var outcome : skipoutcomes) };
  var
    weare : skipstates;
begin
  weare := skipping;
  repeat
    if eof then weare := atendoffile else
      if input↑ = ' ' then get (input) else
        weare := atadatum
```

```
        until weare <> skipping;
        outcome := weare
    end { Skip };


begin { program body }
    nextpile := 1;   noofcards := 0;   score := 0;
    direction := clockwise;   situation := dealing;
    GetNextCard (thecard, situation, newsituation);
    situation := newsituation;

    while situation = dealing do
    begin
      Deal (thecard, score, nextpile, direction);
      noofcards := noofcards + 1;
      if noofcards = packsize then
        situation := fullpackdealt else
      begin
        GetNextCard (thecard, situation, newsituation);
        situation := newsituation
      end
    end;

    case situation of
    fullpackdealt :
      begin
        writeln ('Full pack dealt');   CheckNoMore
      end;
    invaliddatum :
      writeln ('Illegal card representation supplied');
    toofewcards :
      writeln ('Too few cards supplied')
    end { case };
    writeln ('Number of cards dealt : ', noofcards);
    writeln ('Final score : ', score)
end.
```

Figure 9.12

9.6 Exercises

*1. (a) Define two symbolic types for Exercise 7.9.1: one to classify supposed
       triangles according to 7.9.1(b), but including "invalid"; one to identify
       triangles as in 7.9.1(c).
   (b) Write a procedure to classify and, if valid, identify a supposed triangle.
   (c) Write a program which applies this procedure to a sequence of supposed
       triangles.

*2. Modify your program for Exercise 8.5.1 to use symbolic types for months and days.

3. Introduce subrange types to your earlier programs.

†4. (a) Write a program to locate a chosen playing card within a shuffled deck of fifty-two cards. Each card is coded as two characters—e.g. *AH* (ace of hearts), *3S* (three of spades), *9C* (nine of clubs), *TD* (ten of diamonds), *KS* (king of spades), etc. The cards are supplied to the computer as a sequence of codes with no space occurring between the two characters of the code but with several spaces and ends of lines possibly occurring between codes. The chosen card is specified at the front of the data. The program is to state the position of the card within the deck.

(b) Modify your program to accept a portion of a pack with the sequence of card codes terminated by the dummy card *0Z*. If the desired card is not located the program should state how many cards were supplied.

†5. A carpet manufacturer controls his looms by computer. He supplies the computer with a series of colour codes indicating the order in which different colours are to be fed to the looms. Light shades used are yellow, cream, pink, and orange; dark shades used are red, blue, and green; and the code used for each colour is its initial letter. All his patterns are such that colours used must be alternately light and dark. Write a program to check that a series of colour codes terminated by *Z* does satisfy this condition.

†*6. Botanists on field study can sample flora by stretching a string between two pegs driven into the ground and, working from one end, classify each plant touching the string. Associated with each plant is a numeric code and the final sample is represented as a sequence of positive integers terminated by zero. For any two species *s1* and *s2* it is interesting to know how many plants were examined before at least one of each species was encountered.

(a) Assume both species are present and write a program to produce the desired figure.

(b) Modify your program to cater for both species not necessarily being encountered.

Part C

DATA STRUCTURES

Throughout the previous chapters, each item of data we have processed has been independent of all other items. A distinct constant or variable was used to represent each item and no explicit relationship existed between any two (except for formal–actual correspondence of parameters). In this part of the book we shall see how a number of items can be grouped together and how hierarchical relationships between different items can be established.

The data structuring facilities of Pascal are presented in order of increasing complexity.

10

Sets

The basic idea of a set was introduced in Chapter 5 and various examples of constant sets have appeared since. Each set was represented by a group of expressions, each of the same ordinal type (this is called the "base" type of the set), separated by commas and enclosed within the set constructors [and]. One particular constant set we shall find useful, but have not yet met, is [ ], the empty set. You can think of a set as a bag capable of holding a collection of values of some base type. The empty set corresponds to an empty bag. A better analogy is to liken a non-empty set to an attendance register. Beside each name in the register (each possible value within the set) is either a tick (that value is a member of the set) or a cross (that value is not a member of the set). The register has space beside each name for only one tick or one cross and so, no matter how many times we tick a person present (or mark a person absent), there is only one tick (or cross) beside the name. Also, it is impossible to determine the order in which names have been ticked. A set in Pascal (as in mathematics) displays these same characteristics. Each of the expressions

> *[2 . . 5, 7, 11]*
> *[11, 7, 2 . . 5]*

and

> *[5, 11, 3, 4, 3 . . 5, 2, 7, 7]*

denotes the same set.

The set is an appropriate data structuring mechanism to apply when we wish to refer to a group of ordinal values but are concerned with neither the order in which these values are stored within the set nor the number of times a value has been put into the set. Bear in mind, as explained in Chapter 5, that both the size of a set and the range of values it may contain are implementation dependent.

Within a set, a subrange $\alpha . . \beta$ is ignored if $ord\,(\alpha) > ord\,(\beta)$. In this case $[\alpha . . \beta]$ denotes the empty set. The set

> *[i + 1 . . j, 12, i * j]*

will contain no more than two members if $i >= j$. It will contain only one member, the value 12, if $i = 4$ and $j = 3$.

We can define set types and declare set variables. To specify a set type we precede the base type (or its name) by the two reserved words **set of**. Assuming the existence of all the scalar types defined in Chapter 9, the following declarations are valid:

type
    pieces   = **set of** *chesspieces;*
    coloursets = **set of** *colours;*
    agesets   = **set of** *1 .. 120;*
    vowelsets = **set of** *'A' .. 'U';*
    heats   = **set of** *(verycold, cold, cool, warm, hot, veryhot);*

var

    defenders : *pieces;*
    primaries : *coloursets;*
    vowels   : *vowelsets;*
    alphabet : **set of** *'A' .. 'Z';*
    votingages : **set of** *18 .. 64;*

We can assign appropriate set values to set variables:

    primaries := [red, yellow, blue];
    vowels := ['A', 'E', 'I', 'O', 'U'];
    alphabet := ['A' .. 'Z'];

Program transparency is often improved when sets are "named" in this way.

10.1 Set operations

Pascal permits us to compare and to manipulate sets. We shall define set operations in terms of two sets X and Y and, for purposes of illustration, we shall assume the existence of the following six sets:

    S1 : the set of all integers in the range 1 to 20,
    S2 : the set of all even integers in the range 1 to 20,
    S3 : the set of all integers in the range 1 to 20 which are divisible by 3,
    S4 : the set of all integers in the range 1 to 20 which are divisible by 4,
    S5 : the set of all integers in the range 1 to 20 which are divisible by 5, and
    S6 : the set of all integers in the range 1 to 20 which are divisible by 6.

We could construct these sets in Pascal with the following assignments:

    s1 := [1 .. 20]
    s2 := [2, 4, 6, 8, 10, 12, 14, 16, 18, 20]
    s3 := [3, 6, 9, 12, 15, 18]
    s4 := [4, 8, 12, 16, 20]
    s5 := [5, 10, 15, 20]
    s6 := [6, 12, 18]

10.1.1 Set comparison

In Pascal, four relational operators ($<=$, $=$, $<>$, $>=$) are applicable to sets.

$X = Y$ is *true* if X and Y contain exactly the same members:

> $s5 = [5, 10, 15, 20]$
> $s1 = [1 .. 10, 18, 14, 3 .. 20]$
> $[2 .. 1] = [\ ]$

$X <> Y$ is *true* if X and Y do not contain exactly the same members:

> $s1 <> s2$
> $s6 <> [6, 12, 18, 24]$
> $[''] <> [\ ]$

$X <= Y$ is *true* if X is "included in" Y. This is the case if X is empty or if all the members of X are also members of Y:

> $[\ ] <= s4$
> $s5 <= s1$
> $s6 < s3$
> $s6 <= [18, 12, 6]$

$X >= Y$ is *true* if X includes Y ($X >= Y$ is the same as $Y <= X$):

> $[0] >= [\ ]$
> $s2 >= s4$
> $s5 >= [10]$
> $s6 >= [18, 12, 6]$

Every set (even the empty set) includes the empty set. In mathematics the notations $X < Y$ and $Y > X$ are used to imply "strict inclusion" of X within Y, and exclude the case $X = Y$. Pascal does not provide an operator to test strict inclusion but this can easily be programmed: $(x <= y)$ **and** $(x <> y)$ tests strict inclusion of x within y.

Example 10.1

Assuming i, j, k, and n are each of the same ordinal type and have ordinal numbers within the range accommodated by sets, simplify the boolean expressions

1. $(i = n)$ **and** $(j = n)$ **and** $(k = n)$
2. $(i = n)$ **or** $(j = n)$ **or** $(k = n)$. ☐

Using sets we can write these as

1. $[i, j, k] = [n]$
2. n **in** $[i, j, k]$

Alternatively we can express (2) as

> either $[n] <= [i, j, k]$
> or $[i, j, k] >= [n]$ ■

An expression equivalent to (1) above appeared in Figure 7.14. The body of the function *allonrbank* involves the expression

> *here* **and** *cabbage* **and** *goat* **and** *wolf*

This is really an abbreviated form of

> *(here = true)* **and** *(cabbage = true)* **and** *(goat = true)* **and** *(wolf = true)*

because *here*, *cabbage*, *goat*, and *wolf* are boolean variables. As in our solution to expression (1) we can write this as

> *[here, cabbage, goat, wolf] = [true]*

or, better in the context of Figure 7.14,

> *[here, cabbage, goat, wolf] = [onrbank]*

In the same program, the function *situation* involves the expression

> *(cabbage = there)* **and** *(goat = there)* **or**
> *(goat = there)* **and** *(wolf = there)*

This can be written

> *([cabbage, goat] = [there])* **or** *([goat, wolf] = [there])*

Example 10.2

Given four variables *a*, *b*, *c*, and *d* whose type is a small enumerated type, simplify the expression

> *(a = c)* **and** *(b = d)* **or** *(a = d)* **and** *(b = c)*   □

Using sets we can write this as

> *[a, b] = [c, d]*   ■

Example 10.3

Assuming that any sequence of letters can be called a "word", consider all the three-letter words which can be formed from the letters *PASCAL*. Write a program to print all those which are not anagrams of *CAP* and in which each letter is different.   □

The simplest way to generate three-letter words is with three nested loops:

```
for l1 := firstletter to lastletter do
  for l2 := firstletter to lastletter do
    for l3 := firstletter to lastletter do
      writeln (l1, l2, l3)
```

We require that all three letters are different. We ensure that *l1* and *l2*

```
program ThreeLetterWordsFromPascal (output);
  const
    firstletter = 'A';  lastletter = 'S';
    space = ' ';
    wordsperline = 10;

  type
    letters = firstletter .. lastletter;

  var
    l1, l2, l3 : letters;
    givenword, anagram, word : set of letters;
    wordcount : 1 .. wordsperline;

begin
  givenword := ['P', 'A', 'S', 'C', 'A', 'L'];
  anagram := ['C', 'A', 'P'];
  wordcount := 1;
  for l1 := firstletter to lastletter do
    for l2 := firstletter to lastletter do
      if l2 <> l1 then
        for l3 := firstletter to lastletter do
          if not (l3 in [l1, l2]) then
          begin
            word := [l1, l2, l3];
            if (word <= givenword) and (word <> anagram) then
            begin
              write (l1, l2, l3, space);
              if wordcount = wordsperline then
              begin
                writeln;  wordcount := 1
              end else
                wordcount := wordcount + 1
            end
          end;
  writeln
end.
```

OUTPUT :

ACL	ACS	ALC	ALP	ALS	APL	APS	ASC	ASL	ASP
CAL	CAS	CLA	CLP	CLS	CPL	CPS	CSA	CSL	CSP
LAC	LAP	LAS	LCA	LCP	LCS	LPA	LPC	LPS	LSA
LSC	LSP	PAL	PAS	PCL	PCS	PLA	PLC	PLS	PSA
PSC	PSL	SAC	SAL	SAP	SCA	SCL	SCP	SLA	SLC
SLP	SPA	SPC	SPL						

Figure 10.1   Example 10.3

differ if we follow the second **do** by

 if $l2 <> l1$ **then**

and we then ensure that $l3$ differs from both $l1$ and $l2$ if we follow the third **do** by

 if not ($l3$ **in** $[l1, l2]$) **then**

We wish to consider only words which can be formed from the letters *PASCAL* so we include the test

 $[l1, l2, l3] <= ['P', 'A', 'S', 'C', 'A', 'L']$

and we make *firstletter* = 'A' and *lastletter* = 'S'. We detect anagrams of *CAP* with the test

 $[l1, l2, l3] = ['C', 'A', 'P']$

Notice that such simple tests would not suffice if letters could occur more than once.

The full program is given in Figure 10.1. The program can easily be modified to take a different given word and to exclude other anagrams. ■

10.1.2 Set manipulation

The effect of set operations is often illustrated diagrammatically by "Venn diagrams" with sets represented as enclosed areas.

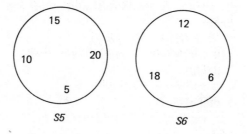

These two sets are "disjoint"—they have no members in common. If two sets are not disjoint, their areas intersect.

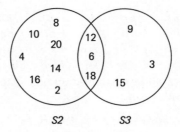

If one set includes another, one area contains the other (unless the two sets are equal, in which case the areas coincide).

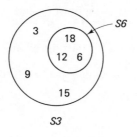

10.1.2.1 *Set union*

The union of two sets X and Y (usually written $X \cup Y$) is a set which contains all the members of both sets X and Y. A value is a member of $X \cup Y$ if it is a member of X **or** a member of Y (or a member of both). Diagrammatically, the union of two sets X and Y is represented by the shaded portion of the diagram below.

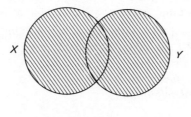

$$X \cup Y$$

$$X \cup Y = Y \cup X$$
$$X \cup Y = X \text{ if } X \text{ includes } Y$$
$$X \cup X = X$$

In Pascal, the union of two sets is implied by the operator $+$:

> v **in** $(x + y)$

is equivalent to

> $(v$ **in** $x)$ **or** $(v$ **in** $y)$

Example 10.4

(a) $S2 \cup S3$ is the set of all integers in the range 1 to 20 which are divisible by 2 or 3 (or both):

> $s2 + s3 = [2, 3, 4, 6, 8, 9, 10, 12, 14, 15, 16, 18, 20]$

(b) *S2 + S6* is the set of all integers in the range 1 to 20 which are divisible by 2 or 6 (or both). This is *S2* because *S2* includes *S6* (any number divisible by 6 is divisible by 2):

$$s2 + s6 = [2, 4, 6, 8, 10, 12, 14, 16, 18, 20]$$

(c) we could have constructed *s2* by putting all the even numbers in the range 1 to 20 into the empty set:

```
s2 := [ ];
for i := 1 to 20 do
    if not odd (i) then
        s2 := s2 + [i]
```

Example 10.5

Extend the card playing program of Figure 9.12 to check that the same card is not played twice. □

We need to keep a record of all the cards played. The set is the obvious data structure to use because each card will be a member of a set only once (at most) and we can disregard the order in which cards have been dealt. Each card in the pack is known by a unique name with two constituents: a rank (two, three, ..., king, ace) and a suit (clubs, diamonds, hearts, spades). Rather than use one set with fifty-two possible members it is better to use four sets, one for each suit. We introduce two types:

denominations = (two, three, four, five, six, seven, eight, nine, ten, jack, queen, king, ace);

dealsets = **set of** *denominations;*

and four set variables:

clubsdealt, diamondsdealt, heartsdealt, spadesdealt : dealsets;

each initialized to *[ ]*.

Within the procedure *ReadaCard* we must now identify each supplied card uniquely by determining both its rank and its suit. We then check that it is not in the appropriate set of cards already dealt. If it is, we terminate the program; if it is not, we add it to the set. The revised version of *ReadaCard* is in Figure 10.2.

A call of *CheckDuplicate* may change the value of *cardtype* so, as usual, we emphasize the fact by supplying *cardtype* as a variable parameter. When *CheckDuplicate* is called, the value of *cardtype* should be *plain* or *court* and so, to improve security, we should adopt the approach we applied earlier to *Deal*: we should use a value parameter to check the current card type and a variable parameter to return the resultant card type. This is not done in Figure 10.2.

We are now considering a further outcome, *cardplayedtwice*, so the data type *states* must be extended to include *cardplayedtwice* (in such a way that

```
0   procedure ReadaCard (var card:cards;  var outcome:readoutcomes);
1     type
2       carddigits = '2' .. '9';
3       digitranks = two .. nine;
4       cardcategories = (plain, court, illegal, duplicated);
5     var
6       cardtype : cardcategories;
7       rank : denominations;
8
9     procedure CheckDuplicate (thiscard : denominations;
10          var thoseplayed : dealsets;  var category : cardcategories);
11    begin
12      if thiscard in thoseplayed then
13        category := duplicated
14      else
15        thoseplayed := thoseplayed + [thiscard]
16    end { Check Duplicate };
17
18    function denom (n : carddigits) : digitranks;
19      var
20        name : digitranks;
21        c : carddigits;
22    begin
23      name := two;
24      for c := '3' to n do
25        name := succ (name);
26      denom := name
27    end { denom };
28
29  begin { Read a Card }
30    if input↑ in ['J', 'Q', 'K', 'A'] then
31    begin
32      cardtype := court;
33      case input↑ of
34        'J' : rank := jack;
35        'Q' : rank := queen;
36        'K' : rank := king;
37        'A' : rank := ace
38      end { case }
39    end else
40      if input↑ in ['2' .. '9'] then
41      begin
42        cardtype := plain;  rank := denom (input↑)
```

```
43      end else
44        if input↑ = '1' then
45        begin
46          get (input);
47          case input↑ = '0' of
48            true :
49              begin
50                cardtype := plain;   rank := ten
51              end;
52            false :
53              cardtype := illegal
54          end { case }
55        end else
56          cardtype := illegal;
57
58   get (input);
59   if input↑ in ['C', 'D', 'H', 'S'] then
60   case input↑ of
61     'C' : CheckDuplicate (rank, clubsdealt, cardtype);
62     'D' : CheckDuplicate (rank, diamondsdealt, cardtype);
63     'H' : CheckDuplicate (rank, heartsdealt, cardtype);
64     'S' : CheckDuplicate (rank, spadesdealt, cardtype)
65   end { case } else
66     cardtype := illegal;
67
68   case cardtype of
69     plain :
70       begin
71         card := plaincard;   get (input)
72       end;
73     court :
74       begin
75         case input↑ of
76           'H', 'D' : card := redcourt;
77           'C', 'S' : card := blackcourt
78         end { case };
79         get (input)
80       end;
81     illegal :
82       outcome := invaliddatum;
83     duplicated :
84       outcome := cardplayedtwice
85   end { case }
86 end { Read a Card }
```

Figure 10.2   Example 10.5

this new state will be contained within the subrange *readoutcomes*) and the case-statement at the end of the program must include an appropriate limb prefixed by *cardplayedtwice:.* ∎

10.1.2.2 *Set intersection*

The intersection of two sets X and Y (usually written $X \cap Y$) is a set which contains only those values common to both X and Y. A value is a member of $X \cap Y$ if it is a member of X **and** a member of Y. Diagrammatically, the intersection of two sets X and Y is represented by the shaded portion of the diagram below.

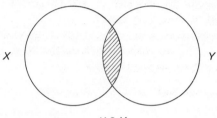

$X \cap Y$

$X \cap Y = Y \cap X$
$X \cap Y = Y$ if X includes Y
$X \cap Y =$ the empty set if X and Y are disjoint
$X \cap X = X$

In Pascal, the intersection of two sets is implied by the operator $*$:

   v **in** $(x * y)$

is equivalent to

   $(v$ **in** $x)$ **and** $(v$ **in** $y)$.

Example 10.6

(a) $S2 \cap S3$ is the set of all integers in the range 1 to 20 which are divisible by both 2 and 3. This is $S6$ because all such integers will be divisible by 6:

   $s2 * s3 = s6$

We could have constructed $s6$ with the assignment

   $s6 := s2 * s3$

(b) $S3 \cap S6$ is the set of all integers in the range 1 to 20 which are divisible by both 3 and 6. This is $S6$ because $S3$ includes $S6$ (any integer divisible by 6 is divisible by 3):

   $s3 * s6 = s6$

266

(c) $S4 \cap S6$ is the set of all integers in the range 1 to 20 which are divisible by both 4 and 6:

s4 * s6 = [12]

(d) $S5 \cap S6$ is the set of all integers in the range 1 to 20 which are divisible by both 5 and 6. This is the empty set because the smallest positive integer divisible by both 5 and 6 is 30:

s5 * s6 = [ ] ■

Example 10.7

Extend the word producing program of Figure 10.1 to exclude all words which do not contain at least one vowel. □

If *word* is the set of letters in the current potential word and *vowels* is the set ['A', 'E', 'I', 'O', 'U'] we wish to exclude the word if *word* and *vowels* are disjoint. We therefore extend the test

(word <= givenword) **and** (word <> anagram)

to

(word <= givenword) **and** (word <> anagram) **and**
(word * vowels <> [ ]) ■

10.1.2.3 *Set difference*

The difference (sometimes called the "relative complement") of two sets X and Y (usually written $X - Y$) is a set which contains those members of X which are not members of Y. A value is a member of $X - Y$ if it is a member of X **and not** a member of Y. Diagrammatically, the difference of two sets X and Y is represented by the shaded portion of the diagram below.

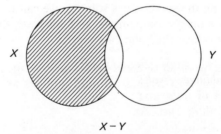

X - Y

$X - Y$ and $Y - X$ are different (unless $X = Y$)
$X - Y = X$ if Y is empty or X and Y are disjoint
$X - X = [ ]$

In Pascal the difference of two sets is implied by the operator $-$:

v **in** (x - y)

is equivalent to

$(v$ **in** $x)$ **and not** $(v$ **in** $y)$.

Example 10.8

(a) $S1 - S2$ is the set of all integers in the range 1 to 20 which are not divisible by 2. This is the set of all odd integers in the range 1 to 20:

$s1 - s2 = [1, 3, 5, 7, 9, 11, 13, 15, 17, 19]$

(b) $S2 - S1$ is the set of all even integers in the range 1 to 20 which are not in the range 1 to 20. Obviously this is the empty set:

$s2 - s1 = [\ ]$

(c) $S6 - S5$ is the set of all integers in the range 1 to 20 which are divisible by 6 but not by 5. This is $S6$ because $S6$ and $S5$ are disjoint:

$s6 - s5 = s6$

(d) We could have constructed $s2$ by removing all the odd integers from $s1$:

```
s2 := s1;
for i := 1 to 20 do
    if odd (i) then
        s2 := s2 - [i]    ■
```

Example 10.9

Reconsider Example 7.9. the man with the wolf, goat, and cabbage. The man has with him a collection of things and there is another collection on the opposite bank. There is only one goat, one wolf, and one cabbage, and we are not interested in the order in which he acquires them, so this example is an obvious candidate for sets. □

At any point during the search for a solution we can represent the state by two sets: *thisside*, the man's companions, and *otherside*, the collection on the other bank. We introduce the following types:

```
passengers = (none, cabbage, goat, wolf);
residents  = cabbage .. wolf;
collections = set of residents;
outcomes  = (failure, success);
depths    = 0 .. maxdepth;
```

and the heading of *Try* becomes

procedure *Try* (*thisside, otherside* : *collections; prevpassenger* : *passengers;
                    depthleft* : *depths;* **var** *outcome* : *outcomes*)

The top level call is

Try ([cabbage, goat, wolf], [ ], none, maxdepth, outcome)

and the global variable *outcome* has type *outcomes*.

Within procedure *Cross* we simulate an unaccompanied crossing by interchanging the two sets:

> *Try (otherside, thisside, none, depthleft − 1, result)*

This assumes that *Try* contains a local variable *result* of type *outcomes*. If the man takes something with him we take his companion from *thisside* and put it into *otherside* with a call of the form

> *Try (otherside + [companion], thisside − [companion], companion,*
>   *depthleft − 1, result)*

We check that the companion is available with a test of the form

> *companion* **in** *thisside*

The initial state is conveniently represented and river crossings are easy to simulate, but detection of the goal state is less straightforward. We cannot use

> *otherside = [ ]*

because we do not know which side *otherside* is unless we know where the man currently is. We could keep track of the man's position as in Figure 7.14 but another approach is to "mark" one bank. If we place something on the right bank and never move it then we must have reached the desired state if we ever have *otherside = [ ]*, because only the left bank can be empty. We introduce the data type

> *companions = (none, cabbage, goat, wolf, rightbankmarker)*

define *passengers* as the subrange

> *none .. wolf*

and extend *residents* to be the subrange
> *cabbage .. rightbankmarker*

The top level call of *Try* becomes

> *Try ([cabbage, goat, wolf], [rightbankmarker], none, maxdepth, outcome)*

We must ensure that no attempt is ever made to transport the right bank marker. We introduce the subrange type

> *realpassengers = cabbage .. wolf*

and attempt accompanied crossings with a procedure *TryToTake* declared local to *Try*:

> **procedure** *TryToTake (thing : realpassengers;* **var** *result : outcomes);*
> **begin**
>   **if** *(thing* **in** *thisside)* **and** *(prevpassenger <> thing)* **then**

```
  begin
    Try (otherside + [thing], thisside − [thing], thing,
        depthleft − 1, result);
    if result = success then
      SayManTakes (thing)
  end
end { Try To Take (thing) }
```

Now that passengers are represented by an enumerated type we can attempt different crossings within a loop rather than testing each case explicitly. The final program is given in Figure 10.3. As in Figure 7.14, this program does not encourage solo crossings from right to left but could be modified to do so. ■

```
program ManCabbageGoatWolfWithSets (input, output);
  const
    maxdepth = 9;
  type
    companions = (none, cabbage, goat, wolf, rightbankmarker);
    passengers = none .. wolf;
    residents = cabbage .. rightbankmarker;
    collections = set of residents;
    outcomes = (failure, success);
    depths = 0 .. maxdepth;
  var
    outcome : outcomes;

  procedure Try (thisside, otherside : collections;
                 prevpassenger : passengers; depthleft : depths;
                 var outcome : outcomes);
    type
      realpassengers = cabbage .. wolf;
      relations = (hostile, peaceful);

    procedure SayManTakes (thing : realpassengers);
    begin
      write ('Man takes ');
      case thing of
        cabbage  : writeln ('cabbage');
        goat     : writeln ('goat');
        wolf     : writeln ('wolf')
      end { case }
    end { Say Man Takes (thing) } ;
```

```
function situationonotherside : relations;
begin
   if ([goat, cabbage] <= otherside) or
      ([goat, wolf] <= otherside) then
      situationonotherside := hostile
   else
      situationonotherside := peaceful
end { situation on other side } ;


procedure TrySoloTrip (var result : outcomes);
begin
   case prevpassenger of
   cabbage, goat, wolf :
      begin
         Try (otherside, thisside, none, depthleft − 1, result);
         if result = success then
            writeln ('Man crosses alone')
      end;
   none :
   end { case }
end { Try Solo Trip } ;


procedure TryToTake (thing : realpassengers;
                           var result : outcomes);
begin
   if (thing in thisside) and (prevpassenger <> thing) then
   begin
      Try (otherside + [thing], thisside − [thing], thing,
         dpethleft − 1, result);
      if result = success then
         SayManTakes (thing)
   end
end { Try To Take } ;


procedure Cross (var consequence : outcomes);
   const
      firstthing = cabbage;  lastthing = wolf;
   var
      result : outcomes;
      thing : realpassengers;
      state : (trying, cantdoit, doneit);
begin
   result := failure;
   thing := firstthing; state := trying;
```

```
        repeat
          TryToTake (thing, result);
          if result = success then state := doneit else
            if thing = lastthing thing state := contdoit else
              thing := succ (thing)
        until state <> trying;

        if result = failure then
          TrySoloTrip (result);
        consequence := result
      end { Cross } ;

    begin { Try }
      if otherside = [ ] then outcome := success else
        if depthleft = 0 then outcome := failure else
          case situationonotherside of
            peaceful : Cross (outcome);
            hostile   : outcome := failure
          end { case }
    end { Try } ;

begin { program body }
  writeln ('Man, cabbage, goat and wolf are initially on ',
    'the left bank of the river');
  writeln;
  writeln ('The actions the man is to perform will be listed ',
    'in reverse order');
  writeln;

  Try ([cabbage, goat, wolf], [rightbankmarker], none,
    maxdepth, outcome);
  writeln;

  case outcome of
    success :
      writeln ('All are now safely on the right bank');
    failure :
      writeln ('No solution has been found')
  end { case }
end.
```

Figure 10.3   Example 10.9

10.1.2.4   *operator precedence*

The relative priorities of the Pascal set operators are the same as when these operators are applied to other operands. So, with sets as with arithmetic operands,

$$x * y + z = (x * y) + z$$

and

$$x - y * z = x - (y * z)$$

Example 10.10

Give Pascal expressions in terms of *s1, s2, s3, s4, s5* and *s6* defined earlier for each of the following sets:

(a) The set of all odd integers in the range 1 to 20 which are divisible by 3:

$$(s1 - s2) * s3$$

(b) The set of all integers in the range 1 to 20 which are divisible by either 2 or 3 but not both:

$$s2 + s3 - s2 * s3$$

and, because $s2 * s3 = s6$, we can write this as

$$s2 + s3 - s6$$

(c) The set of all integers in the range 1 to 20 which are divisible by neither 3 nor 5:

$$s1 - s3 - s5$$

which is the same as

$$s1 - (s3 + s5)$$ ■

10.2   Exercises

1. Write a program to validate the data for a transferable vote election in which each voter places some or all of the candidates in order of preference. A voter must not vote for any candidate more than once. Candidates are numbered consecutively from 1 and the preferences of each voter are supplied in order on one line.

*2. Write a program which counts the number of different letters contained in a given word and prints them out in alphabetical order.

*3. Write a program to offer a computer dating service. The details of each client are supplied on one line in the form

   sex interests name

The sex is indicated by one of the letters *M* and *F* and the interests are specified as a sequence of initials of the following:

   sport, politics, religion, art, music, travel, dancing, films

If the details of a new applicant are supplied in the same format as the first line of input, your program is to produce a list of names of this person's compatible partners. Two people are considered compatible if they are of opposite sex and share at least one common interest.

*4. Write a program to generate prime numbers using the "sieve of Eratosthenes". All odd integers in the range 3 to $n(n>2)$ are placed in the sieve. The numbers 1 and 2 are quoted as primes and then the remaining primes are listed by repeatedly printing the smallest number in the sieve and removing it and all its multiples from the sieve.

Use a set to represent the sieve and take n to be 1 less than the maximum set size accommodated by your implementation.

†5. If you can run programs from a terminal write a program to play "cows and bulls". The computer "chooses" {see later} a four-digit number which you have to determine by supplying four-digit numbers until you hit upon the required number. For each number you supply, the computer tells you how many distinct digits your number has in common with the sought number and how many digits of your supplied number are not only present in the sought number but occupy the correct position. The object of the game is to determine the number in as few attempts as possible.

If the chosen number is *4335* the supplied numbers together with the computer's responses might be as follows:

```
0123   1 present   0 placed
4567   2 present   1 placed
8967   0 present   0 placed
4012   1 present   1 placed
4352   3 present   2 placed
4553   3 present   1 placed
4332   2 present   3 placed
4335   3 present   4 placed
```

To get the computer to "choose" a number you can invent a function $f(x)$ to produce an integer in the range *0* to *9999*. You can then supply a value v at run-time and use $f(v)$ as the chosen number. Alternatively, you could arrange for the program to read four digits and then ask a friend to type a number secretly.

A game equivalent to this long-standing computer pastime is commercially available under a different name.

11

Records

Procedures and functions allow us to group together statements which are logically connected; statements which are all concerned with one logically distinct process. Records provide a similar grouping facility for data items. A record is a collection of objects, each of which is said to occupy a "field" of the record. Fields may be of any data type. A distinct name is associated with each field and access to individual items within a record is via these field identifiers.

To illustrate the concept of records we return to the election example of Figure 7.6. Whenever we wish to accumulate some vote counts we must specify the terminator which will signify the end of the sequence and supply a variable for the return of the total.

These two things are therefore logically connected. We can emphasize their connection by combining them into one record. We declare the following data type:

> *parties* =
> **record**
>   *terminator* : $-2 .. -1$;
>   *total* : $0 .. maxint$
> **end** { parties };

and introduce two variables

> *lunar, martian* : *parties;*

We can visualize each variable as a box subdivided into two compartments: one called *terminator* and capable of holding a vote terminator and the other called *total* and capable of holding an integer in the range $0 .. maxint$.

```
procedure TotalVotes (var party : parties);
   var
      votecount, totvotes : 0 .. maxint;
begin
   totvotes := 0;   read (votecount);
   repeat
      totvotes := totvotes + votecount;
      read (votecount)
   until votecount = party . terminator;
   party . total := totvotes
end { Total Votes }
```

Figure 11.1

To select a field of a record we follow the record variable by the appropriate field identifier and separate the two by a dot. Thus

   $lunar . terminator := -1$

and

   $martian . terminator := -2$

are two legal assignment statements.

A procedure to accumulate vote counts now has the form shown in Figure 11.1. The parameter is transferred as a variable because we need the ability to change part of the record. If the parameter were transferred as a value, assignments within the procedure body to fields of *party* would be local. They would affect only the local copy constructed when the procedure is entered; the actual parameter supplied would remain unchanged. Notice that we have sacrificed some security: a vote terminator could now be corrupted within the procedure.

When a value parameter is transferred a local copy is made each time the procedure is entered. This entails overheads of both time and space. Efficiency considerations suggest that very large records should be transferred as variables to avoid these overheads. We shall ignore this aspect throughout this chapter.

Example 11.1

Write a procedure to sum two distances, each recorded to the nearest inch, in yards, feet, and inches.   □

The obvious way to represent each distance is as a record with three

276

fields:

```
distances =
  record
    yards  : 0 .. maxint;
    feet   : 0 .. 2;
    inches : 0 .. 11
  end { distances }
```

A procedure to sum two distances will have two input parameters (the two supplied distances) and one output parameter (to return the sum). The procedure is given in Figure 11.2. A function cannot deliver a result of record type so we must resist the temptation to define

function *sumofdistances (d1, d2: distances): distances;* ∎

As with variable declarations we can concatenate the definition of two fields of the same type. The two declarations

```
complexnumbers =
  record
    realpart, imagpart : real
  end
```

and

```
complexnumbers =
  record
    realpart : real;
    imagpart : real
  end
```

are equivalent.

A record may be assigned "bodily" to a record variable (unless any field of the record is of file type; see Chapter 12).

```
procedure SumDistances (d1, d2 : distances; var total : distances);
  var
    inchsum : 0 .. 22;
    feetsum : 0 .. 5;
  begin
    inchsum      := d1.inches + d2.inches;
    total.inches := inchsum mod 12;
    feetsum      := d1.feet + d2.feet + inchsum div 12;
    total.feet   := feetsum mod 3;
    total.yards  := d1.yards + d2.yards + feetsum div 3
  end { Sum Distances }
```

Figure 11.2   Example 11.1

Example 11.2

Define

procedure *FindLarger (d1, d2: distances;* **var** *longer: distances)*

to assign to *longer* the larger of two distances *d1* and *d2*. If the two supplied distances are equal, *longer* is to acquire the same value. □

To determine which distance is the larger we must first compare the number of yards. Only if these agree need we compare the number of feet and then only if these agree need we compare the number of inches. The procedure is given in Figure 11.3. ■

Two record types defined independently to have the same structure are distinct types. For the types

redflowers =
   record
      heightinmm: 10 .. 2000;
      noofpetals: 1 .. 20
   end { red flowers }

and

blueflowers =
   record
      heightinmm: 10 .. 2000;
      noofpetals: 1 .. 20
   end { blue flowers }

the two variables

poppy: redflowers

and

violet: blueflowers

```
procedure FindLarger (d1, d2 : distances; var longer : distances);
begin
   if d1.yards > d2.yards then longer := d1 else
    if d2.yards > d1.yards then longer := d2 else
     if d1.feet > d2.feet then longer := d1 else
      if d2.feet > d1.feet then longer := d2 else
       if d1.inches > d2.inches then longer := d1 else
       longer := d2
end { Find Larger }
```

Figure 11.3   Example 11.2

278

have incompatible types. The assignment

violet := *poppy*

is invalid. This is a useful technique to adopt when we have a number of things with the same structure but which must be processed in distinct groups.

Section 9.2.1 introduced the notion of using different names for one type (*pressures* = *real* and *temperatures* = *real*) but in such a way that the types are regarded as identical. If we wish to increase security and insist that pressures and temperatures are kept strictly apart we can define each type as a record with one field:

pressures = **record**
                value : *real*
        end;
temperatures = **record**
                    value : *real*
                end;

For two variables

p : *pressures*

and

t : *temperatures*

the values of interest are *p.value* and *t.value* and the assignment

p := *t*

is invalid.

The equality of two records of the same type cannot be tested bodily with =; the comparison must be made on a field by field basis.

One record may contain another: the details that an employer keeps of an employee might well include a date of birth. A date is most conveniently represented as a record with three fields:

const
    past = *1900*; *future* = *2050*;
type
    sexes = (*male, female*);
    marrystates = (*single, divorced, bereaved, married*);
    months = (*jan, feb, mar, apr, may, jun, jul, aug, sep, oct, nov, dec*);
    dates =
    record
        day   : *0..31*;
        month : *months*;
        year   : *past..future*
    end { *dates* };

```
employees =
    record
        sex : sexes;
        birthdate : dates;
        maritalstatus : marrystates
    end { employees };
```

A type must be declared before it can be used (but see Chapter 14) so it is impossible to declare records which would otherwise be infinite. For example,

```
type
    t1 = record
            a: t2
         end;
    t2 = record
            b: t1
         end;
```

is illegal.

11.1   The with-statement

Several references to fields of the same record are often made within a short section of program. In such a circumstance the with-statement offers an economization of notation. A with-statement has the form

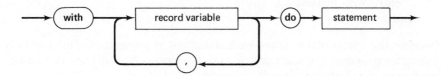

and extends the scope of the variables listed so that, within the qualified statement, field names may be used as though they were simple variables without the need to be prefixed by the record name. Consider the construction of an employee record for a married female employee born on 17th October 1942:

```
var
    lady: employees;
    ...
    lady.sex := female;
    lady.maritalstatus := married;
    lady.birthdate.day := 17;
    lady.birthdate.month := oct;
    lady.birthdate.year := 1942;
```

Using with-statements this sequence of assignments can be written

```
with lady, birthdate do
begin
  sex := female;
  maritalstatus := married;
  day := 17;
  month := oct;
  year := 1942
end { with lady, birthdate }
```

The form

```
with lady, birthdate do ...
```

is equivalent to

```
with lady do
  with birthdate do ...
```

Better, for this example, is the form

```
with lady do
begin
  sex := female;
  maritalstatus := married;
  with birthdate do
  begin
    day := 17;   month := oct;   year := 1942
  end { with birthdate }
end { with lady }
```

because the range of the inner with-statement is minimized. This not only enhances program transparency, it may be more efficient than the earlier version, particularly on a small computer.

Within the qualified statement no attempt must be made to alter (bodily) any of the variables listed between **with** and **do**.

11.2 Record Variants

There may be a need to process objects which can be represented by similar, but different, records. The most appropriate representation is often provided by record variants.

Take the case of dates as defined in the previous section. Only seven of the twelve months have thirty-one days; to increase security a date involving one of the other five months should be represented by a similar record but with a different upper bound specified for the day. The following record type safeguards against such nonsensical references as 31st April and 30th

February:

```
dates =
  record
     year :  past .. future;
     case month: months of
        feb:
          (febday  :  1 .. 29);
        apr, jun, sep, nov:
          (shortmonthday  :  1 .. 30);
        jan, mar, may, jul, aug, oct, dec:
          (longmonthday : 1 .. 31)
  end { dates }
```

Note the following points:

1. A record may have only one variant part and this must follow any invariant fields (but there need not be invariant fields).
2. The declaration of the field whose value determines which particular variant of the record is current is incorporated within the definition of the variant part of the record. This field is called the "tag field" and may be of any (named) ordinal type. Whenever a new value is assigned to the tag field, fields associated with the previous variant cease to exist and those associated with the new variant come into existence with undefined values. Reference to a field of any variant other than the current variant constitutes an error.
3. The fields of each variant must be enclosed within parentheses. In the above example each variant comprises only one field.
4. Even within different variants all field identifiers must be distinct.
5. No **end** is paired with **case.**

Returning to the example, a record of type *dates* has three fields. As previously, *year* and *month* are two of these but there is no longer a field called *day.* Instead, the record will contain one of the fields *febday, shortmonthday,* or *longmonthday;* the current value of *month* dictates which. To reduce the possibility of referring to a variant which does not exist, make it your usual practice to refer to a variant only in a section of program in which the tag field is explicitly set or within a case-statement which uses the tag field as its selector. This latter technique is illustrated in the procedure of Figure 11.4. This procedure increments a date by one day.

The procedure distinguishes leap years but the data type *dates* provides February with twenty-nine days whether or not the year is a leap year. For complete security (so far as the data structure can provide) we could make the data structure distinguish leap years. Try it when you have gained more experience with variants! You will find that the record definition becomes more complex and, accordingly, processing a record becomes more complicated. The importance of security cannot be overemphasized but there are

```
procedure Increment (var date : dates);


   function AtEndOfMonth : boolean;
   begin
     with date do
     case month of
       feb:
           { A year divisiible by 100 is a leap year only if it is
             divisible by 400. Any other year is a leap year if it is
             divisible by 4. }
         if (year mod 400 = 0) or
            (year mod 4 = 0) and (year mod 100 <> 0) then
            AtEndOfMonth := febday = 29
         else
            AtEndOfMonth := febday = 28;
       apr, jun, sep, nov:
         AtEndOfMonth := shortmonthday = 30;
       jan, mar, may, jul, aug, oct, dec:
         AtEndOfMonth := longmonthday = 31
     end { case }
   end { At End Of Month };


   procedure ChangeToFirstOfNextMonth;
   begin
     with date do
     begin
       if month = dec then
       begin
         month := jan; year := year + 1
       end else
         month := succ (month);

       case month of
         feb:
           febday := 1;
         apr, jun, sep, nov:
           shortmonthday := 1;
         jan, mar, may, jul, aug, oct, dec:
           longmonthday := 1
       end { case }
     end { with date }
   end { Change To First Of Next Month };
```

```
begin { Increment }
  if AtEndOfMonth then
    ChangeToFirstOfNextMonth else
  with date do
  case month of
    feb:
      febday := febday + 1;
    apr, jun, sep, nov:
      shortmonthday := shortmonthday + 1;
    jan, mar, may, jul, aug, oct, dec:
      longmonthday := longmonthday + 1
  end { case }
end { Increment }
```

Figure 11.4

---

times when the improved security achieved by tailoring a record definition
to accommodate further variants must be weighed against the increased
program complexity which will inevitably result. For example, compare the
procedure of Figure 11.4 with the much simpler version needed for the
original, less secure, definition of *dates*:

```
procedure Increment (var date: dates);
  function AtEndOfMonth: boolean;
    { as in Figure 11.4 but with day replacing
      febday, shortmonthday and longmonthday }
  ...

begin
  if AtEndOfMonth then
  begin
    if month = dec then
    begin
      month := jan;   year := year + 1
    end else
      month := succ (month);
    day := 1
  end else
    day := day + 1
end { Increment }
```

A record variant may be empty. Reconsider the female employee of
Section 11.1. If she is married we may wish to record her husband's date of
birth and, for completeness, her husband's sex. If her marital status is not

```
procedure PrintDetails (person : employees);

  procedure Give (date : dates);
  begin
    with date do
      writeln (day :2, '/', ord(month) + 1 :2, '/', year mod 100 :2)
  end { Give };

begin { Print Details }
  with person do
  begin
    write ('sex : ');
    case sex of
      male   : writeln ('male');
      female : writeln ('female')
    end { case };

    write ('date of birth : ');  Give (birthdate);

    write ('marital status : ');
    case maritalstatus of
      married:
        begin
          writeln ('married');
          case spousessex of
            male   : write (' husband');
            female : write (' wife')
          end { case };
          write (' ' ' s date of birth : ');
          Give (spousesbirthdate)
        end;
      single:
        writeln ('single');
      divorced:
        writeln ('divorced');
      bereaved:
        case sex of
          male   : writeln ('widower');
          female : writeln ('widow')
        end { case }
  end { with person }
end { Print Details }
```

Figure 11.5

married then such information does not exist. The type definition becomes

```
employees =
  record
    sex : sexes;
    birthdate : dates;
    case maritalstatus : marrystates of
      married:
        (spousesbirthdate : dates;
         spousessex : sexes);
      single, divorced, bereaved:
        ()
  end { employees }
```

Notice that the parentheses are present even when a variant is empty. When one variant comprises more than one field (as is the case for *married)* the field definitions are separated by semi-colons. References to fields of this record are illustrated in the procedure of Figure 11.5. This procedure assumes the original (invariant) definition of the data type *dates.*

Record variants as we have described them, utilizing a tag field, are known as "discriminated unions". As a final note on variants it must be mentioned that Pascal permits "free unions" which do not incorporate a tag field (no tag field identifier appears in the record definition). Free unions are dangerous because they offer little safeguard against erroneous references to variants which are not supposed to exist. Consequently they are not illustrated in this book.

11.3 Packed records

Within a record definition **record** may be preceded by the reserved word **packed** to indicate that storage is to be economized. Consider the data type

```
dates =
  record
    day   : 1 .. 31;
    month : months;
    year  : 0 .. 99
  end { dates }
```

with *months* defined as previously. Each record of this type will occupy three locations within the computer; one for each field. Most of the space in these locations will be unused so storage can be saved if more than one field is packed into one location.

Suppose the computer stored information in decimal and each location could hold six decimal digits. The "largest" date, 31st December 1999, would be represented as follows:

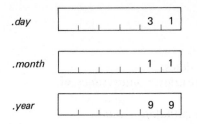

.day

.month

.year

The day and year would be stored as supplied and the month would be represented by its ordinal number. By packing, we can reduce the storage required to one location.

3	1	1	1	9	9

.day .month .year

The computer stores information in binary rather than decimal but the same principle applies. Typically each location (called a "word") in a small computer holds sixteen binary digits (abbreviated to "bits") and, in a large computer, possibly as many as sixty. The binary equivalents of the three integers above are as follows:

    31   11111   (five bits)
    11   1011   (four bits)
    99   1100011   (seven bits)

The total number of bits needed is sixteen, so the whole record could be accommodated within one word. To achieve this economy we use a packed data type:

    dates =
      packed record
          day   :0..31;
          month : months;
          year   :0..99
      end { dates }

Record fields within a packed record will not be packed unless they are, themselves, of a packed type. Within a record of the following type

    shirts =
      packed record
          size   : (small, medium, large);
          colour   : (blue, green, yellow, brown, orange);
          dateoflastorder : dates;
          quantityinstock : 0..100
      end { shirts }

the field dateoflastorder will be packed only if dates is a packed type.

This saving of storage has the further advantage that the time required for operations performed upon entire records should be reduced. Bodily assignment of a record and transfer of a record as a value parameter, each of which involves copying the whole record, will take less time if there are fewer locations to copy. Accessing an individual field, on the other hand, will probably take longer because of the unpacking involved. It must also be borne in mind that extra instructions to perform this unpacking will appear in the machine code. If the number of accesses to a record is high, it is therefore possible that use of a packed record could even increase the overall storage requirement!

A value cannot be assigned to a record variable unless both the value (the record to be assigned) and the variable have identical type, and so the assignment is not permitted if one is packed and the other is not. It is a simple matter to pack or unpack a record field by field. A similar constraint applies to the correspondence of actual and formal parameters and, further, a component of a packed record must not be supplied as an actual variable parameter.

11.4 Exercises

1. Modify your solution to Exercise 7.9.8 to utilize a record type to represent complex numbers.
†2. (a) Define a record type to hold a person's date of birth, sex, and marital status (married, single, divorced, bereaved).
   (b) Write a procedure to marry two people on a specified date. The procedure should check that both are eligible for marriage: old enough, of opposite sex, and not already married. If the marriage is permissible the procedure must update the status of both partners.
3. (a) Define a record type with three fields to represent the time of day in the usual twelve-hour format {e.g. 10.47 am}.
   (b) Modify your solution to Exercise 2.7.6 to utilize this type.
†*4. (a) Define a record type to represent a car by storing the make, model code, engine size, colours available, price, and insurance rating. Define any new types used within your record definition.
   (b) Write a procedure to accept input in some appropriate format and to create a car record.
   (c) Write a procedure to print a car's details.
*5. (a) Define a record type (with variants) to represent any true triangle as classified by your procedure of Exercise 9.6.1. For an equilateral triangle only one length need be stored, an isosceles triangle needs two, and a scalene triangle requires three. Lengths should be stored in decreasing order of magnitude.
   (b) Define a function to classify a pair of triangles as congruent {identical}, similar {of the same type and with corresponding pairs of sides displaying a constant ratio}, related {of the same type but not similar}, or unrelated {of different types}.

12

Files

Various types of file occur in computers but Pascal caters for only one: the "sequential file". Henceforth, any unqualified use of the word "file" implies a sequential file.

A file is a linear sequence of data items (called the "components" of the file). Each item must be of the same type and this may be any type which neither is a file type nor involves a file type. The limit that your computer will impose to the permitted length of the sequence is so large that we can assume there is no limit.

Associated with any file f is a "file buffer variable" $f\uparrow$. When items are being read from the file $f\uparrow$ stores a copy of the component which is next in the sequence. For example, the component type of the standard file *input* is *char* and, as we know, *input*$\uparrow$ holds a copy of the next character of the file. When an item is being written to the file, $f\uparrow$ is used to hold the value that is to be written.

We have already met the two "external" files *input* and *output*. These are called "textfiles" and have some special properties. We shall discuss textfiles and external files later; first we consider general files "local" to the program.

12.1 Local files

At any one time a file is in either "read-mode", when it may be read (the sequence may be scanned linearly from left to right), or "write-mode", when it may be written (items may be appended to the right-hand end). The mode of a file may be changed within a program but a file should not be read when it is in write-mode; nor should it be written when in read-mode.

A file f is set to read-mode by the procedure call

reset (f)

This places a copy of the first component of the file in the file buffer (unless the file is empty, in which case $f\uparrow$ is undefined). Values are then read from f by a call of the standard procedure *read* with f supplied as the first parameter:

read (f, this, that, . . . , theother)

We can define the effect of *read* in terms of the more primitive operation *get*. *get*(*f*) moves along the file and places a copy of the next component in the file buffer. It should be apparent that

> *read (f, thing)*

is equivalent to

begin
    thing := *f*↑; *get (f)*
end

and

> *read (f, a, b, . . . , c)*

has the same effect as

begin
    a := *f*↑; *get (f)*;
    b := *f*↑; *get (f)*;
    . . .
    c := *f*↑; *get (f)*
end

Variables supplied to *read* must have a type compatible with the component type of the file.

The predefined boolean function *eof* is applicable to any file and accepts the file name as a parameter. Thus

> *eof (f)*

detects the end-of-file condition for the file *f*. When *eof(f)* is *true*, *f*↑ is undefined. Any attempt to read beyond the end of a file constitutes an error.

The procedure *readln* and the function *eoln* may be supplied with a file name but are applicable only to textfiles; other files do not embody the concept of a line. As we have seen, the file name may be omitted from a call of *read*, *readln*, *eof*, or *eoln*. The standard file *input* is then assumed.

A file *f* is set to write-mode by the procedure call

> *rewrite (f)*

This erases any previous contents of the file (and consequently *eof(f)* is *true* and *f*↑ is undefined). When the mode of a file is changed to read-mode no further writing to the file should be performed until the file has been emptied (by *rewrite*). A change to read-mode should be regarded as "freezing" the file until it is emptied ready for regeneration. Implementations differ on this, but you will always be safe if you assume these constraints.

Values are written to *f* by a call of the standard procedure *write* with *f* supplied as the first parameter:

> *write (f, this, that, . . . , theother)*

As with *read*, we can break *write* into more primitive operations. The predefined procedure *put* appends a copy of the file buffer to the file and leaves the file buffer variable undefined. Thus

> *write (f, thing)*

is equivalent to

> **begin**
> $f\uparrow := thing;$ *put (f)*
> **end**

and

> *write (f, a, b, . . . , c)*

has the same effect as

> **begin**
> $f\uparrow := a;$ *put (f);*
> $f\uparrow := b;$ *put (f);*
>   . . .
> $f\uparrow := c;$ *put (f)*
> **end**

Values supplied to *write* must have a type compatible with the component type of the file.

The procedures *writeln* and *page* are applicable only to textfiles. If no file name is supplied to a call of *write, writeln,* or *page* the standard file *output* is assumed. When files other than the two standard external files *input* and *output* are in use it is good practice to supply the appropriate file name to all calls of file handling procedures.

To define a file type the component type is preceded by the two reserved words

> **file of**

A file is an appropriate data structure to use when we wish to scan a sequence in one direction.

Example 12.1

In a certain examination the maximum number of marks a candidate can attain is 100. A group of students sits the examination and the marks obtained are supplied as data to a program which is to give the average mark and to state, to the nearest integer, the percentage of students obtaining a mark above the average. Write the program. □

We can compute the average by counting and summing the supplied marks. To determine how many exceed the average we must scan the entire set again and compare each mark with the average. We cannot scan the input file more than once so we must store the input data in such a way that we can scan it again. This suggests the use of a local file.

The program is given in Figure 12.1. The procedure *ReadAndAverage* generates a file of marks and then initializes the file for reading. Within *noabove* the file is again reset. This is superfluous in this program but keeps the function tidy: it prevents the function displaying a side-effect. Upon return from *noabove* the global environment, and, in particular, *markfile*, is the same as it was prior to entry. ∎

```
program MarksAboveAverage (input, output);
  const
    maxmark = 100;
    maxstudents = 500;
  type
    marks = 0 .. maxmark;
    students = 0 .. maxstudents;
  var
    markfile : file of marks;
    noofstudents : students;
    averagemark : real;


  function noabove (bound : real;  n : students) : students;
      { Reads marks from markfile and counts those above bound. }
    var
      student, count : students;
      mark : marks;
  begin
    count := 0;
    for student := 1 to n do
    begin
      read (markfile, mark);
      if mark > bound then
        count := count + 1
    end;
    reset (markfile);
    noabove := count
  end { no above };


  procedure ReadAndAverage
          (var studentcount : students;  var meanmark : real);
          { Transfers marks from input to markfile, counts the
          students, and computes the mean of the marks. }
```

292

```pascal
  var
    mark : marks;
    student : students;
    marktotal : 0 .. maxint;

  procedure SkipSpaces;
  begin
    while (input↑ = ' ') and not eoln (input) do
      get (input);
    if eoln (input) then
      readln (input)
  end { Skip Spaces };

  begin { Read And Average }
    marktotal := 0;   student := 0;
    rewrite (markfile);
    repeat
      read (input, mark);   write (markfile, mark);
      marktotal := marktotal + mark;   student := student + 1;
      SkipSpaces
    until eof (input);
    reset (markfile);
    studentcount := student;
    meanmark := marktotal / student
  end { Read And Average };

begin { program body }
  ReadAndAverage (noofstudents, averagemark);
  writeln ('Total number of students : ', noofstudents :4);
  writeln ('Mean mark : ', averagemark :7:2);
  writeln (noabove (averagemark, noofstudents) :4,
         ' marks exceed the mean ')
end.
```

Figure 12.1   Example 12.1

No relational operators are defined for files. To determine whether two files are equal they must be compared component by component. A procedure to compare two files is given in Figure 12.2.

Bodily assignment of files is not permitted; copying of a file must be achieved one component at a time:

```pascal
  type
    things = ... ;
```

```
var
  f1, f2 = file of things;
  thing: things;
...
```

{The following code effects the (illegal) assignment f2 := f1.}

```
reset (f1);   rewrite (f2);
while not eof (f1) do
begin
  read (f1, thing);   write (f2, thing)
end
```

```
type
  things = ... ;
  thingfiles = file of things;
  compstates = (comparing, mismatch, firstshorter, secondshorter,
                boththesame);
  compoutcomes = mismatch .. boththesame;
...
procedure CompareFiles
    (var f1, f2 : thingfiles;
    function samethings (thing1, thing2 : things) : boolean;
    var outcome : compoutcomes);
  var
    conclusion : compstates;
begin
  reset (f1);   reset (f2);   conclusion := comparing;
  repeat
    if eof (f1)  and eof (f2) then conclusion := boththesame else
      if eof (f1) then conclusion := firstshorter else
        if eof (f2) then conclusion := secondshorter else
          if samethings (f1↑, f2↑) then
          begin
            get (f1);   get (f2)
          end else
            conclusion := mismatch
  until conclusion <> comparing;
  outcome := conclusion
end { Compare Files }
```

Figure 12.2

The loop body is equivalent to

```
begin
    thing := f1↑;    get (f1);
    f2↑ := thing;    put (f2)
end
```

We can, of course, save the superfluous copying to and from *thing:*

```
begin
    f2↑ := f1↑;    put (f2); get (f1)
end
```

Transfer of a value parameter entails the construction of a local copy. Consequently all file parameters must be transferred as variables.

Example 12.2

A group of botanists on field study has recorded the frequency of occurrence of a certain plant at different heights above sea level. When their data is supplied for processing each frequency count is followed by the corresponding altitude, expressed to the nearest metre. Write a program to print these frequencies in ascending order with each frequency accompanied by the altitude. □

```
program FrequencySort (input, output);
    const
        maxfreq = 500;
        maxobs = 2000;
        maxaltitudes = 1000;
        noperline = 5;
    type
        frequencies = 0 .. maxfreq;
        samplesizes = 0 .. maxobs;
        altitudes = 0 .. maxaltitudes;
        observations =
            record
                freq : frequencies;
                alt : altitudes
            end { observations };
        obsfiles = file of observations;
    var
        obsfile1, obsfile2 : obsfiles;
        scan, sizeofsample : samplesizes;
```

```
procedure MoveAllButTheSmallest
              (var this, there : obsfiles; scan : samplesizes);
  { Copies this to there but for this observation with the
    smallest recorded frequency, which is output. }
  var
    smallobs : observations;
begin
  reset (this); rewrite (there); read (this, smallobs);
  while not eof (this) do
    if smallobs.freq <= this↑.freq then
    begin
      write (there, this↑);   get (this)
    end else
    begin
      write (there, smallobs); read (this, smallobs)
    end;
  write (output, smallobs.freq :4, ' (', smallobs.alt :4, ') ');
  if scan mod noperline = 0 then
    writeln
end { Move All But The Smallest };
procedure ReadObservations
              (var obsfile : obsfiles; var noofobs : samplesizes);
  var
    obscount : samplesizes;
begin
  rewrite (obsfile); obscount := 0;
  repeat
    obscount := obscount + 1;
    with obsfile↑ do
      readln (input, freq, alt);
      put (obsfile)
  until eof (input);
  noofobs := obscount
end { Read Observations };
begin { program body }
  ReadObservations (obsfile1, sizeofsample);
  for scan := 1 to sizeofsample do
    if odd (scan) then
      MoveAllButTheSmallest (obsfile1, obsfile2, scan)
    else
      MoveAllButTheSmallest (obsfile2, obsfile1, scan);
  writeln
end.
```

Figure 12.3   Example 12.2

Many different techniques exist for sorting numbers into ascending order. For the moment we consider a simple "selection sort"; we shall meet some more interesting methods later.

The frequencies will be printed in ascending order if we repeatedly scan the data, each time removing and printing the smallest frequency encountered. The need for repeated scanning of a sequence of values suggests the use of a local file. The program is given in Figure 12.3. ∎

The prohibition of comparison, assignment, and value transfer of files applies also to any data type which includes a file type. A record with a field of file type would be an example.

12.2   Textfiles

The predefined type

  text

facilitates the declaration of textfiles:

var
  f : *text;*

A textfile is a file of characters subdivided into lines by the inclusion of "line-markers". These markers are generated by *writeln*, recognized by *eoln* and *readln*, and interpreted as the space character by *read*.

We are familiar with the use of the two external text files *input* and *output*. Manipulation of local text files follows a similar pattern but they must be initialized with *reset* or *rewrite* and may be regenerated and scanned many times. The procedures *reset* and *rewrite* should not be applied to the files *input* and *output*.

12.3   External files

No mention has been made of the representation of files within the computer. Files are conventionally associated with storage devices outside the main store of the computer, typically magnetic tapes and disks. Consequently, the main use of files in a program is to communicate with the external environment. In particular, files generated by one program can be stored and read by another program or, perhaps, by a future run of the same program. To achieve this we must use "external" files.

Any external files a program is to use must be specified in the program heading at the top of the program. Only the names of the files are quoted here; the types of the files are specified by declarations within the variable declaration part at the outermost block-level of the program. The program of Figure 12.3 can save the sorted file for future use if we introduce an external file

program *SortFrequencies (input, output, sortedobs)*

and extend the variable declarations to include

sortedobs : obsfiles

Before we enter the loop within the program body we initialize *sortedobs* with the call

rewrite (sortedobs)

and, within *MoveAllButTheSmallest*, write to *sortedobs* rather than *output* with

write (sortedobs, smallobs)

Although the program accesses an external file the name of the file (*sortedobs*) is local to the program. You may have to supply further information, outside the Pascal program, to associate this "formal file" with an actual file of your computer. This relates to the operational environment and does not form part of the Pascal program itself, so no further mention of it is made here. You must consult your own installation for details.

12.4 Case study 4

A common application of computers is to monitor stock levels in the retail and manufacturing industries. The need to record and continually update large amounts of information suggests a need for files. The design and implementation of a stock control system is a large project, but a suitably simplified example will give us the flavour of the processes involved.

We invent a hypothetical company dealing with a few thousand different items. From time to time some items may be discontinued (when the stock level falls to zero all references to the item are removed from the system) and, occasionally, new items are introduced. Associated with each item is a reorder level and reorder quantity. When stock of an item falls to (or below) the reorder level for that item then, unless it is a discontinued line, an order for the appropriate quantity must be issued. As supply and demand fluctuate reorder levels and quantities may be subject to change. Each item is identified by a reference number (an integer in the range 1 to 10,000) and stock of any one item never exceeds 1,000.

At the end of each week the stock records must be updated to reflect the week's transactions. Each transaction will involve either a sale or the receipt of reordered stock.

In a realistic environment much more information would be relevant. Associated with each item there might be an English description, the name and address of the supplier, the date of the last order, details of any outstanding orders, quantities stocked at different depots, etc. Details of a transaction will obviously include the reference number and quantity of the item involved. Also included, for a sale, could be the branch concerned, the name of the salesperson, the price and whether the sale was for cash or credited to an account, and, for the receipt of goods, the depot acquiring the goods, the value of the consignment, and the name of the delivery driver. For our example we shall ignore these additional features.

12.4.1 System analysis

As usual, we start our design process at the top. Notice that we have been using the word "system". This may refer to one program, a suite of programs, or a combination of "software" (programs) and "hardware" (the pieces of equipment which constitute the computer itself). In the present case the system must comprise a suite of intercommunicating programs. We have tasks to perform at different times: stock levels must be updated weekly; reorder information may be changed at any time; the range of items stocked may be reduced or extended at any time. Communication between programs must be via external files.

The first step in our design process is to decide how many programs we shall need and what files they must access or construct. When designing one program we first consider the top-level structure to determine the procedures and parameters needed. We are doing the same thing for our stock control system but with programs in place of procedures.

It seems sensible to use at least two programs: one, run each week, to update the stock levels and issue reorders and another, run whenever necessary, to modify reorder information or change the range of items stocked. Both programs must have access to a file containing up-to-date stock information; this is called the "master file" and will be accessed within the programs as a read-only file. Each program must produce a new master file and so must be given a second file to use in write-mode. The stock update program must be supplied with details of the week's transactions. These could be supplied, in the order in which they become available, via the standard file *input*, but a moment's consideration of the nature of a sequential file suggests that this is inappropriate. Because a file cannot be scanned backwards several scans of the master file will be necessary unless the order in which the transactions are supplied is the same as that in which the stock items are stored. The best approach is to store stock items in some well-defined order (say, in ascending order of reference number) and to supply the stock update program with a sorted transaction file. This entails first presenting the transactions to a sort program. They can be supplied via *input* and a file must be provided to contain the sorted sequence. A similar approach can be adopted for the item modification program; rather than have the computer search through several thousand records each time we wish to change one it is better to store the modifications in a file (this is known as "batching") and then, before the next weekly update, perform all the modifications in one run.

On this basis, the system needs four programs:

program *SortTrans (input, output, sortedtrans)*
{produces a file of sorted transactions}
program *SortMods (input, output, sortedmods)*
{produces a file of sorted modifications}
program *StockUpdate (oldstock, newstock, nexttransaction, output)*
{produces an updated stock file}
program *ItemModify (oldstock, newstock, nextmod, output)*
{modifies reorder information or range of items stocked}

Notice that all the program parameter lists include *output*. This enables each program to report on the presence, or absence, of errors in the supplied data. In addition, each program should be supplied with a file to store all erroneous data. This data could then be corrected and resubmitted.

We focus our attention on the update program.

12.4.2 Stock updating

From our discussion of the situation so far we could probably define record types to represent items and transactions but, in general, the fields needed by a record may not be apparent until their processing is considered. So, in accordance with our philosophy of not doing things until we have to, we concentrate first on the overall structure of the program. Once the external files have been initialized the updating can commence but, in case the master file and the transaction file have not been supplied correctly, it is as well to first check that neither file is empty. The form of the program is illustrated in Figure 12.4.

Before we worry about the stock updating process we can incorporate *UpdateStock* as a dummy routine and test the overall program structure. We need give little concern to the data types *items* and *transactions*; we can make them both, say, *integer*. If we now write two simple programs, one to produce an integer file and one to print an integer file, we can test our system. We generate empty and non-empty integer files and supply various combinations to our update program and print the files produced, if any. By now your confidence (or, more important, your ability) may be such that you do not need to do this. Remember: the amount of program you generate or change at any one step must be governed by your ability to do it correctly!

We now turn our attention to updating the master file. As usual, we make a number of simplifications for our first attempt. We shall assume that each transaction concerns a different item and that each reference number quoted does correspond to an item stocked. We ignore consideration of reorder information and discontinued items.

For each transaction we must scan the master file (copying records to the new stock file) until we reach the record to be updated. According to whether the transaction denotes a sale or receipt of goods we then deduct

300

```
program StockUpdate (oldstock, newstock, nexttransaction, output);
  type
    items = ... ;
    transactions = ... ;
  var
    oldstock, newstock : file of items;
    nexttransaction : file of transactions;

  procedure CopyOldToNew;
  begin
    repeat
      write (newstock, oldstock↑);   get (oldstock)
    until eof (oldstock)
  end { Copy Old To New };

  procedure UpdateStock;
    ...

begin { program body }
  reset (nexttransaction); reset (oldstock); rewrite (newstock);
  if eof (oldstock) then
    writeln ('The master stock file is empty!')
  else
    if eof (nexttransaction) then
    begin
      writeln ('No transaction have been supplied');
      CopyOldToNew
    end else
    begin
      UpdateStock;
      writeln ('All transactions have been processed')
    end
end.
```

Figure 12.4

the quantity sold or add the quantity received. The updated record will be written to the new stock file when we scan for the next record to be updated. When all the transactions have been processed any remaining records in the master file must be copied to the new file.

A procedure implementing this is shown in Figure 12.5. The procedure *Seek* is to scan the master file copying records to the new file until the desired record is located, and the procedure *CopyOldToNew* is as in Figure

```
procedure UpdateStock;
    {  Assumes all reference numbers refer to items stocked.
       Assumes each transaction concerns a different item.
       Assumes all stock is current.
       Ignores reorder information. }
begin
  repeat
    with nexttransaction↑ do
    begin
      Seek (refno);
      with oldstock↑ do
      case saleorreceipt of
        sale    : qtyinstock := qtyinstock − qtysold;
        receipt : qtyinstock := qtyinstock + qtyreceived
      end { case }
    end { with nexttransaction↑ };

    get (nexttransaction)
  until eof (nexttransaction);

  CopyOldToNew
end { Update Stock }
```

Figure 12.5

12.4. Notice that the statement qualified by

with *nexttransaction*↑ **do**

must not include

get (nexttransaction)

This has the effect of assigning a new value to *nexttransaction*↑ but a variable quoted in a with-list must not be altered (bodily) within the qualified statement. For a similar reason the call

Seek (refno)

must not occur within the statement qualified by

with *oldstock*↑ **do**

Notice, too, that a suitable choice of file name, such as *nexttransaction*, can aid readability when the file is used, as with

get (nexttransaction)

Before we can test the procedure we must define *Seek* and supply an appropriate definition for *items* and *transactions*. The data structures we require are apparent from the processing we wish to perform:

```
const
    maxrefno = 10000;
    maxstock = 1000;
type
    refnos = 1 .. maxrefno;
    stocks = 0 .. maxstock;
    transtypes = (sale, receipt);
    items =
        record
            refno : refnos;
            qtyinstock : stocks
        end { items };
    transactions =
        record
            refno : refnos;
            case saleorreceipt : transtypes of
                sale   : (qtysold : stocks);
                receipt: (qtyreceived : stocks)
        end { transactions };
```

It might appear that there is little point in having a record variant within *transactions* when both variants have the same type; all we achieve is the use of different names for quantities sold and quantities received. However, as the program is expanded to cope with a more realistic environment it is likely that information representing a sale will differ from that representing a receipt. Refinement of the program will be easier if we introduce the variant now.

We can supply a simplified version of *Seek*. Rather than search the master file for a particular item it need only read the next record. We can now test our first draft of *UpdateStock* as soon as we have set up a master file and a transaction file and acquired the ability to print a master file. We can easily write three simple programs to do this; they are shown in Figures 12.6, 12.7, and 12.8. When we are satisfied with this suite of programs we can improve *Seek* (as in Figure 12.9) and test the update program again.

The program needs no refinement to cater for a sequence of transactions referring to the same item. Because *Seek* uses a while-loop it will read no records from the stock file if it is repeatedly called with the same parameter. So, if a batch of transactions is supplied for one item the stock record for that item will be successively updated. Nevertheless, our program will be improved if we process each batch with a repeat-loop within the present repeat-loop of *UpdateStock*. The fact that the program accepts batches of transactions will be explicit and future refinements concerning batches will

```
program SetUpTransFile (input, transfile, output);
  const
    maxrefno = 10000;
    maxstock = 1000;
  type
    refnos = 1 .. maxrefno;
    stocks = 0 .. maxstock;
    transtypes = (sale, receipt);
    transactions =
      record
        refno : refnos;
        case saleorreceipt : transtypes of
          sale    : (qtysold : stocks);
          receipt : (qtyreceived : stocks)
        end { transactions };
  var
    transfile : file of transactions;
    code      : 'R'..'S';

begin
  rewrite (transfile);
  repeat
    with transfile↑ do
    begin
      read (code, refno);
      case code of
        'S':
          begin
            saleorreceipt := sale; readln (qtysold)
          end;
        'R':
          begin
            saleorreceipt := receipt; readln (qtyreceived)
          end
      end { case }
    end { with transfile↑ };

    put (transfile)
  until eof (input);

  writeln ('Transaction file has been constructed')
end.
```

Figure 12.6

```
program SetUpMasterFile (input, output, master);
  const
    maxrefno = 10000;
    maxstock = 1000;
  type
    refnos 1 .. maxrefno;
    stocks = 0 .. maxstock;
    items =
      record
        refno : refnos;
        qtyinstock : stocks
      end { items};
  var
    master : file of items;

begin
  rewrite (master);
  repeat
    with master↑ do
      readln (refno, qtyinstock);
    put (master)
  until eof (input);

  writeln ('Master file has been constructed')
end.
```

Figure 12.7

be simplified. The inner loop is a three-state process terminating when either the end of the transaction file is reached or the item quoted by the incoming transaction is not the same as the one before. We introduce a variable

status : (sameitem, endofbatch, endoffile)

transform the original repeat-loop to

```
repeat
  Seek (nexttransaction↑.refno);
  status := sameitem;
  repeat
    with oldstock↑, nexttransaction↑ do
    case saleorreceipt of
      sale  :qtyinstock := qtyinstock − qtysold;
      receipt: qtyinstock := qtyinstock + qtyreceived
```

```
program PrintMasterFile (master, output);
    ... { as in Figure 12.7 }

begin
  reset (master);
  writeln (output, 'Ref. No      Qty in Stock');
  while not eof (master) do
  begin
    with master↑ do
      writeln (output, refno :6, qtyinstock :12);
    get(master)
  end;
  writeln ('End of master file')
end.
```

Figure 12.8

```
  end { case };

  get (nexttransaction);
  if eof (nexttransaction) then
    status := endoffile
  else
    if nexttransaction↑.refno < > oldstock↑.refno then
      status := endofbatch
until status <> sameitem

until eof (nexttransaction)
```

and run the program with a file of batched transactions.

To consider reorder information the program must check the updated stock level after each batch of transactions. We follow the inner repeat-loop

```
procedure Seek (n : refnos);
    { Assumes the desired reference no. is present. }
begin
  while oldstock↑.refno <> n do
  begin
    write (newstock, oldstock↑);  get (oldstock)
  end
end { Seek }
```

Figure 12.9

by

```
with oldstock↑ do
  if qtyinstock <= reorderlevel then
    Reorder (oldstock↑)
```

and indicate the need to reorder an item with a procedure of the form

```
procedure Reorder (item : items);
begin
  with item do
    writeln ('Reorder', reorderqty, ' of item', refno)
end { Reorder }
```

In a practical environment a file of orders would be constructed and a subsequent run of another program would print the order forms and even address the envelopes.

We must refine the definition of *items*:

```
items =
  record
    refno : refnos;
    qtyinstock, reorderlevel, reorderqty : stocks
  end
```

and modify the other programs in the suite appropriately before we can make a further test run.

To cater for discontinued items we introduce another field to *items*

```
itemiscurrent : boolean
```

and avoid reordering discontinued items:

```
with oldstock↑ do
  if itemiscurrent and (qtyinstock < = reorderlevel) then
    Reorder (oldstock↑)
```

To remove discontinued items the program moves on to the next stock record if the stock level of a discontinued item falls to zero:

```
if (oldstock↑.qtyinstock = 0) and not oldstock↑.itemiscurrent then
begin
  writeln ('item ', oldstock↑.refno : 6, ' is no longer stocked');
  get (oldstock)
end
{ the call get (oldstock) prohibits the use of with oldstock↑ do
  to prefix the if-statement }
```

Again, this modification must be reflected in other programs of the suite.

```
procedure UpdateStock;
   var
      status : (sameitem, endofbatch, endoffile);
      stocklevel : integer;
      success : boolean;
begin
  repeat
     Seek (nexttransaction↑.refno, success);
     if success then
     begin
        status := sameitem;
        stocklevel := oldstock↑.qtyinstock;
        repeat
           with nexttransaction↑ do
           case saleorreceipt of
              sale   : stocklevel := stocklevel − qtysold;
              receipt : stocklevel := stocklevel + qtyreceived
           end { case };
           get (nexttransaction);
           if eof (nexttransaction) then
              status := endoffile
           else
              if nexttransaction↑.refno <> oldstock↑.refno then
                 status := endofbatch
        until status <> sameitem;

        if (stocklevel >= 0) and (stocklevel <= maxstock) then
        begin
           with oldstock↑ do
              if itemiscurrent and (stocklevel <= reorderlevel) then
                 Reorder (oldstock↑);
              if (stocklevel = 0) and not oldstock↑.itemiscurrent then
              begin
                 writeln ('Item', oldstock↑.refno :6, ' is no longer stocked');
                 get (oldstock)
              end else
                 oldstock↑.qtyinstock := stocklevel
        end else
        begin
           writeln ('Item', oldstock↑.refno :6,
                    ' : updated stock level is in error');
           writeln (' Old stock record has not been updated')
        end
     end else
```

308

```
    begin
        writeln ('No stocked item has reference number ',
                nexttransaction↑.refno :6);
        get (nexttransaction)
    end
  until eof (nexttransaction);
  CopyOldToNew
end { Update Stock }
```

Figure 12.10

12.4.3   Data validation

Data output by one program and intended as input for another may be
known to be correct. All other input data must be checked. The sort
programs must check that each transaction or modification request is correctly supplied; they can then call sort routines which can assume that the
data is correct. The modification program must check that items to be
discontinued are currently stocked and that new items to be added are not.
The update program must ensure that each reference number quoted in the
transactions does correspond to a stocked item. Before writing a record to
the new stock file the new stock level must be guaranteed to be in the range
0 to 1,000. The simplest way to achieve this is to hold the stock level in a
local integer variable and write the updated record to the new stock file only

---

```
procedure Seek (n : refnos; var found : boolean);
  var
      state : (scanning, gotit, pastit, endoffile);
begin
  state := scanning;
  repeat
    if eof (oldstock) then state := endoffile else
      if oldstock↑.refno = n then state := gotit else
        if oldstock↑.refno > n then state := pastit else
        begin
            write (newstock, oldstock↑);   get (oldstock)
        end
  until state <> scanning;
  found := state = gotit
end { Seek }
```

Figure 12.11

if the new stock level is sensible. We can thus accommodate a value outside the desired subrange without the Pascal run-time system trapping the error and aborting execution. The modified update procedure is shown in Figure 12.10 and the revised version of *Seek* in Figure 12.11.

So far as our simplified stock control system is concerned the update program is now complete. We leave the development of the system at this stage. Implementation of the other programs is left as an exercise for the reader.

12.5 Exercises

†*1. Write a procedure to merge two integer files. Two files are supplied and each contains a sequence of integers in ascending order. A third file is to be produced and must contain all the supplied values in ascending order.

2. Extend the data validation program of Exercise 10.2.1 to construct a file in which each voter's preferences appear as a sequence of candidate numbers followed by 0. No consideration is to be given to any voter who votes for a candidate more than once or nominates a non-existent candidate.

*3. Modify the computer dating program of Exercise 10.2.3 so that appropriate information for all clients is held in an external file and each new client is introduced via *input*. In addition to producing a list of compatible partners for a new client the program is to extend the client file to include the newcomer.

*4. (a) Include the procedure of Exercise 11.4.4(b) within a program to construct an external file of cars.

(b) Write a program to print details of all available cars which might suit a customer. The customer specifies, via *input*, the minimum and maximum engine capacities to be considered, the highest insurance group tolerated, and the price limit.

5. Implement a simple text editor to edit an external textfile. The editor is to copy from one file to another subject to changes specified by commands supplied via *input*. Include at least the following commands:

CLα   Copy the next α lines.
CCα   Copy the next α characters.
DLα   Delete the next α lines.
DCα   Delete the next α characters.
Iβ...   Insert all text typed between this occurrence of the character β and the next; β may be any character absent from the text to be inserted.
CE   Copy to the end of the file.
DE   Delete the remainder of the file.

†6. Write a program which processes the vote file produced by the program of Exercise 2 and declares the outcome of the election. Assume there will be no more than five candidates.

Until a winner emerges {one candidate has an overall majority} or a tie is declared {all remaining candidates have an equal number of votes} votes are repeatedly counted and, each time, the candidate(s) with fewest votes is (are) eliminated. Votes cast for a candidate are ignored once the candidate has been eliminated. During a count, each voter is regarded as having voted for (at most) one candidate: the highest preference still eligible.

7. As outlined in Exercise 10.2.4 prime numbers may be generated using a device known as the sieve of Eratosthenes. Write three programs, each representing

310

the sieve differently, to produce all primes in the range *1* to *n* for arbitrary *n*. The representations to be used are

    file of *boolean,*
    file of *0 . . maxint,* and
    file of *sieves*

where *sieves* is the set type used for the solution to Exercise 10.2.4.

13

Arrays

An array is effectively a fixed-length, random-access local file. In common with a file, an array comprises a linear sequence of components all of the same type. For an array, there are no restrictions upon component type but the length of the sequence is fixed within the type definition. The fundamental difference between arrays and Pascal's sequential files lies in the access mechanisms. The concepts of read-mode and write-mode do not apply to an array and no access order is specified: any element may be accessed (and updated) by reference to its position in the sequence. Positions within the sequence are denoted by a sequence of ordinal values which constitute the "index type" of the array. One array element corresponds to each value of the index type.

In its simplest form an array type definition has the following form:

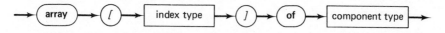

As already stated, the component type may be any type but the index type must be ordinal. Consider an example:

type
    days = *0 . . 31;*
    months = *(jan, feb, mar, apr, may, jun, jul, aug, sep, oct, nov, dec);*
var
    daysin : **array** *[months]* **of** *days;*

The index type of the array variable *daysin* is *months* and its component type is *days*. This means that *daysin* comprises twelve variables, each of type *days*.

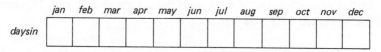

The mathematical name for such a construct is "vector". Each component variable is identified by "indexing" (the mathematical term is "subscripting") the array: the index (or subscript), enclosed between square brackets, follows the array name. So *daysin [jun]* and *daysin [dec]*, for example, are *days* variables and can be used just as any other *days* variable could be:

   daysin [jun]:= 30

and

   daysin [jul]:= daysin [jun]+1

are both valid assignment statements.

The power of arrays stems from the fact that a subscript may be any expression whose type is compatible with the declared index type:

   daysin [succ (nov)]:= daysin [pred (pred (may))]

is a valid assignment. Naturally, if the index type is a subrange type the value of the subscript must fall within range. For the type

   summermonths = jun . . aug

and variables

   summerholidaysin : **array** *[summermonths]* **of** *days*

and

   m : months

the expression

   summerholidaysin [m]

is legal only if the value of *m* lies in the subrange *jun . . aug.*

Use of a named type as the index type of an array is not mandatory but is good programming practice. We shall usually adopt this convention.

Example 13.1

Write a program to produce a frequency count of all letters occurring in a piece of English text.   □

This entails keeping a count for each of the twenty-six letters of the alphabet. We must examine each character of the text and, if it is a letter, increment the appropriate count. We could use twenty-six explicitly-named variables and perform the count update with a 26-limb case-statement, but the process is much neater if we record the counts in an array. The program is given in Figure 13.1.   ■

Notice how the processing performed upon an array governs the choice of the array name. In a context where an array is processed bodily, as in

   Construct (lettercounts)

```pascal
program LetterFrequencies (input, output);
    { Constructs a frequency count of upper case letters occurring
      in the data. }
  type
    letters = 'A' .. 'Z';
    frequencies = 0 .. maxint;
    freqcounts = array [letters] of frequencies;
  var
    lettercounts : freqcounts;


  procedure Construct (var occurrencesof : freqcounts);
    var
      thisletter : letters;
      alphabet : set of letters;
  begin
    for thisletter := 'A' to 'Z' do
      occurrencesof [thisletter] := 0;
    alphabet := ['A' .. 'Z'];      { Assumes A to Z are contiguous. }

    while not eof (input) do
    begin
      if input↑ in alphabet then
        occurrencesof [input↑] := occurrencesof [input↑] + 1;
      get (input)
    end
  end { Construct };


  procedure Display (var occurrencesof : freqcounts);
    var
      letter : letters;
  begin
    writeln ('Letter   Occurrences');
    for letter := 'A' to 'Z' do
      writeln (letter :4, occurrencesof [letter] :12)
  end { Display };


begin { program body }
  Construct (lettercounts);  Display (lettercounts)
end.
```

Figure 13.1   Example 13.1

we choose a name which implies the whole collection that the array represents; in a context where reference is made to individual elements, such as

occurrencesof [thisletter] := 0

we choose a name which implies one element and choose names for subscripts in conjunction.

Example 13.2

The decoding program of Figure 7.8 performs a mapping from one set of values {characters} to another {letters, digits, and question mark}. A vector often provides the neatest implementation of such a mapping. □

We store digit codes in one vector and letter codes in another and initialize both before the decoding process is entered. Initialization involves a process similar to the decoding process of the original program but, whereas the original program does this for every non-blank character of the input, our new approach does it thirty-six times {once for each decimal digit and once for each letter of the alphabet}. The decoding process for each significant character is now achieved by one array access. The saving would be significant for large volumes of input. The program is given in Figure 13.2. ■

Example 13.3

In Example 10.5, the card playing program of Figure 9.12 was modified to check for duplicated cards. Cards dealt were recorded in four sets {*clubsdealt, diamondsdealt, heartsdealt,* and *spadesdealt*} and a case-statement {line 60 of Figure 10.2} selected an appropriate set. We can replace the four explicit sets by an array of four sets:

dealt : **array** *[suits]* **of** *dealsets*

where *suits* is the symbolic type

(clubs, diamonds, hearts, spades)

and perform the selection with a subscript *suit,* of type *suits,* declared local to *ReadaCard.* □
Lines 60 to 65 of Figure 10.2 become

```
begin
    suit := suitwithinitial (input↑);
    CheckDuplicate (rank, dealt [suit], cardtype)
end else
```

and the function *suitwithinitial* could, of course, use an array to map the letters *C, D, H,* and *S* on to the four suits. Later in the program {lines 75 to 78} taxonomy of court cards can now be made more transparent by using

```
program DecodeWithArrays (input, output);
    { Decoding process for one character :-
    [0, 1, . . . , 9] < - > [9, 8, . . . , 0]
    [A, E, I, O, U] < - > [B, F, J, P, V]
   [C, G, K, Q, W] < - > [D, H, L, R, X]
        [M, S, Y] < - > [N, T, Z]
      Everything else → ? }
const
   space = ' ';  query = '?';
type
   digits = '0' .. '9';
   letters = 'A' .. 'Z';
var
   digitchars : set of digits;
   alphabet : set of letters;
   dcodeof : array [digits] of digits;
   lcodeof : array [letters] of letters;

procedure Decode (ch : char);
begin
   if ch in alphabet then write (lcodeof [ch]) else
      if ch in digitchars then write (dcodeof [ch]) else
      write (query)
end { Decode };

procedure DecodeWord;
begin
   repeat
      Decode (input↑);  get (input)
   until input↑ = space
and { Decode Word };

procedure SetUpCodesDigitcharsAndAlphabet;
   var
      d, dcode : digits;
      l : letters;
      vowels : set of 'A' .. 'U';
begin
   digitchars := ['0' .. '9'];
   alphabet := ['A' .. 'Z'];
   vowels := ['A', 'E', 'I', 'O', 'U'];

   dcode := '9';  dcodeof ['0'] := '9';
   for d := '1' to '9' do
```

```
    begin
      dcode := pred (dcode);   dcodeof [d] := dcode
    end;


    for l := 'A' to 'Z' do
      if l in vowels then lcodeof [l] := succ(l) else
       if pred (l) in vowels then lcodeof [l] := pred(l) else
        if pred(pred(l)) in vowels then lcodeof [l] := succ(l) else
         if pred(pred(pred(l))) in vowels then lcodeof [l] := pred (l) else
          if l in ['M', 'S', 'Y'] then lcodeof[l] := succ (l) else
           lcodeof[l] := pred(l)
  end { Set Up Codes Digitchars And Alphabet };


  procedure SquashSpaces;
  begin
    if (input↑ = space) and not eoln then
    begin
      write (space);
      repeat
        get (input)
      until eoln or (input↑ <> space)
    end
  end { Squash Spaces };


begin { program body }
  if eof then
    writeln ('No message has been supplied') else
  begin
    SetUpCodesDigitcharsAndAlphabet;
    repeat
      SquashSpaces;
      while not eoln do
      begin
        DecodeWord; SquashSpaces
      end;
      readln; writeln
    until eof
  end
end.
```

Figure 13.2   Example 13.2

```
procedure PrintOctal (n : integer);
  const
    maxoctallength = 10;
  var
    octaldigit : array [1 .. maxoctallength] of 0 .. 7;
    i : 0 .. maxoctallength;
begin
  if n = 0 then writeln (0 : 1) else
  begin
    if n < 0 then
    begin
      write ('-');   n := -n
    end;
    i := 0;
    repeat
      i := i + 1;
      octaldigit [i] :=n mod 8;
      n := n div 8
    until n = 0;
    for i := i downto 1 do
      write (octaldigit [i] :1);
    writeln
  end
end { Print Octal }
```

Figure 13.3   Example 13.4

the value of *suit*:

```
case suit of
  hearts, diamonds : card := redcourt;
  clubs, spades    : card := blackcourt
end {case}   ■
```

Example 13.4

The programs developed in Examples 6.7 and 7.6 both print an integer in octal form. Arrays provide a third alternative. If a positive integer is repeatedly divided by 8 the remainders are the digits of its octal representation produced in reverse order. They can be stored as consecutive elements of an array and then printed in the appropriate order.   □

The procedure of Figure 13.3 does this.   ■

Example 13.5

The frequency sort program of Figure 12.3 uses two files *(obsfile1* and *obsfile2)* and supplies them in the appropriate order to two calls of *MoveAllButTheSmallest.* One call would suffice if we were to use an array of files and supply appropriate subscripts to select individual files. □

In the variable declaration part of the program we would replace the two explicit files by an array of two files

>   *obs* : **array** *[0 . . 1]* **of** *obsfiles*

and the program body would become

```
begin
    ReadObservations (obs[1], sizeofsample);
    for scan := 1 to sizeofsample do
        MoveAllButTheSmallest (obs [scan mod 2], obs [(scan + 1) mod 2],
                                            scan);
    writeln
end.
```

We *could* do this but it would hardly be worthwhile; the original program is more transparent so we should stick to it! ■

Example 13.6

Returning again to the program of Figure 12.3 we see that a bound is quoted for the number of observations. We can therefore store the observations in an array rather than a file:

>   *obs* : **array** *[samplesizes]* **of** *observations*

Because an array can be updated in situ we need not repeatedly transfer records from one array to another; we can sort the records within one array. We modify our algorithm accordingly. □

We can separate the two logically distinct processes: sorting and printing. When sorting the array we commence each scan at the position after that at which the previous scan commenced and thereby examine one element fewer each time. During a scan we ensure that the smallest value encountered during that scan is located at the left-hand end of the portion of the array covered by the scan: if we find a value smaller than that currently sitting at the left-hand end, we interchange the two. This removes the current smallest from future consideration because, when the scan is completed, this value is now in part of the array which will not be accessed during subsequent scans. The process is described as an "exchange" sort.

The program body is

```
begin
    Collect (theobservations);
    Sort (theobservations);
    Print (theobservations)
end
```

Often, not all the elements of an array are used. This is so here: the number of array elements allocated is *maxobs* but the number of observations supplied is probably fewer. Consequently, we often wish to associate with an array the number of elements currently in use. This immediately suggests use of a record. The variable *theobservations* is a record containing the observations and their number.

The complete program is given in Figure 13.4. The parameters of *Collect* and *Sort* must be transferred as variables because the values of their components are going to change. The procedure *Print*, on the other hand, should take a value parameter. As was mentioned in Chapter 11, copying a large parameter (such as an array of a thousand or more records) incurs a significant overhead, so efficiency considerations encourage the use of a variable parameter. ■

Example 13.7

The case study of Chapter 12 demonstrated the need to search a file for some specified component. The sequential nature of a file permits only linear search: we scan from left to right until we locate the desired item or, as in the procedure *Seek* of Figure 12.11, we discover that the item is absent. We often need to search an array but, because of the ability to access array elements randomly, we can devise more sophisticated searching techniques. If the elements of an array are unordered then we may have to resort to linear search, but if the elements are stored in some particular order we can use this fact to our advantage. If elements are stored in ascending order, as is achieved by the program of Figure 13.4, we can apply a method called "binary chopping". □

We examine the entry positioned at the middle of the sequence: if the length of the sequence is odd there is a unique middle entry; if the length is even we take the value immediately to the left of centre. If this is the value we seek we terminate the search; if not, we compare it with the value we seek. Because the elements in the array are ordered, the comparison tells us which half of the sequence will contain the desired value, if it is present. If the desired value is less than the value currently examined it must lie in the first half; if not, it must lie in the second. We have effectively chopped the array in two: we need now consider only one half. We apply the same approach to the appropriate half of the array and repeat this process, considering a smaller section of the array each time, until either we locate the desired entry or we "exhaust" the search. {We have chopped the table so much that there is nothing left!}

This technique can be applied to any component type for which an ordering can be defined. In particular, this can be any ordinal type, string type (see Section 13.1), or record type with a field of either of these types. A procedure to apply a binary search to an array with components of ordinal

```
program SortFreqsWithAnArray (input, output);
  const
    maxfreq = 500; maxobs = 2000; maxaltitude = 1000;
    noperline = 5;
  type
    frequencies = 0 .. maxfreq;
    samplesizes = 0 .. maxobs;
    altitudes = 0 .. maxaltitude;
    observations =
      record
        freq : frequencies;
        alt : altitudes
      end { observations };
    obscollections =
      record
        obs : array [samplesizes] of observations;
        noofobs : samplesizes
      end { obs collections };
  var
    theobservations : obscollections;

  procedure Collect (var theobs : obscollections);
    var
      obscount : samplesizes;
  begin
    obscount := 0;
    with theobs do
    begin
      repeat
        obscount := obscount + 1;
        with obs [obscount] do
          readln (freq, alt)
      until eof;
      noofobs := obscount
    end { with the obs }
  end { Collect };

  procedure Print (var theobs : obscollections);
    var
      ob : samplesizes;
  begin
    with theobs do
    begin
      for ob := 1 to noofobs do
```

```
      begin
        with obs[ob] do
          write (freq :4, ' (', alt :4, ') ');
        if ob mod noperline = 0 then
          writeln
      end { for ob }
    end { with theobs };
    writeln
  end { Print };

  procedure Sort (var theobs : obscollections);
    var
      first, ob : samplesizes;
      smallobs : observations;
  begin
    with theobs do
    begin
      for first := 1 to noofobs − 1 do
      begin
        smallobs := obs [first];
        for ob := first + 1 to noofobs do
          if obs[ob].freq < smallobs.freq then
          begin
            obs[first] := obs[ob];   obs[ob] := smallobs;
            smallobs := obs[first]
          end
      end { for first }
    end { with the obs }
  end { Sort };

begin { program body }
  Collect (theobservations);
  Sort (theobservations);
  Print (theobservations)
end.
```

Figure 13.4   Example 13.6

---

or string type is shown in Figure 13.5. It assumes the following environment:

```
const
    endoftable = ... ;
type
    span = 1 .. endoftable;
    things = ... ;
    thingtable = array [span] of things;
```

```
    procedure BinChopSearch ( itemwanted : things; var itemat : thingtable;
        var present : boolean; var position : span);
    var
        bottom, middle, top : span;
        state : (stillchopping, foundattop, foundatmiddle, givenup);
    begin
        bottom := 1; top := endoftable; state := stillchopping;
        repeat
            if top = bottom then
                case itemat [top] = itemwanted of
                    true : state := foundattop;
                    false : state := givenup;
                end { case } else
            begin
                middle := (top + bottom) div 2;
                if itemwanted < itemat [middle] then top := middle - 1 else
                    if itemwanted > itemat [middle] then
                        bottom := middle + 1
                    else
                        state := foundatmiddle
            end
        until state <> stillchopping;

        present := state in [foundattop, foundatmiddle];

        if present then
            case state of
                foundattop    : position := top;
                foundatmiddle : position := middle
            end { case }
    end { Bin Chop Search }
```

Figure 13.5   Example 13.7

and searches the whole array. Incorporation of an additional parameter (the position of the last array slot occupied) would permit the procedure to be applied to an array which is not full. Notice the order in which comparisons with the middle entry are made. To be most aesthetically pleasing one of the first tests a program should make in a search loop is "Is what I'm looking at what I want?". However, for binary search, efficiency suffers if we test equality before we test relative magnitude. This is because, in general, we will hit elements we do not want far more often than we hit an element we do want. Consequently, for about half of our probes, we should know which marker (top or bottom) to move after making only one comparison. It is immaterial which one of the two other tests we then make. ∎

Those of you who are mathematically minded will be interested to observe that the expected number of accesses needed to locate an arbitrary entry within a sequence of length n is of the order of $n/2$ for linear search and of the order of log_2n for binary chopping. As n gets larger, so does the difference between $n/2$ and log_2n. The saving achieved by binary chopping is highlighted by considering a few sample values:

n	$n/2$	log_2n
2	1	1
8	4	3
32	16	5
128	64	7
1,024	512	10
32,768	16,384	15

For large n the difference is quite staggering, isn't it? What might surprise you even more is that methods significantly better than binary chopping exist, particularly for "dynamic" tables where new entries are continually being added. So, if a program frequently needs to search for entries in an array, then, unless the number of entries to be searched is small, or the entry sought will almost always be near the front, or the sought entries are batched {as were the transactions for the stock update program in Case Study 4}, or ascending order is expensive to maintain {perhaps because new entries are being added and old ones removed}, you will not use linear search, will you? The best access technique for arrays and any other random access files utilize "hash tables". Description of these is beyond the scope of this book, but if you are a serious programmer you must learn of them.

Example 13.8

Preliminary discussion of the stock control system of Case Study 4 suggested that an English description of each stocked item might be recorded. A description can be stored as an array of characters. □

```
const
    maxdescriptionlength = 30;
type
    desclengths = 1 .. maxdescriptionlength;
    descriptions = array [desclengths] of char;
    ...
    items =
    record
        refno : refnos;
        name : descriptions;
        qtyinstock, reorderlevel, reorderqty : stocks;
```

> *itemiscurrent : boolean*
> **end** *{ items }*

Rather than record the number of significant characters in a name we can simply space-fill to the right. Printing the name of an item is straightforward:

> **procedure** *Describe (this : description);*
>   **var**
>   *ch : desclengths;*
> **begin**
>   **for** *ch : = 1* **to** *maxdescriptionlength* **do**
>   *write (this [ch]);*
>   *writeln*
> **end** *{ Describe }* ∎

Relational operators cannot be applied to arrays {other than strings; see Section 13.1} but assignment is permitted. An array may be bodily assigned to an array variable of an identical type. An item's description could be changed by array assignment:

> **var**
>   *newname : descriptions;*
>   *item : items;*
> . . .
> *item.name : = newname*

13.1 Packed arrays and strings

Arrays, like records, may be packed. The reserved word **packed** precedes **array** in the declaration. Each component of an array will, itself, be packed only if the component type is a packed type. Two predefined procedures *pack* and *unpack* exist. For two arrays

> *a* : **array** *[b1 .. b2]* **of** *t*

and

> *pa* : **packed array** *[pb1 .. pb2]* **of** *t*

with identical component type *t*, the statement

> *pack (a, i, pa)*

packs successive elements $a[i]$, $a[succ(i)]$, . . . into *pa* until *pa* is full, and the statement

> *unpack (pa, a, i)*

unpacks the whole of *pa* into successive elements $a[i]$, $a[succ(i)]$, ... Consequent constraints are that the array *a* must not be declared to have fewer elements than *pa* and *i* must be in the range *b1* to *b2* and such that processing does not "fall off the end of" *a*. Expressed mathematically, the constraint on *i* is

$$ord(b1) \le ord(i) \le ord(b2) - ord(pb2) + ord(pb1)$$

Data stored in an array should be held in packed form when the array is being processed bodily, with perhaps the occasional reference to components. Data should not usually be in packed form if repeated reference is being made to components.

In the data structure described in Example 13.8 item descriptions should be packed because reference is unlikely to be made to individual characters:

descriptions = **packed array** *[desclengths]* **of** *char*

An exception to this would be the reading of a description from a textfile (*input*, say). It must be read one character at a time and this entails repeated component accesses. Efficiency may be improved, therefore, if the characters are read into an unpacked array and then packed into the record:

```
var
    item : items;
    here : desclengths;
    namech : array [desclengths] of char;
. . .
for here := 1 to maxdescriptionlength do
    read (namech [here]);
pack (namech, 1, item.name).
```

Strings as described in Chapter 1 are (constant) packed arrays of characters. The implied index type is the integer subrange 1 to the length of the string, but a string constant must not be subscripted. A packed character array variable whose index type is an integer subrange with the lower bound 1 is called a string variable. String variables share features common to other arrays and, in addition, string constants may be assigned to them, two strings may be compared by applying the usual relational operators (ordering is dependent upon the underlying character set) and a string may be supplied as a parameter to *write* or *writeln*.

If the *name* field of an item is of string type the procedure *Describe* is not needed. The name may be written directly:

writeln (item.name)

If we wish to suppress the trailing spaces (at the right-hand end of the description) we can store the description in a record and incorporate its length:

```
descriptions =
    record
        title : packed array [desclengths] of char;
```

326

```
    length : desclengths
  end { descriptions }
```

A name is then written using formatted output:

```
  with item.name do
    write (title : length)
```

If strings are compared or assigned, the type of the variables or constants involved must be identical. This implies that, if a string constant is assigned to a string variable, extra spaces may be needed:

```
  with item.name do
    begin
      title : = 'Nurdling Flange Mk 2          ';
          { a description must contain 30 characters }
      length : = 20
    end
```

Example 13.9

When a program is run from a terminal a common requirement is for the program to repeat some process *P* until the user tires of this.   □

After each execution of *P* the program must ask the user whether or not processing is to continue:

```
  type
    replies = packed array [1 .. 3] of char;
  var
    reply : replies;
    . . .
  repeat
    P;   writeln ('Would you like another go?');
    Accept (reply)
  until reply = 'NO '
```

A more sophisiticated approach is

```
  var
    reply : replies;
    sensiblereplygiven : boolean;
    . . .
  repeat
    P;   writeln ('Would you like another go?');
    Accept (reply, sensiblereplygiven);
    while not sensiblereplygiven do
    begin
      writeln ('Pardon?');   readln;
      Accept (reply, sensiblereplygiven)
```

```
        end
   until reply = 'NO   '
```

or even

```
   type
      attempts = 1 .. maxint;
      . . .

   var
      reply : replies;
      sensiblereplygiven : boolean;
      attempt : attempts;

   procedure Criticize (this : attempts);
      const
         noofmessages = 6;
   begin
      case this mod noofmessages of
         1 : writeln ('Pardon?');
         2 : writeln ('What?');
         3 : writeln ('Eh?');
         4 : writeln ('I still don"t understand');
         5 : writeln ('Are you using rude words?');
         0 : begin
               writeln ('I"m getting sick of this : I"ll ask you again');
               writeln ('Would you like another go?')
             end
      end { case }
   end { Criticize };
   . . .

   repeat
      P;   writeln ('Would you like another go?');
      attempt := 1;   Accept (reply, sensiblereplygiven);
      while not sensiblereplygiven do
      begin
         Criticize (attempt);   readln;
         attempt := attempt + 1;   Accept (reply, sensiblereplygiven)
      end;
      if attempt > 3 then
         writeln ('Sense at last—Thank You!')
   until reply = 'NO   '   ∎
```

13.2 Multi-dimensional arrays

When the component type of an array is, itself, an array type the array is said
to be multi-dimensional. This term is used because we can picture the data

328

structure in several dimensions. Assume the existence of the types

> *months = (jan, feb, mar, apr, may, jun, jul, aug, sep, oct, nov, dec)*
> *years = 1976 .. 1980*
> *rainfalls = real*

and

> *monthlyrains =* **array** *[months]* **of** *rainfalls*

The data type

> *rainfigures =* **array** *[years]* **of** *monthlyrains*

can be pictured as a two-dimensional table:

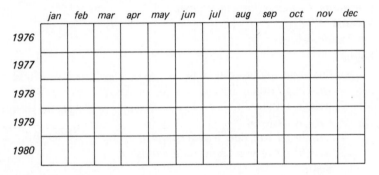

with five rows {*1976, 1977, . . . , 1980*} and twelve columns {*jan, feb, . . . , dec*}.
For variables

> y : *years*
> m : *months*

and

> *rain : rainfigures*

> *rain [y]*

is a vector of twelve real variables representing the monthly rainfalls for the
year y, and

> *rain [y] [m]*

is one element of this vector and, hence, a single real variable representing
the rainfall for month *m* of year *y*. Because such doubly subscripted
expressions are common when two-dimensional arrays are used Pascal
permits an abbreviated form. The expression

> *rain [y] [m]*

may be written

> *rain [y, m]*

The principle extends to more dimensions. If the data type *rainfalls* were, itself, an array type, a structure of type *rainfigures* would be three-dimensional. If we include types

> *days* = *1 . . 31*
> *dailyrains* = *real*
> *rainfalls* = **array** *[days]* **of** *dailyrains*

and introduce a variable

> *d : days*

the following expressions are equivalent

> *rain [y, m, d]*
> *rain [y, m] [d]*
> *rain [y] [m, d]*
> *rain [y] [m] [d]*

The first form is the simplest but other forms can be useful on occasions to emphasize a particular interpretation of the structure.

If intermediate array types need not be named, a shorthand notation is available for the declaration of multi-dimensional arrays. The structure of the data type *rainfigures* would have been the same if the declaration had been written

> *rainfigures* = **array** *[years, months, days]* **of** *rainfalls*

Of course, the type of *rain [y]* would not be *monthlyrains*; it would be a distinct type displaying the same structure. It would be impossible, therefore, to supply *rain [y]* as an actual parameter because the corresponding formal parameter must be given a named type and the type of *rain [y]* is not named. Consequently, the shorthand notation for array declarations is of little use if we wish to process subarrays. A term often applied to mean breaking a multi-dimensional array into constituent arrays is "slicing". If we picture a two-dimensional structure as illustrated on page 328, it will be apparent that Pascal arrays can be sliced row-wise only. The speed of machine code access to an array element is proportional to the number of subscripts supplied, so passing a slice of an array to a procedure can increase run-time efficiency.

Notice the effect of **packed** within an abbreviated array declaration:

> **packed array** *[days, 1 . . 9]* **of** *char*

is effectively the same as

> **packed array** *[days]* **of packed array** *[1 . . 9]* **of** *char*

which is not the same as

> **packed array** *[days]* **of array** *[1 . . 9]* **of** *char*

330

Example 13.10

Assuming the following environment:

const
    earliestyear = 1900;   mostrecentyear = 1980;

type
    years = earlierstyear . . mostrecentyear;
    months = (jan, feb, mar, apr, may, jun, jul, aug, sep, oct, nov, dec);
    yearlyrains = **array** *[months]* **of** *real;*
    rainfigures = **array** *[years]* **of** *yearlyrains;*

write

1. a procedure to determine the wettest month of the recorded period,
2. a function to determine which month of the year was the wettest on average, and
3. a function to deliver the wettest year. ☐

1. This entails scanning the entire table to locate the maximum value it contains. The procedure of Figure 13.6 does this. By initializing *maxrain* to a value less than any that will be present in the array we ensure that

```
procedure FindWettestMonth
    (var rain : rainfigures; var month : months; var year : years);
  var
    maxrain : real;
    wetmonth, m : months;
    wetyear, y : years;
begin
  maxrain := -1;
  for y := earliestyear to mostrecentyear do
    for m := jan to dec do
      if rain [y, m] > maxrain then
      begin
        maxrain := rain [y, m];
        wetyear := y;      wetmonth := m
      end;
  month := wetmonth;      year := wetyear
end { Find Wettest Month }
```

Figure 13.6   Example 13.10, part 1

```
procedure FindWettestMonth
    (var rain : rainfigures; var month : months; var year : years);

var
    thisyear, wetyear : years;
    wetmonth, wettestmonth : months;
    fall, maxfallsofar : real;

    procedure GetWettestMonthThisYear (raininmonth : yearlyrains;
        var month : months; var fallinthismonth : real);
        var
        maxsofar : real;
        m, wetmonth : months;
    begin
        maxsofar := -1;
        for m := jan to dec do
        if raininmonth [m] > maxsofar then
        begin
            wetmonth :=m;    maxsofar := raininmonth [m]
        end;
        month := wetmonth;    fallinthismonth := maxsofar
    end { Get Wettest Month This Year };

begin { Find Wettest Month }
    masfallsofar := -1;
    for thisyear := earliestyear to mostrecentyear do
    begin
        GetWettestMonthThisYear (rain [thisyear], wetmonth, fall);
        if fall > maxfallsofar then
        begin
            wettestmonth := wetmonth;    wetyear := thisyear;
            maxfallsofar := fall
        end
    end;
    year := wetyear;    month := wettestmonth
end { Find Wettest Month }
```

Figure 13.7   Example 13.10, part 1

the first execution of the if-statement will perform the assignments

maxrain := rain [earliestyear, jan]
wetyear := earliestyear
wetmonth := jan

In this particular solution the table is searched row-wise: all the months for one year are examined before the next year is considered. The program would work equally well with column-wise scanning: the same month would be examined for every year before the next month is considered. To achieve column-wise scanning we interchange the for-loops:

for *m* := *jan* **to** *dec* **do**
  for *y* := *earliestyear* **to** *mostrecentyear* **do** . . .

If we stick to row-wise scanning we can process each year (each row) as a slice. The procedure of Figure 13.7 does this.

2. The month which is the wettest on average will be that month with the

---

```
function monthwithmaxtotal (var rain : rainfigures) : months;
  var
    month, wettestmonth : months;
    monthsrain, mostrainsofar : real;

  function totalin (m : months) : real;
    var
      year : years;
      total : real;
  begin
    total := 0;
    for year := earliestyear to mostrecentyear do
      total := total + rain [year, m];
    totalin := total
  end { total in };

begin { month with max total }
  mostrainsofar := −1;
  for month := jan to dec do
  begin
    monthsrain := totalin (month);
    if monthsrain > mostrainsofar then
    begin
      mostrainsofar := monthsrain;      wettestmonth := month
    end
  end;
  monthwithmaxtotal := wettestmonth
end { month with max total };
```

Figure 13.8   Example 13.10, part 2

```
function yearwithmaxtotal (var rain : rainfigures) : years;
  var
    y, wetyear : years;
    yearsrain, maxyet : real;

  function totalinyear (raininmonth : yearlyrains) : real;
    var
      total : real;
      m : months;
  begin
    total := 0;
    for m := jan to dec do
      total := total + raininmonth [m];
    totalinyear := total
  end { total in year };

begin { year with max total }
  maxyet := -1;
  for y := earliestyear to mostrecentyear do
  begin
    yearsrain := totalinyear (rain [y]);
    if yearsrain > maxyet then
    begin
      maxyet := yearsrain;      wetyear := y
    end
  end;
  yearwithmaxtotal := wetyear
end { year with max total }
```

Figure 13.9   Example 13.10, part 3

highest accumulated rainfall for the whole period. We need to scan the columns of our table. The function is given in Figure 13.8.

3. We need to scan the rows of the table. The function of Figure 13.9 does this with slicing. ■

Now an example for mathematicians.

Example 13.11

Arrays provide a natural representation of vectors and matrices:

```
const
  n = ... ; m = ... ;
```

type
> *oneton* = $1 .. n$;
> *onetom* = $1 .. m$;
> *nvectors* = **array** *[oneton]* **of** *real*;
> *mvectors* = **array** *[onetom]* **of** *real*;
> *nbymmatrices* = **array** *[oneton]* **of** *mvectors*;
> *mbynmatrices* = **array** *[onetom]* **of** *nvectors*;
> *nbynmatrices* = **array** *[oneton]* **of** *nvectors*.

We consider the computation of

1. the dot product of two vectors,
2. the cross product of two vectors,
3. the transpose of a matrix, and
4. the product of two matrices. ☐

1. In the usual mathematical notation, the dot (or scalar) product of two n-vectors **u** and **v** is

$$\mathbf{u \cdot v} = \sum_{i=1}^{n} u_i v_i$$

```
function dotproduct (var u, v : nvectors) : real;
  var
    i : oneton;
    sum : real;
begin
  sum := 0;
  for i := 1 to n do
    sum := sum + u[i] * v[i];
  dotproduct := sum
end { dot product }
```

2. The cross (or vector) product of an n-vector **u** and an m-vector **v** is the $n \times m$ matrix **A** defined such that $A_{ij} = u_i v_j$:

```
procedure FormCrossProduct (var u : nvectors; var v : mvectors;
                            var a : nbymmatrices);
  var
    i : oneton;
    j : onetom;
begin
  for i := 1 to n do
    for j := 1 to m do
      a[i, j] := u[i] * v[j]
end { Form Cross Product }
```

3. The transpose of a matrix **A** is a matrix **B** defined such that $B_{ij} = A_{ji}$. If we wish to retain the original matrix we must have a second array

available in which to produce the transpose;

```
procedure FormTranspose (var  a : nybmmatrices;
                         var   atran : mbynmatrices);
   var
     i : oneton;
     j : onetom;
   begin
     for i : = 1 to n do
       for j : = 1 to m do
         atran [i, j] : = a[j, i]
   end { Form Transpose }
```

If the original matrix is square and is to be replaced by its transpose we
can perform the transposition in situ:

```
procedure Transpose (var a : nbynmatrices);
   var
     i, j : oneton;
     aij : real;
   begin
     for i : = 1 to n − 1 do
       for j : = i + 1 to n do
       begin { interchange a[i, j] and a[j, i] }
         aij : = a[i, j];   a[i, j] : = a[j, i];   a[j, i] : = aij
       end
   end { Transpose }
```

4. The product of two matrices $\mathbf{A}(n \times m)$ and $\mathbf{B}(m \times n)$ is a matrix $\mathbf{C}(n \times n)$
defined such that the element C_{ij} is the dot product of the ith row-vector
of $\mathbf{A}$ with the jth column-vector of $\mathbf{B}$:

$$C_{ij} = \sum_{k=1}^{m} A_{ik}B_{kj}$$

Ignoring the possibility of slicing we can model a solution directly on this
formula:

```
procedure FormProduct (var  a : nbymmatrices;  var  b : mbynmatrices;
                       var  c : nbynmatrices);
   var
     i, j  : oneton;
     k  : onetom;
     sum  : real;
   begin
     for i : = 1 to n do
       for j : = 1 to n do
```

```
begin { form dot product of ith row of a with jth column of b }
  sum : = 0;
  for k : = 1 to m do
    sum : = sum + a[i, k] * b[k, j];
  c[i, j] : = sum
end
end { Form Product }
```

We can slice a to produce its ith row $a[i]$, but we cannot directly extract the jth column of b:

```
function  dotprod (var  u : mvectors; var  b : mbynmatrices;
                          col : oneton) : real;
  var
    i : onetom;
    sum : real;
begin
  sum : = 0;
  for i : = 1 to m do
    sum : = sum + u[i] * b[i, col];
  dotprod : = sum
end { dot prod }
```

The neatest solution arises if the transpose $(\mathbf{B}^T)$ of $\mathbf{B}$ is available. The value C_{ij} is then the dot product of the ith row-vector of $\mathbf{A}$ with the jth row-vector of $\mathbf{B}^T$, and so we can use the function defined in part 1. We could, of course, transpose $\mathbf{B}$ inside the product procedure but this extra computation would produce an inefficient solution. The following procedure does this for square matrices and performs the transposition in situ:

```
procedure FormSquareProduct (var a : nbynmatrices; b : nbynmatrices;
                             var c : nbynmatrices);
  var
    i, j : oneton;
begin
  Transpose (b);   { this is the second procedure of part 3 }
  for i : = 1 to n do
    for j : = 1 to n do
      c[i, j] : = dotproduct (a[i], b[j])
end { Form Square Product }
```

Notice that b is transferred as a value parameter. This is so that a local copy will be constructed and it is this local copy which is transposed; the actual parameter remains uncorrupted. ∎

Example 13.12

The Case Study of Section 8.1 illustrated some problems of drawing pictures on a device which can print only left-to-right and top-to-bottom. These can be overcome if we represent the "screen" as a two-dimensional array. We build up our picture in any order we choose and, only when it is complete, print it row by row. □

Mathematicians identify matrix elements in the same way as we did rainfall values, by labelling rows in order from top to bottom and columns from left to right. To identify print positions on our screen it is more convenient to adopt the usual $x-y$ cartesian coordinate system with rows numbered (from zero) from bottom to top and columns (from zero) from left to right.

const
    screenheight = ... ;   *screenwidth* = ... ;
type
    heights = *0 .. screenheight;*
    widths = *0 .. screenwidth;*
    screencols = **array** *[heights]* **of** *char;*
var
    screen : **array** *[widths]* **of** *screencols;*

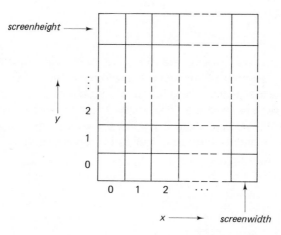

We clear the screen by making every element of *screen* the space character. We then draw our picture by overwriting spaces by other characters at appropriate points. When the picture is complete we print the screen from the top down:

procedure *PrintScreen;*
    var
        row : heights;
        col : widths;

```
begin
  for row : = screenheight downto 0 do
  begin
    for col : = 0 to screenwidth do
      write (screen [col] [row]);
    writeln
  end
end { Print Screen }
```

Let us draw a Christman Tree! To keep the program simple we shall construct the tree entirely from triangles and rectangles.

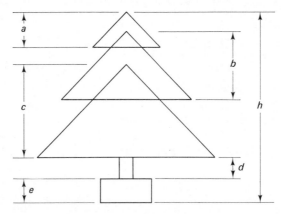

To be general, the process should be defined in terms of parameters indicating the position of the tree on the screen, the number of segments, the size of each segment, the amount of overlap of the segments, and the sizes of the trunk and the tub. You are welcome to do this if you have a few hours to spare! We shall draw a tree of three segments each reaching the centre of the segment above and half as big again. Thus, in the diagram,

$$b = \frac{3a}{2}, \qquad c = \frac{3b}{2}$$

and

$$h = a + \left(b - \frac{a}{2}\right) + \left(c - \frac{b}{2}\right) + d + e$$

The trunk will be $c/4$ high and $c/8$ wide and the tub will be $c/4$ high and $c/2$ wide. So

$$h = a + \left(\frac{3a}{2} - \frac{a}{2}\right) + \left(\frac{9a}{4} - \frac{3a}{4}\right) + \frac{9a}{16} + \frac{9a}{16}$$

$$= a + a\left(1 + \frac{3}{2} + \frac{9}{8}\right) = \frac{37a}{8}$$

and, hence,

$$a = \frac{8h}{37}$$

Because there are only certain positions of the output page at which we can print a character we may not achieve these ratios exactly (unless h is a multiple of 37), but the quality of our tree should suffer little from that! If parameters specify the coordinates of the top of the tree and the overall height, the procedure can deduce everything else. We can specify a pair of coordinates with the data type

> *points* =
> > **record**
> > > *x* : *widths;*
> > > *y* : *heights*
> > **end** { points }

The procedure heading is

> **procedure** *DrawChristmasTree (treetop* : *points; treeheight* : *heights)*

Because we are given the coordinates of the apex of the top triangle we shall draw the triangles in order down the screen. The height of the top triangle is

> *round (8 ∗ treeheight/37)*

and each subsequent triangle grows by 50 per cent. The x coordinate of the apex is the same for each triangle; the y coordinate is less than that for the previous triangle by half the height of the previous triangle. To adhere as closely as possible to the desired ratios and to ensure that the height of the tree produced does not vary much from that requested, we store heights in real form and round to integer when necessary. The structure of this part of the program is

```
var
    realheight : real;
    apex : points;
    segment : 2 .. 3;
...
realheight := 8 ∗ treeheight/37;
apex := treetop;
DrawTriangle (apex, round (realheight));
for segment := 2 to 3 do
begin
    apex.y := apex.y − round (realheight/2);
    realheight := realheight ∗ 1.5;
    DrawTriangle (apex, round (realheight))
end
```

with an obvious interpretation of *DrawTriangle*. The trunk is drawn by

> *apex.y* : = *apex.y* − *round (realheight)*;
> *realheight* : = *realheight/4*;
> *DrawRectangle (apex, round (realheight), round (realheight/2))*

and the tub by

> *apex.y* : = *apex.y* − *round (realheight)*;
> *DrawRectangle (apex, round (realheight), round (realheight* ∗ *2))*

In this form separate procedures must be available to draw triangles and rectangles and the specification of the desired figures is via parameter lists. Data representation is tidied if we introduce a record type with a variant for each shape:

> *shapes* = *(tri, rect)*;
> *triangles* =
>   **record**
>   *apex* : *points*;
>   *triheight* : *heights*
>   **end** { triangles };
>
> *rectangles* =
>   **record**
>   *topcentre* : *points*;
>   *rectheight* : *heights*;
>   *rectwidth* : *widths*
>   **end** { rectangles };
>
> *figures* =
>   **record**
>   **case** *shape* : *shapes* **of**
>   *tri* : *(thetriangle* : *triangles)*;
>   *rect* : *(therectangle* : *rectangles)*
>   **end** { figures }

One procedure now suffices for both shapes so, in the earlier outline,

> *apex* : *points*

is replaced by two variables

> *atriangle, arectangle* : *figures*

and the structure becomes

```
realheight := 8 * treeheight/37;
with atriangle do
begin
  shape := tri;
  with thetriangle do
  begin
   apex := treetop;
   triheight := round (realheight);
   Draw (atriangle);
   for segment := 2 to 3 do
   begin
     apex.y := apex.y − round (realheight/2);
     realheight := realheight * 1.5;
     triheight := round (realheight);
     Draw (atriangle)
   end { segments }
  end { with the triangle}
end { with a triangle };

with arectangle do
begin
  shape := rect;
  with therectangle do
  begin
   topcentre.x := treetop.x;
   topcentre.y := atriangle .thetriangle .apex .y − round (realheight);
   topcentre.y := topcentre.y + 1; { Moving the top up makes the top of
     the trunk coincide with the bottom of the foliage. }
   realheight := realheight / 4;
   rectheight := round (realheight);
   rectwidth := round (realheight/2);
   Draw (arectangle);          { the trunk}

   topcentre.y := topcentre.y − round (realheight);
   topcentre.y := topcentre.y + 1; { Moving the top up makes the top of
     the tub coincide with the bottom of the trunk. }
   rectwidth := round (realheight*2);
   Draw (arectangle)          { the tub }
  end { with the rectangle }
end { with a rectangle }
```

The simplest way to specify the construction of a triangle given its apex p and height h is

Draw a line of length h south-west from p and call the finish point q.
Draw a line of length $2h$ west from q and call the finish point r.
Draw a line of length h north-east from r.

```
procedure Draw (figure : figures);
  type
     directions = (northeast, east, southeast, south,
                       southwest, west, northwest, north);
  var
    corner : points;

  procedure DrawaLine (start : points; length : lengths;
       pointing : directions;  var finish : points);
  ... { see figure 13.11 }

begin { Draw }
  with figure do
  case shape of
  tri :
    with thetriangle do
    begin
      DrawaLine (apex, triheight, southeast, corner);
      DrawaLine (corner, 2*triheight, west, corner);
      DrawaLine (corner, triheight, northeast, corner)
    end;
  rect :
    with therectangle do
    begin
      corner.x := topcentre.x − rectwidth div 2;
      corner.y := topcentre.y;
      DrawaLine (corner, rectwidth, east, corner);
      DrawaLine (corner, rectheight, south, corner);
      DrawaLine (corner, rectwidth, west, corner);
      DrawaLine (corner, rectheight, north, corner)
    end
  end { case }
end { Draw }
```

Figure 13.10

```
procedure DrawaLine (start : points;  length : lengths;
     pointing : directions;  var finish : points);
  const
     nsch = 'I';  ewch = '−';  neswch = '(';  nwsech = ')';
```

```
type
  incvalues = −1 .. 1;
  dirsets = set of directions;
var
  pt : lengths;
  thisch : char;
  xinc, yinc : incvalues;
  xcoord : widths;
  ycoord : heights;

function chartobeprinted : char;
begin
  case pointing of
    north, south          : chartobeprinted := nsch;
    east, west            : chartobeprinted := ewch;
    northeast, southwest  : chartobeprinted := neswch;
    northwest, southeast  : chartobeprinted := nwsech
  end { case }
end { char to be printed };

function increment (posdirs, negdirs : dirsets) : incvalues;
begin
  if pointing in posdirs then increment := 1 else
    if pointing in negdirs then increment := −1 else
      increment := 0
end { increment };

begin { Draw a Line }
  thisch := chartobeprinted;
  xinc := increment ([east, northeast, southeast],
                     [west, northwest, southwest]);
  yinc := increment ([north, northeast, northwest],
                     [south, southeast, southwest]);
  xcoord := start.x;      ycoord := start.y;
  screen [xcoord, ycoord] := thisch;
  for pt := 2 to length do
  begin
    xcoord := xcoord + xinc;      ycoord := ycoord + yinc;
    screen [xcoord, ycoord] := thisch
  end;
  finish.x := xcoord;      finish.y := ycoord
end { Draw a Line }
```

Figure 13.11

Notice that the base of the triangle must be twice its height. This is because we are measuring length in terms of coordinate positions, not true distances. A line of length h drawn south-east will travel h coordinate positions to the right and as many down; a line of length h drawn south-west from the same position will travel h coordinate positions to the left and as many down. A line of length $2h$ is needed to complete the triangle.

A similar approach can be taken for rectangles. The procedure to draw a figure is shown in Figure 13.10. It incorporates the procedure *Draw a Line* of

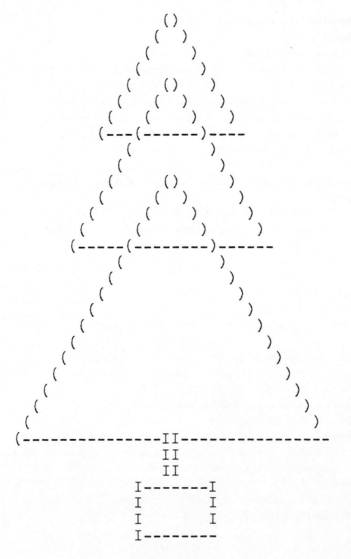

Figure 13.12

Figure 13.11. This assumes that the environment has been extended to include

const
    maxscreendimension = . . . ;
      { maximum of screenheight and screenwidth }
type
    lengths = 0 . . maxscreendimension;

The output from the program body

begin
    ClearScreen;
    top.x : = 30;   top.y : = 35;
    DrawChristmasTree (top, 35);
    PrintScreen
end

in the scope of the variable

    top : points

is shown in Figure 13.12. The figure is elongated because, on the output device used, horizontal spacing (character spacing) is three-fifths that of vertical spacing (line spacing).

13.3   Case study 5

Many computer applications involve the processing of text. We now develop a program to produce a neat version of supplied text. Both left and right margins are to be aligned within a specified page width without splitting words at the end of a line. It is assumed that, within the supplied data, words will be separated by at least one space or end of line, words will contain only letters, digits, hyphens, and apostrophes but will not start with a hyphen, and sentences will contain no punctuation characters other than commas, colons, semicolons, exclamation marks, question marks, and full stops. The character # marks the end of a paragraph.

13.3.1 Outline structure

The program must recognize certain entities in the input data and transcribe them, suitably formatted, to the output stream. It is natural therefore that the composition of these entities and, in particular, their desired layout will influence the structure of the program. The text is composed of paragraphs so the overall program structure will be of the form

repeat
    Paragraph
until *atendoftext*

Each paragraph comprises one or more sentences:

> **repeat**
>   *Sentence*
> **until** *atendofparagraph*

each sentence contains words:

> **repeat**
>   *Word*
> **until** *atendofsentence*

and each word is a sequence of characters:

> **repeat**
>   *Character*
> **until** *atendofword*

Before we worry about producing a suitable output format it will be useful to know that our program can recognize the appropriate entities. Accordingly, we simplify the problem specification and extend our skeletal structure no more than is necessary to facilitate running the program.

The first simplification assumption to make is that the data is correct. Let us assume that each sentence is terminated by a full stop and contains no other punctuation. We can regard any number within the data as a word. We shall ignore layout of the output beyond identifying words, sentences, and paragraphs.

Subject to these simplifications our outline program needs little modification. We can define *Character* to merely copy characters and we must arrange to skip spaces in the data. Basically, spaces separate words so we consider skipping spaces either before or after the call of *Word*. The end of a sentence can be detected only when the full stop has been encountered so we must skip any spaces that may precede the full stop. Consequently, we skip spaces after we have processed a word. Similar reasoning shows that, when processing a paragraph, we must skip spaces after a sentence to locate the paragraph terminator and also after a paragraph to locate the end of the text. In all of these places the skipping process is the same but in each case the first significant (i.e. non-space) character we hope to encounter differs. This suggests that the skipping process should be supplied with a variable parameter, used to indicate the outcome of the skip. The modified program is given in Figure 13.13. Words will be enclosed within parentheses, and all spaces will be skipped. Line markers in the input will be retained. The writeln-statement in *Sentence* ensures that each new sentence will start on a new line and the writeln-statement in *Paragraph* ensures that each new paragraph will be preceded by a blank line. A run of the program with some simple data shows that words, sentences, and paragraphs are recognized.

```
program NeatTextLayout (input, output, neatcopy);
  const
    paraterm = '#';
  type
    skipoutcomes = (startofword, endofsentence, endofpara,
                    endoftext, somethingelse);
  var
    neatcopy : text;
    letters : set of 'A' .. 'Z';
    digits : set of '0' .. '9';
    wordchars : set of char;
    outcome : skipoutcomes;

  procedure Sentence;
    forward;

  procedure Skip (var thingfound : skipoutcomes);
    forward;

  procedure Word;
    forward;

  procedure CopyChar;
  begin
    write (neatcopy, input↑);   get (input)
  end { Copy Char };

  procedure Paragraph;
    var
      reached : skipoutcomes;
  begin
    repeat
      Sentence;   Skip (reached)
    until reached = endofpara;
    get (input);  { skips paragraph terminator}
    writeln (neatcopy)
  end { Paragraph };

procedure Sentence;
  const
    wordstart = '(';  wordend = ')';
  var
    found : skipoutcomes;
```

348

```pascal
begin
  repeat
    write (neatcopy, wordstart);
    Word;   write (neatcopy, wordend);
    Skip (found)
  until found = endofsentence;
  CopyChar;   writeln (neatcopy)
end { Sentence };

procedure Skip {(var thingfound : skipoutcomes) };
  const
    blank = ' ';
  var
    state : (skipping, atsigchar, atfileend);
begin
  state := skipping;
  repeat
    if eof (input) then state := atfileend else
      if input↑ = blank then
        case eoln (input) of {temporary inclusion of line markers}
          true:
            begin
              readln (input);   writeln (neatcopy)
            end;
          false:
            get (input)
        end { case }
      else
        state := atsigchar
  until state <> skipping;

  case state of
    atfileend:
      thingfound := endoftext;
    atsigchar:
      if input↑ in (wordchars − ['-']) then thingfound := startofword
      else
        if input↑ = '.' then thingfound := endofsentence else
          if input↑ = paraterm then thingfound := endofpara else
            thingfound := somethingelse
  end { case }
end { Skip };

procedure Word;
begin
```

```
    repeat
        CopyChar
    until not (input↑ in wordchars)
    end { Word };

begin { program body }
    letters := ['A' .. 'Z'];
    digits := ['0' .. '9'];
    wordchars := letters + digits + ['-', ' ' ' ' ];
    rewrite (neatcopy);
    Skip (outcome);
    if outcome = startofword then
    begin
        repeat
            Paragraph;   Skip (outcome)
        until outcome = endoftext;
        writeln (output, 'A neat copy has been produced')
    end else
        writeln (output, 'Text is improperly supplied')
end.
```

Figure 13.13

We now have four aspects to consider:

1. inclusion of internal sentence punctuation,
2. sensible spacing between words, between sentences, etc.,
3. alignment of left and right margins, and
4. data validation.

We tackle these in the order listed.

13.3.2 Punctuation

A punctuation character is not usually preceded by a space or end of line
{the only exception would be the first of a pair of quotation marks, but this
example is not considering quotations} so it will be useful to make the
program regard a punctuation character as part of the word it follows. We
introduce a set of inner punctuation characters

   punctchars := [',', ';', ':']

and extend skipoutcomes to include

   innerpunctuation

to imply

> *input*↑ **in** *punctchars*

The loop within the body of *Sentence* becomes

> **repeat**
>   *write (neatcopy, wordstart);*
>   *Word;   Skip (found);*
>   **if** *found = endofsentence* **then** *CopyChar* **else**
>   **if** *found = innerpunctuation* **then**
>   **begin**
>   *CopyChar;   Skip (found)*
>   **end**;
>   *write (neatcopy, wordend)*
> **until** *found = endofsentence*

We modify *Skip* to recognize a question mark and an exclamation mark as the end of a sentence, introduce further punctuation into the data, and run the modified program. Every punctuation character should now be bracketed with the word before it.

13.3.3   Spacing

We ignore the influence of the right-hand margin and assume an infinite page width. Each word must be preceded by a space, each sentence must be preceded by an additional space, and each paragraph should start on a new line preceded by three further spaces (thereby making a total of five spaces). We introduce the data type

> *spacings* = *1 . . 3*

and use

> **procedure** *Space (n : spacings);*
>   **const**
>   *blank* = ' ';
> **begin**
>   *write (neatcopy, blank : n)*
> **end** { *Space* }

to print the spaces. The bodies of *CopyChar* and *Space* are short but we use a procedure because their function must obviously change during some future refinement of the program. When margin alignment is considered we shall not know where words and spaces will appear on a line until we reach

the right-hand margin. The procedures *CopyChar* and *Space* will then not
output directly; they will store the output information somewhere (in an
array, for example) to be printed later when the necessary spacing is known.

To achieve normal spacing we precede the call of *Word* (within *Sentence*)
by

    Space (1)

we precede the call of *Sentence* (within *Paragraph*) by

    Space (1)

and we precede the call of *Paragraph* (within the main program body) by

    Space (3)

We can now omit the generation of parentheses around words and can
remove the writeln-statement at the end of *Sentence*. Line markers will still
be retained but a run of the program should show that sensible spacing is
produced.

13.3.4 Margin alignment

We must disregard the line markers in the input and write line markers only
at the end of a paragraph and when the right-hand margin has been reached.
We should accommodate as many words as possible on one line and, if
necessary, insert extra spaces between words until the last character of the
last word (or the punctuation character after it, if there is one) occupies the
last print position of the line. We can do this by building up each line in a
buffer prior to printing:

```
const
    buffersize = ... ;
type
    buffrange = 1 .. buffersize;
var
    linechar : array [buffrange] of char;
```

When the right-hand margin has been reached we shuffle characters around
in the buffer as appropriate and output the buffer when it is in the desired
form. We modify the procedure *CopyChar* and *Space* so that, rather than
output directly to *neatcopy*, they place characters in the buffer. We must
know how much of the buffer is occupied at any time so we introduce an
extended subrange type

    extbuffrange = 0 .. buffersize

and associate an index with the buffer

```
buffer:
  record
    linechar : array [buffrange] of char;
    filled : extbuffrange
  end { buffer }
```

We initialize *buffer.filled* to *0*. The procedure *CopyChar* becomes

```
procedure CopyChar;
begin
  with buffer do
  begin
    filled := filled + 1;   linechar↑[filled]:= input↑;
    get (input)
  end
end { Copy Char }
```

Spaces must not appear at the beginning of a line unless a new paragraph is about to start so the procedure *Space* becomes

```
procedure Space (n : spacings);
  const
    blank = ' ';
  var
    i : buffrange;
begin
  with buffer do
  if not ((filled = 0) and (n = 1)) then
  begin
    for i := filled + 1 to filled + n do
      linechar [i]:= blank;
    filled := filled + n
  end
end { Space }
```

The writeln-statement at the end of *Paragraph* is replaced by the call of a procedure to empty the buffer:

```
procedure EmptyBuffer;
  var
    i : buffrange;
begin
  with buffer do
  begin
```

```
    for i := 1 to filled do
        write (neatcopy, linechar [i]);
        writeln (neatcopy);
        filled := 0
    end { with buffer }
end { Empty Buffer }
```

We can now test the program if we slacken the requirement for right-hand margin alignment. We introduce a page width (less than *buffersize* by, at least, the length of the longest word expected) and terminate a line at the end of the first word (and punctuation if appropriate) which reaches (or exceeds) the specified page width. We do this by including

```
if buffer.filled >= pagewidth then
    EmptyBuffer
```

as the last statement within the repeat-loop of *Sentence*.

When a test run implies that these refinements have been successfully incorporated we modify *EmptyBuffer* so that the information within the buffer is rearranged, if necessary, before it is printed. If *buffer.filled* <= *pagewidth*, we output the buffer unchanged and reset *buffer.filled* to 0. If *buffer.filled* > *pagewidth* we copy the last word entered (and any accompanying punctuation) into another buffer and determine how far the previous word is from the required margin. This tells us the number of spaces we must insert between the remaining words. If we assume that the number of words in the buffer is greater than the number of spaces we have to insert we can work backwards from the right-hand end of the buffer moving words up and inserting an extra space before each one. This is an assumption that a serious program must not make, but its removal is left as an exercise for the reader. The buffer (as far as *pagewidth*) is then output, the word which was removed is placed at the left-hand end of the buffer, and *buffer.filled* is set to indicate the position of its last character.

The form of the final procedure is shown in Figure 13.14. The procedure *SaveLastWord* copies the word most recently placed in the buffer into *lastword* for safe-keeping. Having done this, it can easily find the end of the previous word in the buffer (or any punctuation following the previous word). A variable parameter is supplied to return this position. The procedure is given in Figure 13.15.

MoveWord moves a word along the buffer. The supplied value parameters indicate the position of the end of the word and the distance the word is to be moved. We then need to know the position of the end of the preceding word in the buffer and so, again, a variable parameter is supplied to return this information. Because the first and third actual parameters are the same we could define the procedure to take only two parameters (the second and the third), but the present form stresses that the procedure uses the current

354

```
procedure EmptyBuffer;
  const
    blank = ' ';   maxwordsize = ... ;
  type
    pagerange = 1 .. pagewidth;
    wordsizes = 1 .. maxwordsize;
  var
    noofspaces, endofprevword, sp, lch : pagerange;
    packedline : packed array [pagerange] of char;
    lastword:
      record
        wordch : array [wordsizes] of char;
        start : wordsizes
      end { last word };

  procedure MoveWord (wordend, distance : pagerange;
                      var nextwordend : pagerange);
  ...

  procedure RetrieveLastWord;
  ...

  procedure SaveLastWord (var prevwordend : pagerange);
  ...

begin { Empty Buffer }
  if buffer.filled > pagewidth then
  begin
    SaveLastWord (endofprevword);
    noofspaces := pagewidth − endofprevword;
    for sp := noofspaces downto 1 do
      MoveWord (endofprevword, sp, endofprevword);
    pack (buffer.linechar, 1, packedline);
    writeln (neatcopy, packedline);
    RetrieveLastWord
  end else
  with buffer do
  begin
    for lch := 1 to filled do
      write (neatcopy, linechar [lch]);
    writeln (neatcopy);
    filled := 0
  end
end { Empty Buffer }
```

Figure 13.14

```
procedure SaveLastWord (var prevwordend : pagerange);
  var
    wch : wordsizes;
    lch  : buffrange;
begin
  wch := maxwordsize;  lch := buffer.filled;
  with lastword, buffer do
  repeat
    wordch [wch] := linechar [lch];
    wch := wch − 1;     lch := lch − 1
  until linechar [lch] = blank;
  lastword.start := wch + 1;
  with buffer do
  repeat
    lch := lch − 1
  until linechar [lch] <> blank;
  prevwordend := lch
end { Save Last Word }
```

Figure 13.15

value of *endofprevword* as well as returning an updated value. The full procedure is given in Figure 13.16.

RetrieveLastWord copies the word that we saved in *lastword* into the left-hand end of the buffer and sets *buffer.filled* appropriately. The procedure is given in Figure 13.17.

13.3.5 Data validation

There are two aspects to data validation. On the one hand, there is the defensive element: the program should be tolerant of incorrect data in that it should continue until all the text has been processed even if errors are present. On the other hand, there is the diagnostic aspect: suspected errors in the data should be reported. We leave this second consideration as an exercise for the reader and pursue the first.

In its present form the program treats any unexpected character as the first character of a word and so will not fail if such a character is encountered in a context where a word would be appropriate. The program will run to completion so long as the final paragraph terminator is present, and each sentence immediately preceding a paragraph terminator is correctly terminated.

It is a simple matter to modify the program to cope with missing sentence and paragraph terminators. The presence of a paragraph terminator is tested

```
procedure MoveWord (wordend, distance : pagerange;
                         var nextwordend : pagerange);
   var
      here : pagerange;
begin
   here := wordend;
   with buffer do
   begin
      repeat
         linechar [here + distance] := linechar [here];
         here := here - 1
      until linechar [here] = blank;
      repeat
         linechar [here + distance] := blank;
         here := here - 1
      until linechar [here] <> blank;
      nextwordend := here;
      linechar [here + distance] := blank
   end { with buffer }
end { Move Word }
```

Figure 13.16

```
procedure RetrieveLastWord;
   var
      wch : wordsizes;
      lch  : 0 .. pagewidth;
begin
   lch := 0;
   with buffer, lastword do
   begin
      for wch := start to maxwordsize do
      begin
         lch := lch + 1;    linechar [lch] := wordch [wch]
      end;
      filled := lch
   end { with buffer, lastword }
end { Retrieve Last Word }
```

Figure 13.17

at the end of the loop within the procedure *Paragraph*. The only paragraph terminator which would cause problems if omitted is the very last one because then an attempt would be made to read beyond the end of the input file. The loop termination test should therefore be modified to

> reached **in** [endofpara, endoftext]

and the following

> get (input)

preceded by

> **if** reached = endofpara **then**

The presence of a sentence terminator is checked at the end of the loop within the procedure *Sentence*. The only sentence which would cause problems if improperly terminated is the last one in a paragraph. The outcome of *Skip*, called within the loop, would be *endofpara* or, if the paragraph terminator is missing and this is the last paragraph, *endoftext*. The loop termination test becomes

> found **in** [endofsentence, endofpara, endoftext]

With these modifications the program should persevere until the end of the input file is reached whatever rubbish is supplied as data.

13.4 Exercises

1. Modify the transferable vote election program of Exercise 12.5.6 to accumulate vote counts in an array so that different numbers of candidates may be involved.

2. (a) Write a procedure to read a word and print it backwards. Assume that the word will contain only letters.
   (b) Incorporate this procedure within a program to reverse every word in a sentence. Assume the sentence contains no punctuation other than a full stop immediately following the last word.

†3. Write a program which checks whether the first n characters on one line of data are the same as the first n on the next; n is a user-defined constant.

†*4. Write a program to determine if one word is an anagram of another. The words are supplied left-justified on separate lines.

†*5. A palindrome is a word or phrase which reads the same backwards as forwards if spaces and punctuation are ignored. "Madam, I'm Adam" is a well-known example. Write a program which reads and reproduces a phrase, typed on one line, and determines whether it is palindromic.

†*6. Write a program to sort a set of n integers into ascending order using the following "bubble sort" technique; n is a user-defined constant. The set is scanned from left to right and adjacent values are compared and interchanged if out of order. The scanning process is repeated until no interchanges occur during a scan but one element fewer is examined each time.

7. An integer outside the range [$-maxint$, $maxint$] can be represented by recording its sign and storing its digits in successive elements of an array.

358

Adopting such a scheme and imposing some limit upon the length of an integer, write one procedure to read a long integer, one to write a long integer, and three to process a pair of long integers:

> one to form their sum,
> one to form their difference, and
> one to form their product.

Incorporate these within a program to read four long integers a, b, c, d and print the values $ab + cd$ and $ab - cd$.

8. Write two programs to generate primes in the range 1 to n using the sieve of Eratosthenes {see Exercises 10.2.4 and 12.5.7}; n is to be supplied as a user-defined constant. One program is to represent the sieve as an array of *boolean* and the other as an array of *sieves* where *sieves* is the set type used for the solution to Exercise 10.2.4.

†*9. Write a program to produce Pascal's triangle of binomial coefficients as far as those for some power, specified as a user-defined constant. The triangle below gives coefficients up to the power of six.

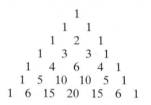

10. When elements are repeatedly added at one end of an array and removed in the reverse order from the same end, the array is said to represent a "stack". The following algorithm uses a stack to transform an "infix" algebraic expression {operators quoted between their operators} into "postfix" form {each operator immediately follows its operands} if we assume all operators have two operands:

> **for each** element in the supplied expression **do**
> > **if** it is an operand **then** output it **else**
> > **if** it is an operator **then**
> > > remove operators from the stack and output them until the stack is empty or there is an opening parenthesis at the top of the stack or the operator at the top of the stack has lower priority than that of the operator currently under consideration and then stack it **else**
> > **if** it is an opening parenthesis **then** stack it **else**
> > **if** it is a closing parenthesis **then**
> > > remove any operators from the top of the stack and output them until an opening parenthesis appears at the top of the stack and then discard this opening parenthesis **else**
> > > something is wrong with the supplied expression;
> > remove any operators from the top of the stack and output them until the stack is empty.

If you apply this algorithm to the expression

$(a+b) * (c-d/(e+f)) = g * h/(i-j)$

you should get

$a\,b+c\,d\,e\,f+/-*g\,h*i\,j-/=$

{corresponding to

$$(((ab+)(c(d(ef+)/)-)*)((gh*)(ij-)/)=)\}$$

Postfix form is of particular relevance to compilers because it requires no parentheses and indicates (reading from left to right) the order in which the operators must be applied when the expression is evaluated. Write a program to convert any Pascal expression containing only parentheses, single character identifiers, and the operators $+$, $-$ (each with two operands), $*$, $/$, $=$, $<$, $>$, & (meaning **and**), and @ (meaning **or**) to parenthesis-free postfix form. Assume the expression contains no spaces but is terminated by a space or end of line.

11. Write a program to evaluate a postfix arithmetic expression. Assume the expression is suitably terminated and contains only numbers and the operators $+$, $-$, $*$, and $/$.

12. Extend your program for Exercise 11 to cater for the relational operators $<$, $>$, $=$, and the boolean operators & (**and**) and @ (**or**).

13. (a) Modify the program for Exercise 7.9.4 to utilize an array rather than a case-statement to achieve translation to Morse Code.

   (b) Extend this program to decode a Morse sentence. Assume that the Morse Code is supplied in the form produced by part (a) and that the decoded sentence can be accommodated on one line. The first line of the data is to comprise either the word *CODE* or *DECODE* to indicate the direction of the translation.

   (c) Check the compatibility of your two directions of translation by storing the translated sentence in a local file, preceded by *CODE* or *DECODE* as appropriate, and then translating it back again. Output the sentence produced: except perhaps for spaces, it should agree with the original sentence.

†*14. The game of Life {published in *Scientific American* **223**(4), October 1970, pp. 120–123} simulates the life cycle of a society of living organisms. The society exists in an infinite two-dimensional array of cells, each cell having eight cells adjacent. Births and deaths occur simultaneously as each new generation is produced.

   A birth occurs in any empty cell with exactly three neighbours (occupied cells); the occupant of a cell with two or three neighbours survives to the next generation; the occupants of all other cells die from either isolation or overcrowding. So, if the initial society comprises four members forming a triangle in adjacent cells the next four generations display the following patterns:

```
                           *           *
       *       * * *      *   *         *           * * *
     * * *     * * *                   *   *         *   *
                 *         * * *        *           * * *
                                        *
       0         1           2          3             4
```

Three eventual outcomes are possible:

1. The society becomes extinct.

2. A steady state is reached {e.g. `* *` / `* *`}.

3. The society oscillates {e.g. `* * *`, `*`/`*`/`*`, `* * *`...}.

Write a program which accepts an initial configuration and displays successive patterns until either a steady state is reached or some predetermined number of generations has been produced.

Adopt a finite space and assume that no organism can live beyond the boundary.

15. Define an algorithm for optimal noughts and crosses play. Represent the board by a two-dimensional array with rows and columns subscripted from -1 to 1. If you have access to a terminal write a program which implements your algorithm and play against your program.

16. Modify a backtracking program (such as those of Figures 7.13 and 7.14 or the solutions to Exercises 7.9.11 and 7.9.12) to print the solution steps in the correct order. Do this by storing the steps in an array while the path from the goal node is being traced and print them only when the sequence is complete.

17. Write a program which applies the postfix transformation described in Exercise 10 but calls a recursive procedure when an opening parenthesis is met rather than stacking it. Assume the entire supplied infix expression is bracketed.

†18. Write a procedure which performs a binary chop search recursively (rather than iteratively).

Exercises 19 to 23 require backtracking programs. In each case the solution steps should be printed in the correct order (see Exercise 16).

†19. Write a program to solve the "n-queens" problem; n queens are to be placed on an $n \times n$ chess board in such a way that no queen is attacking any other. A queen attacks any piece on the same row, column, or diagonal.

†20. (a) Write a program to produce a complete "knight's tour". A knight starts from one corner of an $n \times n$ chess board and, by a sequence of legal moves, must visit every square on the board once and only once. A knight's move is L-shaped: either two squares to one side and one up or down, or one square to the side and two up or down. A solution for $n = 5$ is shown below.

1	14	9	20	3
24	19	2	15	10
13	8	25	4	21
18	23	6	11	16
7	12	17	22	5

(b) What is the smallest value of n for which a complete tour exists?

(c) How many different solutions, starting from the top left-hand corner, exist for $n = 5$?

(d) How many moves does your program attempt before a solution is found for $n = 5$?

(e) If the situation arises that any unvisited square has no unvisited successor {the knight could not move out of this square without revisiting a square already visited} then no solution exists from this position unless this is the only square yet to be visited. Modify your program to recognize this situation and backtrack immediately. Compare this program's run-time with that of the original. How many moves does this version attempt for $n = 5$?

(f) Make the program favour squares with few unvisited successors. To do this, record the moves available at any stage in decreasing order of merit in an array and then attempt moves in this order rather than in the predetermined order dictated by the original program. Again determine the run-time and number of moves attempted.

(g) Rather than maintain a dynamic record of unvisited successors as in part (f), use the number of *possible* successors. A corner square has two possible successors, an edge square adjacent to a corner has three possible successors, and so on. Again determine the run-time and number of moves attempted.

(h) What conclusions do you draw from your results? Do you think these conclusions would hold for all backtracking programs?

†21. (a) Write a program to find a route through a maze. Represent the maze as a two-dimensional array of squares, each marked as either path or hedge. The route, expressed as a sequence of steps in the directions N, S, E, and W, should be printed forwards {not in reverse order}.

(b) Modify your program so that, as in Exercise 20(f), it is steered towards the better moves. At each stage, the first move attempted should, if possible, approach the maze exit.

22. Write a program to play solitaire. The solitaire board has 33 holes arranged as follows:

```
        ×  ×  ×
        ×  ×  ×
  ×  ×  ×  ×  ×  ×  ×
  ×  ×  ×  ○  ×  ×  ×
  ×  ×  ×  ×  ×  ×  ×
        ×  ×  ×
        ×  ×  ×
```

Initially every hole but the central one is occupied by a peg. The object of the game is to determine a sequence of moves to remove all pegs but one, this remaining peg to occupy the central hole. A move can be made only when two pegs and an empty hole are adjacent in a row or column. The move entails jumping one peg over its neighbour into the empty hole and removing the peg jumped over. Moves cannot be made diagonally.

†23. Write a program to solve the "eight-square puzzle" for some specified initial configuration. Eight square tiles, numbered from 1 to 8, are located within a square frame whose area is none times that of a tile. A possible configuration is shown below:

```
+---+---+---+
| 1 | 4 | 2 |
+---+---+---+
|   | 8 | 3 |
+---+---+---+
| 7 | 6 | 5 |
+---+---+---+
```

Tiles can slide, one at a time, within the frame but cannot be lifted. The aim is to produce the following configuration:

1	2	3
8		4
7	6	5

The solution steps, in terms of moving the space up, down, left, and right, should be printed in the correct order.

14

Pointers

The storage required by any variable we have met so far is static in the sense that, once allocated upon entry to the block in which the variable is declared, it is associated with the variable until the block is exited. Pointer variables extend the concept of storage allocation: at any point within the scope of a pointer variable new store can be allocated or store already allocated can be released. Pointers allow hierarchical relationships to be naturally represented and provide flexibility to handle continually varying data structures.

14.1 Pointer types and variables

Given a type t, the type

$$\uparrow t$$

called "pointer to t", is a pointer type "bound" to the type t. A variable v of type $\uparrow t$ can be thought of as pointing to a variable of type t. To access the variable pointed to, the pointer variable is followed by $\uparrow$. Thus $v\uparrow$ is a variable of type t. If we think of the computer store as a collection of pigeon holes, each pigeon hole has a different number stamped on it: this is called its "address". A variable of type $\uparrow t$ records the address of a variable of type t.

Pointer variables allow store to be shared in that several pointers can point to the same object. This has two benefits. First, storage is saved because multiple copies of one object need not be held. Second, information updating becomes more efficient and more secure. If only one copy of an object is stored then only one copy need be changed. This is faster than updating several copies and avoids the possibility of missing some other copies within the updating process.

Case Study 4 of Chapter 12 suggested that a supplier's name and address might be included within a stock item record. This field would occupy most of the store required by a stock item record. It is likely that many items will have the same supplier so much store would be wasted if a copy of the supplier's details were stored in every item record. It is better to store the

364

details once and then have each item record point to a supplier record:

```
firm =
  record
    name    : packed array [1 .. 30] of char;
    address : packed array [1 .. 3, 1 .. 30] of char
  end  { firm };

item =
  record
    . . . ;
    supplier : ↑firm
  end  { item }
```

The firm which supplies an item *i* is

   i.supplier↑

Assignments may be made to pointer variables so long as both sides of the assignment (the variable on the left and the expression on the right) are of the same type. Another item will record the same supplier as item *i* if we use an assignment of the form

   otheritem.supplier := *i.supplier*

Note that this copies only the address of the firm record and not the entire record.

One particular value that may be assigned to any pointer variable, independent of type, is the predefined value **nil**. This is used to mark a variable as "pointing to nothing of interest". We shall see it used shortly.

It is not advisable to write to an external file any records containing pointers. When the file is read, either by a different program or by a subsequent run of the same program, the addresses stored as pointers will probably be meaningless. When the file was written the data pointed to was local to the program and will probably not exist when the file is subsequently read. Although a stock record was used to illustrate the principle of pointers, the technique is probably not the most appropriate if the stock records are to be written to an external file. Instead we would probably have to resort to constructing an array of firms and then storing the appropriate index in the supplier field of each stock record.

14.2 Storage allocation

A pointer variable cannot point to any named variable declared in the program. Pointer variables can point only to anonymous variables created by a call of the standard procedure *new*. If *p* is a variable of type ↑*t*, the statement

   new (p)

creates an anonymous variable of type *t* and makes *p* point to it. The value of *p*↑ is undefined. If pointers are used within item records, we can create an entirely new supplier

> *Fred Bloggs*
> *97 Finkerdiddle Row*
> *Netherwordle*

for an item as follows:

```
new (item.supplier);
with item.supplier↑ do
begin
    name      := 'Fred Bloggs              ';
    address [1]:= '97 Finkerdiddle Row      ';
    address [2]:= 'Netherwordle             ';
    address [3]:= '                         '
end
```

Storage allocated by a call of *new* will be associated with the program until it is explicitly released by a call of the standard procedure *dispose*. If *p* is a pointer variable with a defined value other than **nil**, the statement

> *dispose (p)*

indicates that the storage occupied by the variable *p*↑ is no longer needed. All pointer variables which currently reference this variable become undefined. Use of *dispose* is illustrated in Example 14.1.

If the type of *p* is pointer to a record type with a variant part,

> *new (p)*

will allocate sufficient storage to accommodate the largest variant. If only one variant is to be used and this is not the largest, space may be saved by utilizing the alternative form

> *new (p, v)*

where *v* is the desired tag field value. If the variant part involves a record variant which in turn involves a further record variant, and so on, this form can be extended to

> *new (p, v_1, v_2, . . . , v_n)*

which allocates a variable with variants appropriate for the tag field values $v_1, v_2, . . . , v_n$. The tag field values must be listed in order of their declaration and trailing values may be omitted.

When tag field values are specified, the storage allocated is sufficient only for the variants specified but the tag fields are not given values. Once the tag fields have been given the values indicated, they must not be changed. Also, the variable created must not appear in an assignment statement or as an actual parameter.

If a variable is created by a call of the form

$$new\ (p,\ v_1,\ v_2,\ \ldots,\ v_n)$$

it can be destroyed only by

$$dispose\ (p,\ v_1,\ v_2,\ \ldots,\ v_n)$$

with an identical tag field list.

14.3 Recursive data structures

Whereas it is impossible to have a record type *t1* involving a field of type *t2* if type *t2* involves type *t1*, *t1* may contain a field of type ↑*t2* while *t2* contains a field of type ↑*t1*. To permit the definition of such structures, a type name *t* may be used in the context ↑*t* before the type *t* has been defined. We illustrate this with a simple English–French dictionary:

```
type
    letters     = 'A' .. 'Z';
    wordlengths = 1 .. 20;
    words       = packed array [wordlengths] of letters;
    frenchwords =
        record
            fword    : words;
            engequiv : ↑englishwords
        end { french words };
    englishwords =
        record
            eword      : words;
            frenchequiv : ↑frenchwords
        end { english words };
var
    englishentry : array [letters] of ↑englishwords;
    frenchentry  : array [letters] of ↑frenchwords;
```

To represent an empty dictionary we would set the pointers in the vectors to **nil**:

```
var
    initial : letters;
    ...
for initial := 'A' to 'Z' do
begin
    englishentry [initial] := nil;
    frenchentry [initial] := nil
end
```

The word pair *(dog, chien)* can be entered as follows:

```
var
    engword :↑englishwords;
    frenword :↑frenchwords;
...
new (engword); new (frenword);
with engword↑ do
begin
    eword := 'dog                    ';
    frenchequiv := frenword
end;
with frenword↑ do
begin
    fword := 'chien                  ';
    engequiv := engword
end;
englishentry ['D'] := engword;
frenchentry ['C'] := frenword
```

The resulting data structure is illustrated diagrammatically in Figure 14.1.

In keeping with the terminology for procedure declarations, types such as *englishwords* and *frenchwords* can be described as mutually recursive. Correspondingly, a record type may be directly recursive:

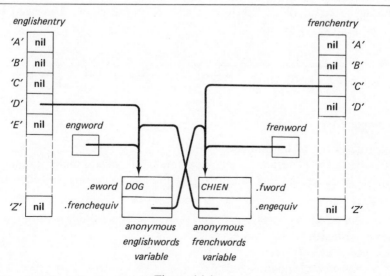

Figure 14.1

```
type
    entries =
      record
          word : words;
          translation : ↑entries
      end { entries }
```

Comparison of this type with the two previous types illustrates a common trade-off between user convenience and security. If French words and English words are both represented by the one type then only one procedure is needed to read a word or to write a word. If distinct types are used there is less possibility of two words in the same language being accidentally linked together as supposed translation equivalents.

Directly recursive types are commonly used in the construction of data structures called "lists" and "trees".

14.4   Lists

A list is a collection of records chained together. Consider the following data type:

```
box =
  record
      thing : ... ;
      next  : ↑box
  end { box }
```

An object of type *box* contains a *thing* and a pointer to another box. We can envisage a chain of such boxes. The end of the chain is marked by the special pointer value **nil**.

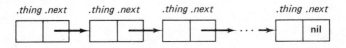

Example 14.1

Construct a list of the integers 1 to 10. □

We repeatedly generate a new box, make its *next* pointer point to the previously generated box, and store an integer value one less each time:

```
type
    intbox =
      record
          int  : 1 .. 10;
          next : ↑intbox
      end { int box };
var
    intlist, newbox : ↑intbox;
```

```
   i : 1 .. 10;
    . . .
 intlist := nil;
 for i := 10 downto 1 do
 begin
    new (newbox);
    newbox↑.int := i;   newbox↑.next := intlist;
    intlist := newbox
 end    ■
```

Example 14.2

Write a procedure to insert a given integer at the right place within a (possibly empty) list of integers stored in ascending order. □

This entails scanning along the list so long as the value currently under inspection is less than the value to be inserted or until the end of the list is encountered. The new value must then be stored within an appropriate

```
procedure Insert (i : integer;   var list : intlists);
   var
      p, prevp, box : intlists;
      state : (scanning, posnfound, listexhausted);
begin
   new (box);   box↑.int := i;
   if list = nil then
   begin
      box↑.next := nil;      list := box
   end else
      if i <= list↑.int then
      begin
         box↑.next := list;      list := box
      end else
      begin
         p := list;      state := scanning;
         repeat
            prevp := p;      p := p↑.next;
            if p = nil then state := listexhausted else
               if p↑.int >= i then state := posnfound
         until state <> scanning;
         prevp↑.next := box;      box↑.next := p
      end
end { Insert }
```

Figure 14.2   Example 14.2

370

record (a box) and this record must be placed in the list. The procedure is given in Figure 14.2. It assumes that *intlists* = ↑*intbox*. As *p* moves down the list *prevp* keeps one step behind. When *p* indicates that the desired position has been found we must insert the new box between *p* and the box to which *p* previously pointed. We could "look ahead" instead of maintaining a pointer to the previous value of *p*:

```
p := list;   state := scanning;
repeat
  if p↑.next = nil then state := listexhausted else
    if p↑.next↑.int >= i then state := posnfound else
      p := p↑.next
until state <> scanning;
box↑.next := p↑.next;   p↑.next := box
```

The version of Figure 14.2 is conceptually simpler. ■

Example 14.3

The procedure of Figure 14.3 removes a specified integer from a list. The integer is assumed to be present in the list. □
   When the sought integer is found the pointer pointing to its *intbox* is adjusted to point to the next *intbox*. The *intbox* containing the integer is then disposed of. ■

Example 14.4

The following procedure prints successive integers in a list. □

```
procedure PrintIntList (list : intlists);
  const
    noperline = 10;
  var
    count : 0 .. maxint;
  begin
    count := 0;
    while list <> nil do
    begin
      write (list↑.int);   count := count + 1;
      if count mod noperline = 0 then writeln
    end
  end { Print Int List } ■
```

   Value transfer is suitable even if the list contains many thousand elements. *list* is a record with two fields; only these two fields will be copied. Notice that the concept of value transfer is slightly different for

```
procedure Remove (i : integer;  var list : intlists);
  var
     thisbox, prevbox : intlists;
begin
  thisbox := list;
  if list↑.int = i then
    list := list↑.next else
  begin
    repeat
      prevbox := thisbox;      thisbox := thisbox↑.next
    until thisbox↑.int = i;
    prevbox↑.next := thisbox↑.next
  end;
  dispose (thisbox)
end { Remove }
```

Figure 14.3   Example 14.3

pointers. For any other data type the actual parameter cannot be altered by local assignments to the formal parameter. This remains true for a pointer but the information pointed to can be altered.

Example 14.5

Using the two procedures of Examples 14.2 and 14.4 the following program prints in ascending order a set of non-zero integers supplied as input and terminated by 0.   □

```
program ListSort (input, output);
  . . .
  var
    i : integer;
    orderedseq : intlists;
  . . .
begin
  orderedseq := nil;
  read (i);
  repeat
    Insert (i, orderedseq);   read (i)
  until i = 0;
  PrintIntList (orderedseq)
end. ■
```

Example 14.6

The English–French dictionary introduced earlier will be improved if words in the same language with the same initial letter can be chained together. □

Each entry requires a pointer to another entry of the same type:

frenchwords =
   record
      fword   :*words;*
      engequiv:↑*englishwords;*
      fnext   :↑*frenchwords*
   end { french words };

englishwords =
   record
      eword   : *words;*
      frenequiv : ↑*frenchwords;*
      enext   : ↑*englishwords*
   end { english words } ■

14.5 Trees

A common requirement is to express a hierarchical relationship between items of data. One data structure often used to achieve this is the tree. A family tree is an example of such a structure. A tree is composed of boxes, each containing more than one pointer (or perhaps a list of pointers) to boxes of the same type. Each box is the destination of only one pointer. The boxes are called "nodes" and the pointers "branches". A node pointed to is called a "successor node" of the node containing the pointer which, in turn, is called the "parent node" or "predecessor node". A node with no successor nodes is called a "terminal node". One node will have no predecessor node: this is called the "root node".

In particular, if each node has no more than two successors the structure is called a binary tree. Use of a binary tree can reduce the number of comparisons involved in the sorting process of Example 14.5. Rather than insert each supplied value within a linear list we hang it at the appropriate place on a tree. We make each node in the tree capable of holding a left and a right branch and construct the tree so that each left successor contains a value less than or equal to the value stored by the parent and each right successor contains a value greater than that stored by the parent. If the values

$$97, -426, 278, -9, -627, 3001, \text{ and } 156$$

are supplied in that order the resultant tree would have the following form:

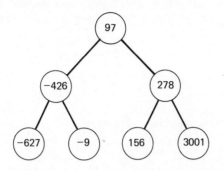

Within the program the tree is represented by the following data type:

```
trees = ↑boxes;
boxes =
    record
        value : integer;
        left, right : trees
    end { boxes }
```

and both *left* and *right* are **nil** for a terminal node.

The most natural way to process a recursive data structure is often with a recursive procedure. A new integer is added to the tree by the following simple recursive procedure:

```
procedure Add (int : integer; var t : trees);
begin
    if t = nil then
    begin
        new (t);
        with t↑ do
        begin
            value := int;   left := nil;   right := nil
        end { with t↑ }
    end else
        with t↑ do
            if int <= value then
                Add (int, left)
            else
                Add (int, right)
end { Add }
```

You might like to produce a non-recursive version!

Printing the integers in ascending order is a simple matter if we use recursion, but is difficult otherwise. The trick is to notice that, given the root node, we must print the left sub-tree, then the value stored at the root, and then the right sub-tree. Printing a sub-tree follows exactly the same pattern. For a terminal node we simply print the value stored. If we ignore line layout, the process is illustrated by the following simple recursive procedure:

```
procedure Print (t : trees);
begin
  if t <> nil then
    with t ↑ do
    begin
      Print (left);   write (value);   Print (right)
    end { with t↑ }
end { Print }
```

14.5.1 Heuristic search

Section 7.7.3 introduced the concept of "state space search"; the program explores legal sequences of states seeking a sequence which transforms a specified initial state into some desired goal state. The search was described in terms of traversing a tree and the tree structure was represented by the program's run-time procedure linkages. Backtracking was achieved by exiting recursive procedures. The resultant search was "depth-first" : each sequence of steps was explored to the depth bound before another sequence was examined.

We can represent the search tree explicitly and then achieve greater flexibility in backtracking. In particular, at any point during the search, we can develop that node which is currently the most promising. The program's search for a solution is then said to be "heuristic".

We grow the tree from the root and test each new state produced until a goal state is reached. We then follow the path from the goal node back to the root to determine the desired sequence of steps. Consequently, the tree must contain back-pointers : each node must point back to its parent. Each node must also store the state it represents and must contain some indication of the operator that was applied to produce this state from that of the parent node.

Using three-element nodes

{ state, operator, parent }

we can apply our problem-solving process without the need for recursion. We maintain a list of states open for development. We repeatedly remove the first member and add its successors until a successor set contains a goal state. The procedure of Figure 14.4 illustrates the basic process and assumes the following types:

```
states = ... ;
operators = ... ;
nodeptrs = ↑nodes;
```

```
nodes =
  record
    state  : states;
    optor  : operators;
    parent : nodeptrs
  end { nodes };

listptrs = ↑nodelists;
nodelists =
  record
    first : nodeptrs;
    next  : listptrs
  end { nodelists }
```

The procedure *Develop* produces the successors of the supplied node and checks them for a goal state. If a goal state is detected *solved* becomes *true* and *goalnode* points to the node containing the goal state; if not, *solved* becomes *false* and *goalnode* remains undefined. Recursion is present within the procedure *TracePathTo*, but only because it simplifies expression of the algorithm; the recursion could be replaced by two loops.

There are different ways that successors can be added to *open* and each gives rise to a different search strategy. If successors are added to the front of *open* the search is depth-first and a depth bound is needed. If successors are added at the end of *open* the search is breadth-first: all sequences of length n are examined before any of length $n + 1$. A breadth-first search does not need a depth bound and guarantees that any solution it finds is a shortest solution.

```
procedure Search (startstate : states;
        procedure Develop (node : nodeptrs; var newnodes : listptrs;
              var solved : boolean; var goalnode : nodeptrs);
        procedure Name (op : operators) );
    var
      open, successors : listptrs;
      node, goalnode : nodeptrs;
      status : (searching, goalfound, openisempty);
      solved : boolean;

    procedure Add (these : listptrs; var list : listptrs);
    . . .

    procedure TracePathTo (here : nodeptrs);
    begin
      if here↑.parent <> nil then
```

376

```
      begin
        TracePathTo (here↑.parent);   Name (here↑.optor)
      end
    end { Trace Path To (here) };

  begin { Search }
    new (node);
    with node↑ do
    begin
      state := startstate;        parent := nil
    end { with node↑ };

    status := searching;
    repeat
      Develop (node, successors, solved, goalnode);
      if solved then
        status := goalfound else
      begin
        Add (successors, open);
        if open = nil then
          status := openisempty else
        begin
          node := open↑.first;     open := open↑.next
        end
      end
    until status <> searching;

    case status of
      goalfound:
        TracePathTo (goalnode);
      openisempty:
        writeln ('No solution exists')
    end { case }
  end { Search }
```

Figure 14.4   Basic search process

The search becomes heuristic if nodes open for development are held in decreasing order of merit so that the node at the front of the list is the one currently most promising. We define an evaluation function to produce, for each node, a value indicative of the difference between the state stored and a goal state. The better a state appears to be the lower its evaluation. If the data type *nodes* is extended to include the field

value : $0 .. maxint$

```
procedure Add (these : listptrs; var list : listptrs);
  var
    rest : listptrs;

  procedure Insert (this : listptrs; var list : listptrs);
  begin
    if list = nil then
    begin
      this↑.next := list;   list := this
    end else
      if this↑.first↑.value < list↑.first↑.value then
      begin
        this↑.next := list;   list := this
      end else
        Insert (this, list↑.next)
  end { Insert };

begin { Add }
  while these <> nil do
  begin
    rest := these↑.next;   Insert (these, list);
    these := rest
  end
end { Add }
```

Figure 14.5

```
program HeuristicIntegerTransformation (input, output);
  const
    addint = 3;   subint = 4;   multint = 2;
  type
    operators = (add, subtract, multiply);
    states = integer;
    nodeptrs = ↑nodes;
    nodes =
      record
        state  : states;
        value  : 0 .. maxint;
        optor  : operators;
        parent : nodeptrs
      end { nodes };
```

```
    listptrs = ↑nodelists;
    nodelists =
      record
        first : nodeptrs;
        next : listptrs
      end { node lists };
var
  initialint, finalint : states;


function foundfinalint (this : states) : boolean;
begin
  foundfinalint := this = finalint
end { found final int };


procedure NameOperator (op : operators);
begin
  case op of
    add      : writeln ('Add ', addint :1);
    subtract : writeln ('Subtract ', subint :1);
    multiply : writeln ('Multiply by ', multint :1)
  end { case }
end { Name Operator };


procedure Search ...
    { as in Figures 14.4 and 14.5 }


procedure Transform (node : nodeptrs; var newnodes : listptrs;
    var goalfound : boolean; var goalnode : nodeptrs);

  procedures AddNewNode (int : states;  op : operators);
      { updates goalfound and goalnode if int is a goal state }
    var
      nodeptr : nodeptrs;
      listptr : listptrs;
  begin
    new (nodeptr);
    with nodeptr↑ do
    begin
      state := int;  value := abs (int − finalint);
      optor := op;  parent := node;
      if value = 0 then
      begin
        goalfound := true;  goalnode := nodeptr
      end
    end { with nodeptr↑ };
```

```
      new (listptr);
      listptr↑.first := nodeptr;   listptr↑.next := newnodes;
      newnodes := listptr
   end { Add New Node };


 begin { Transform }
   newnodes := nil;   goalfound := false;
   AddNewNode (node↑.state + addint, add);
   if not goalfound then
   begin
      AddNewNode (node↑.state − subint, subtract);
      if not goalfound then
         AddNewNode (node↑.state * multint, multiply)
   end
 end { Transform };


begin { program body }
  read (initialint, finalint);
  writeln ('Initial integer : ', initialint);
  writeln ('Final integer : ', finalint);
  writeln;


  if initialint = finalint then
     writeln ('Initial state constitutes a goal state')
  else
     Search (initialint, Transform, NameOperator)
end.
```

INPUT:
  8   37

OUTPUT:
Initial integer: 8
Final integer: 37

Multiply by 2
Multiply by 2
Add 3
Add 3
Subtract 4
Add 3

Figure 14.6   Heuristic search

the procedure of Figure 14.5 maintains the appropriate ordering. A more efficient version could be written and, again, recursion is convenient but not necessary.

Definition of a suitable evaluation function is usually very difficult. In the case of the integer transformation problem of Example 7.8, an effective function is simply the absolute magnitude of the difference between the current integer and the desired final integer. The program of Figure 14.6 tackles the integer transformation problem heuristically.

14.6 A sample data structure

To illustrate a more elaborate data structure we consider one example: a chess-playing program. The program is one player; the other may be human or another program. A program to play chess must play legally and, preferably, well. To play legally, little more need be known than the position of each piece on the board. To play well, the program must be able to evaluate such aspects as mobility, attacking power, defence of the king, and control of the centre. Approaches fall between two extremes. Little information need be stored, and the evaluations computed whenever needed or a full data structure representation of each state of the game can be maintained. The second approach requires more store but may save time because the program is better able to detect probable good moves and little computation is required to evaluate any position of interest. The data structure should be designed, as program development dictates what information must be available. Nevertheless, we ignore the playing process itself except to note in passing that it uses backtrack programming. To choose a move from any given position the program traverses a "look-ahead tree". It considers all possible moves and, for each, all possible replies, and each possible response to each reply, and so on, to some depth. A single play by one player is called a half move. A program cannot begin to play reasonable chess until it can detect (and avoid) pins and forks, and this requires a four half-move look-ahead. There are typically at least thirty moves available at any one time in the middle game, so a four half-move look-ahead can involve more than a million positions $\{30^4 = 810,000\}$. A good chess-playing program must look further than four half moves, so improvements to the basic approach have been developed to enable deep look-aheads to be performed in a realistic time.

We concentrate on the development and initialization of a data structure to represent a state of the game. The game is played on a two-dimensional board of sixty-four squares, so a sensible representation of the board is

array *[rows, columns]* **of** *squareptrs*

where

squareptrs = ↑*squares*

and *rows* and *columns* are both the integer subrange $1..8$. It is assumed that "we" (i.e. the program) are playing from rows 1 and 2 and our opponent's pieces initially occupy rows 7 and 8. The need for *squareptrs* rather than *squares* will soon be apparent.

Each square has a position (denoted by its row and column) and a possible occupant:

```
pieceptrs = ↑pieces;
squares = record
              row : rows;
              col : columns;
              occupant : pieceptrs
          end { squares }
```

The occupant is stored as *pieceptrs* rather than *pieces* to make moving a new piece to the square efficient. Rather than copy all the information for the new occupant we simply assign a pointer to it.

An empty board can now be generated:

```
var
    square  : array [rows, columns] of squareptrs;
    r : rows;   c : columns;
    . . .
for r : = 1 to 8 do
    for c : = 1 to 8 do
    begin
      new (square [r, c]);
      with square [r, c]↑ do
      begin
        row := r;   col := c;   occupant := nil
      end
    end
```

Representation of a piece must contain its type and owner and, for completeness, might well include the square it occupies:

```
piecenames = (pawn, knight, bishop, rook, queen, king);
owners = (me, you);
pieces = record
             name  : piecenames;
             owner : owners;
             residence : squareptrs
         end { pieces }
```

The reasons for using *squareptrs* rather than *squares* are analogous to those for using *pieceptrs* within a *squares* record. Also, the mutual recursion would not be possible if the pointers were omitted. It is the use of *squareptrs* here which necessitates the use of *squareptrs* in the representation of the board.

Each player uses a number of pieces. These are most conveniently handled as a list:

```
colours = (black, white);
piecelists = ↑pieceboxes;
pieceboxes = record
                piece : pieceptrs;
                next  : piecelists
             end {piece boxes};

players = record
                colour : colours;
                men : piecelists
          end { players }
```

The two sets of chessmen can be initialized by

```
case mycolour of
white  : begin
              queenfile : = 4;   kingfile : = 5
         end;
black  : begin
              queenfile : = 5;   kingfile : = 4
         end
end { case };
my.colour : = mycolour;   my.men : = nil;
SetPieces (my, me, queenfile, kingfile);
SetPawns (my.men, me);
your.colour : = yourcolour;   your.men : = nil;
SetPieces (your, you, queenfile, kingfile);
SetPawns (your.men, you)
```

using the variables

```
my, your : players;
mycolour, yourcolour : colours;
queenfile, kingfile : columns;
```

The procedures *SetPieces* and *SetPawns* are given in Figures 14.7 and 14.8.

To determine all the legal moves of one piece we can scan the board in appropriate directions from the current position of the piece and construct a list of potential sites. Typically, unless a king is in check, the moves available to most pieces, from one move to the next, do not change. The only pieces affected are those that are potential tenants of a square which another piece has either just occupied or just vacated. Determination of all possible moves is therefore faster if a list of potential sites is maintained for each piece and appropriate lists updated each time a move is made. This process is helped if

```
procedure SetPieces (var player : players;   meoryou : owners;
                          qfile, kfile : columns);
   var
      rank : rows;
      list : piecelists;

   procedure Place
         (nameofpiece : piecenames;   row : rows;   col : columns;
          var list : piecelists);
      var
         box : piecelists;
   begin
      new (box);
      with box↑ do
      begin
         next := list;   list := box;
         new (piece);
         with piece↑ do
         begin
            name := nameofpiece;   owner := meoryou;
            residence := square [row, col];
            residence↑.occupant := piece
         end { with piece↑ }
      end { with box↑ }
   end { Place };

begin { Set Pieces }
   list := player.men;
   case meoryou of
      me  : rank := 1;
      you : rank := 8
   end { case };
   Place (rook, rank, 1, list);      Place (rook, rank, 8, list);
   Place (knight, rank, 2, list);    Place (knight, rank, 7, list);
   Place (bishop, rank, 3, list);    Place (bishop, rank, 6, list);
   Place (queen, rank, qfile, list);
   Place (king, rank, kfile, list);
   player.men := list
end { Set Pieces }
```

Figure 14.7

```
procedure SetPawns (var men : piecelists; meoryou : owners);
  var
    r : rows;   c : columns;
    manbox, pawnlist : piecelists;
begin
  case meoryou of
    me  : r := 2;
    you : r := 7
  end { case };
  pawnlist := men;
  for c := 8 downto 1 do
  begin
    new (manbox);
    with manbox↑ do
    begin        { place new man on list }
      next := pawnlist;   pawnlist := manbox;
      new (piece);
      with piece↑ do
      begin        { make it a pawn }
        name := pawn;   owner := meoryou;
        residence := square [r, c];
        residence↑.occupant := piece
      end { with piece↑ }
    end { with manbox ↑ }
  end { for c };
  men := pawnlist
end { Set Pawns }
```

Figure 14.8

each square maintains a list of potential tenants:

```
squarelists = ↑squareboxes;
squareboxes = record
                site : squareptrs;
                next : squarelists
              end { square boxes };

pieces = record
           name : ...;   owner : ...;   residence : ...;
           sites : squarelists
         end { pieces };
```

```
squares = record
            row:...;   col:...;   occupant:...;
            tenants : piecelists
         end { squares }
```

The procedure of Figure 14.9 will record the fact that the occupant of square *source*↑ can move to square *dest*↑. Initially only the knights and the pawns are able to move. Assuming that sites and tenants have been initialized to **nil**, the knights' moves can be initialized by two procedure calls:

InitialKnightMoves (1, 3);   InitialKnightMoves (8, 6)

using

```
procedure InitialKnightMoves (fromrow, torow : rows);
begin
   RecordMove (square [fromrow, 2], square [torow, 1]);
   RecordMove (square [fromrow, 2], square [torow, 3]);
   RecordMove (square [fromrow, 7], square [torow, 6]);
   RecordMove (square [fromrow, 7], square [torow, 8])
end { Initial Knight Moves }
```

A similar approach, but using a for-loop, can be applied to the pawns. For simplicity, we have ignored the complications caused by a pawn's capturing moves differing from its normal moves.

To introduce the concepts of attack and defence the data structure can incorporate lists of attackers and defenders. Associated with each piece can be lists of pieces attacking it, pieces it is attacking, pieces defending it, and pieces it is defending:

```
pieces =
   record
      name:...;   ...   sites :...;
      attackers, defenders, targets, wards : piecelists
   end { pieces }
```

For example, one of the opponent's rooks could be initialized as follows:

```
var
   rk, kt, pwn : pieceptrs;
   ...
rk := square [8, 1] ↑.occupant;
kt := square [8, 2] ↑.occupant;
pwn := square [7, 1] ↑.occupant;
Add (rk, kt↑.defenders);
Add (kt, rk↑.wards);
Add (rk, pwn↑.defenders);
Add (pwn, rk↑.wards)
```

```
procedure RecordMove (source, dest : squareptrs);
   var
      siteptr : squarelists;
      tenptr : piecelists;
begin
   with source↑.occupant↑ do
   begin
      new (siteptr);
      with siteptr↑ do
      begin
         next := sites;   site := dest
      end { with siteptr↑ };
      sites := siteptr
   end { with source ↑ .occupant };

   with dest↑ do
   begin
      new (tenptr);
      with tenptr↑ do
      begin
         next := tenants;   piece := source↑.occupant
      end { with tenptr ↑ };
      tenants := tenptr
   end { with dest ↑ }
end { Record Move }
```

Figure 14.9

using

```
procedure Add (pce : pieceptrs; var list : piecelists);
   var
      p : piecelists;
begin
   new (p);
   p↑.piece := pce;   p↑.next := list;
   list := p
end { Add }
```

Development of this data structure has illustrated how relationships can be represented by pointers and records. We abandon the example at this point and leave the interested reader to consider what further information might be stored. In particular, the program must know when a king is in check and when en passant capture is possible and must know if a king has been moved {a king cannot be castled once it has been moved}. Some, if not all, of this information should be held within the data structure.

14.7 Exercises

1. Modify your programs for Exercises 13.4.10, 13.4.11, 13.4.12, and 13.4.17 so that each stack is represented, not by an array but by a linked list.
*2. Computers are often used to simulate real world situations. These often involve queueing: people queueing in a shop, ships waiting to dock, lorries waiting to be unloaded, car components waiting to be assembled. A common queueing discipline is first-in, first-out (as opposed to a stack which is first-in, last-out). The queue is a linear sequence with entities added at one end and removed from the other. Within a computer a convenient representation is as a chained list with a pointer to each end.

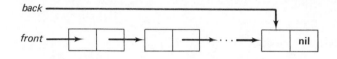

Define a record type to represent a queue, storing the queue length and the two pointers, and write the following function and two procedures:

function *empty (queue : queues) : boolean*
to detect an empty queue;
procedure *join (item : items;* **var** *queue : queues)*
to add an item to the end of a queue;
procedure *leave (***var** *item : items;* **var** *queue : queues)*
to remove an item from the front of a queue.

3. Introduce pointers to your program for Exercise 13.3.14, the game of Life. Prior to each cycle, one pointer is to indicate the current colony and another is to indicate where the new colony is to be generated. These two pointers must be interchanged for each new generation.
*4. Extend your record type for Exercise 11.4.2 to include a list of immediate relatives (parents, children, brothers, and sisters) and, for a married person, the spouse. Correspondingly, modify the marrying procedure to forbid the marriage of immediate relatives and to update the spouse information for a legal marriage.
*5. (a) Produce a non-recursive version of the procedure *Add* of Figure 14.5.
   (b) Assuming the data type *trees* defined in Section 14.5 introduce a suitable type *depths* and write

procedure *Find (n : integer; tree : trees;* **var** *found : boolean;*
var *boxcontainingn : boxes;* **var** *depthofn : depths)*

to seek the integer *n* within the given tree. *found* is to indicate whether *n* is present. The two other variable parameters are to be given appropriate values only if *n* is located.

6. Modify the programs of Exercise 13.4.16 and replace the array by a list.
7. Modify your programs for Exercises 13.4.20(f) and 13.4.21(b) so that the moves available at any stage are stored as a list rather than held in an array.
†8. (a) Supply heuristic programs for Exercises 7.9.11, 13.4.21, and 13.4.23. These

programs should be able to tackle problems with longer solutions than could the earlier versions.
(b) Encourage your programs to seek short solutions.
9. (a) Define a record type (with variants) to represent an operand of an algebraic expression assuming that an operand is a letter, an integer, or an operand–operator–operand triplet and that the operators available are $+$, $-$, $*$, and $/$.
(b) Write a procedure to read a fully bracketed triplet and represent it by a binary tree using the data type defined in part (a). A fully bracketed triplet has the form (*operand operator operand*) where each *operand* is a letter, an integer, or a fully bracketed triplet.
(c) Write a• procedure to output the fully bracketed form of an algebraic expression represented by a given tree.
(d) Write a program to read a fully bracketed triplet y and a letter x and to print the analytic partial derivative $\partial y/\partial x$. This should appear as either a single term or a fully bracketed triplet.
(e) If your program does not produce simplified output, modify it so that it does. for example, the program of part (d), supplied with

$$((a*x)+(b*x))$$

may well produce

$$(((a*1)+(0*x))+((b*1)+(0*x)))$$

when $(a+b)$ would suffice.
†10. Write a program to print a supplied message in large letters. Adopt your own conventions as to the number of words that will appear on one line. Each letter should be composed of several occurrences of the letter printed in normal size. For example,

```
PPP    AA     SS    CC     AA    L
P  P A    A S  S C   C A    A L
P  P A    A S      C     A    A L
PPP  AAAA   SS   C      AAAA L
P    A    A    S C     A    A L
P    A    A S  S C   C A    A L
P    A    A  SS    CC   A    A LLLL
```

Make your program economize on space by generating only those letters needed and storing these only once.

Part D

EXCEPTIONAL CONTROL TRANSFER

15

The Goto-Statement

During the execution of a program, control passes sequentially from one statement to the next. The execution of one statement may involve nested control transfers. For example, a procedure call implies a transfer of control to (and subsequent return from) the procedure body and control transfers will occur within the body. A repeat-loop involves a conditional transfer from the end of the loop back to the beginning.

The goto-statement is a simple device enabling control to be transferred unconditionally from one place to another. This action is called a "jump".

15.1 Statement labels

Any statement which is to be the destination of a jump must be prefixed by a label and the two separated by a colon. A statement label is an unsigned integer. Statement labels are quite distinct from case labels and each must be declared in the declaration part preceding the statement part in which it appears as a prefix. Within any block in which a statement label appears the label must be declared once, and only once, and used as a statement prefix once, and only once.

LABEL DECLARATION

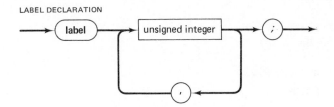

Label declarations must precede any other declarations occurring at the same block level. The catch-phrases introduced earlier to aid memorizing the order of declarations must be extended to account for this:

Let's Cook Textured Vegetable Protein
Little Cats Tails Vary Profusely
Little Chillies Taste Very Pungent

392

Control is transferred to a labelled statement by a goto-statement.

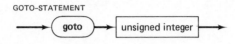

GOTO-STATEMENT

Execution then continues from the destination statement as though control had reached there naturally.

A jump cannot be made into a procedure body, with-statement, repeat-statement, while-statement, if-statement, case-statement, or compound statement.

15.2 Use of goto-statements

The disjoint control flow which results from the use of a goto-statement is a damaging factor and so this statement should be used as little as possible. In some older languages its use must, unfortunately, be great, but in Pascal you will rarely need it. The only use you make of it should be to abort a process prematurely. This will involve transferring control forwards to the end of the process; you should never explicitly transfer control backwards.

A common example of this occurs during data validation. We often need to make a number of checks on supplied data, performing some processing after each successful check but abandoning the current record immediately an invalid datum is detected. Assuming the existence of boolean functions *check1, check2, check3, . . .*, the overall structure might be

```
GetNextRecord;
repeat
  if check1 then
  begin
    . . . ;
    if check2 then
    begin
      . . . ;
      if check3 then
      begin
        . . .
        . . .
      end { check 3 }
    end { check 2 }
  end { check 1 };
  GetNextRecord
until allrecordsprocessed
```

If there are many such checks the nesting of the program logic becomes excessive. One way to reduce the textual nesting is to introduce procedures:

```
GetNextRecord;
repeat
  if check1 then
  begin
    . . . ;
    Check2etc
  end;
  GetNextRecord
until allrecordsprocessed
```

with

```
procedure Check2etc;
begin
  if check2 then
  begin
    . . . ;
    Check3etc;
  end
end { Check 2 etc }
```

and so on.

The nesting of the program logic itself can be reduced by inverting the tests and using goto-statements:

```
label 999;
. . .
GetNextRecord;
repeat
  if not check1 then goto 999;
  . . . ;
  if not check2 then goto 999;
  . . . ;
  if not check3 then goto 999;
  . . . ;
  . . . ;
999:
  GetNextRecord
until allrecordsprocessed
```

This approach could have been used in Figures 7.13 and 7.14. The procedure *Cross* of Figure 7.14 would have the form shown in Figure 15.1.

Another common situation is the need to exit from a set of nested loops. For example, consider a section of program to determine three integers in

```
procedure Cross (var solnfound : boolean);
  label 1;
  var
    solved : boolean;
begin
  if cabbage = here then
  begin
    Try (not here, not cabbage, goat, wolf, depthleft − 1, solved);
    if solved then
    begin
      writeln ('Man takes cabbage'); goto 1
    end
  end;
  if goat = here then
  begin
    Try (not here, cabbage, not goat, wolf, depthleft − 1, solved);
    if solved then
    begin
      writeln ('Man takes goat'); goto 1
    end
  end;
  if wolf = here then
  begin
    Try (not here, cabbage, goat, not wolf, depthleft − 1, solved);
    if solved then
    begin
      writeln ('Man takes wolf'); goto 1
    end
  end;
  Try (not here, cabbage, goat, wolf, depthleft − 1, solved);
  if solved then
    writeln ('Man crosses alone');
1:
  solnfound := solved
end { Cross }
```

Figure 15.1

the range 1 to 100 which satisfy some particular condition:

VERSION 1

```
var
  solved : boolean;
  i, j, k : 1 .. 100;
. . .
```

```
solved := false;
i := 1;
repeat
  j := 1;
  repeat
    k := 1;
    repeat
      if condition (i, j, k) then solved := true else
        if k < 100 then k := k + 1
    until solved or (k = 100);
    if not solved and (j < 100) then j := j + 1
  until solved or (j = 100);
  if not solved and (i < 100) then i := i + 1
until solved or (i = 100)
```

Conceptually simpler is

VERSION 2

```
label 1;
var
  i, j, k : 1 .. 100;
  . . .
for i := 1 to 100 do
  for j := 1 to 100 do
    for k := 1 to 100 do
      if condition (i, j, k) then goto 1;
1:  . . .
```

Before you decide that this trick simplifies programming and you will use it for all non-deterministic loops from now on, we shall examine some defects of this approach and I shall try to impress its dangers upon you.

First, transparency. Throughout the book it has been stressed that the intent of a program should be apparent from the program text. Further, the overall effect of one level of program logic should be apparent without the need to examine lower levels of logic. For example, the structure

```
s := s0;
repeat
  . . .
until s <> s0;
case s of
  s1: . . . ;
  s2: . . . ;
  s3: . . .
end { case }
```

immediately presents itself as a non-deterministic loop with three possible outcomes of interest. if the states have been carefully named the intended effect of this section of program should be obvious without looking inside the repeat-statement. Contrast this with Version 2 of the three-integers example. The three outermost levels of logic {the three for-statements} are not transparent; they do not clearly state the intent of the program. In fact, they blatantly deceive! Each states that the situation is deterministic and that a hundred iterations of the loop will be performed. The true intent of the loops is not apparent until the very bottom level of logic {**goto** *1*} is examined. In such a small section of program this can perhaps be excused, but do not underestimate its undesirability in general.

Second, disjoint control flow. In our three-integers example we will presumably wish to know, upon exit from the process, whether the process was successful or not. In Version 1 we simply follow the outermost repeat-loop by

   if *solved* **then** ... **else** ...

and we have maintained our usual sequential flow of control. In Version 2 we must precede the labelled statement by any statements we wish to be obeyed if no suitable set of integers is found:

```
      ...
   for i := 1 to 100 do
      for j := 1 to 100 do
         for k := 1 to 100 do
            if condition (i, j, k) then goto 1;
      ...;      { statements to be obeyed if
                  no suitable set is found }
   1 :...       { statements to be obeyed if
                  a suitable set is found }
```

But this is not enough. If no solution is found control will pass from the nested loops to the desired statements; then control will pass sequentially to the statements which were supposed to be obeyed only if a solution was found! We could, of course, overcome this by using another goto-statement:

```
   label 1,2;
      ...
   for i := 1 to 100 do
      for j := 1 to 100 do
         for k := 1 to 100 do
            if condition (i, j, k) then goto 1;
      ...;      { statements for failure }
   goto 2;
   1 :...;   { statements for success }
   2 :...
```

This disjoint flow of control must be avoided. It makes programs less transparent, more error prone, and more difficult to modify later. If you find yourself writing something resembling this latest version tear it up and think again!

If you use a goto-statement in a context such as Version 2, borrow the idea of a boolean (or symbolic) variable from Version 1:

```
    . . .
    solved := false;
    for i := 1 to 100 do
       for j := 1 to 100 do
          for k := 1 to 100 do
             if condition (i, j, k) then
             begin
                solved := true;   goto 1
             end;
    1: if solved then . . . else . . .
```

This not only reduces the disjoint control flow; the appearance of *solved* immediately before and after the nested loops implies that the for-loops are, perhaps, not deterministic after all.

15.3 In conclusion

In the strictest sense a goto-statement is never needed. However, there are occasional circumstances where its use can simplify the nested logic that would otherwise arise. In such a circumstance think very carefully before you introduce the goto-statement and use it only if you are absolutely sure that the resulting program is more transparent. If in doubt, leave it out!

APPENDIXES

Appendix A

Pascal Syntax Diagrams

In these diagrams an attempt has been made to imply some semantics. For example, the sections

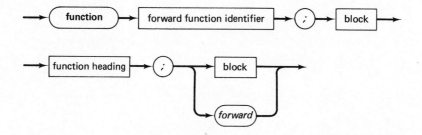

of the diagram for a block imply that the result type of a function is omitted only when the function has been previously defined as a forward reference. However, the semantics are not completely specified: the (illegal) form

   $- true$ **in** $(a$ **mod** $b)$

is accommodated by the syntax diagram for an expression.

The following entities are referred to but not defined:
constant identifier, ordinal constant identifier,
numeric constant identifier, integer constant identifier,
symbolic identifier, variable identifier,
ordinal variable identifier, type identifier,
real type identifier, ordinal type identifier,
structured type identifier, pointer type identifier,
file identifier, field identifier, procedure identifier,
function identifier, forward procedure identifier,
forward function identifier;

array variable, record variable, file variable,
pointer variable;

ordinal expression, boolean expression;

character.

The definition of "character" is implementation dependent. Interpretation

402

of the others is intuitively obvious. For example a numeric constant identifier is either *maxint* or a user-defined constant of type integer or real, a symbolic identifier is the name of a value of symbolic type, a structured type identifier is the name of a structured type and an ordinal expression is an expression of some ordinal type.

All the identifiers are syntactically equivalent to

> identifier

and the variables are syntactically equivalent to

> variable

PROGRAM'

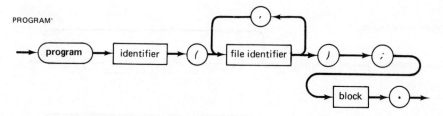

BLOCK

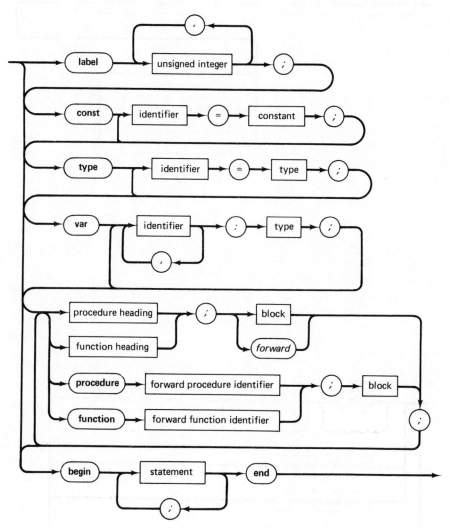

404

PROCEDURE HEADING

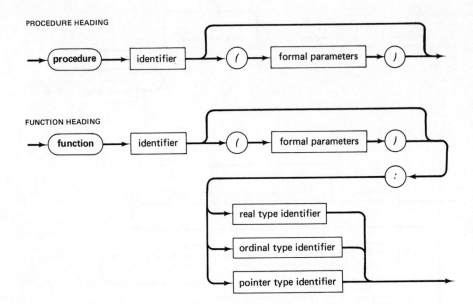

FUNCTION HEADING

FORMAL PARAMETERS

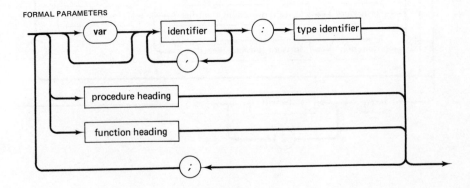

405

TYPE

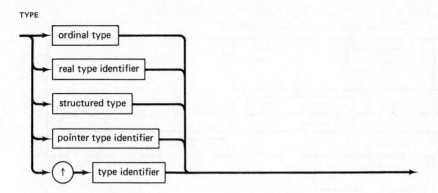

ORDINAL TYPE

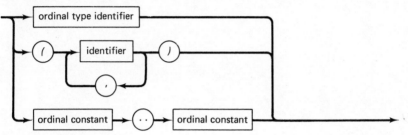

STRUCTURED TYPE

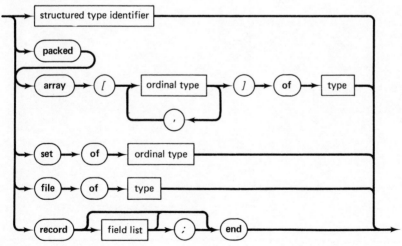

406

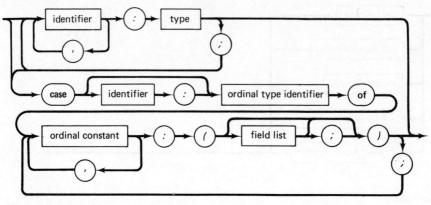

407

STATEMENT

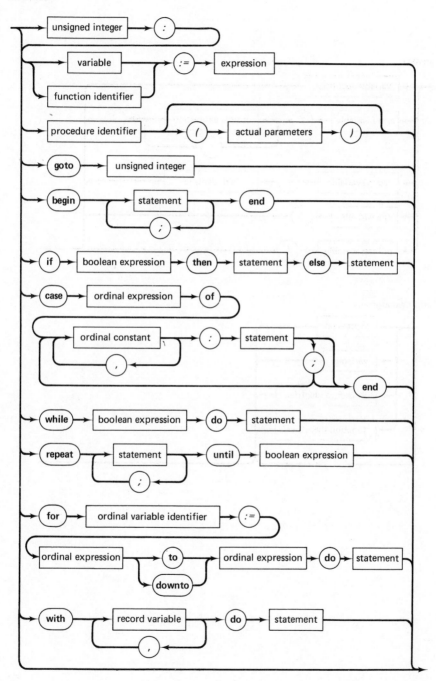

408

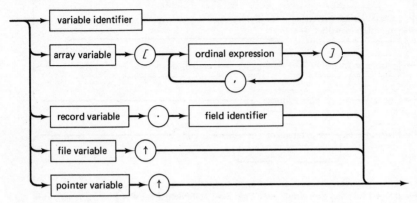

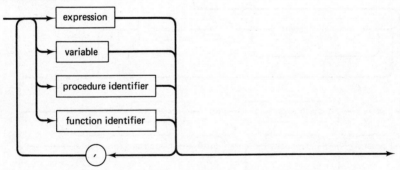

EXPRESSION

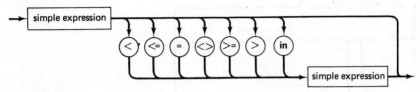

SIMPLE EXPRESSION

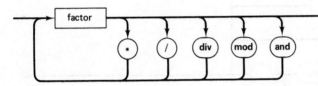

TERM

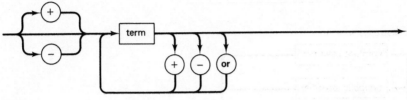

FACTOR

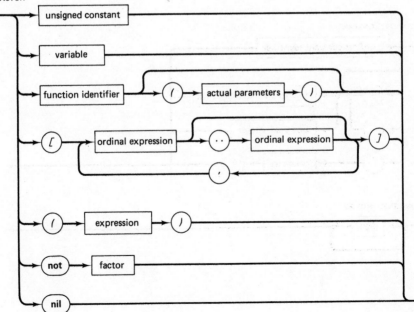

CONSTANT

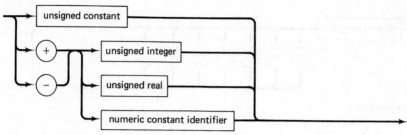

UNSIGNED CONSTANT

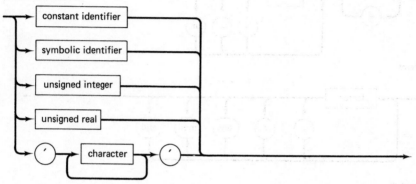

ORDINAL CONSTANT

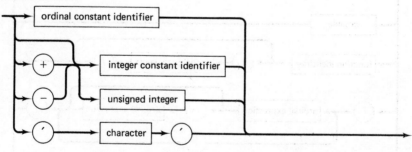

UNSIGNED INTEGER

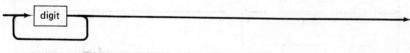

UNSIGNED REAL

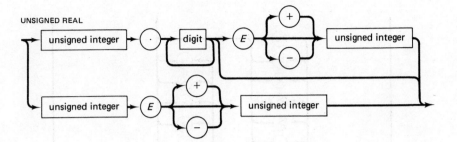

412

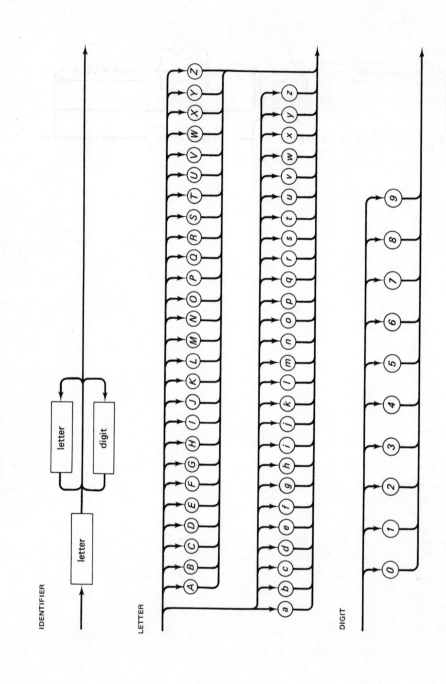

IDENTIFIER

LETTER

DIGIT

Appendix B

Reserved Words

Reserved words cannot be used as identifiers.

and	downto	if	or	then
array	else	in	packed	to
begin	end	label	procedure	type
case	file	mod	program	until
const	for	nil	record	var
div	function	not	repeat	while
do	goto	of	set	with

Appendix C

Predefined Identifiers

These identifiers could be redefined within a Pascal program but this would usually be a foolish thing to do.

Constants

    false   *maxint*   *true*

Types

    boolean   *char*   *integer*   *real*   *text*

Files

    input   *output*

Procedures

dispose	*get*	*new*	*pack*	*page*	*put*	
read	*readln*	*reset*	*rewrite*	*unpack*	*write*	*writeln*

Functions

abs	*arctan*	*chr*	*cos*	*eof*	*eoln*
exp	*ln*	*odd*	*ord*	*pred*	*round*
sin	*sqr*	*sqrt*	*succ*	*trunc*	

Directive

    forward

Appendix D

Operators

For the purpose of defining operators, any operand of type s, where s is a subrange of type t, is treated as if it were of type t, and any operand of type **set of** s is treated as if it were of type **set of** t.

Arithmetic operators

Operator	Operation	Type of operands	Type of result
+	addition	integer/real	integer/real
−	subtraction	integer/real	integer/real
*	multiplication	integer/real	integer/real
/	division	integer/real	real
div	integer division	integer	integer
mod	modulo reduction	integer	integer

The operators + (identity) and − (negation) may also be used with only one operand. For any arithmetic operator, the result is of type real if an operand is of type real.

Boolean operators

Each boolean operator requires its operand(s) to be of type boolean and produces a result of type boolean.

Operator	Number of operands	Operation
not	1	logical inversion
and	2	logical *and*
or	2	logical *or*

Relational operators

Each relational operator requires two operands and produces a result of type boolean. With the exception of **in**, both operands must have the same

416

type (subject to the interpretation of the opening paragraph of this appendix) unless one is real and the other integer.

Operator	Operation	Type of operands
= < >	equal to, not equal to	real, ordinal, string, set, pointer
< >	less than, greater than	real, ordinal, string
<=	less than or equal to	real, ordinal, string, set
>=	greater than or equal to	real, ordinal, string, set
in	set membership	left: ordinal type *t*
		right: **set of** *t*

When applied to sets, the operators <= and >= denote set inclusion.

Set operators

Each set operator requires two operands, each of some set type *t*, and produces a result of the same type *t*.

Operator	Operation
+	set union
−	set difference
*	set intersection

Priorities of operators

1 {highest} : **not**
2   : * / **div** **mod** **and**
3   : + − **or**
4 {lowest} : = `<>` <   > < = > = **in**

Subject to these priorities and to the effect of brackets, operators are applied from left to right.

Appendix E

Some Character Sets

ISO/ASCII

	0	1	2	3	4	5	6	7	8	9	10	11	12	13	14	15
0																
16																
32		!	"	#	$	%	&	'	(	)	*	+	,	−	.	/
48	0	1	2	3	4	5	6	7	8	9	:	;	<	=	>	?
64	@	A	B	C	D	E	F	G	H	I	J	K	L	M	N	O
80	P	Q	R	S	T	U	V	W	X	Y	Z	[	\	]	↑	_
96		a	b	c	d	e	f	g	h	i	j	k	l	m	n	o
112	p	q	r	s	t	u	v	w	x	y	z	{			}	~	

The ordinal number of a character is the sum of its row number and column number. In the table above the space character has ordinal number 32; all the other gaps correspond to "control characters" which cannot be printed.

Sets of sixty-four characters are common: four are displayed below.

ICL 1900 series

	0	1	2	3	4	5	6	7	8	9	10	11	12	13	14	15
0	0	1	2	3	4	5	6	7	8	9	:	;	<	=	>	?
16		!	"	#	£	%	&	'	(	)	*	+	,	−	.	/
32	@	A	B	C	D	E	F	G	H	I	J	K	L	M	N	O
48	P	Q	R	S	T	U	V	W	X	Y	Z	[	$	]	↑	←

Prime P300/P400

	0	1	2	3	4	5	6	7	8	9	10	11	12	13	14	15
0		!	"	#	$	%	&	'	(	)	*	+	,	−	.	/
16	0	1	2	3	4	5	6	7	8	9	:	;	<	=	>	?
32	@	A	B	C	D	E	F	G	H	I	J	K	L	M	N	O
48	P	Q	R	S	T	U	V	W	X	Y	Z	[	\	]	↑	←

CDC Scientific set

	0	1	2	3	4	5	6	7	8	9	10	11	12	13	14	15
0	:	A	B	C	D	E	F	G	H	I	J	K	L	M	N	O
16	P	Q	R	S	T	U	V	W	X	Y	Z	0	1	2	3	4
32	5	6	7	8	9	+	−	*	/	(	)	$	=		,	.
48	≡	[	]	%	≠	→	∨	∧	↑	↓	<	>	≤	≥	¬	;

ASCII with CDC ordering

	0	1	2	3	4	5	6	7	8	9	10	11	12	13	14	15
0	:	A	B	C	D	E	F	G	H	I	J	K	L	M	N	O
16	P	Q	R	S	T	U	V	W	X	Y	Z	0	1	2	3	4
32	5	6	7	8	9	+	−	*	/	(	)	$	=		,	.
48	#	[	]	%	"	_	!	&	'	?	<	>	@	\	↑	;

Appendix F

Exercise Notes and Hints

Exercises 1.4

3. Try two different approaches:
   (1) Convert the yards to inches and the feet to inches.
   (2) Convert the yards to feet and add to the original feet before converting from feet to inches.
8. Avoid duplication: compute the tax payable and store it in a variable so that it can be printed and added to the net price to produce the total cost.
10. You cannot store a four-letter word in one variable; you must use four character variables.
11. Use *readln* to move from one line of input to the next.

Exercises 2.7

3. $\alpha^2 - \beta^2 = (\alpha - \beta)(\alpha + \beta)$
   All working should be with integers and any division should be performed with **div**.
4. Watch out for the case where the tiles fit exactly: for 8-inch tiles and a room of 10 feet the amount to be cut from the last tile is 0 inches and not 8. Your first attempt will probably give the wrong answer.
5. Compute the change

   $$change := 100 - cost$$

   and then repeatedly reduce the value of this variable as successive (decreasing) denominations are considered.
      When you have read Chapter 4 you might like to improve your program so that only coins to be paid are listed {i.e. remove the zero cases}.
6. Notice that direct addition does not work: adding 4 minutes to 1458 gives 1502, not 1462.

Exercises 3.4

2 and 3. The position in the alphabet is not the position in the lexicographic ordering—it is the position relative to the letter A.

420

Exercises 4.5

2. This can be done neatly by introducing a variable to represent the letter wanted. First pick up the "smaller" of the first two letters supplied and then change this value only if the third letter is smaller.

It can also be done by using no variables other than the three needed to store the letters. Try it both ways.

5. (a) You could test to see if the square on any side was equal to the sum of the squares on the other two, but it would be nice to incorporate the philosophy of Exercise 4.5.2 and determine the longest side first.
   (b) Each side of a triangle is shorter than the sum of the other two sides. The computation constituting part (a) must not be obeyed if the three lengths do not constitute a triangle.

6. The second letters need be compared only if the first agree. The third letters need be compared only if the first and second agree.

This program can benefit from use of a boolean variable when you have read Chapter 5.

7. If the person has not had a birthday yet this year the age is the difference between the two years; if the person has had a birthday this year the age is one greater.

8. To convert an integer to real form, either add 0.0 or multiply by 1.0 (before adding anything to it):

$$(maxint + maxint) * 1.0$$

will generate overflow but

$$maxint * 1.0 + maxint$$

will not. To avoid use of *real* you must write a test such as

$$\alpha + \beta > maxint$$

in the form

$$\alpha > maxint - \beta$$

11. Use case-statements to add *st*, *nd*, *rd*, or *th* and to name the month.
12. Use

   if *age* < 17 **then** . . . **else**
     if *age* <= 20 **then** . . . **else**
       . . .

to determine the age group and, for each group, discriminate the three risks with a case-statement. This is a lengthy business; a neater approach is possible when you have read Chapters 9, 12, and 13.

Exercises 5.5

2. Test parity with the standard function *odd*. Use a set of primes for the other test.
3. Your program must not attempt to read more letters than are provided.

Exercises 6.5

4. The number of digits in a positive integer is given by the number of times the integer can be divided by 10.

6. An integer n cannot have a factor (other than itself) greater than $\sqrt{n}$ so you could test integers in decreasing order, starting with *trunc (sqrt (n))* until a factor is found.
   Alternatively, you could find the smallest factor and use this to compute the largest.

12. $n!$ increases dramatically as n increases. Test your program with small values of n.

14. Use a case-statement to discriminate the operators.

17. As the x_i are read, accumulate their sum and the sum of their squares.

18. You could test all integers from 1 to n as potential factors but, as with Exercise 6.5.6, you should be able to reduce this range to 1 to $\sqrt{n}$.

19. Use two loops, one within the other.

20. Use two (nested) loops designed so that the control variable of the second can never take a value previously taken by the control variable of the first.

Exercises 7.9

3. (b) $(n \geq m)$ **and** $(m > 0)$ $\Rightarrow$ $hcf(n, m) = hcf(m, n \bmod m)$
   $(n > m)$ **and** $(m = 0)$ $\Rightarrow$ $hcf(n, m) = n$
   $\qquad\qquad n < m$ $\Rightarrow$ $hcf(n, m) = hcf(m, n)$

10. The trick is to spot that

    moving n discs from *left* to *right* entails moving
    $\qquad n - 1$ discs from *left* to *centre*,
    $\qquad\quad 1$ disc from *left* to *right*, and then,
    $\qquad n - 1$ discs from *centre* to *right*.

Exercises 9.6

4, 5, and 6. Use a variable of symbolic type to control the multi-exit loops.

Exercises 10.2

5. To choose a number you could use a function such as the following:

```
type
    fourdigits = 0 .. 9999;
function f (x: real) : fourdigits;
    var
        big, less: real;
    begin
        big := abs (x) * maxint;
        less := trunc (big/10000) * 10000.0;
        f := trunc (big − less)
    end {f}
```


Exercises 11.4

2. When you have read Chapter 13, extend your solution to include the person's name and, in the event of a marriage, to update the wife's surname. Then introduce a record variant to store a wife's maiden name.

4. Use a symbolic type to represent the make and either an integer or a letter to

indicate the model. When you have read Chapter 13 return to this example and store the model (and possibly the make) as a string.

Exercises 12.5

1. Use a three-state scalar type: *(merging, endoff1, endoff2)*.
6. The following example illustrates the transferable vote election process for five candidates:

Ballots:
```
1  3  4  2  5
5  4  3  1
2  1  5  3  4
3  2
5  4  2
1  2  3
4  3  1
2  5  3  4
3  5  1  2  4
1  4  5
```
Count 1:1 (3 votes), 2 (2 votes), 3 (2 votes), 4 (1 vote), 5 (2 votes)
No overall majority—candidate 4 is eliminated.
Count 2:1 (3 votes), 2 (2 votes), 3 (3 votes), 5 (2 votes)
No overall majority—candidates 2 and 5 are eliminated.
Count 3:1 (4 votes), 3 (5 votes)
Candidate 3 has an overall majority and so is declared the winner.

Exercises 13.4

3. Do this in three different ways:
   (1) Use two packed arrays and test equality bodily.
   (2) Use two unpacked arrays and compare the two sequences character by character.
   (3) Store the first sequence in an array but test the second character by character as it is read.

   You might like to extend your programs to cater for both lines not containing at least *n* characters.
4. One word is an anagram of another if it contains the same letters with the same frequencies. If no letter could occur more than once in a word we could use a set, but we need to record the frequency of occurrence so we use an array. Count the frequency of each letter in each word and compare the two.
5. Store the phrase in an array but skip spaces and punctuation as the phrase is being read. Check for a palindrome by scanning from both ends towards the centre.
6. Store the values in an array (*int*, say). Scan elements 1 to $n-1$ interchanging int_i and int_{i+1} if $int_i > int_{i+1}$: this guarantees that the largest value is now stored as int_n. Consequently the second scan need be only from 1 to $n-2$.
   If no interchange occurs during a scan the sequence must be stored in ascending order. Use a boolean (or two-valued symbolic) variable to indicate whether interchanges have occurred.
9. Generate successive lines of the triangle in situ in a one-dimensional array by starting at the right-hand end and scanning backwards, summing adjacent values.

The first and final values are always 1 so need not be stored (but storing one of them may simplify your algorithm).

14. Represent the cells as a two-dimensional array. **Either** use two-valued symbolics *(empty, occupied)* and, when counting neighbours, check whether a cell is a corner cell, edge cell, or inner cell **or**, alternatively, use three-valued symbolics *(empty, occupied, outofbounds)* and surround the boundary by a band of *outofbounds* cells.

    Use two arrays: one to store the current generation and one to hold the next. Prior to each new generation either copy the new array into the old one (by bodily assignment) or arrange for the "other" array to be used (this was achieved for files in Figure 12.3).

18. The recursive procedure must take at least two parameters: to indicate the bottom and the top of the current sub-table being searched.

19. Represent the board as a two-dimensional array of squares, each square marked *occupied, attacked,* or *available* as appropriate.

    Clearly, each row (and each column) must contain one (and only one) queen. Seek a solution by placing a queen in successive rows (or columns), each time trying only available squares and, after each placing, updating all the squares under the lady's influence. If no available square exists (in the row or column under consideration) for a queen the program must backtrack (the queen most recently placed must be moved and all squares under her influence returned to *available*). If the *n*th queen has been placed, a solution has been found. The solution is not a sequence of steps; a suitable printing of the board will suffice.

    Modify your program to produce *all* the solutions.

20. (a) You could represent the board as a two-dimensional array of squares, each marked with an integer in the range $[0, n^2]$, indicating the move which brought the knight to that square $(0 => $ as yet unvisited). To simplify detection of moving off the board, you might like to enclose the board within two bands of squares marked out of bounds (perhaps -1). A nicer representation of each square, and one which will give you practice with record variants, is as a record with a tag field of the symbolic type *(empty, outofbounds, occupied)* and with a variant indicating the move if *occupied*.

    (e) Extend the representation of a square to include the number of unvisited squares accessible from that square. Update this information each time a new move is considered.

    (f) Use the additional information supplied by the extension of part (e) to order the moves.

    (g) This is a simplification of part (e). Retain the number of successors initially available and do not update this information.

21. Represent the maze by a two-dimensional array of four-valued symbolics *(visited, unvisited, exit, hedge)*. Extend the boundary by enclosing the entrance within a hedge (to avoid stepping out via the entrance). Display the solution by printing the maze using one character for the hedge, one for each visited square, and a space for each unvisited square.

23. Prevent your program moving the same tile on two successive moves.

Exercises 14.7

8. (a) Exercise 7.9.11—aim to get the cannibals across the river.
    Exercise 13.4.21—record the coordinates (row and column) of the exit and attempt to minimize the distance from it.
    Exercise 13.4.23—the evaluation function must take account of the sequencing of the tiles as well as the displacement of each tile from its intended destination.

424

(b) Include the depth within each evaluation. Extend the definition of a node to include its depth so that this information is readily available.

10. Generate each letter needed in a two-dimensional array. Access these via a vector of pointers, each initially **nil**. Build up each line of the message as a list (or vector) of pointers to letters.

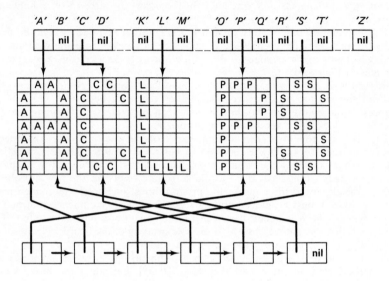

Index

abs 39, 41, 60, 414
address 363, 364
algorithm 3, 13, 166, 233
anagram 258–260, 266, 357, 422
and 84–87, 415, 416
arctan 42, 105, 414
array 311–362
  packed 324–327
assertion 198, 243

backtrack 163–176, 183–184, 197, 360, 374, 380
batch 298, 323
block 142, 144, 215, 363, 391
branch 166, 372

card
  playing 241, 251, 262, 314
  punched ix, 31
case study 185–196, 199–208, 241–250, 297–309, 345–357
chr 53, 222, 414
comment 8, 9, 137, 213
compatibility 49, 218, 232, 278, 289, 290, 312
compiler 3, 9, 10, 14, 91, 125, 177, 180, 198, 211, 219, 233, 359
condition
  auxiliary 123, 227
  dominant 123, 227
constant 14–15, 80–83, 218, 224, 233, 237
correctness 19, 187, 198, 240, 299
cos 42, 414

data 13
  sentinel 110–116, 229
  validation 78, 236, 238, 240, 308–309, 355–357, 392
dispose 365–366, 414
div 38, 43, 415, 416, 419

editor 309
efficiency 63, 68, 74, 127, 131, 132, 142, 211, 233, 275, 280, 319, 322, 329, 363, 380, 381
eof 84, 110, 116–118, 289, 414
eoln 83, 116, 289, 296, 414
Eratosthenes, sieve of 273, 309, 358
error 4, 8, 10, 17, 19, 37, 39, 40, 52, 84, 87, 117, 151, 198, 211, 214, 219, 221, 232, 235, 236, 240, 281, 285, 289, 299, 309, 355, 396
execution 4, 8, 10, 211, 236, 309
exp 42, 414
exponentiation 42

factor 120–125, 134, 135, 225, 421
  highest common 134, 182
factorial 46, 135, 421
false 58, 59, 61, 65–66, 80, 83, 92, 96, 169, 217, 414
Fibonacci sequence 36, 97–101, 127, 134
field 274, 285
  tag 281, 285, 365
  width 5
file 288–310
  buffer variable 288
  external 288, 296–297, 298, 364
  formal 297
  local 288–296
format 33–35, 132, 326
forward reference 157–158, 162, 366
function 151–157, 221 (*see also* routine)

game (*see also* puzzle)
  chess 163, 380–387
  cows and bulls 273
  Life 359, 387, 423
  noughts and crosses 360
  solitaire 163, 361
get 55, 56, 117, 289, 414

identifier   7, 12, 218, 413, 414
  scope   144–145, 202, 217, 218
in   90–91, 219, 227, 415, 416
indentation   9
input   24–31, 49, 54–57, 84, 222
input   24, 56, 84, 111, 116, 237, 288, 289, 290, 296, 298, 414
input↑   56–57, 116, 117, 288

jump,   *see* statement, goto

label
  case   66–68
  statement   391–392
lexicographic order   51, 52, 419
library   180
line printer   ix, 4, 33, 51
list   10, 368–372, 382, 384, 385, 387
ln   42, 414
loop   95–136, 393–395
  decremental   128–130
  deterministic   126–130
  incremental   126–128
  multi-exit   120–126, 224–229, 421
  non-deterministic   95–126, 395

machine code   x, 3, 14, 24, 68, 287, 329
matrix   333–336
maxint   37, 39, 40, 46, 78, 199, 357, 414, 420
mean   135, 182, 290
memory, *see* store
mod   38, 43, 415, 416
Morse code   ix, 182, 359

negation   63–64, 84, 123
new   364–366, 414
nil   364, 365, 368
node   166, 372
  parent   372, 374
  root   166, 372
not   88–89, 415, 416
number
  binary   47, 105, 286
  complex   74, 183, 276, 287
  fixed point   35, 40
  floating point   6, 42
  octal   105, 161, 317
  ordinal   52, 221, 222, 223, 233, 286, 417
  prime   5, 94, 120–125, 132, 225, 273, 309, 358

odd   83, 88, 414, **420**
operator
  addition   6, 38, 41, 43
  boolean   84–89
  division   38, 41, 43
  multiplication   6, 19, 38, 41, 43
  relational   58, 61, 86, 90, 219, 257–260, 278, 292, 324, 325
  set, *see* set
  subtraction   38, 41, 43
or   88, 415, 416
ord   53, 83, 221, 222, 255, 414
output   ix, 4–6, 31–35, 222, 364
output   7, 288, 290, 296, 299, 414
overflow   37, 46, 48, 119, 164, 420
overprinting   187

pack   324, 414
packed   285–287, 324–327, 329
page   33, 290, 414
palindrome   78, 357, 422
parameter   5, 146–151, 253, 366
  input   147, 243
  output   151, 170, 243
  value   146–147, 171, 181, 243, 262, 275, 287, 294, 319, 336, 370
  variable   147–151, 171, 242, 243, 246, 262, 275, 287, 294, 319, 346, 353
Pascal's triangle   358, 422
pi   15, 27, 104–105
ply   166
pointer   363–388
portability   51, 125, 238
precedence   43, 61, 86, 88, 89, 272, 416
pred   39, 52, 221, 414
priority, *see* precedence
procedure 5,   137–151   (*see also* routine)
program   ix, 3
put   290, 414
puzzle (*see also* game)
  beakers   184
  eight square   361, 423
  Hanoi, towers of   183, 421
  knight's tour   360, 423
  maze   163, 361, 423
  missionaries and cannibals   183, 423
  queens   360, 423

queue   387

read 24–25, 49, 56, 105, 288, 289, 296, 414
readln 24, 27–30, 49, 56, 116, 289, 296, 414, 419
record 274–287
  packed 285–287
  variant 280–285, 302, 340, 365, 388
recursion 153, 158–176, 182–184, 360, 373, 374, 380, 381
  data structure 279, 366–368
  direct 158–161
  infinite 159, 279
  mutual 161–163
refinement 185, 190, 199, 243, 302
reset 288, 296, 414
rewrite 289, 296, 414
root
  cube 181
  quadratic equation 46, 74–76, 80–82
  square 134
round 39, 414
routine 137
  dummy 196–197, 299
  formal 176–181

search
  binary 319–323, 360, 423
  breadth-first 375
  depth-first 374, 375
  hash 323
  heuristic 174, 374–380, 387
  linear 288, 319, 323, 331–333
  steered 361
security 211, 212–214, 217, 219, 233, 240, 278, 280, 281, 283, 363, 368
selector 64, 281
  boolean 65–66
  ordinal 66–69
semantics 4, 17
set 90–91, 255–273, 420
  constructors 90
  difference 266–269, 416
  empty 255, 257
  inclusion 257, 261, 416
  intersection 265–266, 416
  union 261–265, 416
side-effect 151, 153, 246, 291
sin 42, 414
slice 329, 332, 333, 336
sort
  bubble 357, 422
  exchange 318
  insertion 371

selection 296, 317–318
  tree 372–374
sqr 39, 41, 414
sqrt 42, 414
stack 358, 387
standard deviation 135, 182
state indicator 224–229
statement 3
  assignment 17–24, 39, 147, 153, 216, 218, 246, 275, 276, 278, 287, 292, 293, 324, 326, 364, 366, 371
  case 64–69, 227, 281, 420, 421
  compound 69–71, 97, 127, 137, 196
  empty 8, 66, 196
  for 126
  goto 391–397
  if 58–64, 72–78, 85–89, 127, 227
  repeat 101–110, 225, 227
  while 96–101
  with 279–280, 301
store 14, 19, 68, 211, 275, 285, 287, 296, 363, 380, 388
  allocation 142, 147, 160, 363, 364–366
string 5, 6, 15, 319, 324, 325–327, 422
succ 39, 52, 414, 221
syntax 4
  diagram 10

taxonomy 229–232, 314
terminal ix, 4, 10, 24, 31, 33, 51, 84, 273, 326, 360
testing 185, 188, 196–199, 217, 243, 299
textfile 116, 288, 289, 290, 296
time 19, 119, 174, 211, 275, 287, 380, 382
transferable vote election 272, 309, 357, 422
transparency 19, 63, 74, 123, 132, 139, 171, 211, 212–214, 217, 219, 224, 225, 227, 243, 256, 280, 314, 318, 395, 396, 397
trapezium rule 135
tree 164, 174, 215, 372–374, 380, 388
  Christmas 338–345
true 58, 59, 61, 65–66, 80, 83, 92, 96, 169, 217, 414
trunc 39, 414
type
  anonymous 215, 229
  array *see* array
  base 90, 218, 255, 256

type, *continued*
  boolean 58, 65–66, 80–94, 169, 217, 414
  char 15, 51–57, 222, 414
  component 288, 289, 290, 311, 319, 324, 327
  enumerated *see* type, symbolic
  file *see* file
  host 218, 232
  index 311, 312
  integer 15, 37–40, 46, 218, 414
  named 215, 229, 239, 281, 312, 329
  ordinal 40, 66, 90, 221, 232, 240, 255, 281, 311, 319
  pointer, *see* pointer
  real 6, 15, 40–42, 47–49, 78, 218, 414
  record, *see* record
  scalar 16, 37, 40, 58, 152
  set, *see* set
  string, *see* string
  subrange 211, 218, 232–241, 312
  symbolic 211, 217–232
  text 296, 414
  user-defined 215

union
  discriminated 285

  free 285
  set 261–265, 416
unpack 324, 414

variable 14, 16
  anonymous 364, 365
  array 311
  boolean 91–94, 123, 170
  character 52
  control 126, 131, 421
  declaration 16
  file buffer 288
  integer 17, 39, 40
  pointer 363–364
  real 17, 42
  record 274, 276, 287
  set 256
  string 325, 326
  subrange 232
  symbolic 218
vector 311, 314, 333–334

write 5, 31–35, 105, 289, 290, 325, 414
writeln 5, 31–35, 105, 290, 296, 325, 414